THE REPRESENTATION AND REALITY OF WAR

THE BRITISH EXPERIENCE

David Gordon Wright, 1937–95

THE REPRESENTATION AND REALITY OF WAR

THE BRITISH EXPERIENCE

Essays in Honour of David Wright

EDITED BY KEITH DOCKRAY AND KEITH LAYBOURN

SUTTON PUBLISHING

First published in in the United Kingdom in 1999 by
Sutton Publishing Limited · Phoenix Mill
Thrupp · Stroud · Gloucestershire · GL5 2BU

British Library Cataloguing in Publication Data
A catalogue record for this book is available from the British Library

ISBN 0 7509 1861 6

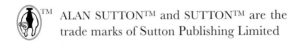

ALAN SUTTON™ and SUTTON™ are the trade marks of Sutton Publishing Limited

Typeset in 10/12pt Baskerville.
Typesetting and origination by
Sutton Publishing Limited
Printed in Great Britain by
Bookcraft, Midsomer Norton, Somerset.

CONTENTS

ACKNOWLEDGEMENTS

M any people have helped us in gathering together information about David Gordon Wright (1937–95). Most of the contributors have provided some reflections and remembrances. In addition, John O'Connell, Robert Perks, Graham Townend and Tony Saul have supplied us with useful material on David as a colleague, research supervisor and lecturer. In the early days of preparation we also discussed the commemorative volume with David's eldest son, Tim. We would also like to thank the *Telegraph and Argus* (Bradford District Newspapers) for permitting us to reproduce part of a photograph which shows David. Jane Crompton, Christopher Feeney, Sarah Moore and the staff at Sutton Publishing have offered excellent help and advice in the production of this *Festschrift*. The University of Huddersfield has generously contributed towards its production.

LIST OF ABBREVIATIONS

ABCA	Army Bureau of Current Affairs
BACIE	British Association of Commercial and Industrial Education
BIAE	British Institute for Adult Education
BSP	British Socialist Party
BWL	British Workers' League (later National Democratic Labour Party)
BWP	British Way and Purpose Scheme
CEA	Council for Educational Advance
COs	Conscientious Objectors
Comintern	Communist International
CPGB	Communist Party of Great Britain
ECCI	Executive Committee of the Communist International
HCCL	Huddersfield Council for Civil Liberties
HWORC	Huddersfield Workers' Own Recruiting Committee
ILP	Independent Labour Party
LCC	London County Council
LEA	Local Education Authority
LSEC	Labour and Socialist Election Committee
LMS	London Municipal Society
MST	Military Service Tribunals
NCC	No-Conscription Councils
NCF	No-Conscription Fellowship
NCLC	National Council of Labour Colleges
NCW	National Council of Women
NDLP	National Democratic Labour Party
NUS	National Union of Students
NUT	National Union of Teachers
NUWSS	National Union of Women's Suffrage Societies
OU	Open University
PLP	Parliamentary Labour Party
SWMF	South Wales Miners' Federation
TUC	Trades Union Congress
UDC	Union of Democratic Control
USRC	Unionist Social Reform Committee
WEA	Workers' Educational Association
WMF	Workers' Municipal Federation

LIST OF CONTRIBUTORS

Michael Bartholomew, who recently retired as Open University Staff Tutor in Arts, Yorkshire Region, has contributed numerous sections to published Open University course units and books.

Keith Dockray, a Fellow of the Royal Historical Society, retired as Senior Lecturer in Medieval and Early Modern History at the University of Huddersfield in 1994. Author of *Richard III: A Reader in History* (1988), *Richard III: A Source Book* (1997), *Edward IV: A Source Book* (1999), and numerous articles on later medieval and early modern England, he is currently working on *Henry VI, the Wars of the Roses and the End of the Lancastrian Dynasty: A Source Book*.

Brendan Evans, Pro-Vice Chancellor and Professor of Politics at the University of Huddersfield, has published a range of articles and books on British politics, political ideology and the politics of the labour market, including *The Politics of the Training Market: From Manpower Services Commission to Training Enterprise Councils* (1992). Joint author, with Andrew Taylor, of *From Salisbury to Major: Continuity and Change in Conservative Politics* (1996), he is currently writing a book on *The Impact of Thatcherism*.

John A. Hargreaves, twice winner of the Yorkshire History Prize and an Associate of the Royal Historical Society, is head of Humanities, Howden Clough High School, Batley, West Yorkshire. Author of numerous articles and currently editor of the *Transactions of the Halifax Antiquarian Society*, he is now writing a new history of Halifax.

J.A. Jowitt is Director of the Centre of Continuing Education at the University of Bradford. His publications include *Victorian Bradford* (co-editor with David Wright, 1981), *Model Industrial Communities in Mid-Nineteenth Century Yorkshire* (editor, 1986), *Employers and Labour in the English Textile Industries 1850–1939* (co-editor, 1988), *Mechanization and Misery* (1992) and *The Centennial History of the Independent Labour Party* (co-editor, 1992).

Keith Laybourn, Professor of History at the University of Huddersfield and a Fellow of the Royal Historical Society, has written about fifty articles and twenty-two books, most recently *Britain on the Breadline* (1990), *The Rising Sun of Socialism* (1991), *A History of British Trade Unionism* c. *1770–1990* (1992), *The Centennial History of the Independent Labour Party* (co-editor, 1992), *The General Strike of 1926*

(1993), *The Guild of Help and the Changing Face of Edwardian Philanthropy* (1994), *The Evolution of British Social Policy and the Welfare State* (1995) and *Socialism in Britain 1881–1951* (1997). General Editor of the Sutton Modern British History Series, he has two books about to appear, and is currently working on the history of the Communist Party of Great Britain and compiling a reader on debates in twentieth-century British history.

Cyril Pearce, Senior Lecturer in History and Education at Bretton Hall College, near Wakefield, associated with the University of Leeds, has written several articles and a book on *The Manningham Mills Strike*.

J.A.G. Roberts, a Fellow of the Royal Historical Society and formerly Principal Lecturer in History at the University of Huddersfield, has written several articles and four books: *China Through Western Eyes: the Nineteenth Century* (1991), *China Through Western Eyes: the Twentieth Century* (1992), *A History of China Vol. 1: Prehistory to c. 1800* (1996) and *Modern China: An Illustrated History* (1998).

William Stafford, Professor of Politics at the University of Huddersfield and a Fellow of the Royal Historical Society, has written numerous articles and three books: *Socialism, Radicalism and Nostalgia: Social Criticism in Britain 1775–1830* (1987), *Mozart's Death: A Corrective Survey of the Legends* (1991) and *John Stuart Mill* (1998).

Andrew Taylor, Professor of Politics at the University of Huddersfield, has written numerous articles and four books, mainly on British politics, the politics of coal mining, and trade union history. Joint author, with Brendan Evans, of *From Salisbury to Major: Continuity and Change in Conservative Politics* (1996), he is currently writing a history of the National Union of Mineworkers.

David Taylor, Dean of Music and Humanities at the University of Huddersfield and a Fellow of the Royal Historical Society, has written many articles on agriculture, policing, crime and gender, the pamphlet *'A Well-Chosen, Effective Body of Men': The Middlesbrough Police Force, 1841–1914* (1995), and two books: *The New Police in Nineteenth-Century England: Crime, Conflict and Control* (1997) and *Crime, Policy and Punishment* (1998).

Philip Woodfine is Principal Lecturer in History at the University of Huddersfield and a Fellow of the Royal Historical Society. Co-editor, with Jeremy Black, of *The British Navy and the Use of Naval Power in the Eighteenth Century*, he has written numerous articles on eighteenth-century political, diplomatic and social history. His book *Britannia's Glories: the Walpole Ministry and the 1739 War with Spain* was published by the Royal Historical Society in 1998 and he is currently working on a new biography of Sir Robert Walpole.

INTRODUCTION:
D.G. WRIGHT (1937–95)

Keith Dockray and Keith Laybourn

David Gordon Wright, to whom this volume of essays is dedicated, died at his home in Gloucestershire on 4 December 1995. A gifted historian, a dedicated researcher and a first-rate lecturer, he was also a notably caring tutor, a generous, supportive and self-effacing colleague and, above all, a most compassionate human being. His range of interests and expertise was wide: the French Revolution, for David one of the truly formative events of modern European history, regularly provided a focus for his scholarly attention; Napoleon, a highly skilled politician and a 'military genius' who 'raised the art and science of war to new heights', fascinated him; and his deep knowledge of nineteenth- and twentieth-century English literature, not least the novels of Charles Dickens, George Eliot and Thomas Hardy, and the poetry of Gerard Manley Hopkins, clearly informed his judgements on social history. Among the finest writers on nineteenth-century popular radicalism and Chartism, David Wright ranks, alongside his early mentor Jack Reynolds, as one of the best recorders of Bradford's history. Above all, he sought to understand and explain warfare and its impact, whether in France during the 1790s, the Napoleon-dominated Europe of 1796–1815 or the First World War of 1914–1918. For David Wright, moreover, warfare was no dry-as-dust academic pursuit, particularly the Second World War, under the shadow of which he spent his early years: the enormous loss of life resulting from the Holocaust, for instance, and the mass bombing of British and German cities during the War affected him deeply. Indeed, many of the history staff at Huddersfield Polytechnic in the 1970s and the 1980s can remember the emotionally-charged lecture on the bombing of Dresden he delivered on more than one occasion, Philip Woodfine in particular:

> He could analyse the evidence but he could not simply talk about the devastating human losses as matters of record. David recalled how he had once given a similar talk to an Open University Summer School group, and afterwards found himself in the bar along with colleagues and students. Suddenly overwhelmed by all he had been discussing, and feeling it was quite obscene to be where he was, he put down his drink and went quietly to bed.[1]

Certainly, it is highly appropriate that the ethics and nature of warfare, and its impact on politics, society and the men and women who lived through it, should form the unifying theme of this *Festschrift*.

As David Wright once ironically reflected, his birth on 31 October 1937 occurred a week before the death of James Ramsay MacDonald, Labour's first Prime Minister. David was born in Little Horton, a Bradford suburb, into a middling working-class family: indeed his father was a trade unionist, and, although David had distinct personal reservations about the role of collective organizations such as trade unions, he was always proud of his working-class roots.[2] The highlight of his early school career, seemingly, came in 1945 when he became class ink monitor, the 'most eminent post I've ever held', he once assured Philip Woodfine. Once he reached secondary school age, David became a pupil at Grange Grammar School, Bradford, where Jack Reynolds, already an eminent local historian, not only gave him confidence and helped him to overcome his natural shyness and pronounced stutter but also fired his latent interest in, and enthusiasm for, history.[3] In 1956 he obtained a place at Manchester University to read Modern History, Economics and Politics and, after graduating with a second-class honours degree in 1959, embarked upon a postgraduate diploma in education.[4] Then, in September 1960, he returned to Grange Grammar School as an assistant master in the department headed by Jack Reynolds, and when his former mentor joined the staff at Bradford College of Advanced Technology (now the University of Bradford), he succeeded him as head of history at the school.[5]

While at Grange, David Wright embarked on a Leeds University doctorate under the guidance of A.J. Taylor, Asa Briggs and Donald Read and, despite the pressures of full-time schoolteaching, successfully completed his thesis on nineteenth-century Bradford politics (and obtained his PhD) in 1966.[6] Shortly afterwards, he became Lecturer in History at City of Leeds Carnegie College (now part of Leeds Metropolitan University). Then, in 1971, he secured an appointment as Senior Lecturer in History at Huddersfield Polytechnic; he became Principal Lecturer in the mid-1970s; and, eventually, Reader in History. Also in 1971 he joined the part-time staff of the Open University and, for over twenty years, taught both interdisciplinary and specialist history courses (mainly, but not entirely, on the nineteenth and twentieth centuries), conducted seminars in the evenings and on Saturdays, and spent many weeks at Summer Schools (held at host universities ranging from York to East Anglia) where he found himself teaching alongside historians such as Arthur Marwick and Clive Emsley, both of whom he much admired.[7] At Huddersfield, until his early retirement in 1988 (partly as a result of ill-health), he played a key role in establishing flourishing BA and MA degrees, as well as inspiring his younger colleagues – not least the joint editors of this *Festschrift*![8] Early on, he was much involved in Certificate of Education courses, not only putting on history modules but also supervising students on teaching practice in local schools: he particularly enjoyed encouraging, and advising, mature students embarking on a career in the classroom.[9] As a teacher himself, David was immensely conscientious and hard-working, both for Huddersfield Polytechnic and the Open University, and probably at his best when formally lecturing. More able students, in particular, much appreciated his carefully crafted, thought-provoking and often challenging lectures, as Graham Townend, an undergraduate at Huddersfield between 1976 and 1979, recalls:

> One thing I will always remember about David is a lecture to the Historical Association he gave when I was in my second year at Huddersfield. The room was full and as David spoke – the subject was Gladstone – you knew that you were witnessing something special. It was one of those rare occasions when the lecturer and his subject are one. You felt that David was speaking about Gladstone almost from the heart and the effect was spellbinding.[10]

Most of David's teaching concentrated on British and European history 1789–1945, where he was particularly fond of introducing students to literary source material and, indeed, literature itself: George Eliot's *Middlemarch*, for instance, was a set book for his long-running Special Subject on Mid-Victorian England, as was John Stuart Mill's *On Liberty*. Yet he could be notably versatile: for many years he taught a course on political philosophy with Bill Stafford (relishing, especially, Rousseau's *Social Contract* and, more surprisingly perhaps, J.S. Mill's essay on *The Subjection of Women*); and, for a while, he even joined Pauline Stafford and Keith Dockray's tutorial team covering later medieval history with first year BA students.[11] Equally important was David's encouragement of historical research, whether by supporting his younger colleagues in their endeavours or supervising MPhil and PhD students himself.[12] Even after his early retirement, he continued to teach part-time for several years, both for Huddersfield and the Open University, as well as maintaining a role in promoting research.

Although an intensely private man where his personal problems and misfortunes were concerned, David Wright was always sympathetic to the needs and plight of others. Many of his former colleagues at Huddersfield and the Open University had occasion to be greatly touched by his personal concern for their welfare, for he was always highly sensitive to pain and suffering, caring and compassionate in response.[13] When David first arrived at Huddersfield in 1971, the aura of fastidious non-worldliness, and delight in presenting an old-fashioned image, that later became so characteristic of him, had hardly begun to develop:

he was, then, still a young man of thirty-four years, often to be seen wearing a safari jacket. By the mid-1970s, however, he had abandoned that kind of outfit, and became very much more the traditional schoolmaster both in style and attitude.[14] Pipe-smoking – and David in the later 1970s was rarely to be seen not puffing at one or other of his many pipes – obviously complemented such an image nicely; even when, in the 1980s, he began virtually chain-smoking cigarettes, they were almost invariably menthol and held, Noel Coward-like, in a cigarette holder.[15] What never changed was his single-mindedness, as his long time colleague at Huddersfield John O'Connell recalls:

> . . . he had no ambition to be anything other than an academic. He had no inclination – and would not have been suited – to be 'promoted' into an administrative job. He was certain of his course, and single-minded in other ways. I remember being left feeling idly self-indulgent when he told me that he did not take a Sunday paper because it was a waste of valuable time to read one.

Even more striking, perhaps, was David Wright's pride in both his Englishness and the English literature he so enjoyed reading, also highlighted by John O'Connell:

> I did not know until then [the day of the Memorial Service] of David's attachment to the novels of Thomas Hardy (and doubtless the poems) and, most surprisingly to me, the poetry of Gerard Manley Hopkins. I expressed astonishment [to Brendan Evans] to learn that he was a devotee of the writings of a Jesuit priest. . . . But Brendan explained what should have been obvious: that what he found attractive in Hopkins was his Englishness, which is – if there is one key – the key to understanding David.[16]

When, in the mid-1970s, Sir Isaiah Berlin was lured to Huddersfield Polytechnic by his former postgraduate research student Bill Stafford – an invitation enthusiastically accepted, so he asserted, as a means of escaping the hot-house atmosphere surrounding the election that very day of his successor as President of Wolfson College, Oxford! – he talked at length to the history staff, most particularly David Wright; moreover, when David temporarily left the company, Sir Isaiah promptly expressed the opinion that 'there goes a fine mind'. This was high praise indeed from one of the great intellectuals of the twentieth century, for Berlin had clearly detected in David subtleties of thought found only in exceptionally able historians. And Graham Townend, who, after completing his BA at Huddersfield in 1979, went on to conduct successful research for a PhD at Edinburgh University, recollects that:

. . . when I used to come into the department, [David] was usually to be seen in his room peering at a microfilm reader looking at material on Chartism. . . . He was perhaps proof that scholarship is not just about an endless list of publications which seems to be so much the thing these days. . . . My supervisor at Edinburgh, Harry Dickinson, once said he always thought David was more an academic than he was. . . .[17]

David did indeed have a first-rate mind and was an historian of great dedication and ability. Remarkably, he completed his part-time Leeds PhD on Bradford politics between the 1830s and 1880s in a little over three years (in 1966), despite many pressing family and job-related commitments. From then on, although teaching always took priority over research, he produced a steady stream of books and articles revealing not only his wide range of historical interests but also an ever more compelling empathy with nineteenth- and twentieth-century English literature: most importantly, he published on the French Revolution, Napoleon and the Revolutionary and Napoleonic Wars; popular radicalism in nineteenth-century England, particularly Chartism and political protest in his native Bradford; Leeds, Bradford and the American Civil War; and the Great War of 1914–1918.

David Wright's heart-felt interest in the heroic struggle for democratic rights in Britain, and his desire to encourage sixth-formers and undergraduates to appreciate its importance, led him to produce his *Democracy and Reform, 1815–1885* in 1970, a volume in the Longman Seminar Studies in History series (of which he was a great advocate) which sold more than 50,000 copies in the 1970s.[18] Many years later, in 1988, there followed his immensely perceptive *Popular Radicalism: The Working Class Experience, 1780–1880*.[19] In both these books, and several articles, David examined the impact of Chartism, and suggested that it was a powerful radical tradition, just as much as more recent labourist and socialist ideologies, that helped shape the emergence of the working class and democratic rights in Britain. Such an interpretation derived, in part at least, from the local and regional work David first undertook when researching his doctorate. Indeed, he published several important articles and pamphlets specifically drawing upon an ever-burgeoning knowledge of politics and society in his beloved West Riding of Yorkshire, culminating in a volume of essays on *Victorian Bradford*, jointly edited with Tony Jowitt and, appropriately, dedicated to Jack Reynolds, his old mentor.[20]

David's studies of popular radicalism in England led him, in the early 1970s, to develop a growing interest in the French Revolution, Napoleon and the Revolutionary Wars of 1789–1815. This resulted in two books, again in the Longman Seminar Studies in History series, containing not only the required analysis of historical debates and well-chosen illustrative documents but also a wealth of original research. *Revolution and Terror in France, 1789–1795*, published in

1974, was remarkable not least for making sense, in a clear, coherent and stimulating manner, of the extraordinary twists and turns of France's most turbulent years.[21] *Napoleon and Europe*, published in 1984, reflects not only David's fascination with Corsica's most famous son but also his firm belief in the role of great men in history. Indeed, David Wright's own complex and many-sided personality had strange echoes in that of Napoleon, a political and military genius who demonstrated an almost mystical belief in his destiny as a latter-day Prometheus, created a vast empire and fundamentally reformed the institutions of France. When writing of the Napoleonic legend, moreover, David penned a truly purple passage:

> . . . each writer, and indeed each reader, constructs his own Napoleon from the mass of evidence available. More books have been written on Napoleonic France and Europe than days have elapsed since Napoleon's death in 1821. The shelves of libraries are weighed down by biographies, monographs and detailed analysis of policy. His military career, government and administration, personality, sex life, even his very anatomy, have been subjected to minute scrutiny. Books continue to pour from the presses, containing every possible argument, including allegations that he was slowly changing into a woman, or was poisoned by arsenic contained in the wallpaper at Longwood, his residence on St Helena.[22]

David Wright's penchant for studying war and its impact, so evident in *Napoleon and Europe* and, indeed, his earlier work on the American Civil War's influence on Yorkshire politics and society, is also apparent in a 1978 article exposing the propagandist activities of writers such as Thomas Hardy, H.G. Wells, Rudyard Kipling and Arnold Bennett – men whose peculiarly high profile made them invaluable props for a wartime government – during the early years of the First World War.[23] Aptly, too, his very last publication, in 1991, was a Huddersfield Polytechnic History pamphlet entitled *The Great War: A Useless Slaughter?* As a man whose own father had been gassed and badly wounded at the Somme and Passchendaele, he certainly recognized how deep an impact the Great War of 1914–1918 has had on the national psyche:

> Even though the Great War ended a lifetime ago, the Western Front remains deeply embedded in our culture. For the generation born before the Second World War, the Menin Gate at Ypres, recording the names of 55,000 missing dead, is one of the most sacred places on earth. The first day of the battle of the Somme (1 July 1916), when the British Army suffered 60,000 casualties, including 20,000 dead, is the blackest day in our history. There remain in 1991 in British Legion homes 400 men blinded by mustard or chlorine gas on the Western Front. We are still moved by the courage, discipline and loyalty of the men who fought in such a war. . . .

Nevertheless, David's perceptive analysis of the evidence resulted in a far more sober and balanced assessment than that encapsulated in Ludendorff's characterization of British soldiers as 'lions led by donkeys' or Clemenceau's conclusion that 'war is too serious a matter to be left to generals'.[24]

Not only David Wright himself but many of his former colleagues and research students have worked on warfare and its impact: no better theme could have been chosen for a *Festschrift* dedicated to his memory, particularly since so many of the papers bear the stamp of his posthumous influence. The majority, too, are on nineteenth- and twentieth-century topics obviously linked, whether directly or indirectly, to his own work and historical legacy. Keith Dockray's, alone, concerns seventeenth-century England, but even he raises matters very much within the scope of David's historical perception and scholarly expertise. Indeed, the paper has its genesis in a final year BA course on 'Yorkshire and the Civil War' which the author taught at Huddersfield Polytechnic for several years in the late 1970s and early 1980s, a course which owed much to David Wright's encouragement. Three features of the resulting discussion might well have appealed to him: it very much concerns the West Riding of Yorkshire, especially Bradford, focus of so much of David's own historical attention; it concentrates upon narrating and explaining political and military events there during the English Civil War, mainly through the analysis of contemporary and near-contemporary evidence; and it particularly highlights literary source material and its shortcomings, as David did in both his teaching and writing. Raising fighting forces, maintaining discipline over them and ensuring they were fit and able for combat was clearly a major problem for commanders in the seventeenth-century Civil War. Securing and holding on to seamen for ships-of-war proved no less a headache during the 1790s, as Philip Woodfine so graphically demonstrates: indeed, battling most constructively and productively with hitherto neglected and often intractable King's Bench records, he vividly portrays the activities of English naval press gangs during the era of the French Revolutionary Wars, as well as exposing the abuse of much-vaunted constitutional liberties and the consequences of impressment for ordinary sea-faring folk. John Hargreaves, spanning both the later eighteenth and early nineteenth centuries, focuses on Halifax and the impact of external wars on religion and popular protest in this growing West Riding industrial town. Specifically, he argues that Evangelicals in Halifax were divided in their response to the American and French Revolutions but that, throughout the 1830s and 1840s, a significant minority were committed to a widening of the parliamentary franchise, favouring 'French principles and French conduct' and the 'revolutionary experiment'. For David Wright, raised a Methodist, eventually becoming an Anglican, and greatly influenced in his personal life and writings by religion, all this would have proved fascinating, not least in the context of his own work on the impact of the American Civil War in the West Riding.

David's own political, social and moral stance was clearly influenced by the writings of John Stuart Mill and, of course, the morality of war – much evident in the papers of William Stafford and J.A.G. Roberts – interested him deeply and often featured in his own historical analysis. Bill Stafford reconstructs J.S. Mill's early Bentham-inspired optimism, and traces his intellectual journey towards a more complex and cautious position, in an elegant and coherently argued paper (based on a comprehensive knowledge of Mill's notably scattered observations on warfare) that would, no doubt, have delighted David Wright. Although Mill produced no up-dated theory of *jus in bello* (since, for him, civilized states were less likely to commit war crimes anyway), believed in the rule of international law (or, rather, international convention) and argued that only defensive war can truly be justified, he proved far from consistent: for instance, since he saw the American Civil War as the North's righteous struggle against the slavery of the South, that war, at least, could be justified – as a necessary confrontation between civilization and barbarism. For Bill Roberts, however, the rules and restrictions of just war, if they ever really existed (and they seem to have been less evident in the history of China than in the rest of the world), certainly provide an important key to understanding the behaviour of James Bruce, 8th Earl of Elgin, when in the Far East between 1857 and 1860, most notably the nature of his occupation of Guangzhou (Canton) in the late 1850s and his sanctioning of the burning of the fabulous Summer Palace in Beijing (Peking) in 1860. 'No human power shall induce me to accept the office of oppressor of the feeble', he recorded in his journal, and, certainly, Elgin rejected the idea of terrorizing the civilian population of Guangzhou. When pressed almost beyond endurance by Chinese mistreatment of both British and French prisoners in 1860, however, he reluctantly sanctioned the destruction of the Summer Palace, as an essentially utilitarian response to less than ethical behaviour by the Chinese (but he refused to authorize any assault on the Forbidden City).

Politics and war, two of David Wright's major interests, are combined in Andrew Taylor's detailed and analytical essay on the Conservative Party and its attempt (between 1911 and 1922) to create political stability within the context of mass democracy: in particular, he challenges the notion that Bonar Law's Conservative Party needed to develop an explicit social policy since what was required, and what the Conservative leadership managed to bring about, was the creation of political stability and party unity. The First World War, in fact, helped reaffirm the Conservative Party's belief that 'pragmatism not class, social reform or ideology' should drive its politics. As well as finding the sheer complexity of political responses to war enthralling (and the political machinations engendered by the First World War were complex indeed), David Wright also enjoyed wielding the axe as a slayer of myths (as he certainly did in both *Napoleon and Europe* and his pamphlet on the Great War). Tony Jowitt and Keith Laybourn also have myths firmly in their sights in their iconoclastic co-authored paper on the Bradford Independent Labour Party, particularly the myth that arose during the First World War of the ILP as a pacifist organization. Clearly, several of the leaders did oppose the war effort but very few were pacifists: rather, many opposed the war not on principle so much as for what it was. The Bradford ILP, certainly, contained members holding a variety of viewpoints: a few pacifists, rather more who opposed the First World War because of its questionable objectives, and even a significant number who actually supported the War (as a vehicle for accelerating the decline of capitalism). And many actually joined up and fought at the front because, quite simply, they preferred the British political system to the Hun. Perhaps in Huddersfield men holding anti-war views were both more numerous and more fixed in their views than their Bradford neighbours. Certainly, Cyril Pearce makes a powerful case for concluding that enthusiasm for the Great War there was less marked and more equivocal than conventional portrayals of the national mood might lead us to expect. Not only were anti-war views more tolerated in Huddersfield than most places, there developed in the town a broad-based, extensive and well-organized anti-war community, particularly once conscription was introduced in the spring of 1916. As a result, even though the town's Liberal ruling élite did eventually accept the need to fight and reluctantly acknowledged the necessity of conscription, Huddersfield managed to escape the worst excesses of wartime jingoism.

Two twentieth-century papers in this collection can be linked, very clearly, to both David Wright's literary interests and his powerful sense of Englishness. Inspired by the fact that his own maternal grandfather had fought in the same regiment as the Irish working-class writer and poet Patrick Macgill, David Taylor finds his subject reflecting two apparently conflicting perspectives on the First World War: the romantic and the tragic. Much of what Macgill wrote, whether poetry or prose (and this self-educated former navvy has bequeathed us both) appears to conform to now conventional portrayals of the First World War along the lines of Joan Littlewood's powerful and highly satirical 1960s musical concoction *Oh, What a Lovely War!*: the sense of pessimism, of futility in the face of overwhelming odds, of expectation that an inevitable death is just around the corner, and, of course, the yawning chasm between officers and the 'poor bloody infantry' (highlighted by the fact that, even in the trenches, class divisions persisted). Yet, as David Taylor convincingly argues and demonstrates, Macgill's writings also convey very strongly the romance of war, even under the terrible conditions in which he often found himself: the sense of solidarity with his fellow soldiers, of shared experience, of camaraderie, and of fierce pride in being a rifleman. Even in the darkest days of the war, a certain optimism and sense of positive self-image can be detected in Macgill's remarkable outpourings. H.V. Morton, the prolific, if now largely forgotten, travel writer who forms the subject of Mike Bartholomew's elegantly constructed essay, was clearly touched by both the First and the Second World Wars. What would have appealed most to David Wright about Morton, however, is his quintessential Englishness. *In Search of England*, published in 1927 after six months travelling, presents an essentially mythological England, a rural, agricultural, tranquil, unchanging place which might never have experienced the traumas of the Great War. Twelve years later, in 1939, Morton embarked on another tour of England, the results published in 1940 as *I Saw Two Englands*, one in peace and the other in war. Here, however, there is a significant postscript where Morton leads a group of First World War veterans across a moonlit harvest field in search of reported German parachutists. Later on, moreover, he produced a further book entitled *Atlantic Meeting*, specifically based upon his personal experiences as one of two journalists who accompanied Churchill to meet Roosevelt in August 1941. For Mike Bartholomew, though, it is the extent to which Morton encapsulates the myth of Englishness – with his emphasis on the parish, the rural, and the Arcadian 'land of lost content' – that provides his lasting appeal.

Both Keith Laybourn and Brendan Evans, in the final two papers, focus upon the relationship between war and politics during the Second World War. Keith Laybourn, indeed, sets himself the awesome task of unravelling the reasons why the Communist Party of Great Britain supported the British war effort on 3 September 1939, moved to opposing it just over a month later and, finally, after Germany launched its invasion of the Soviet Union in June 1941, once more changed its line and henceforth supported Churchill's wartime government. Evidence points to the divisions within the CPGB on the question of war but, clearly, whatever doubts the leadership and rank and file may have had, it was Stalin, the needs of the Soviet Union and the Comintern that determined the Party's action. David Wright would certainly have appreciated the close attention to detail required in order to explain why the CPGB adopted three, if not four, different positions in no time at all. No doubt, too, his attention would have been firmly engaged by Brendan Evans' investigation into how far postwar further education reflected wartime priorities and aspirations. The Second World War was certainly a decisive moment in British history: it reshaped politics, saw the inauguration of the modern welfare state and, indeed, determined the very framework of postwar politics in Britain. Nevertheless, caution must be exercised and the extent to which the war brought about fundamental change not exaggerated. As Brendan Evans suggests, the Conservatives, who dominated the wartime coalition, when 'confronted with a tidal wave' in favour of radical upheaval 'kept cool and diverted it'. This seems to have been particularly true of adult, technical and further education. Since war had revealed real technical weaknesses in British industry, concessions had to be made there. However, in the areas of adult and further education, equivocation and division ruled. Although the Beveridge Report provided substantial backing for the development of further education, the voluntary sector, including the Workers' Educational Association and the British Institute of Adult Education, was split over the precise role the state might legitimately play. In the end, such disarray enabled ministers to get away with issuing a circular, just two weeks after the implementation of the 1944 Education Act, declaring that Local Education Authorities need not, after all, submit schemes for further education: an outcome hardly likely to have won the approval of David Wright.

Of all viable literary genres the *Festschrift* could be said to be the most corpse-like with its ritual valediction. Yet, so its editors believe, this is certainly no dull tome, as lifeless as a marble monument. Rather, it is a worthy testimony to the immensely lively and productive research of David Wright himself and the continuation, since his retirement, subsequent illness and early death, of much fruitful labour in a field of studies so close to his heart. All the contributors to this volume are either ex-colleagues, collaborators or students of his and the book's publication is a highly appropriate tribute to one of the finest historians of his generation, offered in his honour with great respect, real gratitude and deep affection for a man we all miss profoundly.

Notes

1 Philip Woodfine to Keith Laybourn, undated letter.

2 David was always proud of his family background and occasionally commented wryly on episodes of his family's history, for instance in a letter he sent to Philip Woodfine around Christmas 1991: 'To see Scissett [near Huddersfield, where Philip lives] was poignant. It takes me back to Mafeking night in 1900 when a handsome chap from Burton-on-Trent took a 17-year old lass into a cornfield near Scissett and had a night of love under the stars. She bore a daughter in 1901 – that daughter was my mother. I never saw my real grandfather (he did a QFO!), but I saw my real grandmother once – in 1947. My mother was brought up by her mother's sister and husband (always regarded by her as "Ma" and "Pa", and grandma and granddad to me). All very Hardyesque. No doubt Scissett (then coal-mining) is now all yuppie and puritan. TV instead of good *alfresco* shagging?!!!'. Philip rightly comments that this letter, written in David's invariable fountain pen ('a piece of conservatism on which he prided himself, though with his handwriting the typewriter was always an improvement') both encapsulates his more relaxed conversational style and provides valuable clues about how his background shaped the man and his interest in social history. David also once mentioned, in conversation with Keith Laybourn and Keith Dockray, that one of his grandfathers, who lived to be a hundred, recalled hearing Joseph Chamberlain speak in 1886, and that his great, or great-great, grandfather had seen Napoleon on board the *Bellerophon* as he sailed into exile on St Helena.

3   Even in his later life David's stutter occasionally returned, at times of stress, and the fact that he was a heavy smoker (both pipe and cigarettes) is probably a further pointer to his nervous disposition; moreover, although Jack Reynolds fostered the historian, he never managed to convince him of the fascination of cricket: for David, cricket was 'the most tedious game ever invented', rivalled only by football for which he had little time either.

4   Later in life, David claimed that, as a student, he drank a great deal of beer, and also enjoyed dressing smartly: certainly several of his colleagues at Huddersfield remember a photograph, probably taken in 1957 or 1958, where he most nearly resembled Buddy Holly or, perhaps, a besuited six-foot-one-inch Teddy Boy. During one of his summer vacations he worked at a bakery in Goole and was delighted to discover that Philip Woodfine – a child at that time – had actually been living in the next street: he always relished the chances and coincidences of life. Both at school and university, despite an aversion to cricket and football, David mainly enjoyed sport, but individual rather than team games. Indeed, he was a fine sportsman in his own right, particularly excelling at boxing and swimming. While at Manchester he became university light-heavyweight boxing champion and always enjoyed recalling how he had sparred with Floyd Patterson only a week or so before Patterson knocked out Brian London in the first round of their heavyweight title fight; also, at the Bradford Swimming Club, he played a role in the training of Anita Lonsborough, who won the 200 metres breaststroke for women at the 1960 Olympics.

5   Soon after his return to Bradford, David married Valerie, his girlfriend throughout his grammar school days. They had three children – Tim, Simon and Victoria – all born in the early to mid-1960s. Clearly, in the years that followed, David's family meant a great deal to him and they, in turn, helped to provide a homely environment in the book-filled house at Shipley, near Bradford, where he spent very many years of his adult life. All this helped facilitate his academic work and, in his 1984 study of *Napoleon and Europe*, he specifically expressed his gratitude 'to my daughter Victoria for both encouragement and criticism'. Valerie's premature death, in 1986, affected David profoundly, not least in leading him to question his religious beliefs: raised a Methodist, he had finally converted to Anglicanism (his wife's religion) in the mid-1970s but, in his last years, Christianity no longer provided the firm spiritual and moral comfort it once had. Even so, it was fitting that a moving Memorial Service for David, attended by many of the contributors to this *Festschrift*, as well as his children and Shipley friends, should have been held at St Paul's Church, Shipley, on 22 December 1995. He was actually buried on a grassy Cotswold hillside, very reminiscent of a Pennine foothill, overlooking Stroud in Gloucestershire.

6   Several anecdotes about David's years as a schoolmaster, and their lasting impact on him even after he moved into higher education, are worth recording. Philip Woodfine, for instance, recollects that 'he was always marked by his days as a schoolmaster. I remember once talking to a group of students together, on a course we taught jointly [at Huddersfield Polytechnic]. As we walked away together he positively hissed, "no first names in front of the students, *please*". He was always formal in that way. Remember the glee with which he used to tell his curiously old-fashioned story about the days when his all-male staff was joined by a young attractive woman? He was mortally embarrassed at the lunch table when a very senior teacher, who only knew her through the excited chit-chat of the young bucks like David, leaned courteously towards her and enquired: "And how are you finding the school, Miss Bedworthy?"' Keith Laybourn's first memory of David, indeed, is as a schoolmaster who

had come to the newly-formed University of Bradford in 1966, to talk to one of Jack Reynold's groups: 'He was young, dynamic and spoke about Chartism with passion.' And, perhaps significantly, David had a photograph of himself as a schoolmaster in his study at Huddersfield, sporting an academic gown and surrounded by a class of boys, very much the traditional grammar school photograph of the 1960s.

7 John O'Connell, formerly Dean of Humanities at Huddersfield Polytechnic, recalls, in a letter to Keith Dockray dated April 1998, that during his time at Huddersfield David Wright 'led two lives: as well as being on the staff of the Polytechnic, he was on the staff of the Open University. That he did both jobs and, of course, his writing, is his great achievement. His attachment to the OU was often brought home to me, perhaps most clearly shortly after he retired. I was made to realize that, though he had early-retired from the Polytechnic, he had not retired from the OU.' Indeed, although he had no real ambition to be anything other than an academic (and would probably have found an administrative appointment intolerable, anyway), David did once consider the possibility of taking a post as Open University Staff Tutor in Arts for the Yorkshire region: fortunately, he never did so (although he did act as Assistant Staff Tutor from time to time), not least because it left open a vacancy for Mike Bartholomew, one of the contributors to this *Festschrift*. David Wright's Open University career also provides evidence that, although by temperament a traditionalist in matters educational, he could on occasion be unexpectedly radical: for instance, he was always rather uncomfortable with the fact that, during his time, virtually all OU courses required students to sit three-hour examinations and once he wrote to *Sesame* (the Open University student newspaper) advocating a complete rethink on this.

8 Keith Laybourn recollects an occasion when, in about 1974, both he, David Wright and most of the Huddersfield history staff were enlisted into providing seminars for an Historical Association Sixth Form Conference at Bradford University. David remembered that he had once taught Keith and announced dramatically: 'Keith Laybourn once sat at my feet.' Pauline Stafford, a force to be reckoned with long before she attained her present eminence in early medieval studies, enquired provocatively whether or not that was at primary school. David's smiling response was to say 'I felt that', even though by the mid-1970s he already enjoyed projecting himself in the role of the aged schoolmaster (even wearing a sports jacket with reinforced arm patches from time to time).

9 Keith Dockray remembers jointly supervising, with David, a student on teaching practice in the early 1970s, when he not only expressed great admiration for the traditional down-to-earth approach to history teaching of the middle-aged woman who was head of history at the school but also made a whole series of helpful and *practical* suggestions to the student. Another of David's colleagues at Huddersfield in the 1970s, Tony Saul, in conversation with Keith Dockray, recalled his similarly practical advice to a student struggling to cope with a class of boisterous fourteen-year-olds: find the biggest boy in the class and, whether he has done anything wrong or not, expel him from the classroom and let him kick his heels in the corridor for the rest of the lesson (a draconian but notably effective remedy when put to the test).

10 Graham Townend to Keith Dockray, letter dated January 1996. Keith Dockray also remembers this lecture vividly, not least David's dry wit when considering the odder aspects of Gladstone's private life. David was, in fact, a stalwart of the Historical Association, serving as president of the Bradford branch from 1975 to 1980.

11 Both for Huddersfield and the OU David gave a high priority to marking, and commenting on, student assignments, and getting work back quickly; moreover, he was always encouraging in his remarks on essays and ready to acknowledge quality with high marks. His concern to recognize the achievements of his students, and firm belief in the valuable role of such occasions, explains his almost invariable attendance at Huddersfield graduation ceremonies and also, very frequently, Open University ones as well.

12 David's research students included both John Hargreaves and Cyril Pearce, contributors to this volume. John Hargreaves, besides remembering David as a thoughtful and challenging lecturer, emphasizes (in a letter to Keith Laybourn, dated December 1996) how he 'always found him a sympathetic and patient supervisor and valued his succinct and encouraging observations on my work'. Robert Perks, now Curator of Oral History at the British Library, has similar recollections of David as supervisor of his 1985 PhD (on 'New Liberalism and the Challenge of Labour in the West Riding of Yorkshire with special reference to Huddersfield'). For several years, moreover, David Wright was a member of the history panel of the Council for National Academic Awards, the body responsible for supervising the award of degrees in the Polytechnic sector.

13 On one occasion, when there had been a mining disaster in Yorkshire, he sought out Keith Laybourn and, in all gravity, expressed the hope that his father, who was a miner, had not been involved, while Philip Woodfine recalls the note David sent to him when his father died: 'It was in Latin, and almost illegible, as was his way, but it was a gesture of real sympathy and kindness, and curiously comforting.'

14 Keith Laybourn remembers that David's distinctive style was to refer to his 'day and age', giving the impression of being ten or twelve years older than he actually was: specifically he recollects a young female member of the Education Department at Huddersfield, probably in her early thirties, remarking that he was such nice company for one so old! Yet he could be very much a man of contrasts. For a few years he even relinquished his car to his wife Valerie, choosing instead to ride an ancient motor cycle to-and-fro from work, clad most incongruously in full biker's gear. Behind the old-fashioned image, moreover, there remained a powerful radical streak, as demonstrated by his then unfashionably liberal views on homosexuality: sexual orientation did not matter, he once remarked to Keith Dockray in the mid-1970s, and people should be judged as people, not in terms of their gender preferences when it came to bedmates. David's liberal sexual attitudes also covered the massive, undoctored tom cat which ruled the roost in his Shipley home for a number of years and provided real companionship following his wife's death: he was inordinately proud of its nightly sexual adventures in the gardens of respectable suburbia which, he frequently asserted, resulted in utter feline exhaustion every morning, and he was devastated when it died.

15 Often the pipe-smoking David contrived to smother both students and colleagues in clouds of smoke, as well as frequently combining the arduous tasks of pipe-cleaning and conducting tutorials. Later, the cigarette-smoking David used occasionally to barter his Consulate menthol cigarettes for Keith Dockray's standard Benson and Hedges: a pair of hopeless addicts of the noxious weed, indeed!

16 John O'Connell to Keith Dockray, letter dated April 1996.

17 Graham Townend to Keith Dockray, letter dated January 1996.

18 D.G. Wright, *Democracy and Reform, 1815–1885* (London, Longman, 1970).

19 D.G. Wright, *Popular Radicalism: The Working Class Experience, 1780–1880* (London, Longman, 1988).

20 D.G. Wright, 'A Radical Borough: Parliamentary Politics in Bradford 1832–1841', *Northern History*, iv, 1969; D.G. Wright, 'Bradford and the American Civil War', *Journal of British Studies*, viii, 1969; D.G. Wright, 'Leeds Politics and the American Civil War', *Northern History*, ix, 1974; D.G. Wright, 'The Bradford Election of 1874', in J.A. Jowitt and R.K.S. Taylor (eds), *Nineteenth Century Bradford Elections* (Bradford, Leeds Extra-Mural Department, 1979); D.G. Wright and J.A. Jowitt, *Victorian Bradford* (Bradford, Bradford Metro, 1981). See also D.G. Wright, *The Chartist Risings in Bradford*, (Pamphlet, Bradford, Bradford Libraries, 1986) and D.G. Wright, 'The West Riding Textile District in Mid-Nineteenth Century Yorkshire', in J.A. Jowitt (ed.) *Model Industrial Communities in Mid-Nineteenth-Century Yorkshire* (Bradford, Bradford University Press, 1986).

21 D.G. Wright, *Revolution and Terror in France, 1789–1795* (London, Longman, 1974).

22 D.G. Wright, *Napoleon and Europe* (London, Longman, 1984), pp. 94–5.

23 D.G. Wright, 'The Great War, Government Propaganda and English "Men of Letters", 1914–1916', *Literature and History*, vii, 1978.

24 D.G. Wright, *The Great War: A Useless Slaughter?* (Huddersfield, Huddersfield Pamphlets in History and Politics, 1991), p. 1.

1

BRADFORD, LEEDS AND THE CIVIL WAR IN THE WEST RIDING OF YORKSHIRE: LITERARY SOURCES AND THEIR INTERPRETATION

Keith Dockray

Once England dissolved into Civil War in the late summer of 1642, it was perhaps inevitable that the West Riding of Yorkshire rapidly became a major battleground between contending Royalists and Parliamentarians. Although sparsely populated and notably deficient in good quality agricultural land, over 300 gentry families were seated there: a minority, such as the Saviles of Thornhill near Dewsbury (whose head, Sir John Savile, was raised to the peerage in 1628) and the Ingrams of Temple Newsam near Leeds, were knightly houses generously endowed with estates; most belonged to the ranks of middling-to-small gentry; and, significantly, almost a third had pronounced Puritan leanings. Even more significantly, by the early seventeenth century the West Riding had become home to, and its economy increasingly dependent on, well-established coal, iron and cloth industries, and their development had been accompanied by the growth of small but vigorous urban communities, most of which were to experience military action during the Civil War. Barnsley, Rotherham and Sheffield, for instance, had emerged as centres for coal, iron and metal-working: Sheffield, indeed, was already nationally known for its cutlery. Similarly, Wakefield, Halifax, Bradford and Leeds were all textile towns, very much reliant on a local woollen cloth industry that had grown markedly since the later Middle Ages: economic depression in the industry in the 1630s, especially in the context of mounting government financial demands and Laudian assaults on Puritanism, might, indeed, go far to explain the degree of support for Parliament in towns like Halifax and Bradford during the Civil War. Not that any of these towns were large, even by the modest standards of the time. Leeds and Wakefield were probably the biggest: Leeds, where many West Riding clothiers had premises, was even described, in 1639, as one of the most populous towns in England with about 12,000 people (although 6,000 is probably nearer the mark). Halifax and Bradford were considerably smaller, perhaps home to 2,500–3,000 inhabitants apiece: of the two, Halifax probably had the edge in terms of cloth production but it was lowly Bradford that was to experience the most dramatic events of the Civil War in the West Riding.[1]

Politically, the West Riding was notably disturbed during early Stuart times, largely as a result of a great feud between two of its most powerful knightly families: the Saviles of Thornhill and the Wentworths of Wentworth Woodhouse. Sir John Savile and Sir Thomas Wentworth, in particular, were both men of great ambition and their rivalry dominated West Riding political life for more than a decade from about 1617; Savile ingratiated himself with James I's favourite George Villiers, Duke of Buckingham, while Wentworth emerged as one of the government's leading critics in the Commons; and both had strong support in the West Riding. By the mid-1620s many substantial local gentry, particularly men active in county administration, were backing Wentworth, while Savile, whose estates were concentrated there, enjoyed much support in the cloth-producing districts around Leeds, Wakefield and Halifax, especially clothiers whose interests he ostentatiously promoted. Both Savile and Wentworth were raised to the peerage in June 1628 but when, shortly afterwards, Buckingham was murdered, Wentworth seized advantage of his rival's weakened position, accused him of accepting bribes from recusants, and not only helped engineer his resignation as Vice President of the Council of the North but also, in December 1628, secured the Lord Presidency of the Council for *himself*. Now the most powerful man north of the Trent, having at his disposal very considerable resources of patronage, Wentworth continued to enjoy, in the 1630s, much influential support; nevertheless, his self-interested ruthlessness inevitably aroused significant opposition as well, not least in the West Riding where Thomas, Lord Fairfax, for one, emerged as a prominent critic. Non-parliamentary taxation, ranging from knighthood fines in the early 1630s to Ship Money later in the decade, helped fuel discontent, as did the implementation of Laudian religious policies by Richard Neile, Archbishop of York. Puritan gentry in the West Riding particularly resented Neile's anti-Puritan offensive; so, too, did vocal Puritan communities in industrial centres such as Bradford, Leeds, Halifax, Wakefield and Sheffield. The Puritan citizens of Bradford, for instance, came into conflict with the ecclesiastical authorities over the appointment of a master to the local grammar school and when, in 1635, Neile gave the post to a man of Laudian inclinations, did their level best to secure his removal. Not surprisingly, when heavy-handed Laudian policies provoked rebellion in Scotland in 1638 and Charles I looked particularly to the north of England for financial and military support, there was a marked lack of enthusiasm: the West Riding knight Sir William Savile, for instance, not only refused to bring his troop of horse to York for training but also became embroiled in deep intrigue with Thomas, Lord Wentworth's enemies both at Court and in Yorkshire. In the end, indeed, shortage of both men and money forced the king, in 1639, to abandon his projected campaign in Scotland for the time being.

The behaviour of Charles I and his government in 1640 served to intensify the crisis: Laud's unpopular religious measures continued unabated; a new writ for Ship Money was issued; and there were fresh demands to levy troops for war against the Scots. In Yorkshire, not least in the West Riding, discontent continued to mount, and there is interesting evidence of local gentry petitioning the king in the summer of 1640, particularly complaining of the military demands being made upon them, the cost of maintaining troops when assembled and, inevitably, their unruly behaviour while no actual campaign was in progress. When the Scots seized the initiative in August 1640, advanced over the border, defeated a royal army and occupied Northumberland and Durham, the prospect of their marching south into Yorkshire clearly added to the anxieties already rife among local landowners; as for the king, he had no choice but to conclude a humiliating treaty with his rebellious Scottish subjects at Ripon and call the Long Parliament. Although Yorkshire sent thirty MPs to Westminster in November 1640, none of the newly developed West Riding urban communities were represented. In view of this, and the considerable pressure brought to bear on electors in both the county and ancient boroughs by Thomas, Lord Wentworth (now Earl of Strafford), it is surely significant that only five of the Yorkshire members who were returned can be described as pro-government. Among the thirty, interestingly enough, the diarist and Knaresborough MP Sir Henry Slingsby (a firm Royalist throughout the Civil War) was to vote against Strafford's attainder in April 1641, while the county member Ferdinando, Lord Fairfax (who rapidly became commander-in-chief of Parliamentary forces in Yorkshire once war commenced) helped frame the indictment condemning him. Clearly, during the first few months of the Long Parliament, Yorkshire critics of Charles I's government must have been well pleased not only by Strafford's execution but also the abolition of the discredited Council of the North. Even so, they remained apprehensive, particularly men of Puritan persuasions whose fear of Roman Catholicism (even more alarming than Laudianism) knew no bounds once Ireland erupted in rebellion in October 1641: indeed, for many of them, this might well have seemed but the precursor of a Catholic uprising in England and the imposition of Popish tyranny! Nonsense it may have been, but the king's behaviour, particularly his attempted *coup d'état* in January 1642, did nothing to allay their suspicions, especially in the West Riding clothing towns where anti-Catholic hysteria went hand-in-hand with severe recession in the local textile industry. In March 1642 Charles I, having abandoned London to Parliament, took up residence in the city of York: at best he seems to have received a lukewarm reception in Yorkshire, not least at Hull where he was refused admission in April and again in July. Nevertheless, during the spring and summer of 1642, the nationwide resurgence of Royalism (as alarm grew at the intentions and behaviour of Parliament) found expression in Yorkshire as well: even though a large gathering of freeholders on Heworth Moor on 3 June gave the king a decidedly mixed reception, support for his cause was growing (albeit particularly among Yorkshire Catholics and none too significantly in the West Riding), and the king's summons to local gentry to assemble in arms at York on 4 August seems to have elicited a decent response. Even so, Charles I's decision to abandon York for Nottingham (where he raised the standard of war on 22 August) must reflect, in part at least, disappointment at his reception in Yorkshire over the preceding few months.

Not that the Royalist historian Edward Hyde, Earl of Clarendon chose to portray Yorkshire's response to Charles I's dilemma in this way. On the contrary, when describing the king's arrival at York in March 1642, he recorded that he 'found his reception there to be equal to his expectation, the gentry and men of ability of that great and populous county, some very few excepted, expressing great alacrity for his majesty's being with them'. At the outbreak of Civil War, Clarendon tells us:

> The greatest part of the gentry of that populous country [of Yorkshire], and very many of the common people, did behave with signal fidelity and courage to the king's service. . . . There were very few gentlemen, or men of any quality, in that large county who were actively or factiously disaffected to his majesty. . . .

Even Clarendon had to admit, however, that 'Leeds, Halifax and Bradford, three very populous and rich towns (which depending wholly on clothiers naturally maligned the gentry) were wholly at their [the Parliamentarians'] disposition'. Clarendon has many fine qualities as a historian and, as a close adviser and minister of Charles I throughout the Civil War, often had much valuable inside information: even so, he has to be treated with great caution as a source for northern history, he frequently confused and misrepresented events and, when it came to military matters, he was particularly prone to become unreliable and unconvincing.[2]

Equally problematic, if for rather different reasons, is Margaret, Duchess of Newcastle's *Life* of her husband. Royalist commander in the north from December 1642 until the disaster at Marston Moor early in July 1644, William Cavendish, Duke of Newcastle has been much criticized, both in his own lifetime and since, for his generalship. Perhaps it was with a view to putting the record straight that his second wife published her *Life* in 1667 (just under a decade before her husband's death in 1676). If so, her efforts enjoyed little success, at any rate if Samuel Pepys' reaction (in March 1668) is typical: the diarist could hardly have been more scathing when referring to 'the ridiculous history of my Lord Newcastle, written by his wife, which shows her to be a mad, conceited, ridiculous woman, and he an ass to suffer her to write what she writes to him and of him'. C.H. Firth, the *Life*'s modern editor, was often notably critical too, particularly of the duchess's treatment of her husband's military career. Are such strictures justified? Certainly, it is a notably fulsome biography, with Margaret determined to present her husband in as favourable a light as she could, emphasizing, wherever possible, his good qualities and achievements, while tending to gloss over his failings and mistakes. Yet, although having to rely on what others could tell her about Newcastle's military career, she could obviously consult her husband himself and clearly also learned much from his secretary John Rolleston. Moreover, the picture she presents of a conscientious commander who enjoyed the loyalty of his subordinates, willingly sought advice from men whose military knowledge and experience exceeded his own, and did not shirk from getting in on the action himself, is, as P.R. Newman has emphasized, more balanced and credible than is often allowed. For instance, while by no means a triumph of military planning and execution, his West Riding campaign of 1643 did result in a considerable victory at Adwalton Moor on 30 June, and, in the battle, he both commanded in person and courageously fought on foot; as for the Royalist defeat at Marston Moor, blame must be firmly placed on the shoulders not of Newcastle but of Prince Rupert.[3]

Perhaps the most valuable Royalist narrative of political and military events in Yorkshire from early 1639 to July 1644, not least the West Riding campaigns of 1642/3, is provided by Sir Henry Slingsby of Scriven near Knaresborough. Slingsby himself, moreover, was in the thick of many of these events, and his comments on their significance are often perceptive. For instance, he sat as MP for Knaresborough in the Short Parliament of April/May 1640, 'which was so unfortunate that it lasted but three weeks without having done anything to content either king or country'; returned by Knaresborough again to the Long Parliament, he fully appreciated the implications of its early deliberations. 'Great expectance there is of a happy Parliament', he declared, 'where the subject may have a total redress of all his grievances'; moreover, he observed, 'they fear not the dissolving of Parliament, for the Scots are at Newcastle with an army fortified'. From the beginning, Slingsby was a firm Royalist: he was among the fifty-nine MPs who voted against Strafford's attainder in April 1641; in May 1642 he was commissioned by the king to command the trained bands of the city of York; and, soon after the commencement of the Civil War, he received a further commission from the Earl (later Marquess and Duke) of Newcastle to raise a volunteer regiment of foot. Thereafter, he played a prominent part in the northern campaigns of 1643 and 1644, culminating in his fighting for the king at Marston Moor, and, in the later stages of the war, fought in both the West Country and the Midlands, notably at the battle of Naseby in

June 1645. Following Charles I's defeat in 1646 he was judged a malignant for refusing to abandon the Royalist cause, his estates were sequestered and, eventually, he was executed in 1658 for allegedly plotting against the Cromwellian regime.

Sir Henry Slingsby's so-called 'diary' is, in reality, a memoir, not a journal kept on a day-to-day (or even month-to-month) basis: rather, it appears to have been compiled in full at a later date. Frequently vague when it came to precise dates, selective in the events covered, and less detailed as a source for campaigning in Yorkshire 1642–4 than either Margaret, Duchess of Newcastle's *Life* or Thomas, Lord Fairfax's *Short Memorial of the Northern Actions*, Slingsby's account is none the less invaluable: it is a notably honest and often self-effacing memoir, written by an intelligent man who avoided pejorative innuendoes about his opponents or the twisting of facts to show himself in a favourable light, and containing generally accurate descriptions of events as well as astute comments on their nature and significance. Slingsby is especially interesting on men's motives, not least his own (where we are left in no doubt as to his personal conviction of the rightness of the Royalist cause), and he is never more perceptive than in his analysis of the situation facing Yorkshire in the autumn of 1640:

> The charge this year hath been so grave to this country, by impositions and taxes laid upon it, and by the waste which is made by the soldiers that are billeted here, that men are at a stand which course to take. . . . The fear they apprehend by that which hath befallen their neighbours in Northumberland and the Bishopric of Durham, from the Scots army that lies there yet amongst them, hath made many both here and in the Bishopric to forsake their houses and neglect, so that it is greatly to be feared we shall find both the value of our lands and rents to fall and abate very much.

When writing of the Civil War itself, moreover, Slingsby provides valuable evidence of the mechanics of fighting (particularly the problems of raising, mustering and paying men), as well as vividly bringing home to us just what campaigning entailed.[4]

No narrative of the northern war has been more influential than that bequeathed by Sir Thomas Fairfax, who succeeded his father Ferdinando as 3rd Lord Fairfax in 1648. Like his father, he had emerged as a firm supporter of Parliament by the summer of 1642 and, when war broke out, he became second-in-command to Ferdinando (appointed generalissimo of northern Parliamentary forces in August 1642) as general of the horse. Thereafter, he played a very active – indeed leading – role in the West Riding campaign of 1642/3, showing great personal courage, a capacity to inspire his men and a willingness to take the offensive even when the odds were against him. Early successes included the taking of Leeds in January 1643 and the storming of Wakefield in May, although, arguably, his failures in battle at Seacroft Moor near Leeds at the end of March and Adwalton Moor near Bradford at the end of June 1643 had far greater strategic significance: indeed, following the fall of Bradford to the Royalists (an almost inevitable consequence of Adwalton), he found himself forced into an ignominious retreat to Hull. In the spring of 1644, however, he played a major role in the strategically vital Parliamentarian victory at Selby; at Marston Moor he commanded the horse of the right wing; and, in the mopping-up operations that followed, he contrived to get himself wounded not once but twice! Certainly, by early 1645, such was his military reputation that he became commander-in-chief of the New Model Army. Many years later, towards the end of the 1660s, Fairfax composed his *Short Memorial of the Northern Actions, during the war there, from the year 1642 till the year 1644*. A very personal document, firmly based on Fairfax's own experiences during the first couple of years of the Civil War (as he recollected them), the *Short Memorial* vividly brings the war to life as its author re-lived his many daring deeds. Certainly, he had none of Sir Henry Slingsby's capacity for self-deprecation, as is only too evident in his dramatic recital of personal courage in the face of adversity when retreating from Leeds to Hull in the summer of 1643:

> And now I had been at least twenty hours on horseback, after I was shot [at Selby]: and as many hours before. . . . [At Barton] I lay down a little to rest; if it were possible to find any in a body so full of pain; and [in] a mind so full of anxiety and trouble. . . . So passing [the] Humber, we arrived at Hull; our men faint and tired: [and I] myself having lost all, even to my shirt; for my clothes were made unfit to wear, with rents and the blood which was upon them.

Recently, indeed, P.R. Newman has subjected Fairfax's memoir to searching criticisms, commenting, in particular, on his memory lapses, his tendency to distort events, his willingness to play down (or even ignore) matters that reflected badly on him, as well as highlighting evidence of Fairfax's misinterpreting or disobeying his father's orders. At the very least, it is now clear, the *Short Memorial* must be treated with considerably more caution than has traditionally been the case.[5]

Historians have always been cautious about the *Autobiography* of Joseph Lister. Born in Bradford in 1627, Lister enjoyed a solidly Puritan upbringing before becoming, at the age of fourteen, apprentice to a local clothier. Before long he found himself caught up in the dramatic events that marked the early stages of the Civil War in Bradford, at any rate if we are to believe his *Autobiography* (probably written not long before his death in 1709) where he relived with a vengeance the traumatic experiences of his formative years. Habitually emotional and long-winded, often petty and frequently irritating, Lister's memoir is none the less interesting in presenting the singular viewpoint of a West Riding Puritan clothier who recorded much about Bradford's experiences in the Civil War not to be found anywhere else. Lister's Puritanism certainly comes across very strongly in his discussion of the origins of the Civil War: he saw the war, in fact, as fought for the defence of 'true religion' against the dark forces of Papal tyranny, and put particular stress on the outbreak of Catholic rebellion in Ireland in the autumn of 1641, as a result of which 'many thousand protestants of all ages, sexes, and degrees, were put to death'. This, he declared, made a tremendous impact on Protestant opinion in England:

> . . . great fear came upon the protestants in England, these villains giving it out that what they had done there was by the king's commission, and that in a little time the English protestants . . . should drink of the same cup.

Typically, Lister then supplies a splendid local anecdote of his own, featuring the 'holy Mr Wales', Puritan minister at Pudsey near Bradford, a man wont to 'spend six or seven hours in praying and preaching, and rarely go out of the pulpit'. On one particular day, he recollected, a man:

> . . . came and stood in the chapel door, and cried out with a lamentable voice. 'Friends', said he, 'we are as good as dead men, for the Irish rebels are coming; they are come as far as Rochdale, and Littleborough, and the Batings, and will be at Halifax and Bradford shortly.' . . . Upon which the congregation was all in confusion, [the] Irish Massacre being but lately acted, [and] the people's hearts failed them with fear; so that the Rev. Mr Wales desired the congregation to compose themselves as well as they could, while he put himself and them into the hands of Almighty God by prayer. . . .

The Civil War, Lister believed, resulted from the policies of the king, aided and abetted by 'the constant solicitation of the bloody queen, together with the swarms of Jesuits and evil affected councillors, bishops and men of great estate, place and trust'; in particular, he declared, they:

> . . . all put their hands together to destroy Christ's interest in the nation, and betray their trust every way to the utter ruin and overthrow of religion, and to cut off the lives of all the Protestants, and so have enslaved this land to Rome, the mother of harlots, whose kingdom is established by God.

As for the war itself, Lister saw Parliament as very much carrying out the will of God and, not surprisingly, he chose to concentrate on Bradford's role, emphasizing the strong commitment of the town and its surrounding area to the Parliamentary cause:

In this war Bradford was deeply engaged; the generality of the town and parish, and the towns about, stood up for the Parliament, and though it was not easy to keep, yet they threw up bulwarks about it; and the inhabitants were firm to the cause, and to one another, to the very taking of the town. . . .

Predictably, Lister is at his most dramatic when describing the fall of Bradford to the Royalists in the summer of 1643:

But oh! what a night and morning was that in which Bradford was taken! what weeping and wringing of hands! none expecting to live any longer than till the enemies came into the town, the Earl of Newcastle having charged his men to kill all, man, woman and child, in the town. . . .[6]

Another West Riding Parliamentarian who tried his hand at autobiography was Captain John Hodgson of Coley Hall, near Halifax. Little is known of him beyond what can be gleaned from his *Memoirs* (essentially a pocket-book) but he seems to have been a minor Yorkshire gentleman or yeoman from the Hipperholme district. Although not having a great deal to offer on the West Riding campaigns of 1642–4, what he does say is both splendidly personal and clearly partisan. Rather harshly dubbed 'an honest-hearted, pudding-headed Yorkshire Puritan' by Thomas Carlyle in the nineteenth century, Hodgson certainly saw the Civil War very much as a rearguard action against the dangers of Roman Catholic tyranny. Parliament, he wrote with some gusto, had:

. . . declared their fears and jealousies, that there was a popish party about the king carrying on a design to alter religion; that the war with Scotland was procured to make way for it; that the rebellion in Ireland was framed in England, and should have been acted here.

He particularly emphasized his own religious motivations in becoming involved in the fighting. 'When I put my hand to the Lord's work', he declared, 'I did it not rashly but had many an hour and night to seek God, to know my way.' He first took up arms in December 1642 in response to Sir William Savile's attack on Bradford; he fought in Sir Thomas Fairfax's army at Leeds in January 1643; and he was present at the storming of Wakefield in the May of that year. Between these two successes, however, there had been the Parliamentary failure at Seacroft Moor at the end of March 1643, described by Hodgson as a total rout. Indeed, he tells us:

I was there sore wounded, shot in two places, cut in several, and led off into a wood by one of my soldiers. . . . With much ado he got me to Leeds in the night, and it was a considerable time before I was cured.

He was soon in trouble again, following the battle of Adwalton Moor and the fall of Bradford to the Royalists in the summer of 1643. In fact, he asserted:

> Many were taken prisoners; myself was stripped into my shirt, and driven in amongst the rest. After they had kept us two or three days, they had us to Leeds. . . .

Released soon afterwards, he made his way to Rochdale in Lancashire where he 'fell sick of a fever'. Nevertheless, in the years that followed, he continued to play an active role in Parliamentary campaigning, including taking part in the sieges of Pontefract castle in 1645 and 1648. Clearly, Puritanism was his driving force throughout: indeed, soon after the restoration of Charles II in 1660, John Hodgson, 'a great fanatic', was reported as organizing a meeting of 'a hundred fanatics, ministers and others' at his home.[7]

Contemporary and near-contemporary narratives must be regarded as fundamental to any reconstruction of military campaigning in Bradford, Leeds and the West Riding during the Civil War but their evaluation and interpretation can be greatly aided by consulting the records of central administration, local records, newsbooks, tracts, official and semi-official letters, and private correspondence. Particularly valuable are the relevant volumes in the *Calendar of State Papers, Domestic*, series, containing a great variety of interesting material, most notably official and semi-official letters. Once the king had left London early in 1642, however, these volumes become more and more dominated by letters written from the provinces to the Parliamentary leaders in the capital: for instance, a communication of 24 May 1642 reported that the king 'has summoned the freeholders, copyholders and substantial farmers of this country to be here at York on Friday next'; another, of 4 June 1642, recorded that, at this meeting on Heworth Moor outside York, 'there was the greatest appearance of people that ever I saw in this county'; and a newsletter of 17 June 1642 declared the royal Court at York to be 'full of Lords and many of the House of Commons', adding that 'the gentlemen of these northern parts are very forward in offering their service' but also that 'there is no likelihood' at present 'of levying a war on the Parliament'. Not dissimilar material can be found in John Rushworth's *Historical Collections*, a remarkable contemporary compilation combining the author's own firmly pro-Parliament narrative of events with an extensive selection of record material. In the same category, perhaps, are John Vicars' *Parliamentary Chronicles*, where Vicars, another convinced Parliamentarian, put together in narrative form a considerable amount of contemporary material: indeed, this is invaluable for the ill-documented West Riding campaign of January to April 1644.[8]

Apart from narratives such as the *Life of Newcastle* and Sir Henry Slingsby's *Diary*, the Royalist viewpoint on the West Riding campaigns can best be gleaned from the collection of newsbooks (or journals) familiar to historians under the name *Mercurius Aulicus*. Sponsored by Charles I's Court, and published weekly in

Oxford from January 1643 to September 1645, these semi-official Royalist periodicals set new standards in journalism including, on occasion, graphic accounts of events in the West Riding such as the Parliamentarian defeat at Seacroft Moor on 30 March 1643, Sir Thomas Fairfax's seizure of Wakefield a few weeks later on 21 May, and the Royalist victory at Adwalton Moor on 30 June 1643.[9] Many contemporary tracts survive too: most notably, from the Parliamentarian standpoint, there is *The Rider of the White Horse*, a pamphlet celebrating the triumph of the townsmen of Bradford over the odds when the town was besieged in December 1642, and, from the Royalist perspective, the *Express Relation*, an account of Adwalton Moor and the fall of Bradford to the Earl of Newcastle.[10] All such sources, given their propagandist purpose, need to be treated with great caution; nevertheless, they often provide detail not to be found anywhere else and have certainly been much used by historians of the Civil War.

Finally, as far as sources are concerned, much can be learned from private correspondence, and here pride of place must surely go to the Fairfax letters, long recognized as a rich archive for West Riding history in the 1640s. These include letters sent both to and from members of the Fairfax family. In the former category, letters written by Thomas Stockdale, an ardent West Riding Puritan, in 1641/2 are particularly informative. On 23 December 1641, for instance, he expressed considerable concern about Roman Catholics when writing to Ferdinando, Lord Fairfax: 'I hear of no order yet to come into the country to restrain the daily concourse of recusants, [whose] consultations may conduce to the prejudice both of Church and Commonwealth'. Ferdinando, Lord Fairfax himself wrote at considerable length from Selby to the Parliamentarian Committee of Safety in London on 10 December 1642 painting a sorry picture of the problems he was encountering in resisting the Royalists, while there are frequent letters from Sir Thomas Fairfax to his father. On 9 January 1643, for instance, he reported from Bradford that 'these parts grow very impatient of our delay in beating them [the Royalists] out of Leeds and Wakefield, for by them all trade and provisions are stopped, so that people in these clothing towns are not able to subsist'; a fortnight later, on 27 January, he wrote from Wakefield suggesting, optimistically, that 'if we could join all our forces, your lordship might resolve of some notable design'; but, back in Bradford on 20 April 1643, he was gloomily reporting that 'this town is very weak' and that he had been unable to meet a request for aid from a Penistone delegation, advising them instead 'to seek help from Rotherham and Sheffield'. Of course, such letters are often far from being disinterested records of events, but they do have an immediacy lacking in narrative sources.[11]

Clearly, virtually none of the surviving sources for Bradford, Leeds and the Civil War in the West Riding – even apparently impersonal records – can be regarded as entirely impartial: this is why there has been so much diversity in their interpretation. From the beginning of the war, there was considerable support for Parliament, particularly in the West Riding clothing towns and among middling gentry living in the vicinity of Bradford and Leeds. The Parliamentarian leadership certainly looked to this region for support, and seemingly got it, reflecting, perhaps, both the degree of economic depression and the strength of local Puritanism. As Ferdinando, Lord Fairfax emphasized on 10 December 1642: 'I have hitherto supported this army by the loans and contributions, for the most part, of the parishes of Leeds, Halifax and Bradford, and some other small clothing towns adjacent, being the only well-affected people of the country.'[12] Far more West Riding gentry became Royalist than Parliamentarian, however, particularly local knights: in the Huddersfield area, for instance, Sir Thomas Beaumont of Lascelles Hall enrolled in Sir William Savile's Royalist army on the outbreak of war and, in 1643, was appointed governor of Sheffield castle on the king's behalf; Sir John Kaye of Woodsome, likewise, served on the Royalist side; and Sir John Ramsden of Longley Hall was eventually taken prisoner fighting for the king at Selby in April 1644. Many of the principal strongholds in the West Riding were soon garrisoned for the king, too, including Pontefract, Sandal, Tickhill and Knaresborough castles. Even a minority of rich clothiers supported Charles I, although most were for Parliament, as were many yeomen, farmers, artisans and weavers.

When the king departed from Yorkshire early in August 1642, he left behind him as lieutenant-general of the county Henry Clifford, Earl of Cumberland, apparently the man the local gentry wanted but hardly ideal for the job; fortunately his deputy, Sir Thomas Glemham, was a professional soldier and tailor-made for the task. Charles I had also toyed with the idea of arresting the potentially dangerous Ferdinando, Lord Fairfax and his son Sir Thomas but had decided against it: thus they were available, when the call came, to assume command of Parliamentarian forces in Yorkshire. In August and September 1642, however, many Yorkshire notables were still hoping to keep the county neutral: indeed, on 29 September, a group of prominent Royalists and Parliamentarians put their names to a neutrality pact, pronouncing a 'general amity betwixt all the gentry and others of this county' and undertaking to disband their armies. Since a powerful section of Yorkshiremen rejected it out of hand, and Parliament rapidly condemned it as well, the pact has little more than curiosity value, and, anyway, by this time civil war was already becoming a reality, not least in the West Riding.[13] The Royalists, although lacking an effective command structure under Cumberland's ineffectual leadership, certainly made an effort to secure both Leeds and Bradford in October 1642. Most notably, having established a presence in Leeds, Sir William Savile determined, on 23 October, to launch an assault on Bradford. The town, unwalled and situated in a hollow surrounded by hills, was not easy to defend, particularly against artillery attack. Nevertheless, according to Joseph Lister:

> . . . it was made a little garrison; and though it was not easy to keep, yet [the townsmen] threw up bulwarks about it. . . . When the enemies approached the town, horsemen were sent to Halifax, Bingley and the small towns about, who presently took the alarm, and came with all speed, and such arms as they had, and stuck close to the inhabitants, and did very good service.

If Lister's recollections are to be relied upon, however, threat soon turned to farce:

> [The Royalists] brought two great guns with them, and planted them directly against the steeple. . . . But God so ordered it that a great snow shower fell, [and] one of the great guns burst, which so disheartened them that they went away of their own accord. . . .[14]

Clearly encouraged by this, Bradford's defenders gleefully followed the retreating Royalists to Leeds and, within a few days, enough Parliamentarian reinforcements arrived there, as Sir Henry Slingsby puts it, to persuade 'Sir Thomas Glemham to quit the place' since 'the force he had was not able to encounter his adversary'.[15] These puny events, engaging no more than a few hundred men on either side, are, perhaps, typical of the early stages of the Civil War in the West Riding: dramatic they may have been for those caught up in them, but they had little if any strategic significance.[16] In December 1642, however, everything changed when William Cavendish, Earl of Newcastle, not only took over from Cumberland as Royalist commander but also brought with him a far more powerful army than any so far seen.

Now began a sustained Royalist campaign in the West Riding which was to culminate, albeit after a number of setbacks, in spectacular success in the summer of 1643. On 10 December 1642 Ferdinando, Lord Fairfax gloomily reported Newcastle's strength as 'far too potent to be resisted by the small power which I have', a conclusion occasioned, in part at least, by a successful Royalist assault on Tadcaster a few days earlier and probably not altered by his son's daring (but, arguably, self-indulgent) lightning strike on Sherburn-in-Elmet soon afterwards.[17] Newcastle now launched a major offensive against the West Riding clothing region. Royalist forces under the command of Sir William Savile occupied Leeds and Wakefield and, on 18 December, Bradford was besieged. Events there are dramatically described in *The Rider of the White Horse*, a Parliamentarian tract probably based on the report of an eye-witness actively involved in defending a town 'most unable to resist' such an onslaught. Even so, whereas in Leeds, 'the malignant rumour being predominant', the Royalists 'easily converted the town into their temper', Bradford proved an altogether different kettle of fish.

Although there were also 'malignant spirits' there, they failed to prevent the town's inhabitants mounting a vigorous defence against appalling odds, remarkable not least because 'all our trained soldiers, with their arms, were with the Lord Fairfax'. Moreover, throughout an engagement probably lasting most of the day, Royalist ordnance battered the town:

> You see the Lord's mercy to us: that which was planted against the steeple never hit it; another intended for the scouring of Kirkgate, [though] many of their bullets hit the houses, and some the street, yet was nobody at all hurt therewith. . . . [Eventually] the terror of the Lord and of us, falling upon them, sending their foot and artillery foremost, away they went (using their feet better than they used their hands) and about fifty of our muskets after them; which courage in ours did most of all astonish the enemy.[18]

Bradford triumphed, in fact, and it was a victory for the townsmen themselves: neither Sir Thomas Fairfax nor his field army played any part. And, although the successful defence of a small West Riding town against an ill-organized Royalist assault had no great strategic significance, it had tremendous propaganda potential (as the Fairfaxes clearly recognized), as well as temporarily putting an end to Newcastle's hopes of fully subduing the region.

Early in 1643, indeed, the Parliamentarians themselves took the initiative when they turned up in considerable force outside Leeds on 23 January. As Ferdinando, Lord Fairfax reported three days later:

> . . . on Monday last he [Sir Thomas Fairfax] drew his forces out of Bradford, and marched to Leeds, where Sir William Savile commanded in chief. My son first summoned them by trumpet to yield, which being refused, the assault began. . . . The people do observe that Sir William Savile, and the chief commanders on the other side, soon after the fight began, fled by secret ways towards Pomfret [Pontefract], and their men after them by degrees. . . .[19]

News of the disaster at Leeds seems to have unnerved the Royalist garrison in Wakefield into abandoning the town, and, for a few weeks, the Parliamentarians looked set to capitalize on their successes in the West Riding. It was not to be. Instead, on 30 March 1643, the Royalists under General George Goring inflicted a crushing defeat on Sir Thomas Fairfax's army at the battle of Seacroft Moor near Leeds. Typically, Fairfax was reluctant to shoulder his full weight of blame, remarking that:

> . . . our men, thinking themselves more secure, were more careless in keeping order; and while their officers were getting them out of houses where they

sought for drink, it being an exceedingly hot day, the enemy got, another way, as soon as we, to the Moor. . . . They, seeing us in some disorder, charged us both in flank and rear. The countrymen presently cast down their arms and fled. The foot soon after: which, for want of pikes, were not able to withstand their horse. Some were slain; and many taken prisoners. Few of our horse stood the charge. Some officers, with me, made our retreat with much difficulty. . . . Yet we got to Leeds. . . .

Even Fairfax admitted, however, that this was 'one of the greatest losses we ever received', while John Hodgson openly criticized the Parliamentarian leader for 'exceeding his commission at the request of the clubmen', as a result of which 'at Seacroft they fell upon us and totally routed us'.[20]

Perhaps Newcastle could, and should, now have seized Leeds by storm but, instead, the Royalists chose to reoccupy Wakefield, raid Barnsley and then march south to take Rotherham and Sheffield.[21] Rotherham fell on 4 May 1643.[22] Sheffield capitulated soon after.[23] Sir Thomas Fairfax, meanwhile, had marched to Bradford in the immediate aftermath of Seacroft Moor and, clearly, Parliamentarian spirits there were at a low ebb.[24] Presumably it was partly to boost both his own and his men's morale that, on 21 May 1643, Fairfax launched a daring, albeit potentially foolhardy, raid on Wakefield and secured possession of the town once more.[25] But, as so often with Fairfax's more impulsive gestures, it bore little military fruit: it did, however, enable supplies once more to get through to Halifax, Bradford and Leeds; it resulted in the taking of 1,500 prisoners, among them General Goring; and, no doubt, it administered a timely blow to Royalist prestige. Nevertheless, the balance of military advantage still lay firmly with the Royalists who, by June 1643, were ready for a major and sustained campaign against the West Riding clothing towns. As John Hodgson put it:

Not long after this [Fairfax's seizure of Wakefield] appears the Earl of Newcastle with a formidable army. It was observed by some that the land was like Eden before him and behind him as a barren wilderness.[26]

Clearly, Newcastle's eyes were firmly set on Bradford but, before reaching his goal, he had to fight a major battle on Adwalton Moor on 30 June. This proved a disaster for the Parliamentarians, but for Margaret, Duchess of Newcastle it was certainly a triumph for her husband's personal leadership, with:

. . . the field totally won by my Lord, notwithstanding he had quitted 7000 men to conduct her Majesty [to Oxford], besides a good train of artillery, which in such a conjuncture would have weakened Caesar's army. In this victory the enemy lost most of their foot, about 3000 were taken prisoners, and 700 horse and foot slain, and those that escaped fled into their garrison at Bradford, amongst whom was also their General of the Horse [Sir Thomas Fairfax].[27]

Ferdinando, Lord Fairfax, had, in fact, gambled and lost at Adwalton Moor and, as a result, Bradford now lay helpless before Newcastle's victorious army, particularly once the Parliamentarian commander-in-chief left the town for Leeds. Nor did his son Sir Thomas, after fleeing first to Halifax and then to Bradford, baulk at abandoning the townsmen to their fate once the hopelessness of Bradford's situation became apparent. Inevitably, as John Hodgson sadly recorded, once the Royalists 'drew up their whole army, and besieged us in Bradford, [and] planted their pocket-pistols [probably the demi-cannon familiarly known as Gog and Magog] and mortar-pieces against the kirk and town', surrender became the only option.[28] Leeds, never so solid for Parliament as Bradford anyway, capitulated soon after. Before long even Sir Thomas Fairfax had abandoned the West Riding and found refuge in Hull. Royalist supremacy there must now have appeared not only firm but virtually irrevocable.

Yet, by the summer of 1644, the situation in the West Riding had been completely transformed and Royalist power almost wiped out. For most of the summer and autumn of 1643 an uneasy calm prevailed in much of the region: Royalist control was a reality but it was not oppressive and, apart from occasional local flair-ups on the Lancashire border and in the vicinity of Hull (which continued to hold out for Parliament despite the Earl of Newcastle's efforts to secure it), there was little military activity. All this changed early in 1644, not least as a result of the arrival in the north of a Scottish Parliamentarian army under the terms of the Solemn League and Covenant, and the West Riding once more became home to determined military campaigning. Even before the Scots invaded, there was small-scale fighting in January 1644, particularly in the vicinity of Halifax, and it soon fell to the Yorkshire knight Sir John Belasyse (recently appointed governor of York) to maintain Royalist control of the West Riding against a mounting Parliamentarian resurgence. Clearly, Belasyse soon found himself severely overstretched, not least in the West Riding once Sir Thomas Fairfax despatched John Lambert to recover the region and its clothing towns for Parliament. John Hodgson, who was in Lambert's force, described how:

We marched out of Cheshire to Sowerby, and from then to Halifax, and back to Keighley, and so to Bradford. . . . We found the enemy at Bradford [on 3 March 1644], but they over-run the kirk. Our horse [was] put to flight but our foot gave them such a salute with shot as made them run for it.[29]

Soon afterwards Lambert mounted a successful assault on Hunslet near Leeds and there was also fighting in the vicinity of Kirklees near Dewsbury.[30] Belasyse now decided that the time was ripe for decisive action in the West Riding, moving his main army to Leeds and settling on Selby as his principal operational base. On 25 March 1644 Belasyse launched a major attack on Bradford but, after heavy fighting, failed to take the town and eventually withdrew back to Leeds.[31] Once more the initiative passed to the Parliamentarians. Sir Thomas Fairfax marched from Cheshire to the West Riding, took Leeds and, despite Belasyse's efforts to prevent their meeting, joined forces with his father at Ferrybridge.[32] Then, on 11 April 1644, the two Fairfaxes and Lambert launched a major attack on Belasyse's Royalist army. The resulting battle of Selby proved the undoing of the Royalists not only in the West Riding but, ultimately, the north of England as a whole. Most of their infantrymen were either killed or captured; Belasyse himself, wounded in the fighting, ended the day a prisoner; and, before long, the victorious northern Parliamentarians had joined the Scots and Oliver Cromwell's Eastern Association army in perhaps their most famous triumph of the entire Civil War: the battle of Marston Moor, fought on 2 July 1644. Sir Henry Slingsby, for one, certainly recognized Selby's significance as 'a fatal blow to us' and 'the very dawning of that day which brought prosperous success to Parliament'; while Clarendon declared that the defeat of Sir John Belasyse at Selby by Sir Thomas Fairfax 'so let loose all the king's enemies in the northern parts, which was lately in the king's devotion, that his friends were in great distress in all places'.[33] Certainly, the combined impact of Selby and Marston Moor soon rendered the West Riding, for all practical purposes, a Royalist-free zone as Charles I's supporters laid down their arms in considerable numbers and, one by one, Royalist castles capitulated: for instance, Sheffield's governor Sir Thomas Beaumont surrendered on 11 August 1644, Knaresborough fell on 20 December and, on 21 July 1645, even the stubborn Royalist garrison in Pontefract castle at last threw in the towel. For the West Riding, in fact, the Civil War was now virtually at an end.

Clearly, the effects of warfare on Bradford, Leeds and the West Riding since the autumn of 1642 had been considerable: the physical damage to buildings, the billeting of soldiers and their often unruly behaviour, the cost of feeding and paying fighting men and, most of all, the frequent disruption of normal economic activity. Perhaps conditions were never worse than in the spring and early summer of 1643, as graphically recorded by Sir Thomas Fairfax in a letter of 23 May.[34] No doubt Fairfax had every reason, when writing to London at this time, to paint as black a picture as possible, but it is clear that West Riding economic and social life – especially the cloth industry and trade – *was* severely disrupted by military campaigning and all it entailed. Not until after the great Royalist defeats at Selby and Marston Moor, and the virtual ending of campaigning in the

West Riding, could local communications be effectively re-established, more or less normal trade be resumed, and the region begin to recover from the economic impact of war.

Notes

This chapter has its genesis in a final year BA course on *Yorkshire and the Civil War* which I taught at Huddersfield Polytechnic for several years in the late 1970s and early 1980s, a course that owed much to David Wright's encouragement. I have drawn heavily on my lectures (first written in 1977) and on a collection of primary sources put together to provide material for seminar discussion.

1   In recent years our knowledge and understanding of West Riding history during the Civil War has been greatly enhanced by the research and publications of P.R. Newman, especially 'The Royalist Army in Northern England 1642–1645' (2 vols, unpublished D.Phil thesis, University of York, 1978); 'The Civil War in Bradford', in *The Siege of Bradford* (Bradford Libraries and Information Service, pamphlet, 1989), pp. 9–26; 'The Defeat of John Belasyse: Civil War in Yorkshire, January–April 1644', *Yorkshire Archaeological Journal*, 52, 1980, pp. 123–33. My own debt to Newman is apparent throughout this chapter. From an earlier generation, C.H. Firth's pioneering work deserves particular mention, especially the introduction to his edition of Margaret Duchess of Newcastle's *Life of William Cavendish Duke of Newcastle* (London, Routledge, 1886). Much of value and relevance is also to be found in J.T. Cliffe, *The Yorkshire Gentry from the Reformation to the Civil War* (London, Athlone Press, 1969); A. Fletcher, *The Outbreak of the English Civil War* (London, Edward Arnold, 1981); C.V. Wedgwood, *The King's War 1641–1647* (London, William Collins, 1958); P. Young and R. Holmes, *The English Civil War: A Military History of the Three Civil Wars 1642–1653* (London, Eyre Methuen, 1974).

2   Edward Hyde, Earl of Clarendon, *The History of the Rebellion and Civil Wars in England*, ed. W. Dunn Macray (6 vols, Oxford, 1888), especially vol. 2, pp. 1, 14, 284–7, 464.

3   *Life of Newcastle.*

4   *The Diary of Sir Henry Slingsby of Scriven*, ed. D. Parsons (London, Longman, 1836), esp. pp. 48, 64–5, 60–1.

5   Thomas, Lord Fairfax, *A Short Memorial of the Northern Actions, during the War there, from the year 1642 till the year 1644*, in *An English Garner*, vol. 2, *Stuart Tracts 1603–1693*, ed. E. Archer (1909), pp. 365–98, especially pp. 385–6.

6   *The Autobiography of Joseph Lister of Bradford*, ed. A. Holroyd (Bradford, 1860), esp. pp. 7–9, 11, 13.

7   *Memoirs of Captain John Hodgson of Coalley-Hall near Halifax, touching his conduct in the Civil Wars, and his troubles after the Restoration*, in *Original Memoirs written during the Great Civil War*, ed. J. Ritson (Edinburgh, 1806) esp. pp. 95–100.

8   *Calendar of State Papers, Domestic (CSPD), Charles I*, vol. 18 1641–1643, vol. 19 1644, especially vol. 18 pp. 330, 334, 342; John Rushworth, *Historical Collections* (1821 edn), vols. 3, 4 and 5; John Vicars, *Parliamentary Chronicles*, 3 vols (1644).

9   *Mercurius Aulicus*, in *The English Revolution III, Newsbooks 1, Oxford Royalist* (vol. 1, London, Cornmarket Press, 1971), esp. pp. 174–5, 283–4, 349–51.

10   *The Rider of the White Horse and his Army, their late good success in Yorkshire*, in *The Siege of Bradford*, pamphlet, pp. 27–31; *An Express Relation of the Passages and Proceedings of his Majesty's Army, under the*

Command of his Excellence the Earl of Newcastle, against the Rebels under the Command of the Lord Fairfax and his Adherents, in *Life of Newcastle*, Appendix, pp. 215–17. The British Library holds a large collection of such Civil War tracts, most of them still unpublished since the 1640s but much cited in secondary sources: British Library, Thomason Tracts.

11 *The Fairfax Correspondence: Memoirs of the reign of Charles I*, ed. G.W. Johnson (2 vols, 1848), especially vol. 2, p. 299; *Memorials of the Civil War, comprising the correspondence of the Fairfax family with the most distinguished personages engaged in that memorable contest*, ed. R. Bell (2 vols, 1849), especially vol. 1 pp. 25–30, 33–4, 35–6, 44–5. Several letters written by the Earl of Newcastle during the early 1640s can be found in Firth's edition of the *Life of Newcastle*, especially pp. 192–5. In 1873 Abraham Holroyd included a number of interesting letters and papers in his *Collectanea Bradfordiana* (Bradford, 1873) as well as Thomas Lord Fairfax's *Short Memorial of the Northern Actions*, *The Rider of the White Horse* and extracts from John Vicars' *Parliamentary Chronicles*. In 1861 W.H.D. Longstaffe edited, for the Surtees Society, Nathan Drake's *Journal of the First and Second Sieges of Pontefract Castle 1644–5*, an invaluable record by a local man actually present in the castle during the Parliamentarian sieges of Pontefract; in the same series, in 1877, C. Jackson edited the *Life of John Shaw*, a brief autobiographical sketch by a West Riding Puritan preacher who provides an eye-witness account of the taking of Rotherham by the Royalists early in May 1643: Surtees Society, vol. 37, 1861, vol. 65, 1877. In 1882 G. Duckett published several letters of June 1642 in the *Yorkshire Archaeological Journal* (vol. 7, 1882); the same journal, in 1884, printed Thomas Lord Fairfax's *Short Memorial of the Northern Actions* (vol. 8, 1884); and, in 1908, the *Bradford Antiquary* reprinted John Hodgson's *Memoirs* (vol. 12, 1908).

12 Bell, *Fairfax Memorials*, vol. 1, pp. 25–30.

13 A. Woolrych, 'Yorkshire's Treaty of Neutrality', *History Today*, 6, 1956, especially p. 702.

14 Lister's *Autobiography*, p. 11. Sir Thomas Fairfax's *Northern Actions*, pp. 365–6, in similar vein, tells how: 'We drew out close to the town to receive them. They had advantage of the ground, the town being compassed with hills, which made us more exposed to their cannon shot, from which we received some hurt. Yet notwithstanding our men defended the passages, which they were to descend, so well that they got no ground of us. And now, the day being spent, they drew off; and returned back again to Leeds.'

15 Slingsby's *Diary*, pp. 78–9; Fairfax's *Northern Actions*, p. 366, similarly, relates how 'we marched to Leeds' where 'the enemy having notice of it, quitted the town in haste'.

16 In the same category as Royalist attempts to secure Leeds and Bradford was Sir Thomas Glemham's attack on Wetherby in November 1642, described in characteristically egocentric terms by Thomas, Lord Fairfax, *Northern Actions*, pp. 366–7: 'About six of the clock in the morning, they [the Royalists] set upon us with 800 horse and foot. The woods thereabout favoured them so much that our scouts could get no notice of them; so no alarm was given till they were ready to enter the town, which they might soon do for the guards were all asleep in houses. . . . Myself only was on horseback. . . . One came running to me, and told me, the enemy was entering the town. I presently galloped to the court of guard, where I found not above four men at their arms; as I remember, two foot sergeants and two pike men, [who] withstood with me when Sir Thomas Glemham, with about six or seven commanders more, charged us: where, after a short but sharp encounter, [they] retired. And in this time more of the guard were gotten to their arms. But I must confess I know of no strength, but the powerful hand of God, that gave them this repulse. Afterward they made another attempt. . . .

And here again, there fell out another remarkable providence. During this conflict our magazine was blown up: which struck such a terror in the enemy, thinking we had cannon (which they were informed we had not), that they instantly retreated'. Slingsby's *Diary*, pp. 83–4, presents a no less graphic account of this 'sore scuffle between two [Glemham and Fairfax] that had been neighbours and intimate friends'.

17 Bell, *Fairfax Memorials*, vol. 1, pp. 25–30; Fairfax's *Northern Actions*, pp. 368–9, 372–4; Slingsby's *Diary*, pp. 85–7; *Life of Newcastle*, pp. 14–16.

18 *The Rider of the White Horse*, in *Siege of Bradford*, pp. 27–31. Another important account of events in Bradford on 18 December is to be found in a letter despatched from Selby by Ferdinando Lord Fairfax on 29 December 1642, *An English Garner*, vol. 2, pp. 369–70n, where he particularly emphasized the substantial Royalist force confronting Bradford's townsmen who 'had not in all above 80 muskets, the rest being armed with clubs and such rustic weapons; with which small force they put the cause to trial with the great strength of the enemy'. A contemporary tract, penned by an eye-witness in Bradford just three days after the siege on 21 December, ibid., vol. 2, p. 371n, similarly stressed the bravery and determination of the townsmen in the face of artillery bombardment. Lister's *Autobiography*, pp. 11–12, chose to highlight the fate of 'a stout, gallant [Royalist] officer', commanding a company of foot, [who] 'came running down a field, shaded with a hedge, intending to come running into the church, and so cut off the men both in the church and steeple. But the men in the steeple, having a full view of their design, ordered a few men to meet them, and give them a charge. And the commander coming first, two of the townsmen met him, and struck him down: he cried out for quarter, and they poor men, not knowing the meaning of it, said "aye, they would quarter him", and so killed him'. Hodgson's *Memoirs*, pp. 93–5, not surprisingly, particularly emphasized the part played by men from Halifax after 'several neighbours came into Halifax vicarage to the chapels, to crave the assistance of such as were able and willing, that they would afford their help to rescue their poor besieged neighbours, who were threatened with nothing less than destruction'. Hodgson's own congregation at Coley chapel was among those approached, with the result that 'many of us did put our hands to the plough with much resolution'.

19 Ferdinando, Lord Fairfax to the Speaker of the House of Commons, 26 January 1643, Rushworth's *Historical Collections*, vol. 5, pp. 125–7. John Hodgson, who was in Fairfax's force at Leeds, recorded in his *Memoirs*, pp. 96–7, how 'Sir Thomas drew us down into the bottoms towards Leeds, and, by degrees, we entered the town near the water side, and our force broke in on the other side, and met in the market-place, and beat out their horse and foot, and put them all to run'. Sir Thomas Fairfax himself, in *Northern Actions*, pp. 371–2, recollected later that 'the business was hotly disputed for almost two hours: but, after, the enemy were beaten from their works. The barricades were soon forced open into the streets: where the horse and foot resolutely entering, the soldiers cast down their arms, and rendered themselves prisoners. The governor and some chief officers swam the river and escaped'. A Royalist report, in *Mercurius Aulicus*, p. 59, clearly hoped to minimize the humiliation at Leeds by playing down the size of the king's garrison: 'Some of the rebels in Yorkshire . . . surprised the town and castle of Leeds, from which they had been valiantly repulsed not long before, wherein were Sir William Savile and Sir William Witherington, with two hundred men, many of which were taken prisoners, but most saved themselves'.

20 Fairfax's *Northern Actions*, pp. 374–6; Hodgson's *Memoirs*, pp. 97–8. Margaret, Duchess of Newcastle, predictably, emphasized the importance of her husband's astute planning in bringing about the 'total rout' of a 'much greater' Parliamentarian force (although, in fact, the two armies at Seacroft Moor were probably of similar size), *Life of Newcastle*, p. 20. A report in *Mercurius Aulicus*, pp. 174–5, both praised Goring and scathingly recorded how Sir Thomas Fairfax, finding himself forced 'to save his horse by losing his foot, fled away to Leeds'.

21 A report in *Mercurius Aulicus*, pp. 212–13, suggested that Newcastle withdrew his forces from the vicinity of Leeds 'to save the effusion of Christian blood' and 'to preserve the town from plundering'; while the *Life of Newcastle*, p. 21, certainly puts a favourable gloss on Newcastle's actions after Seacroft Moor.

22 John Shaw, vicar of Rotherham, was actually in the town when it fell, recording how, 'when the little powder that the town had was spent', the townsmen 'upon honourable terms' yielded it up, terms that were not observed since 'when the enemy entered [they] not only plundered the town but made all the commanders and soldiers prisoners' (Shaw's *Life*, pp. 136–7). Margaret, Duchess of Newcastle, by contrast, stressed how her husband 'showed such clemency' to the common soldiers in Rotherham 'that very many willingly took up arms for his Majesty's service' (*Life of Newcastle*, p. 21).

23 According to Newcastle's wife, *Life of Newcastle*, p. 22, when the Parliamentarian garrison in Sheffield 'came to hear of my Lord's hitherto victorious army, they fled away from thence into Derbyshire, and left both town and castle (without any blow) to my Lord's mercy'. A report in *Mercurius Aulicus* of 9 May 1643, pp. 240–1, recorded that: 'Rotherham and Sheffield, two towns of principal note in the West riding of Yorkshire, both which before had contributed very largely to the aid of Leeds, were yielded up unto his Majesty; by getting which his Majesty had obtained two convenient passes, the one by Sheffield into Derbyshire, the other by Rotherham into those parts of Nottinghamshire; [and] that, besides the use his Majesty might have of the Sheffield cutlers, for which that town is very famous, in the employment of his armoury, there were found 1400 arms in Rotherham fit for present use, together with five thousand pounds in ready money.'

24 As indicated, for instance, in a letter sent by Sir Thomas Fairfax to his father on 20 April 1643 (Bell, *Fairfax Memorials*, vol. 1, pp. 44–5).

25 Even Fairfax himself made no bones about admitting that the successful storming of Wakefield was 'more a miracle than a victory', but that did not prevent him penning a full account of it in *Northern Actions*, pp. 31–3. A contemporary Parliamentarian tract describing the action was printed under the title 'A Miraculous Victory . . . at Wakefield' (*An English Garner*, vol. 2, pp. 377–8n). By contrast, a Royalist report of 28 May 1643 regarded it as 'the greatest loss that has befallen his Majesty in the North during the course of all this war' (surely an exaggeration!); nevertheless, in so far as it had already provoked vigorous Royalist counter-measures, it might yet prove 'to be the occasion of a greater good in bringing the war there to a speedy end' (*Mercurius Aulicus*, pp. 283–4).

26 Hodgson's *Memoirs*, pp. 98–9.

27 *Life of Newcastle*, pp. 24–5. Slingsby's *Diary*, pp. 96–7, provides a valuable (if brief) account of both the circumstances resulting in the battle (Parliamentarians and Royalists alike resolving to give battle yet neither knowing of the other's intentions) and the battle itself, ending when 'Stockdale – who stood at my Lord Fairfax's elbow – advised my Lord not to hazard the rest [of his men], seeing all was lost, but to shift for himself: so that they [the Parliamentarians] were totally routed'. A

Royalist report of 3 July 1643 described the battle in some little detail, particularly noting that Newcastle 'so animated the whole army that they charged with unexpressable courage, and so amazed the rebels with the bravery of their coming, that the rebels soon fell into confusion' (*Mercurius Aulicus*, pp. 349–50). Another Royalist version of events can be found in the *Express Relation*, a contemporary tract, in *Life of Newcastle*, Appendix, pp. 215–16. From the Parliamentarian side, Lister's *Autobiography*, p. 12, put defeat down to treachery; while Fairfax's *Northern Actions*, pp. 378–81, likewise highlighted treasonable behaviour by 'one Colonel Skirton, a wild and dangerous man', as instrumental in discouraging Parliamentarian troops who 'began to flee and so we were soon routed'.

28 Hodgson's *Memoirs*, pp. 99–100. Sir Thomas Fairfax, in the most substantial account we have of the fall of Bradford and its aftermath, predictably made every effort to justify *his* less than admirable behaviour (*Northern Actions*, pp. 381–4). Joseph Lister wallowed in the misery of it all while, at the same time, providing splendid detail: for instance, he recalled that the Royalists 'were encamped at Bolling Hall, so near the town on that side of it, that they planted some of their guns against the steeple, and gave it many a sad shake' (Lister's *Autobiography*, pp. 12–13). From the Royalist side, the *Express Relation*, similarly, stressed how 'our cannon dismounted their drakes upon the top of the steeple, and battered the steeple so as none could stay on it, where they had many musketeers, and so we got both ends of the town'; moreover, he added, 'news was brought us from Halifax that all the forces were run from thence, [and] so we are possessed of that town' (*Life of Newcastle*, Appendix, pp. 216–17).

29 Hodgson's *Memoirs*, p. 103. John Vicars' *Parliamentary Chronicles* described the events in Bradford and its vicinity in a little more detail, and commented approvingly that 'this valiant Colonel Lambert, after [a] brave victory so fortunately achieved, presently entered into Bradford and regarrisoned it for the use of Parliament' (*Collectanea Bradfordiana*, p. 92). When news of this minor resurgence reached London, the Parliamentarian leadership there wrote to Ferdinando, Lord Fairfax on 5 March 1644: 'We have considered the opportunity that is now offered for reducing and assuring Yorkshire whilst the Marquis of Newcastle has drawn the greatest part of his forces towards the north to oppose the Scots, and how necessary it is to hinder all further levies there to increase his army, which the better to effect, we have written to Sir Thomas Fairfax to forthwith march into the West Riding with all his horse, and take with him two regiments of foot out of Lancashire. We desire that you will also take the field with as great force of horse and foot as you can, and joining with Sir Thomas Fairfax, make the best advantage you can of the present opportunity' (*CSPD, Charles I*, vol. 19, 1644, p. 35).

30 Bell, *Fairfax Memorials*, vol. 1, p. 94; Vicars' *Parliamentary Chronicles*, in *Collectanea Bradfordiana*, pp. 92–3.

31 Slingsby's *Diary*, pp. 102–3, where the author ruefully remarked on the 'strange fortune we have had' at Bradford, 'for until his excellency [Newcastle] took it after the battle upon Adwalton Moor, we never attempted anything upon it but received an affront, once by Sir Thomas Glemham, once by my Lord Goring, and now by Colonel Belasyse'; Vicars' *Parliamentary Chronicles*, in *Collectanea Bradfordiana*, p. 93.

32 *CSPD, Charles I*, vol. 19, 1644, p. 103; Slingsby's *Diary*, p. 105.

33 Slingsby's *Diary*, pp. 105–6; Clarendon's *History of the Rebellion*, vol. 3, p. 325. For Margaret, Duchess of Newcastle, it was both 'a great misfortune' and an 'utter rout' (*Life of Newcastle*, pp. 35–6); while a Royalist report of 26 April 1644 rightly predicted that 'by this disaster the rebels were like to get too much power in Yorkshire': *Life of Newcastle*, pp. 35–6; *Mercurius Aulicus*, pp. 959–60. The

Parliamentarian leadership in London certainly had every reason to celebrate the 'good success that God has been pleased to give [Lord Fairfax] and his son with their joined forces against the town of Selby', particularly the rich haul of Royalist notables, common soldiers and weaponry that fell into Parliament's hands as a result (*CSPD, Charles I*, vol. 19, 1644, p. 125).

34 Sir Thomas Fairfax to the Speaker of the House of Commons, 23 May 1643, as quoted in D.F.E. Sykes, *The History of Huddersfield and its vicinity* (1898), p. 233: 'The Earl of Newcastle's army do now range over all the south-west parts of this country, pillaging and cruelly using the well-affected party; and here about Leeds, Bradford and Halifax, being a mountainous and barren country, the people now begin to be sensible of want, their last year's provisions being spent, and the enemies' garrisons stopping all the provisions, both of corn and flesh and other necessaries, that were wont to come from the more fruitful countries to them; their trade utterly taken away, their poor grow innumerable, and great scarcity to relieve them; and this army which now lies amongst them to defend them from the enemy cannot defend them from want, which causes much murmers and lamentations among the people: and for the army itself, it is so far in arrears, and no way appearing how they shall either be supplied with money or succour as they grow very mutinuous.'

2

'PROPER OBJECTS OF THE PRESS': NAVAL IMPRESSMENT AND HABEAS CORPUS IN THE FRENCH REVOLUTIONARY WARS

Philip Woodfine

Naval press gangs have usually been assigned a colourful but minor role in popular histories of the eighteenth century. Like so much of nautical lore and practice, they are seen as part of an isolated world of ports and ships, their trades and mysteries, largely closed to most of even the contemporary population. Success in naval warfare, particularly against France, was arguably the single most important guarantor of Britain's place as a leading European power in this period. Yet in modern times the study of this success has been the preserve of specialist scholars. Naval historians have been rather marginal members of the academic community, their concerns treated with at best a distant respect. Conversely, few social historians have been willing to venture into a field – perhaps one should say into waters – regarded as the preserve of naval specialists. The current renewal of interest in military and naval power, and the gearing of the British state to the financial and administrative demands of that power, is likely to break down these barriers.[1] Social historians might fruitfully revisit the evidence of impressment: the compulsory, and often forcible, seizure of individuals who were then taken on board ships of war, or aboard tenders (hired commercial vessels) while waiting to be assigned to a ship. Wartime impressment was rooted in long tradition and, together with the issuing of bounties for volunteers, was the main method used to meet the desperate need of the navy for serviceable seamen. Nicholas Rodger has calculated that in the mid-eighteenth century the demand for seamen in wartime, for the merchant marine and navy taken together, exceeded the supply by around two to one.[2] Nearly a quarter of a century ago, Professor Bromley introduced his survey of naval manning with a call for historians to study impressment for the sake of the light which it can shed on at least part of the experience of the working classes: 'The assumptions and aspirations of those diverse groups of citizens who still style themselves the working class now count for so much in British policy-making that it becomes a matter of urgency to unravel their origins in ancient servitudes and injustices'.[3]

A recent article by a distinguished historian of eighteenth-century popular politics suggests that the subject of impressment into the wartime navy may indeed soon be incorporated into the mainstream of social and political history.[4] Where naval historians have typically seen the manning problem as an operational issue, a special case of the abuse of power and largely confined to the seafaring community, Nicholas Rogers has argued that impressment must be seen 'within the broader framework of labour relations'; it was 'the preferred option of many employers to the problem of manning the fleet'.[5] The central argument put forward by Rogers is one on which further evidence from as many different sources as possible is urgently needed. He contends, in terms familiar since the publication of Douglas Hay's celebrated essay on the criminal law, that the selective use of legal power over the lives and fortunes of the poor was a kind of semi-intuitive collusion between the propertied classes to mould and control those who made up the broad base of the social pyramid.[6] The records of King's Bench, the principal source of evidence explored in this chapter, give little explicit support to this line of reasoning. They do provide one striking example of the exercise of arbitrary power by a wealthy landowner in 1795, though it was a case in which the interests of the propertied classes were in conflict. Three men pressed at the bidding of a local notable were being defended by their employer, the Plymouth brewer John Clark Langmead. The three, Thomas Pitts, Robert Horswell and Thomas Cocks, were maltmen who worked for Langmead and who spent some idle time roaming on land belonging to Henry St John of Mutley. One of them threw a stick, knocking down a grazing duck, and all three were seized by some of St John's servants. St John, instead of having them taken before a magistrate, gave them the alternatives of entering the navy or going to prison. Pitts replied that they would not enter: 'he was ready to be carried before any Justice, but . . . he would as soon be hanged as go on board a King's ship'.[7] None the less, the three were tightly bound and marched to Plymouth dock, to the quarters of Captain Dod of the *Atlas*, and shortly after were carried aboard that ship by a guard of marines. Dod viewed the men as having chosen to enter the service in order to avoid a charge of felony, a view which was subsequently accepted by King's Bench.[8] The assault against property in the form of the duck made the maltmen vulnerable to the law and must have weighed heavily in the decision of the court, since the judges had unambiguous evidence sworn by the three men that they were detained on board the *Atlas* in irons under guard, and had no intention of entering the service.[9] Even such an apparently clear-cut instance of oppressive class rule, however, no doubt had its local dimensions, not given in the legal depositions, of an overbearing and unpopular individual or (perhaps and) of repeated trespass and provocation.

It is easy to agree with the general proposition that the rich were powerful and that the poor were numerous and lived hard, their destinies shaped and controlled by those who had the wealth and property. Distinctions of rank, wealth, education and power ran through the period in every way. Nor is this in any sense unique to the eighteenth century. Historians at the end of the twentieth century must make their way to the British Library through streets in which poverty, squalor and homelessness are still rife, alongside conspicuous consumption and great wealth. We are likely to learn little by dwelling upon the broad issue of inequalities of wealth and power. Rather, it is the narrower question of the nature and extent of discretion which is likely to extend our knowledge of the period. There were many degrees of power, and not every employer can be simply classed among the élite. Few records are likely to survive which explicitly document the manipulative use of impressment by employers, and those administrative and legal records which do exist cannot simply reconstruct for us the habitual attitudes and outlook of those concerned. Were seamen and shore workers cowed and submissive because of the implied threat of the impress, or their employers' power to have them sent into the navy? Or were employers, such as the Plymouth brewer Langmead, harassed by the danger of losing skilled men or useful labourers at a moment's notice? There is not as yet enough evidence to recreate with any confidence the mentalities involved. For Rogers, impressment 'operated like other aspects of the law in the eighteenth century; it allowed for the discretionary favours of the rich and powerful.'[10] However, it should be emphasized that this discretion operated within a known framework of law. To be the object of a press warrant, a man had to be employed at sea or in waterborne occupations in rivers or harbours. Such a man was fair game provided he had reached the age of eighteen and had served more than three years at sea. Landmen of any age were allowed to serve out their three years' apprenticeship to the sea before being (in legal theory) liable to impressment. Seamen in particular trades such as the Greenland fisheries enjoyed exemption from the press for months before their voyage began, provided only that they had signed articles.[11] The common law gave powers to masters and parents, even where statutes might be silent. A boy, William Oliff, who volunteered in 1794, was snatched back against his will by his father when on leave in Chatham. Since a boy under the age of 21 had no power to enter into any contract without the consent of a parent or guardian, the navy could not attempt to recover him.[12] The rights of the individual were a battleground between the navy and the masters or relatives of those whom it impressed, but the court of King's Bench did rule against the navy, and in favour of those rights, in the great majority of contested cases.

The Rogers' argument places considerable stress upon the impressing of vagrants. Though the specific power of the Justices to send vagrants to the Impress officers was supported only by an early eighteenth-century statute, Tudor statute and practice greatly bolstered both the office and duties of the magistrates; their power to adjudge unemployed people as vagrants; and the definitions by which they could do so.[13] Does this, though, mean that justices sent the undesirable, inconvenient or menacing poor into the navy? Little is actually known of the extent of the practice of disposing of vagrants to the wartime navy. The received view is that naval officers rarely accepted vagrant recruits, though considerable numbers were taken into the marines.[14] The records of the court of King's Bench, examined in this chapter, support this contention. Indeed, one case suggests that the powers of the magistrate over the idle and disorderly were limited by the scope of the law. The sitting magistrate at Bow Street in March 1795 had before him one James Watson, seized along with several others in a raid for 'suspected persons' carried out on a public house of bad repute. Watson, when questioned, admitted that he had some years before been on a voyage to India, and the magistrate despatched him to the impress tender. The Admiralty Solicitor advised that Watson could not be retained, on two grounds: 'because it hath been determined in the Court of King's Bench, that a person quitting the Sea Service and betaking himself to a Land Employment, is no longer an Object of a press Warrant', and because in any case the arresting constables had been acting not on a proper press warrant, but on a civil search warrant.[15] King's Bench records, though, are almost certainly the wrong place to look for evidence of vagrant impressment. As the poor would have few legal grounds of challenge, and more importantly no money, then they are unlikely to figure in the very expensive processes of formal legal pleading. To search the surviving Quarter Sessions rolls for evidence of the numbers of vagrants or suspicious characters despatched by Justices to the Impress Service would be a laborious task. It is vital, though, if these arguments are to be properly assessed. Pitt's ministry certainly wanted to impress vagrants. In 1795 a new law was introduced enabling magistrates to levy 'such able-bodied and idle Persons as shall be found' to serve in the navy.[16] This indicates, at least, an official encouragement to press vagrants, and there is little doubt that the idea would have had some, perhaps substantial, popular support. Justices of the peace in London seem to have put the Act into force quite early, to judge by the only King's Bench case examined which directly involved vagrancy. Two Prussian Jews, Joseph David and Solomon Isaac, were 'carrying about and exhibiting a Gallantee Show' when they were taken up on 22 October 1795. They did not have sufficient substance for their support and maintenance, and were not exercising any lawful calling, so the magistrates the next day delivered them to the regulating captain. The plight of these two vagrants is recorded only because they attracted the support of members of the London Jewish community. The first approach to the regulating captains by Mr Fridag, a member of the Jewish community, brought out advice from the Admiralty Solicitor that there were no special grounds to discharge the men: 'there being no Exception in the Act in favor of Foreigners or Jews, and it being by no means contrary to the Spirit of the Laws for manning the Navy to admit of Foreigners in the Service'.[17] An appeal subsequently launched to the magistrates by Abraham Goldsmid of Goodman's Fields was also turned down.[18] This incident suggests that the new law gave a latitude welcomed by the authorities, and it may be that the statute led to an upsurge in vagrant impressments.[19]

There was undoubtedly some public support for the idea of making the idle and able-bodied enter the fleet. One popular entertaining monthly began its June 1790 issue with a purportedly first-hand account of 'Manning the Navy', and devoted its monthly illustrative plate to the scene.[20] The writer claimed to have accompanied a squad from the Impress Service based at the Tower. Two able seamen (heavily stereotyped by nautical oddities of behaviour and speech) were singled out from a captured group and kept for the service. The author expressed what must have been the assumptions of some readers at least about the purpose of the press: 'As I was but a novice in press-matters, I was . . . astonished . . . when our commander discharged the rest of the prisoners, who appeared to be stouter men . . . and fitter objects, being a set of idle vagabonds, most likely thieves, the pressing of whom I thought would be doing an essential service to community; but I was soon given to understand that this circumstance furnished the very reason why they were rejected; that what rendered them burthensome to the public, would render them equally so to a ship, and that half a dozen such fellows were enough to corrupt the whole crew of a first rate man of war . . .'.[21] However, the range of naval stereotypes and clichés was wide and there was no consistency in the discussion of the nature of the service. Just two months later, the same journal assembled a collection of aphorisms under the title of 'Character of a Ship of War', two of which asserted: 'It is the bridewell of the nation, where all the incorrigible viages [sic; vagrants] are sent, to wear out ropes, and make more work for the hempen w[hore]s in London. . . . It is the Devil's academy, where the seven liberal sciences of swearing, drinking, thieving, whoring, killing, cozening, and backbiting, are taught to full perfection.'[22] These very different contemporary views of the nature of warships, and the men taken to man them, encapsulate a problem of interpretation which persists to this day and has importance for social history. Was pressing largely confined to the recruitment of useful seafaring men, and therefore peculiar to the workers of the maritime and coastal world? Or was it used more widely as a tool of social control, to rid society of vagrants or to hold over working men the menace of impressment as a kind of labour discipline?

The specific area of control to which Rogers directs most attention lies in the relations between employers and workers. Whether masters obtained protections for their waterfront employees, or gave character references to have them released from wrongful seizure as vagrants, or conversely gave them up to impressment, he argues that they were enhancing their control over refractory workers and also over potentially sharp rises in labour costs. He contends that, while there was extensive and violent proletarian resistance to the press gangs, the more successful groups in capitalist society did generally, despite occasional inconvenience and loss, collude in and benefit from the practice of impressment. Rogers invokes a general interest of the propertied classes in manning the fleet and protecting commerce and empire. The everyday reality was a complex one, however, not least because the views and needs of particular masters were often sharply at variance with this imagined general class interest. This was certainly true in the merchant marine, when impressment might put more than money at risk. The commodore guarding one convoy returning from the Baltic, when over the Dogger Bank, ordered the ships under his charge to bring to, and sent lieutenants aboard to press men from among them. One of them pressed a landman, George Bullock (fittingly, a former farm labourer), ignoring both the indentures of his apprenticeship to the sea and also an Admiralty protection. The 276 ton *Betsey* was put at some risk, being so far out to sea, by the depletion of the crew. The master 'urged the Inconvenience and Danger this Deponent and the said Ship *Betsey* would be put to if the Crew were lessened in number at that time there being but twelve persons on board and two of them . . . upwards of sixty Years of Age and two under fourteen and which is not a Crew sufficient for a Ship of the Burthen of the said Ship *Betsey*'.[23] Similarly, the master of a small coasting vessel which lost the only carpenter aboard to the press might not be able to proceed to sea, and would experience at the least considerable delay and loss of money, perhaps of livelihood. It had always been the practice in the coal trade, according to one deponent, 'to protect the mates and carpenters of their respective ships being their most useful hands in preference to any other of their Crew'.[24] Of course, carpenters were much in demand aboard naval vessels too, and captains would go some lengths to get them.[25] One was pressed from his collier vessel by a party from the sloop *Sphynx*, who informed the master, Bourn, that they pressed the carpenter on the orders of their Captain, Lucas. Bourn went on board to ask for Davison's release 'but the said Captain Lucas positively refused to release him'.[26] Five days later, the *Sphynx* pressed another carpenter from an incoming collier in the Thames.[27] In such cases, the merchant ships' masters almost invariably claimed that they could neither find another carpenter nor safely put to sea without one. It is hard to say whether this was purely a formula, employed because it was known to have effect with the court, or whether it became formulaic because a genuine difficulty regularly arose.[28]

Ships' masters were also dependent on their mates. One Southampton shipmaster, John King of Emsworth, clearly relied heavily on his nineteen-year old apprentice, William Ellis, who acted as both chief mate and keeper of accounts for his illiterate master who had otherwise only a boy and a crippled seaman with whom to man his 62-ton sloop.[29] Though a writ of habeas corpus was issued by the Court of King's Bench to recover this invaluable young man from the *Aurora* at Spithead, the lieutenant in charge of the Impress Service at Emsworth furnished evidence that Ellis was over eighteen, and had been more than three years at sea. The Admiralty Solicitor, James Dyson, made the comparatively rare suggestion that the Lords of Admiralty should therefore defend the lieutenant at public expense in an action to hold on to Ellis.[30] In cases such as this the conflict appears to be not between the propertied and the plebeian but between the interest of the navy on one hand and that of both employer and employee on the other. In other instances, the navy might seduce the employee at the expense of the employer. One young Scot of twenty-two, who had not long served at sea when he was impressed from a collier, evidently found it congenial to be rated able bodied aboard the frigate *Amazon*. His master 'told this Deponent not to enter and he would endeavour to get him clear'.[31] Instead, after ten days on board, McIntosh did enter the service, and rejected his former master's appeal to have him released.

The grievances of ships' masters found expression as part of a wider public debate over the harmful impact of war. These were years in which views of the war, and the navy, were at best ambiguous. Naval victories could be celebrated and their glamour appropriated to the crown. Admiral Howe's dramatic victory on the first of June 1794 was the occasion of a Grand Naval Gala in Vauxhall Gardens: the Prince of Wales's gallery was opened and illuminated by thousands of variegated lamps and His Royal Highness the Duke of Gloucester gave permission for his own band, in full uniform, to play.[32] Such celebrations were no doubt warmly patriotic occasions for those who could afford the three shillings for admission. The 'apotheosis of George III' can be documented in many instances such as the appearance of the king and queen at Covent Garden later that year, when *God Save the King* was demanded by the audience six times: '*Rule Britannia* was not forgotten, and indeed, no expression of loyalty and respectful attachment was omitted, which could evince the honest and patriotic feelings of a British audience'.[33] This celebration of the navy, so evident in contemporary newspapers, and the linked endorsement of monarchy and country, may help to explain the paradox that there was so little protest against naval impressment. Impressment after all struck at the much-vaunted British personal liberties, supposedly guaranteed under the constitution. This ancient coercive system survived at least in part because schemes for a government registry of suitable seamen like those which existed in France and Spain, though occasionally proposed, were always judged to be the thin edge of an absolutist wedge.[34] Impressment was a glaring abuse of the ancient constitutional liberties and rights of which the English were pleased to imagine themselves possessed, and which were vaunted by both loyalists and reformers in these years.[35] Only the victims of press gangs, one naval pamphleteer argued, suffered 'such a marked deprivation of those rights which the constitution has devolved on all classes of their fellow subjects'.[36] Yet the issue, far from lying at the centre of the debate over rights and liberties, was more often seen as lying within the marginal world of the seaman and therefore not a challenge to normal citizens.

If the constitutional anomaly of impressment was not a burning issue, the costs of conflict with France did make the war highly unpopular, notably in the commercial and trading towns of the kingdom. The corporations of several leading towns presented to the House of Commons petitions respectfully urging them to cease interfering in the internal affairs of France and to promote a speedy peace.[37] The ports most directly affected were galvanized into petitioning when the Commons began to consider a new bill to improve manning by obliging shipowners to furnish men for the navy, in a quota proportioned to the tonnage of their vessels. The response was obvious: where were the shipowners, any more than the navy, to find the numbers of seamen who were suddenly required? A petition from Scarborough pointed out 'the Difficulties that have been experienced during the last Year, of procuring Men for the Merchants Service, wherein the enormous Wages of Six Pounds *per* Month were paid to Seamen of an ordinary Description'.[38] A petition from Sunderland protested:

> That the decrease of Seamen in Time of War is always very great, but at this Juncture it is particularly so, the Dread and Fear entertained of the Impress Service by young Men, in the interior Parts of the Country, prevents Numbers becoming Apprentices to the Sea Service, and several Instances have occurred, during the present War, where Apprentices, contrary to Law, have been impressed into His Majesty's Service, the Consequence is, that the Petitioners are put to great Expence and Inconvenience in procuring the necessary Number of Hands to navigate their Ships, and, not being able altogether to raise able-bodied Seamen, they are oblidged [sic] to accept old and infirm Men, to whom they pay from Eight to Ten Guineas a Piece *per* Voyage Coastwise, who, before the Commencement of the War, were not able to support themselves. . .[39]

In the event, the bill was withdrawn, and speedily replaced by one which imposed a system of quotas levied on ports rather than owners.[40] However, the frictions implied in the petitions from the coastal shipping trade did not go away. Owners and ships' masters, as a matter of deliberate policy, manned their vessels with young men apprenticed to the sea for three years who would be doubly protected, by their age and indentures, from the impress. Even so, the clashes between the navy and the merchant trade were unremitting, as captured in the records of writs sought in the Court of King's Bench. The predations of the press gangs must have been a constant concern of shipowners such as the Hurry family of Great Yarmouth, who had part interests in several ships in the coal and Mediterranean trades. Even in the imperfect sample of surviving King's Bench writs, it appears that they lost an (alleged) apprentice seaman from the *Mary* in January 1795 and no fewer than five apprentices in November 1798, as the *Daedalus* entered North Shields to collect a cargo of coal, as well as an apprentice pressed from the *Withywood* in the Thames in January 1800.[41] Some unfortunate men were pressed twice, sometimes in quick succession. When four apprentices were released from their illegal detention by the navy in January 1795, two of them were immediately impressed again.[42] A young Scot, Donkin McCuie, was impressed twice within the term of an apprenticeship begun in the autumn of 1792.[43] John Reburn, an apprentice aged seventeen, had the misfortune to fall prey to both the Spanish and British navies. Captured from the *Bonito* transport and imprisoned in Cadiz, he was released under cartel, only to be impressed by the *Adamant* when on his voyage to Lisbon, *en route* for home.[44] A young Sunderland man of the same age was taken by a Dunkirk privateer in April 1794 and returned in a cartel ship in September, but promptly impressed by a boat crew from the *Peterel* when he arrived in the Downs.[45] William Smith, a waterman and late Officer of Trinity House, was active in detecting the embezzlement of naval stores in Kent, and in securing convictions at the Assizes. This useful man was impressed in June 1794 and released only in August, by order of the Lords of Admiralty. He was impressed again in April 1795 while actually transporting embezzled stores from a prosecution and despite having on him the Admiral's certificate that he had been discharged from the press by their Lordships.[46]

In this tense situation, which threatened the very survival of some shipping enterprises, recourse to law, through the court of King's Bench, seems to have been quite widespread. In fact, the surviving records of suits in King's Bench probably understate considerably the extent of impressment disputes. They relate only to cases brought within the dates of the legal terms. Term dates varied, but occupied some fourteen to fifteen weeks on average, little more than a quarter of the year. Even during term, applications were usually made, not in court but to the judges in their chambers: between 10 and 10.30 each morning and 3 and 3.30 in the afternoon. The judges also acted at their own houses on Saturdays or in the evenings, or on holy days when the court was not sitting. These papers are recorded along with the court's other business, and form the great majority of cases. Outside term, the same process occurred, and writs were issued in the same way, but recorded separately. Those records, or many of them, survived into the early twentieth century, but were then destroyed, so we now have only the imperfect sample of term time, and no means of checking how typical this was of the whole.[47] The sample is large enough, though, to draw some conclusions about what is going on: some 219 cases between May 1793 and November 1798.[48] The surviving applications for writs of habeas corpus come predominantly from those engaged in the coal and east coast trades. No doubt this was linked to the belief, current at the time, that the North Sea was a valuable nursery of seamen: 'the difficulties of the navigation in the Coal Trade, are admitted to give the seamen derived from it, in point of skill, expertness, patience of fatigue and hardship, an incontestible superiority over those drawn from the other maritime trades of the kingdom'.[49] The great majority of cases are about sea apprentices.

The basic rules and procedures for obtaining a writ of habeas corpus were obviously familiar to sea captains and ship owners, and affidavits were sworn before legal agents in all the leading east coast ports, as well as in London. At the same time, the costly structure of fees and the often considerable delays of King's Bench did weight the odds against all but those with an unanswerable case.[50] Before a writ could be issued, counsel had to be briefed to present the case to the court, one case per day only being allowed to each counsel. Generally, on presentation of an affidavit, the court appointed a day to the commander concerned to show cause why a writ of habeas corpus should not issue. On that day, counsel on both sides would be heard and (usually) the writ would be issued.[51] The standard fee for this service in the 1790s, endorsed on the depositions, was half a guinea, irrespective of other attorney, clerical and administrative fees, right down to the fact that affidavits had to be made out on sixpenny stamped paper, almost the value of a landman's daily pay in the navy.[52] This process had to be repeated on each new application to the court, which meant fresh costs as naval officers moved impressed men from ship to ship, so that a new writ needed to be taken out each time. The service of each writ by an attorney in the relevant port was also presumably expensive, including charges for time spent and fees for an affidavit of service, sworn out as soon as the writ was delivered. These costs were not even ascertainable in advance, particularly as naval commanders did everything in their power to make delivery difficult and cause attorneys to make repeated fruitless trips.[53] In the case of the Plymouth men accused of assaulting a duck, the habeas corpus writ was to be served by an attorney, John Saunders, and by Thomas Reynolds, a commissioner for taking affidavits in King's Bench. They encountered a typically circular progress when they called upon Captain Dod of the *Atlas* on shore and asked for permission to go aboard the ship. Their only hope of doing so was to obtain a written order from the commander to that effect, which 'the said Edmund Dod positively refused to grant on any account'. Dod assured the men instead that they could make use of his name: 'You may tell the Commanding Officer on board, you came from me, and you may then see the Men'. This of course was positively refused when the two lawyers made their fruitless trip out to the ship.[54] In the face of all these costs and delays, the initiative had to rest with the plaintiffs.

It is not surprising, therefore, that the applicants for writs include a number of friends and relatives: a significant minority of affidavits involved links of kin or friendship.[55] London cases were especially likely to feature family members, and usually involved the shore-based impress service, rather than press gangs from ships. John Robson, a corn factor, was the determined father of an apprentice lighterman, under eighteen, who was impressed while moving a lighter barge from one mooring to another, and carried aboard the receiving ship *Enterprize*. Robson senior first preferred an indictment against the two pressing officers at a sessions for the Liberty of the Tower of London. The grand jury found the charge of assault and false imprisonment a true bill, notwithstanding which the young apprentice was transferred on board the *Reasonable*, lying at Spithead. He was released on an order of King's Bench obtained by his father, but only after more than a year of enforced naval service, and therefore with more than a third of his protected apprenticeship elapsed.[56] Friends were particularly likely to be involved in applications involving foreign nationals, where various members of the expatriate communities concerned came forward to help impressed seamen. A typical example was that of the glass cutter and two mariners who gave affidavits to secure the release of fellow German, Freerk Swierman, who had been pressed when homeward bound from the West Indies. The Admiralty refused to release him without papers from his consul proving his nationality; papers which, on that voyage, he could not have with him.[57] Nor is it surprising that writs were sought preponderantly by those with a direct financial interest, the masters of apprentices and the captains or owners of vessels. The typical case found in these records involved a writ obtained by a ship's master for an apprentice in the east coast coal trade, from Yarmouth to Scarborough and Whitby up to North and South Shields, Newcastle-upon-Tyne and Blyth. The predominance of small masters and of family members may be simply a reflection of face-to-face employment patterns in the shipping industry, as in so many small businesses of the time.

These records do reveal that naval officers were not always over scrupulous in their methods. Every commander of a naval vessel knew that no indenture or protection need be taken at face value, but could be dismissed as a possible forgery and referred to the Admiralty.[58] Captain Bollard of the *Sandwich* refused even to look at the indentures and protections of four young sea apprentices from Lowestoft, 'saying he could on no account release them without Orders from the Admiralty'. Two at least of these recruits may have been of limited use to the service, as their first merchant captain scathingly testified: 'from their Behaviour and mode of doing their Duty on their first coming on board the said ship *Mary* this Deponent believes they never did serve at sea before'.[59] Naval officers, midshipmen and petty officers knew that everything possible must be done to deter legal officials and prevent them from setting foot on deck. So long as the process of serving writs could be frustrated, much might be done. An impressed man could be moved from ship to ship, so that the original receiving captain could return the writ with the true, but hardly useful, reply that neither when the writ was served, nor since, had the man been in his custody.[60] The master or friends or relatives of the captured man would then have to spend more money, time and energy to find out the captain who currently held the victim, and to serve the writ afresh. This was the experience of the family and the master of an apprentice bookbinder, Edward Gabriel, in 1798. On 17 May Gabriel absconded from his master, John Handcock, and the next day entered the navy under the name of John Jones. Almost at once he wrote to his master a letter in which he 'expressed a great desire and anxiety to return'. Handcock went aboard the *Zealand* to have him released, but was refused, and Gabriel was swiftly removed aboard the *Wasp*.[61] If a pressed man could be removed into a ship likely to be soon ready for sea, then in practical terms this was a race for his liberty, and one which the navy must often have won. A typical case involved a Swede, Elias Lindby, who notwithstanding his Admiralty protection was impressed while at Jamaica on an English merchant ship. When he reached Chatham on the frigate *Penelope* he got his friends to sue for his freedom. The writ was at first refused by the lieutenant then in command, on the grounds that the captain was not aboard. Before the writ could be served again, Lindby was promptly moved aboard the *Sandwich* and then aboard the *Director*, lying at the Nore and expected to put to sea directly.[62] Two young apprentices, a stonemason and a carpenter, seized by the Impress Service at the Tower, were being urgently reclaimed in early May 1793 from the *Robust*, which was under sailing orders and due to depart within eight days.[63]

The surest way to keep the men captured by the press gangs was to persuade them to enter the service voluntarily, after which no writ could release them, unless they were minors or apprentices who might still be reclaimed.[64] Sometimes, perhaps, the glamour of a seafaring life could work on the imaginations of restive apprentices, particularly when viewed through the mists of alcohol. John Appleton of Houndsditch was apprenticed to his pewterer father, who affirmed that his son 'was induced thro' ill advice & in a state of intoxication to absent himself from the Deponent's Service and to enter on board his Majesty's Ship the *Sandwich*, and hath been since removed to His Majesty's Frigate *Imperieuse* where he is detained against his Will, having applied to the Deponent to procure his discharge'.[65] The navy retained the callow entrant, no doubt a wiser and more sober young man, as one of the quota for the Port of London. Impressed men who did not soon afterwards 'enter' might be physically confined for some time, threatened and cajoled. This was the plight of a sixteen-year old apprentice wheelwright from Swansea, seized by the Impress Service there and confined against his will. His father testified that the crew of the impress tender refused to allow any professional person aboard to take his son's affidavit, 'and in order to intimidate him threaten to send him on Board a Ship of War forthwith'.[66] James Holburn was a landman indentured to the sea for only two weeks when he was impressed in the Thames and taken aboard the *Emerald* in November 1795. His master Christopher Pearson took out a writ of habeas corpus to recover him, boarded the ship and was told by the first lieutenant that if he produced Holburn's indenture and protection 'he doubted not but he would be discharged'. Pearson went back to London for the papers and boarded the *Emerald* again. He testified that 'he was told by the said Captain that he might retire and said he should detain both the apprentice and his Indenture and Protection. That this deponent then demanded the said Indenture of the said Captain which he peremptorily refused to deliver saying he should send them to the Admiralty'.[67] Pearson managed to speak to his apprentice, who told him 'that every means had been made use of both by threats and promises to induce him to enter for the said ship but that he had refused and further said that if they detained him seven years he would not enter. And desired this deponent to use every means in his power to get him clear'.[68]

Merchant seamen and shipowners of course did what they could to improve their own chances in this costly game. The King's Bench records do indicate that merchant sailors exploited the system of claiming protection through indentures to the sea service. William Peverlay claimed to be an apprentice, but the court accepted that Peverlay had already served three years at sea before being indentured.[69] This was almost certainly an attempt to hide behind indentures in order to stay clear of the press. Another canny seaman, Alexander Anderson, was impressed in Edinburgh, and discharged by Sir George Home, the head of the Impress Service there, on the grounds that Anderson occasionally acted as a sailmaker for the navy. By the second time that he was impressed, Anderson had already signed to go on a Greenland ship, the *Raith*, in the coming season, and was therefore exempt.[70] He seems to have been limiting his risks. Seamen and their masters knew the value of protections and apprenticeships, and a regular business may have existed in providing them. A naval officer employed in the Impress Service at Berwick alleged that a shopkeeper, John Moreson, dealt extensively in engaging young men in indentures so they could work at sea from Sunderland and other northern ports without risking impressment.[71] One Yarmouth man apprenticed himself to the sea simply so that for three years he could work safely in the port as a coalheaver. Though this was clearly a device to avoid the press, the navy's hands were tied. The Admiralty Solicitor advised the incensed regulating captain at Yarmouth that the wily dock worker 'never was an Object of the press Warrant', as it could not be proved that the man had used the sea before he was indentured.[72] The huge predominance of the north-eastern ports in the applications made to the court of King's Bench suggests that apprenticeship indentures were a systematic defence against the navy's manning drive on the prized seamen of the coal trade. Elsewhere, exemption from the press was claimed on the ground of customary informal kinds of apprenticeship the legal status of which was at least ambiguous.[73] Not every affidavit sworn before an attorney need be the literal truth, either. In more than one case, men who were claimed for apprentices were in fact out of their time.[74] Two collier crewmen falsely claimed that they were engaged to go on a voyage as Greenland fishermen, and were accordingly exempt.[75] It would be surprising if these were the only false oaths made to evade impressment, especially since in a remarkably large number of cases the indentures of apprenticeship were not produced for the perusal of the court, but merely attested in an affidavit.[76]

It would be surprising also if naval officers, viewing the world from within their own closed circle, had not believed that their merchant counterparts were practising wholesale fraud and deceit to avoid naval service. War must have polarized attitudes and values which were already distinct, and given an edge of righteous indignation to the mission to man the fleet. Doubtless for these reasons, the navy at every level practised slow compliance with writs of the highest court of the land. This amounted to frustrating the court in the exercise of what should have been from a Whig viewpoint its most sacred function, the protection of the liberties of the individual citizen. The court of King's Bench seems to have been seen primarily as one among many civilian groups – corporations, guilds and so on – frustrating a necessary work.[77] Naval contempt for the law could be surprisingly overt. The higher his rank, the more likely an officer seems to have been to dismiss legally served writs as an impertinence. Admiral Skeffington Ludwidge, commanding at the Nore, was pursued to a sloop off Sheerness in early 1799 by an attorney, John Atkins. Atkins could not get aboard, and followed Ludwidge to his office on shore to deliver his writ. There the door was shut on him, but he persisted and got into the admiral's presence, though the writ was still refused. Atkins laid it on the table, and eventually Ludwidge picked it up and referred it to his clerk. Though this constituted a legal service of the writ, the admiral subsequently made no return to it and so those who were seeking to free the sailor concerned had to go back to the court to obtain a rule, to be served on the Solicitor of the Admiralty, to show cause why the writ should not be complied with. Another hapless attorney, officer to the Sheriff of Hampshire, was charged to deliver a writ of habeas corpus for the release of Thomas Browne, and boarded the *Brunswick* in June 1796 to present it to Admiral Richard Rodney Bligh. Before being removed to the *Brunswick*, Browne had been confined for four days in irons aboard the *Royal Sovereign* and given no food but what he received 'from the humanity of the seamen'.[78] Browne was an eating-house keeper and dealer in slops (clothes) and the reason for his ill treatment was that he had lured sailors away from the *Royal Sovereign* into the service of the East India Company. Nothing could persuade Admiral Bligh to respect the legal rights of such a man. He:

> . . . put him [the sheriff's officer] in bodily fear and danger of his Life calling out to some of his Men to get ready a Thirty two pound Shot directing them to affix thereto the said Writ of Habeas Corpus and throw it after this deponent into the Boat then along side the said Ship and did speak and utter many indignant and contemptuous Words and Expressions of and concerning the said Writ of Habeas Corpus and the service thereof throwing it down on the deck with indignation and contempt refusing to obey it or to release the said Thomas Browne though requested so to do. And this deponent further maketh Oath that the said Admiral Bligh compelled this deponent by threats and menaces to take up the said Writ of Habeas Corpus and to quit the Ship and this deponent verily believes if he had not taken up from the deck the said Writ . . . and carried it with him out of the Ship into the Boat he should have been assassinated, he the said Admiral Bligh giving positive orders to some of his Men to throw the thirty two pound Shott after him this deponent if he did go into the Boat without it.[79]

One case which embodies many of the practices which recur in these records is that of James Townshend. Captain Thomas Affleck of the *Alligator* was served with a writ of habeas corpus for Townshend, a sea apprentice to William Hurry of Great Yarmouth. The captain, on taking Townshend, had roundly declared his indenture and protection to be illegal, and subsequently refused to give him up.[80] Affleck defended his contempt of the court's writ with stylish but empty evasion:

> . . . from his inexperience and not knowing the Contents Nature and meaning of such said Writ, and the Consequences of the non Obeyance and Observance thereof and being at that time otherwise much Engaged in the Business and Concerns of his said Profession, and without thinking of or intending any sort of Contempt or disrespect to this Honourable Court by neglecting to make the due and necessary return thereto, which he is now informed he ought to have done, imprudently and unthinkingly suffer'd the same to be destroy'd and thereby deprived himself of the opportunity of making the due and necessary Return thereto, which he should otherwise most certainly have done by inclosing and sending the same to the Secretary of the Board of Admiralty.[81]

Meanwhile, Townshend had been turned over, on the orders of the Admiralty, to the *Stately*, which was then on its way to the East Indies. As usual in such disputed cases, the Admiralty Solicitor advised Affleck to make the matter up, and would not guarantee to pay his expenses. The unusual feature of this case, though, is that the Lords of Admiralty did agree to consider doing so if it became necessary, and in the meantime ordered Dyson, their solicitor, to give Affleck all assistance short of a guarantee of payment. Dyson spent Admiralty money that summer on a local investigation into Townshend, which found 'that he has been a Chimney Sweeper & in various other situations, many bad ones, is a great *rogue* & capable of almost *any Thing* – that there is every reason to think, among his various Employmts., that he has been at Sea at different times long before Sepr. 1793 . . .'.[82] The navy may have felt that they had done a kind of rough justice in impressing a rogue who, having served at sea, was a proper object of the press. This pragmatic approach was part of Admiralty culture, it seems: one man charged with piracy was impressed in 1795 so as to keep him under the navy's hands until the witnesses against him had time to come over from Massachusetts.[83]

The sheer persistence of the naval officers is striking. They knew they would have the approval of their captain and perhaps even the Admiralty for showing keenness. They would probably also have the consensus of the ship behind them, as so many were in the same position. The bulk of pressing was practised by warships seeking to complete their complements and build a safe working crew. They needed men, preferably young and trainable men, and above all they needed men who were used to working seagoing vessels. To find such men, ships' commanders sent out their parties to prey on merchant seamen in the places where they were most likely to be found, aboard their ships or on duties in their boats. Men such as the young Scot caught in a boat in Long Reach in the Thames, towing his becalmed ship, were an easy target.[84] The ships' logs of several of the naval vessels involved in the impressments charted in the King's Bench records do give some insight into the manning crisis. The *Diomede*, for instance, whose captain the Hon. Charles Elphinstone caused great havoc among merchant shipping in the Thames in May 1798, was fitting out a newly built and undermanned ship which had aboard at least sixty Greenwich pensioners. He must have been more than usually keen to find fit young men who knew the ropes.[85] One ship alone, the *Three Brothers*, lost to the *Diomede* its carpenter and five apprentices.[86] Colliers, coasters, fishermen, crews of transports and others were caught up in the constant war for men which the navy had to wage. Professor Baugh has called it 'a sort of game – albeit a grim one – in which certain informal rules came to be observed'.[87] It had its seasons, with a slacker time in the high summer and early autumn. And it had its places: seamen were always vulnerable in rivers such as the Thames, where the next reach could conceal a pressing crew, and vulnerable too when passing naval anchorages such as the Nore, the Downs, or Spithead. Nationally, the bulk of naval impressment could be expected to have taken place when naval vessels swooped on inward bound merchant ships in the Channel.[88] Hardly a trace of this aspect of manning, though, shows up in the records of applications for habeas corpus – not surprisingly, since merchant seamen caught in this way would rarely have legal grounds for such an application, and their impressment game had different rules. It seems clear that the records of both King's Bench and Admiralty show a specific set of tensions, a particular game played out between on one hand the navy and on the other the owners, masters and crews of the north-eastern coal and coasting ships.

The evidence of impressment examined here indicates that it was – so far as those specific records can tell us – an abuse of individual rights which was indeed largely confined to the seafaring community. Naval impressment as it appears in these sources cannot simply be used as a metaphor for the dominance of a wealthy élite over the mass of the people. The navy's reluctant cooperation with the courts, so evident in the records of King's Bench, may be an aspect of the discretionary arrogance of those who enjoyed power, but it does not necessarily tell us anything straightforward about the class interests of employers and property owners ashore. It does, however, point to a clash of military and civilian outlooks and codes of behaviour in wartime. This is a phenomenon which occurs in other areas of life, for example in the tensions set up in local communities by participation in volunteer companies, with their often combative loyalism and amateur military ardour.[89] Naval officers seem to have been imbued with a service ethos and a sense of solidarity against other interest groups, such as guilds and corporations. They were keen to man their ships by any possible means, and ruthless in doing so, confident that in most cases they would have at least the tacit support of their superiors. The emergency of war justified any effort to make ships ready for sea, and naval officers were inclined to regard civilian protests as attempts to evade their responsibility to the crown and nation. They believed, or professed to believe, that most indentures and declarations of age were false, and pressed men wholesale, giving them up only on direct orders from the court or the Admiralty Solicitor. The record of this vigorous resort to pressing does not illuminate for us the plight of the poor in general, but it does tell us a great deal about the hazards of working life for the seagoing labourers and craftsmen of the North Sea.

Notes

1   Lawrence Stone (ed.), *An Imperial State at War: Britain from 1689 to 1815* (London, Routledge, 1994); John Brewer, *The Sinews of Power: War, Money and the English State 1688–1783* (London, Unwin Hyman, 1989); Jeremy Black, *Britain as a Military Power 1688–1815* (London, UCL Press, 1998).

2 Nicholas Rodger, *The Wooden World. An Anatomy of the Georgian Navy* (London, Collins, 1986), pp. 148–9.

3 J.S. Bromley (ed.), *The Manning of the Royal Navy 1660–1815*, Navy Records Society, no. 119 (London, NRS, 1974), p. iii.

4 Nicholas Rogers, 'Vagrancy, Impressment and the Regulation of Labour in Eighteenth-Century Britain', *Slavery and Abolition*, 15: 2, 1994, pp. 102–13.

5 Ibid., p. 111.

6 Douglas Hay, 'Property, Authority and the Criminal Law', in D. Hay, P. Linebaugh, J.G. Rule, E.P. Thompson and C. Wilmslow, *Albion's Fatal Tree: Crime and Society in Eighteenth-Century England* (London, Allen Lane, 1975).

7 Affidavit of Thomas Pitts, 23 April 1795, PRO KB 1/28, Easter 35 Geo III, 18.

8 James Dyson, Admiralty Solicitor, to Evan Nepean, Secretary of the Navy, 19 May and 18 June 1795, PRO ADM 1/3683, unfoliated.

9 Affidavit of Pitts, Houswick and Cocks, 26 May 1795, PRO KB 1/28, Trinity 35 Geo III, 3.

10 Rogers, 'Vagrancy, Impressment', p. 111.

11 E.g. affidavit of Thomas Curry, 14 November 1794, PRO KB 1/28, Michaelmas 35 Geo III, 22.

12 Dyson to Nepean, 1 October 1795, PRO ADM 1/3683, unfoliated.

13 2 & 3 Ann c. 6, cl. 16.

14 Rodger, *Wooden World*, p. 170.

15 Dyson to Nepean, 24 March 1795, PRO ADM 1/3683, unfoliated.

16 *Journal of the House of Commons*, L, p. 480.

17 John Staples and George Story, regulating captains, to Dyson, 10 November 1795, PRO ADM 1/3683, unfoliated. Advice endorsed on letter.

18 Ibid., John Staples and George Story to Dyson, 16 November 1795.

19 This seems implicit in a case which arose in August 1795 in Edinburgh. The regulating captain there sent away a young apprentice, John Gow, to the Nore on the grounds that the young man had been delivered over by the magistrates as a vagrant. It later emerged that this was a pretext, but it would have had no value if the practice had not existed. Dyson to Nepean, 29 August and 29 September 1795, PRO ADM 13683, unfoliated.

20 *The Attic Miscellany, and Characteristic Mirror*, IX (June 1790), pp. 321–3. The folding plate, a feature of the periodical, is full of movement and of figures, their features mostly caricatured, drawn in characteristic style by Samual Collings. On Collings, see B.E. Maidment, *Reading Popular Prints, 1790–1870* (Manchester University Press, 1996), pp. 41–4.

21 *Attic Miscellany*, IX, p. 322.

22 *Attic Miscellany*, XI, (August 1790), p. 413.

23 Affidavits of William Preston, 26 November 1796, and Nicholas Tate, 23 November 1796, PRO KB/129, Michaelmas 37 Geo III, 87.

24 Affidavit of Thomas Mankins, 12 November 1793, PRO KB/128, Michaelmas 34 Geo III, 30.

25 E.g. affidavit of Matthew London the elder of Hackney, carpenter, to recover his son and apprentice Matthew, 10 May 1793, ibid., Easter 33 Geo III, 62.

26 Affidavit of Joseph Bourn, 10 May 1793, ibid., 77.

27 Affidavit of William Wilson, 11 May 1793, ibid., 78.

28 Numerous instances can be found of impressing carpenters. E.g. affidavits of John Thompson, 5 November 1793, PRO KB 1/28, Michaelmas 34 Geo III, 31; James Luke, 2 February 1797, PRO KB 1/29, Hilary 37 Geo III, 37; Thomas Skipsey on behalf of his relation William Skipsey, a landman and carpenter impressed after less than a year at sea, 15 May 1798, ibid., Easter 38 Geo III, 43; George Brown of North Shields to retrieve his chief carpenter, impressed despite his protection, 15 May 1798, ibid., 47.

29 Affidavit of John King, 24 January 1794, PRO KB 1/28, Hilary 34 Geo III, 14.

30 Dyson to Philip Stephens, First Secretary of Admiralty, 16 January 1795, PRO ADM 1/3683, unfoliated.

31 Affidavit of Maitland McIntosh, 17 November 1795, PRO KB 1/29, Michaelmas 36 Geo III, 99.

32 *Morning Post*, 18 June 1794; Linda Colley, 'The Apotheosis of George III: Loyalty, Royalty and the British Nation, 1760–1820', *Past & Present*, 102, 1984, pp. 94–129.

33 *Bath Journal*, 1 December 1794.

34 Bromley (ed.), *Manning of the Royal Navy*, pp. xxxv–xxxvii.

35 Though not without ambiguities, the appeal to tradition can be traced in numerous radical writings: see e.g. Mary Thale (ed.), *Selections from the Papers of the London Corresponding Society 1792–1799* (Cambridge, Cambridge University Press, 1983), pp. 5–9, 106.

36 [Lieutenant John Mackenzie], *Considerations on the Impress Service* (1786), in Bromley (ed.), *Manning of the Royal Navy*, p. 125.

37 For example, York on 6 February 1795, Durham 17 February (with a counter-petition from some leading citizens), Liverpool 19 February; *Journal of the House of Commons (JHC)*, XL, 35 Geo III, pp. 166, 228, 237.

38 Petition of Bailiffs and Burgesses of Scarborough, 16 February 1795, *JHC*, XL, p. 220. Other petitions came from shipping interests in Whitehaven, Newcastle-upon-Tyne and North and South Shields, 17 February, ibid., pp. 225–6.

39 Sunderland petition, 17 February 1795, ibid., p. 226.

40 Royal assent 5 March 1795; *JHC*, L, p. 300; enforcing Act 12 May 1796, *JHC*, LI, p. 790.

41 Affidavits of William Cobb Hurry, 24 January 1795, PRO KB 1/28, Hilary 35 Geo III, 31; Edmund Cobb Hurry, 6 November 1798, and Richard Powles, 1 November 1798, PRO KB 1/30, Michaelmas Geo III, 9; Henry Stephenson, 5 February 1800, PRO KB 1/31, Hilary 40 Geo III, 38.

42 Dyson to Stephens, 12 January 1795, PRO ADM 1/3683, unfoliated.

43 Affidavits of John Wilson, 22 May 1794 and 12 June 1795, PRO KB 1/28, Easter 34 Geo III, 31 and Trinity 35 Geo III, 20; order in PRO KB 21/46, p. 223.

44 Affidavit of Ann Reburn and others, n.d., PRO KB 1/29, Hilary 36 Geo III, 21.

45 Affidavit of Abraham Bywater, in Dyson to Nepean, 28 October 1795, PRO ADM 1/3683, unfoliated. The *Peterel* was the sloop which, three years later, became the first command of Jane Austen's brother Frank: Jane to Cassandra, 28 December 1798, in R.W. Chapman (ed.), *Jane Austen. Letters 1796–1817* (Oxford, Oxford University Press, 1955), p. 23.

46 Dyson to Nepean, 31 March 1795, PRO ADM 1/3683, unfoliated.

47 *Sixty-Ninth Annual Report of the Deputy Keeper of Public Records* (London, HMSO, 1908) pp. 10–11; *Seventieth Annual Report of the Deputy Keeper of Public Records* (London, HMSO, 1909) p. 10.

48 30 in 1793; 68 in 1794; 66 in 1795; 16 in 1796; 9 in 1797; 22 in 1798; 1 in 1799; 1 in 1800. It might be instructive to compare the years 1803–5 with 1793–5. Both these periods were ones of newly-commenced war, and it would be useful to know if, and why, the first years of the war saw less hostility to impressment than did the resumption of war after the Peace of Amiens. Several supplementary volumes of the Home Office papers deal with the issue of resistance to impressment: HO 42/71–4 for 1803 and HO 42/78–9 for 1804.

49 *Report from the Committee appointed to enquire into the State of the COAL TRADE of this Kingdom*, 31 December 1800, p. 643.

50 It is hard to recover the details of fees, but they can be reliably inferred from the work of Richard Gude, who was active in the Crown Office of King's Bench from 1789 to 1823. The tables of Gude's definitive guide to the court show a remarkable range of fees being applied at each stage of resort to it, payments being made to clerks, judges and lawyers and even to door-keepers and other officials. Richard Gude, *The Practice of the Crown Side of the Court of King's Bench, and the Practice of the Sessions, The General Rules of Court, from the Reign of James I to the present Time; And the Statutes relating to the Practice. Together with a Table of Fees, and Bills of Costs. Also, an Appendix of Forms and Precedents* (2 vols, London, 1828; repr. Littleton, Colo, Fred B. Rothman, 1991).

51 This process can be followed in the Rule Books. E.g. the case of Edward Riou of the *Rose*, who had impressed Robert Drydon; rules of 13 and 21 November 1793, PRO KB 21/46, pp. 159, 168.

52 Rodger, *Wooden World*, p. 125.

53. Affidavits of Nicholas Fairlies and Thomas Wilson, 29 April 1793, PRO KB 1/28, Easter 33 Geo III, 36.

54 Affidavit of Thomas Reynolds, 27 April 1795, ibid., Easter 35 Geo III, 18.

55 For cases where details exist, the figures for those swearing affidavits in 1793–5 are as follows. 1793: master 20, master *and* friend or relative 4, friend or relative 5. 1794: 40, 3, 12. 1795: 44, 2, 8.

56 Affidavit of John Robson, 19 May 1794, ibid., Easter 34 Geo III, 26.

57 Affidavits of Herman Hasshaughn and Alfred Arentz, 25 September 1797; of Andrew Hoff, 25 January 1798, PRO KB 1/29, Hilary 38 Geo III, 12. A similar case was that of Peter Torris, a German, his friend Nicholas Augustine expressly stating that he acted at the request of Torris: 2 May 1796, ibid., Easter 36 Geo III, 84.

58 E.g. affidavit of Thomas Reynolds, 2 May 1795, PRO KB 1/28, Easter 35 Geo III, 35.

59 Affidavit of George Betts of Great Yarmouth, master of the *Mary*, Lowestoft, 28 November 1796, PRO KB 1/29, Michaelmas 37 Geo III, 88.

60 This is common in the returns to writs, often endorsed on the back of the original parchment document, and preserved in the Recorda/Writ files; e.g. return to writ for Thomas Swainton, carpenter, by Sir William Sidney Smith, *Diamond*, 28 June 1794, PRO KB 16/21/3, unfoliated.

61 Affidavit of Thomas Gabriel and Thomas Handcock, 18 June 1798, PRO KB 1/30, Trinity 38 Geo III, 34.

62 Affidavit of Elias Peter Lindby, 3 May 1796, PRO KB 1/29, Easter 36 Geo III, 82; affidavit of Andrew Peterson, 27 April 1796, ibid., 53.

63 Affidavits of Lewis Kennedy and Matthew London, 10 May 1793, PRO KB 1/28, Easter 33 Geo III, 61, 62.

64 Officers who allowed runaway apprentices the enlistment bounty could be severely reprimanded by their Lordships. Dyson to Nepean, 14 July and 26 December 1795, PRO ADM 1/3683, unfoliated.

65 Affidavit of John Appleton, enclosed in Dyson to Nepean, 28 October 1795, ibid.

66 Affidavit of Thomas Rees, 24 January 1797, PRO KB 1/29, Hilary 37 Geo III, 25.

67 Affidavit of Christopher Pearson, 28 November 1795, ibid., Michaelmas 36 Geo III, 108.

68 Ibid.

69 Dyson to Nepean, 18 November 1795, PRO ADM 1/3683, unfoliated.

70 Dyson to Nepean, 27 March 1795, ibid.

71 Dyson to Nepean, 20 June 1795, ibid.

72 Dyson to Nepean, 5 September 1795, ibid.

73 'Colts' in the West of England, and unstamped indentures in Scotland: Dyson to Nepean, 16 November and 30 December 1795, ibid.

74 E.g. writ issued to Edward Howorth, commander of the *Enterprize*, and its return, 12 February 1794; PRO KB 16/21, unfoliated.

75 Dyson to Nepean, 26 August 1795, PRO ADM 1/3683, unfoliated.

76 E.g. affidavit of Samuel Wiggins, 7 May 1793, PRO KB 1/28, Easter 33 Geo III, 47.

77 The corporations of ports, not least the City of London, were persistently suspicious of, or hostile to, the Impress Service. E.g. affidavit of William Grieves, 12 November 1793, PRO KB 1/28, Michaelmas 34 Geo III, 30. A case of manslaughter by impress officers in Poole Harbour brought out bitter conflict; Dyson to Stephens, 28 February 1795, Dyson to Nepean, 7 March, 29 June 1795, PRO ADM 1/3683, unfoliated.

78 Affidavit of Thomas Browne, 4 June 1796, PRO KB 1/29, Trinity 36 Geo III, 10.

79 Affidavit of John Handley, 8 June 1796, ibid., 22.

80 Affidavits of William Hurry and Elisha Darby, 24 January 1795, PRO ADM 1/3683, unfoliated.

81 Deposition of Captain Thomas Affleck, March 1795, ibid.

82 John Reynolds to Dyson, 9 July 1795, ibid.

83 Dyson to Nepean, 11 and 28 April 1795, PRO ADM 1/3683, unfoliated.

84 Affidavit of William Robinson, 16 November 1795, PRO KB 1/28, Michaelmas 36 Geo III, 31.

85 Log of the *Diomede* 10 March 1798 to 10 September 1799, PRO ADM 51/1420 part 3; his vigorous pressing led to eighteen surviving writs of habeas corpus in that month alone. Similar motives appear in the logs of the *Rose* 22 June 1793 to 26 March 1794, PRO ADM 51/1151; the *Peterel* 24 October 1794 to 6 June 1795, PRO ADM 51/1143.

86 Affidavits of Matthew Titteroy Gilley, 18 May 1798, PRO KB 1/29, Easter 38 Geo III, 49–51.

87 D.A. Baugh, *British Naval Administration in the Age of Walpole* (Princeton, NJ, Princeton University Press, 1965), p. 156.

88 Baugh, *British Naval Administration*, pp. 155–9; Rodger, *Wooden World*, pp. 180–1.

89 Philip Woodfine, '"Unjustifiable and Illiberal": Military Patriotism and Civilian Values in the 1790s', in B. Taithe and T. Thornton (eds), *War: Identities in Conflict 1300–2000* (Stroud, Sutton Publishing, 1998), pp. 73–94.

3

'Evangelical Piety and Gallic Flippancy': Religion and Popular Protest in Halifax Parish in the Age of Revolution

John A. Hargreaves

The Evangelical vicar of Halifax, the Revd Dr Henry William Coulthurst (1753–1817), addressing the Halifax Volunteer Corps of Infantry at Halifax Parish Church at the height of the French invasion scare in January 1804, implored his congregation to reflect upon 'the scenes of blood, rapine, and devastation which have overspread France, Europe, Africa and the West Indies' since the usurpation of Napoleon Bonaparte. Speculating upon the dire consequences for Halifax of a Napoleonic invasion, he warned that the magnificent Manufacturers' Piece Hall, opened in 1779, 'now the grand repository of our commerce, would instantly be a barrack and this very church a charnel house'. He urged a patriotic disdain for 'French principles and French conduct', concluding:

> He calls you a nation of shopkeepers! Tell him that you are diligent, honest merchants and manufacturers, possessed of manly understanding, that you . . . wish not to wander in the trackless wilds of revolutionary experiments . . . that you will obey the law of your country, that you will submit yourselves to all your governors, that you . . . abhor every pitiful particle of Gallic flippancy or Gallic policy.[1]

To what extent was Coulthurst's unequivocal denunciation of 'French principles and French conduct' in his sermon of 1804 typical of the reaction of Anglican and Nonconformist Evangelicals in Halifax to continental and transatlantic revolution in the last quarter of the eighteenth century and the first half of the nineteenth century? During this period Halifax and its rural hinterland experienced major social and economic dislocation as a consequence of industrialization and urbanization, which resulted in a quadrupling of the population of the town from an estimated 6,360 in 1764 to 25,159 in 1851, paralleled by an almost equally spectacular growth in the population of the parish embracing Halifax from around 41,220 in 1764 to 149,257 in 1851. Increasing numbers of domestic outworkers became absorbed into the new urban factory workforce following the opening of the Halifax branch canal in 1828, which stimulated the development of steam-powered technology by providing plentiful supplies of cheap coal for the mills along the Hebble Valley. This social and economic transformation provided fertile soil for the development of popular protest during the period 1775–1848, inspired by both the American and French Revolutions. It also provided the context for the growth within the emerging industrial town and its vast upland Pennine parish of evangelicalism, which infused both the Established Church and Protestant Nonconformity with a missionary zeal to win the allegiance of an expanding industrial proletariat. This was strengthened by the appointment of Henry William Coulthurst as Vicar of Halifax in 1790, and by the great Yorkshire revival of 1793, which resulted in a spectacular growth of Methodism within the parish. These developments prompted the superintendent minister of the Halifax Wesleyan Circuit, the Revd Charles Atmore, to observe triumphantly in June 1794:

> . . . the great work of God . . . is almost indescribable . . . we have added about 700 persons in our circuit since last conference; the greater part of whom, there is reason to believe, are truly converted to the Lord, and can rejoice in him as their Saviour and Redeemer.[2]

This chapter will explore the relationship between popular protest and evangelicalism, particularly Methodism, in the parish of Halifax from the outbreak of the War of American Independence in 1775 to the overthrow of the July monarchy of Louis Philippe in the French Revolution of February 1848. It will argue that the relationship between popular protest and evangelicalism in Halifax during this period was multi-faceted and dynamic, responding to changing economic, social and political conditions, not least fundamental changes in the character of extra-parliamentary protest itself during the reform crisis of 1830–32. The struggle for the Great Reform Act of 1832, which enfranchised many of the 'diligent, honest merchants and manufacturers' whom Coulthurst had exhorted 'not to wander in the trackless wilds of revolutionary experiments' in 1804, encouraged a growing number of aspiring bourgeois Halifax Evangelicals to participate in political agitation in the 1830s and 1840s. They campaigned, for example, against colonial slavery, Graham's Factory Bill, the Maynooth grant and the Corn Laws, without compromising their predisposition to resist subversive movements perceived as insurrectionary, irreligious or a danger to commercial prosperity and private property.

RADICALISM, LUDDISM AND THE PARLIAMENTARY
REFORM MOVEMENT

Although the release from imprisonment of John Wilkes 'the popular champion of the people's rights' in April 1770 was greeted in Halifax with the 'ringing of bells, fireworks and other demonstrations of joy', it was the political crisis generated by the War of American Independence between 1775 and 1783 which gave birth to the agitation for parliamentary reform in Yorkshire in the late eighteenth century.[3] Moreover, the reform movement – which was sustained during the 1780s by Major John Cartwright's radical constitutional societies, the Revd Christopher Wyvill's Yorkshire Association and Protestant Dissenters in their unsuccessful campaigns for civil and religious liberty – developed against a background of endemic dearth and distress, exacerbated by the war. In 1783, the most serious of a spate of food riots across the Pennines erupted in Halifax, resulting in the execution of two of the leaders of the mob for robbery, the last public hanging to take place in the town.[4]

It was not until 1791–92, however, that an organized popular radical movement developed in the West Riding stimulated by the outbreak of the French Revolution, the publication of Tom Paine's avowedly republican *Rights of Man*, the foundation of the Sheffield Society for Constitutional Information and of the London Corresponding Society. By November 1792, when magistrates at Bingley obliged a Halifax bookseller, who had sold copies of a penny paper, *The French Constitution*, to acknowledge the error of his ways, a Jacobin society had been established at Halifax. At a huge open-air meeting in the town on Easter Monday 1794, plans were approved for a National Convention and, in the following year, the Home Secretary, the Duke of Portland, asked the Halifax attorney Robert Parker to investigate rumours that Jacobins in Elland were involved in plans for an armed insurrection.[5]

Such activity stirred Pitt's government into a policy of repression which continued throughout the wars with Revolutionary and Napoleonic France, but this did not deter the Halifax branch of Major Cartwright's Union Society, founded in October 1812 following a spate of Luddite disturbances, from collecting in under two months some 17,000 signatories for a petition for parliamentary reform. Reform meetings at Soyland, near Ripponden, in December 1816 and January 1817, stimulated by the postwar distress, were also well-attended, but the climax of the postwar parliamentary reform movement followed the massacre at St Peter's Field in August 1819. As the perceptive Tory Anglican diarist Anne Lister commented, Halifax was full of talk 'of the sad work at Manchester' and on Monday 4 October, an estimated 50,000 'male and female reformers' attended a large open-air meeting in the town, which was followed by a patriotic dinner, during which toasts were proposed to: 'The People, the source of all legitimate power'; 'The Saviour of our country, Major

Cartwright' and 'Henry Hunt, the Champion of Liberty' (this was the famous 'Orator' Hunt)[6]. Moreover, in 1820, the ladies of Halifax expressed their radical sympathies by presenting a loyal address to Queen Caroline, the estranged wife of the unpopular King George IV.[7]

Immediately following the outbreak of the War of American Independence, the local clergy took a prominent role in resisting the radical resurgence and in upholding public order. They affirmed with the gentry, merchants, manufacturers and other inhabitants of the town and neighbourhood of Halifax their loyalty to the crown in an address to the Earl of Dartmouth, the Secretary of State for the American Colonies, in November 1775, which expressed their 'grateful sense' of the blessings enjoyed under the reign of George III and their 'protestation' at the conduct of the colonists 'now in open rebellion'.[8] In 1783, a fortnight after the Halifax food riot, the Vicar of Halifax, the Revd Dr Henry Wood, and Joshua Horton of Howroyd, in their capacity as magistrates, proclaimed an order that all corn brought into Halifax 'be publicly exposed for sale in the open market and that no corn or meal be sold privately'.[9]

In 1792, Dr Henry Coulthurst, Wood's successor, chaired 'a very numerous and respectable meeting of the principal inhabitants of the town' at the Talbot Inn 'for the preservation of peace and good order, liberty and property against the various efforts of Levellers and Republicans'.[10] Later, following the Jacobin plot at Elland, which Coulthurst had been instrumental in exposing, he complained to the Home Secretary that there was not a single active magistrate in the whole of 'this very large parish containing 70,000 souls and equal in extent to the county of Rutland'.[11] Consequently, in 1797, Coulthurst was appointed to the commission of the peace, fulfilling a pledge in his first sermon at Halifax Parish Church on 12 December 1790 that:

> . . . when things serious and sacred are trifled with, when the name of God himself is trampled on and despised, surely it is high time . . . to bring forth the spear and stop the way and stand up for the name of the Lord our God.[12]

In 1796, Coulthurst had preached a resoundingly loyal sermon at the University of Cambridge on the anniversary of King George III's accession, from Ecclesiastes, chapter 10, verse 20: 'Curse not the king . . . and curse not the rich in thy bedchamber', a text which he maintained was peculiarly apt in this 'Day of Tumult and Confusion', when 'kings are wantonly cursed and insulted and the rich and opulent are upbraided as the usurpers and piratical invaders of the common property of mankind'. The sermon praised 'the vigorous exertions' of Britain's 'intrepid rulers' in introducing repressive legislation which had 'providentially preserved . . . the just political equilibrium'.[13] Later, during the Napoleonic invasion scare, he reputedly 'put a cockade in the side of his hat and walked in procession with a recruiting party' through the streets of Halifax 'with drums beating and colours flying' in a bid to encourage enlistment.[14]

In June 1812, he warned Earl Fitzwilliam in the wake of the Luddite disturbances that while Halifax had returned to a 'state of calm', he feared that 'at bottom there is a deep laid system of organised Rebellion and Revolution'.[15] He had played an active role in the suppression of the movement and following the proclamation of a royal amnesty in 1813 he obtained oaths of allegiance to the crown from forty-one former Luddites, twenty-five of whom were from his own parish.[16] During the postwar radical agitation, Coulthurst again emerged as a champion of loyalism, when his name headed a declaration of 193 inhabitants of the town of Halifax on 27 January 1817 abhorring 'the daring attempts which are daily made to inflame the minds of the lower orders . . . and to make them dissatisfied with their situation'. The declaration, supported by other local Anglican clergy and laymen, warned that interference in politics would render the lower orders 'the tools of designing men, who, under the mask of patriotism, desire anarchy and revolution' and expressed a determination to energetically oppose 'the blasphemous and seditious doctrines, which are so generally promulgated at the clubs and meetings, which disgrace our country at the present moment' and to support 'our beloved king and our admirable constitution'.[17]

The use of the pulpit of the Halifax Parish Church to proscribe radicalism continued under Coulthurst's successor, the Evangelical Revd Samuel Knight (1757–1827), son of Titus Knight, a convert of John Wesley and the first minister of Square Independent Chapel. Anne Lister recorded in her diary for Sunday 25 August 1822 that Mr Franks, junior, had preached for over 40 minutes:

> . . . as much to put us in love with our political as religious constitution and perhaps, more apt *against* radicalism than *for* the Society for the Promotion of Christian Knowledge, on behalf of which there was a collection after the service.[18]

Prominent local Dissenting ministers also held aloof from the Painite radicalism which emerged during the French Wars. The biographer of Dr John Fawcett (1740–1817) concluded that the scholarly and influential Halifax Baptist divine was:

> . . . a true patriot and well understood the principles of civil and religious liberty; but it was his uniform study to practise himself and to inculcate upon others the rule laid down by his Divine master: 'Render unto Caesar . . .'. The feelings of his heart and the dictates of his judgment led him to cherish the most ardent love for his native country, praying for 'kings and all that are in authority, that we may live a peaceable and quiet life in all godliness and honesty'.[19]

In the highly-charged atmosphere of the period, however, the professed political quietism of at least one other local Dissenting minister did not go unchallenged. The biographer of the Revd Joseph Cockin (1755–1828), Titus Knight's successor at Square Chapel, maintained that the Independent minister 'avowed, without disguise or reserve, the doctrine of passive obedience and non-resistance' and that 'as far as he had any political principles, they were rather courtly', particularly 'as he advanced in years'. He cited two published sermons, 'The Loyal Subject' and 'The Oppressor Punished', the latter a response to the failure of Napoleon's Moscow campaign, as evidence of Cockin's patriotism, and deplored the taunts of Jacobinism directed at Cockin by the *Leeds Intelligencer*, in the *Orthodox Churchman's Magazine* and in a pamphlet on democratic scheming as 'gross insults' incurred because:

> . . . he would not join in abusing and cursing the French; neither would he subscribe his life and fortune to carry on a sanguinary and destructive war which burdened England with taxes . . . and has made the weight of government too heavy for the prosperity of the country.[20]

Members of other Dissenting sects willingly assisted the authorities in maintaining public order at times of crisis. According to Sir Francis Wood, the Deputy Lord Lieutenant of the West Riding, 'several Quakers with whom we talked and reasoned' were willing to take the lead in forming an association for the preservation of the peace at Rastrick, where 'numberless' outrages occurred in the wake of the Luddite disturbances in the summer of 1812.[21]

Of all the Nonconformist sects, however, it was the Wesleyans who were most conspicuously resolute in their opposition to radical protest. John Wesley had visited the Methodist society in Halifax on Monday 20 July 1789, within a week of the storming of the Bastille, on the day that *The Times* had expressed its horror at 'the bloodshed . . . which France now exhibits' unprecedented in European history since the St Bartholomew's Day Massacre of 1572.[22] Wesley, whose initial private sympathy for the 'oppressed people' of America had been superseded by an unambiguously loyalist public stance on the outbreak of the War of American Independence, appears to have made only the most oblique of references to the 'amazing revolutions' in Europe in 1789–90, which he viewed with millennarian optimism as forerunners of an approaching time 'when the earth shall be filled with the knowledge of the glory of the Lord'.[23] Neither his journal, which records that he preached in the evening of Monday 20 July 1789 at Halifax 'to a noble congregation and afterwards spent near another hour exhorting the society', nor local sources reveal in detail the content of his sermon or exhortatory address.[24] However, J.U. Walker, the contemporary historian of Wesleyanism in Halifax, insisted that the 'principal feature' of Wesley's exhortation was 'an earnest desire that his people should ever maintain membership with the Establishment', which apparently commanded 'spontaneous assent' from the Halifax Wesleyans.[25]

The Revds William Thompson (1733–99) and John Pawson (1762–1806), successively superintendent ministers of the Halifax Wesleyan Circuit during the years 1789–93 and presidents of the Wesleyan Conference in 1791 and 1793 respectively, exhibited sharply differing viewpoints about relations with the Establishment after the death of Wesley in 1791. While Thompson favoured strengthening links with the Church of England and public protestations of loyalty to the Pittite administration, Pawson favoured celebrating the sacrament in church hours and 'declaring our love for our King and Country by fasting and praying for them'.[26] Pawson's correspondence from Halifax from 1791 to 1793, which affirms the extraordinary strength of evangelicalism 'on every side' within the town, reveals his own reservations about the writings of Paine in 1792. Although privately recognizing the validity of some of Paine's criticisms of the government, Pawson regretted Paine's rejection of religion, for 'nothing under heaven can make the inhabitants of this land more happy but more religion, and this alas, is not so much as thought of'. He concluded, therefore:

. . . let us meddle as little as possible with state affairs, but let us give up ourselves to our most blessed master and endeavour to be more useful in his hands than ever.[27]

J.U. Walker later maintained that the root cause of the Kilhamite secession at Bradshaw in 1797, when society members joined the Methodist New Connexion, barring the Wesleyan preachers from the chapel, was the introduction of 'the detestable works of Paine' to many members of the society through 'a reading club' and 'debating society'. One of the seceders had apparently boasted: 'mention me a sentiment or paragraph in Paine's *Rights of Man* and I'll tell you the very page where it is to be found'.[28] Moreover, it was the association of Luddism in Halifax with the Painite radicalism of the veteran republican democrat John Baines, 'a man notoriously disaffected to the government', that alarmed the Revd Jabez Bunting (1779–1858), superintendent of the Halifax Wesleyan Circuit, in 1812. Baines organized a vast parade of working men, each wearing white crêpe arm bands, to accompany to the grave at the South Parade Wesleyan Chapel the body of Samuel Hartley (1788–1812), one of two Luddites mortally wounded in the assault on a mill near Cleckheaton on 11 April 1812.[29] Although at the inquest into their deaths it was observed that 'neither of these victims of lawless violence manifested any sense of religion', Hartley was the son of Samuel and the late Elizabeth Hartley, both of whom had chapel connections, and no doubt the family approached Bunting for permission to bury Hartley in the graveyard near his mother.[30]

Bunting, in his first superintendency, was sensitive to the growing criticism in official circles of the looseness of the affiliation of many to Methodism in the disturbed manufacturing districts. He was also acutely aware of the threat to Methodist expansion from Viscount Sidmouth's proposed amendment to the Toleration Bill, which sought to restrict itinerant preaching and which Bunting had condemned as 'a fearful measure', campaigning vigorously in the Manchester and Liverpool districts against the bill and collecting £30 in the Halifax Circuit to help defray the costs of the campaign.[31] So, whatever sympathies he may have felt for the 'members of his flock . . . subjects of grinding misery . . . exposed to the seductions of rash and ignorant men' he decided boldly to denounce 'all violations of the law' and adopt a distinctly circumspect, but essentially pragmatic, attitude towards the Luddite funeral. Accordingly, he allowed Hartley to be buried in the chapel graveyard and was present at the funeral service, but instructed a junior colleague, Mark Dawes, to officiate, thereby upsetting the crowds of mourners, who obliged the young minister to make an undignified exit over the chapel wall after the burial.[32]

On the following Sunday Bunting, refusing to depart from his well-established practice of conducting no more than two services on the Sabbath, declined to conduct an afternoon memorial service for Hartley. However, he again attended the service at which the popular revivalist and politically quietest preacher, Jonathan Saville (1759–1842), preached to 'the largest congregation that ever assembled in Halifax Chapel', with hundreds more standing outside under the watchful eye of constables patrolling 'to keep the peace'. 'At that time, perhaps more than ever', Jonathan Saville later recalled, 'infidelity was busy amongst the lower classes' and in his sermon he pointedly contrasted the eternal destiny of the believer with the ignominious fate of the infidel, arousing strong hostility from the radicals, who hurled stones at Saville as he went to conduct his class meeting. Bunting also regarded himself as a marked man after the episode and his friends judged it hazardous for him to proceed to his country appointments alone.[33]

The role of popular religion in the Luddite disturbances of 1812 excited considerable contemporary discussion. Thomas Broughton, a Barnsley weaver, who turned informer, in a deposition sworn before Sheffield magistrates in August 1812, maintained that in Halifax the Luddites met 'as Dissenters under the cloak of Religion'.[34] While both Broughton's motives for volunteering information and the reliability of his evidence have been discredited, he was not alone in suggesting a link between the disturbances and popular religion. The official report of the Luddite trials at York, published in 1813, commented pejoratively on 'the religious fanaticism which unhappily exists in an excessive degree' in the districts where the disturbances had occurred, while contemporary observers such as Colonel Norton and the Revd Sydney Smith, concluded that some of those executed were Methodists.[35]

Certainly a Methodist hymn had been sung as one group of prisoners, including John Hill (1777–1813), a Greetland cotton spinner, had been led out to the scaffold, but Bunting's own conclusion that none of the York prisoners 'were members of our body' is corroborated by the membership lists in the Halifax Circuit Directory for 1811.[36] Bunting did, however, acknowledge that '6 out of the 17 who were hanged were sons of Methodists' and that one of the fathers, Joseph Hey, was a respected senior Wesleyan local preacher in the Halifax Circuit. In conversation with Thomas Shillitoe and Joseph Wood, two Quakers who undertook pastoral visits to the families of the bereaved after the executions, Wood described Hey as 'a truly pious man', with whom they parted 'in a near sympathy' after he had insisted that they also counsel his other two sons.[37]

Shillitoe and Wood did not make any other specific allusions to Methodists among the families of the bereaved whom they visited, but the Revd Thomas Jackson (1785–1873), Bunting's colleague in the Sowerby Bridge Circuit, prevented the burial of Luddites executed at York in the graveyard of the Greetland Wesleyan Chapel. After consultation with Bunting, Jackson hurried to the chapel and ordered the gates and doors to be secured by strong locks, supported by a local magistrate who maintained that 'as convicts were not Methodists but nominal churchmen', they should be interred 'in the churchyards of the parishes to which they belonged'. 'In these calamitous times', Jackson later wrote in his autobiography:

> I never hesitated to preach obedience to the laws . . . and to warn people against the dangerous courses to which they were incited; yet I was never interrupted in any of my night journeys across the moors.[38]

There is really no doubt at all where local Wesleyan ministers and indeed Anglican clergymen stood on the issue of Luddism. When, shortly after the disturbances, in May 1813 an appreciative address was presented to Joseph Radcliffe – the Huddersfield magistrate who had been the most intrepid opponent of the Luddites, on behalf of the inhabitants of the parish of Halifax – among the 294 signatures, headed by Dr Coulthurst's, were those of Wesleyan ministers Jabez Bunting, William Leach and Zechariah Yewdall, along with prominent Methodist laymen of both Old and New Connexions.[39] Between Halifax Parish Church, where Coulthurst filled the pulpit, and the South Parade Wesleyan Chapel, where Bunting reigned supreme, stood the Crispin Inn, where the veteran Painite radical John Baines had held court and where both the nineteenth-century recorder of the radical tradition, Frank Peel, and the twentieth-century rescuer of the Luddites from 'the enormous condescension of posterity', E.P. Thompson, saw a fusion of the Luddite machine-breaking and the Painite republican movements in Halifax. Whether this fusion was real or imaginary in the minds of contemporaries or in the perception of later historians, both Georgian clerics and Wesleyan ministers believed that a display of strength was required to pre-empt any potential challenge to establish society, and so Bunting 'expressed his unshaken confidence in God and his determination to do his duty'.[40]

However, Bunting also recognized that there were lessons to be learned, confiding to George Marsden after the Luddite executions that:

> . . . the progress of Methodism in the West Riding of Yorkshire has been more swift than solid; more extensive than deep; more in increase of numbers than in the diffusion of that kind of piety which shines as brightly and operates as visibly at home as in the prayer meeting and the crowded lovefeast.[41]

Throughout 1812, Methodist membership, which had begun to recover in the preceding decade from the effects of the Kilhamite secession, continued to grow in Halifax, showing a 5 per cent increase in 1812 and a 12 per cent increase in 1813 if the newly-created Sowerby Bridge Circuit is included in the calculation. In November 1812 the South Parade Chapel, enlarged to accommodate 2,000, was re-opened. 'Our seats are nearly all let', Bunting continued in his letter to Marsden, 'and in the town we have much comfort and considerable prosperity', but 'in the country', he added, 'I expect no good till discipline is fully revived; and that cannot be without risking the division of several societies'.[42] The risk was taken, financial dues enforced and the societies at Salterhebble and Skircoat Green broken up with the loss of most of the members, several class leaders and local preachers, including Joshua Dodgson, who later became a prominent figure in the Wesleyan Reform Movement in Elland.[43] The extent to which, if at all, Luddism or conflicting political attitudes and sympathies were issues in this enforcement of discipline is impossible to assess. Certainly Bunting's insistence that no member of the Methodist society was implicated in the actual disturbances cannot be disproved from the available evidence, though Methodism in 1812, as Bunting himself admitted, had a constituency much wider than those formally identified through membership.[44]

Wesleyan discipline continued to be enforced as machine-breaking gave way to renewed agitation for parliamentary reform. In December 1816, Brother Merchant, a Wesleyan local preacher, was 'charged with attending a political meeting at Ripponden when he should have been in class' and although he subsequently expressed remorse he received 'a severe censure' from the local preachers' meeting.[45] Another Ripponden local preacher, Thomas Cheetham, also acknowledged a conflict of allegiance between religion and politics during the years 1819–20 when he unhappily imbibed the sentiments and temper of those who were for 'correcting abuses and reforming the state' and political subjects became:

> . . . the daily theme of my converse and political writings employed my leisure hours. Thus, my seasons of retirement for spiritual exercises were much neglected . . . [with the result that] the Spirit of God was offended and withdrew leaving me to mourn over my folly.

Moreover, he only recovered from his 'sore evil' when he resolved to 'fear God and honour the king' and 'no more meddle officiously with the affairs of the state', endeavouring to 'live soberly, righteously and Godly in this world'.[46]

Other local Wesleyans, however, found it increasingly difficult to remain aloof from radical politics during the reform crisis of 1830–32, but in the changed political circumstances of those years, some argued that they were supporting the attempts of a Whig government to strengthen the constitution against the threat of revolution by extending the parliamentary franchise. George Buxton Browne, a Halifax Circuit steward and former local preachers' secretary, was among the Halifax requisitioners for parliamentary reform in 1831 and spoke at a public meeting to petition the House of Lords in October 1831, proclaiming that the passage of the Reform Bill through the House of Commons was already evidence that 'truth is mighty and will prevail'. He argued at a reform meeting at the Piece Hall in May 1832 that 'nothing could so much promote the spread of true Christianity as a proper enlargement of the civil liberties of mankind' and that it was no longer an agitation 'of a few, poor and discontented', but 'of persons of property and understanding', who:

> . . . when they talked of reform they did not mean revolution; their object was not to unsettle property, but to establish the liberties of Englishmen on the surest and firmest foundation.[47]

Moreover, early in June 1830, John Broadbent and Francis Noble, both prominent Wesleyans, were among the requisitioners and Abraham Hanson, a Wesleyan local preacher, was among the speakers at a reform meeting which resolved to form the Elland Political Union.[48] In February 1831, Francis Noble, making his debut as a political speaker, confided that circumstances now rendered it necessary that he should publicly identify with the campaign for parliamentary reform. He recalled the political tensions of his youth:

> . . . in company with persons of opposite political principles. The one was a King and Constitution man . . . and the other was styled a Jacobin and every

opprobrious name. The principles that I imbibed were 'King and Constitution' and I do not know that there is an ounce of blood in my veins contrary to that sentiment (Hear, hear). It has been said that the Reformers, in seeking for a change, are attempting to bring about a revolution; but I repel the imputation (Cheers) . . . It is because I deprecate anything of the kind and wish to prevent it from taking place in my day that I take part in this day's proceedings.[49]

Early in October 1831, when the Reform Bill faced rejection in the House of Lords, at a meeting in the schoolroom of Elland Wesley, on the motion of Francis Noble, a petition was launched in support of the bill which collected 1,185 signatures in a single day.[50]

Meanwhile at Halifax in February, prominent Wesleyans like Alexander Grylls Suter, William Denton, John Rayner and John Wilkinson Foster and New Connexion Methodists such as Jonathan Akroyd, George Beaumont, Peter Kenyon Holden and Daniel Ramsden had added their names to a requisition for a meeting to consider petitioning Parliament for parliamentary reform, a meeting which George Beaumont, one of the speakers, declared would long be remembered by the 'friends of freedom in Halifax'.[51] Shortly afterwards a political union was established in Halifax modelled on the Birmingham Political Union, while at Ovenden, a union adopting the more radical model of the National Union of the Working Classes was proposed at a meeting addressed by Abraham Hanson of Elland and chaired by the handloom weaver and former Methodist New Connexion local preacher, Benjamin Rushton, whose continuing appeal remained a source of embarrassment to the circuit authorities.[52] A local preachers' meeting in April 1829 had recorded its disapproval 'of the conduct of our Lightazles' friends in employing Benjamin Rushton to preach', and similar disapproval 'of the conduct of our friends at Ovenden in employing preachers from other bodies' in January 1830 was probably a reference to the same problem.[53]

Rushton, who had been one of the driving forces behind the building of the new Salem Chapel in 1815 before directing his energies towards support of the Methodist New Connexion cause at Ovenden, was already a veteran reformer by 1830. He had been active in radical politics at the time of Peterloo and may have either been expelled or chosen to withdraw from the Methodist New Connexion at the time of Cobbett's appeal to Methodists in 1820–1 to refuse to pay their dues.[54] His Methodist background, continuing grass-roots association with Methodists, and predominantly radical sympathies were characteristic of a generation of local preachers, including the cobbler Abraham Hanson of Elland Wesley and the woolcomber William Thornton of the Round Hill Primitive Methodist Chapel, Northowram. During the 1830s, Hanson and Thornton brought radical instincts into

Methodism and Methodist insights into radicalism until, in the case of the former, expulsion by the Wesleyan authorities, and in the case of the latter, emigration to escape prosecution, severed their increasingly tenuous links with the movement in 1839.[55]

Methodist support for parliamentary reform in Halifax continued unabated throughout 1831, particularly during the crisis caused by the Lords' rejection of the second bill in October. George Beaumont had summed up the expectations of many when he declared that the Lords cannot 'prevent the enlightened, whether in the middle or lower ranks of society from having a mighty influence in the affairs of state' and, following the bill's rejection, William Thornton – arguing that the bill had been 'a healing measure, calculated to make the people loyal, happy and contented and to give stability to the throne and prosperity to the people' – urged on the members of the Halifax Political Union 'the necessity of uniting for the purpose of redeeming the productive classes from that debased degradation to which the borough mongers and the Pitt clubs have reduced them'.[56]

Popular pressure reached its height during the days of May in 1832, when the third Reform Bill was placed in jeopardy by Grey's resignation after the king's initial refusal to create sufficient new peers to ensure the bill's passage. During the crisis, which was ultimately resolved when William IV threatened the House of Lords with the creation of new peers, the Halifax Political Union received an influx of 200 new members, collected 13,700 signatures for petitions delivered to London by a deputation led by George Buxton Browne and organized a massive public meeting at the Piece Hall, addressed by Browne and other speakers, including the New Connexion Methodists Jonathan Akroyd, P.K. Holden and John Rhoebottom, which attracted an estimated attendance of between 25,000 and 30,000.[57]

THE ANTI-SLAVERY MOVEMENT

Following the enactment of the Reform Bill, many Methodists renewed their efforts to secure the abolition of colonial slavery, a distinctly humanitarian cause which had long been viewed sympathetically by the Wesleyan authorities who viewed slavery as an obstacle to missionary expansion in the West Indies.[58] During the essentially non-partisan campaign, which continued until the system of negro apprenticeship was brought to an end in 1838, both the Wesleyan South Parade and Hanover New Connexion Chapels were made available for anti-slavery meetings; liberal- and conservative-minded Methodist ministers like John Bakewell of the New Connexion and William Bunting of the Old Connexion and laymen at both extremes of the political spectrum like G.B. Browne and T.S. Swale attended the same meetings and even, in the latter case, travelled to

London together as delegates of the Halifax Anti-Slavery Society to the Exeter Hall Conference in 1833, while Wesleyan, New Connexion, Primitive and Wesleyan Associationist Methodists across the Calder valley supported petitions to end the system of negro apprenticeship.[59] G.B. Browne, one of a number of leading Wesleyans including A.G. Suter, George Thompson, John Jackson and E.M. Wavell at the forefront of the campaign, never missed an opportunity to commend the cause. Indeed, as early as 1831, at a public meeting to present a loyal address to King William IV, he had added his personal congratulations to the new monarch for having freed by royal proclamation all crown slaves in the colonies; and in 1838, with Victoria on the throne, he made one of his last and most impassioned speeches against negro apprenticeship, arguing that to hold the apprentice 'a single day more in bondage' was 'a crying sin against God'.[60]

THE FACTORY MOVEMENT, TRADE UNIONISM AND THE ANTI-POOR LAW MOVEMENT

Methodist support for the other great Evangelical crusade of the 1830s and 1840s, the campaign for factory regulation, was, however, more ambivalent, partly on account of the involvement in the factory movement of the former Wesleyan minister, Joseph Rayner Stephens, whose resignation in 1834 had produced a secession from the main Wesleyan body in Halifax, and partly because of the vested interests of Methodist manufacturers.[61] In Halifax at least two Wesleyan ministers, William Bunting in 1834 and Amos Learoyd in 1847, revealed their lack of sympathy for the movement, while the Akroyds, the leading Methodist New Connexion manufacturers, masterminded a determined counter-attack on the movement by local manufacturers and Anglican clergy alienated by Oastler's campaign against vicarial tithes.[62] There was, however, consistent support for the Ten-Hour Bill from at least one Wesleyan manufacturer, William Hatton, from working-class radicals with Methodist connections such as Benjamin Rushton and William Thornton, and a degree of sympathy from G.B. Browne, who chaired a factory reform meeting in 1832.[63] However, only when education became the primary issue, as in Sir James Graham's abortive Factory Bill of 1843, was there determined and sustained opposition to a government attempt at factory regulation from the local Wesleyan, New Connexion and Primitive Methodist communities, acting with the approval of their respective connexional authorities.[64]

Trade unionism, although never dominant in an area whose economic structure ensured that the working-class movement developed a stronger political than trade unionist complexion, became a keenly debated issue in 1834 in the wake of the conviction and transportation of the six Dorchester labourers, several of whom were Wesleyans. Conference, which had warned

Methodists in 1833 against involvement with 'associations . . . employing unlawful oaths and threats and force to acquire new members', refused to take up their cause.[65] In April 1834 a Methodist operative wrote anonymously to the *Halifax Guardian*, protesting that 'the power of the unions is of such a nature as to compel members of all religious denominations to place themselves under their demoralizing influence' and in September, the Halifax Wesleyan superintendent minister 'to the great apparent satisfaction' of the local preachers' meeting, 'expressly forbid any local preacher to address a secret order as such'. At Midgley, however, it had become customary for a friendly society to hold their annual Whitsuntide service at the Methodist New Connexion Chapel by 1833.[66]

Although some Halifax Methodists were critical of the New Poor Law at vestry and board of guardian meetings, mainstream Methodists in Halifax appear to have remained aloof from the popular anti-poor-law movement, which was closely associated with the factory movement in the West Riding. At its first public meeting in Halifax – attended by Richard Oastler – William Smith and William Culpan, both former Wesleyan local preachers expelled from the Halifax society in 1834 for their support for J.R. Stephens, proposed and seconded a resolution calling upon 'ministers of religion of all denominations' to come forward and champion the rights of the poor by opposing the New Poor Law. Their speeches were followed by contributions from two other radicals with Methodist backgrounds. William Thornton, drawing on an Old Testament analogy in proposing a resolution denouncing the New Poor Law, maintained that it treated the poor more inhumanely than the Hebrews under Egyptian slavery:

> The Israelites could go about and hear the birds sing; but when the working men of England could not work, they were denied that privilege and compelled to go into a Bastille.

Benjamin Rushton, seconding the resolution, criticized the Whig government's provision of a salary of £15,000 for the new Archbishop of Canterbury, while another speaker criticized the Wesleyan, G.B. Browne, for hypocrisy as a campaigner against slavery in chairing meetings of the board of guardians.[67]

CHARTISM AND THE ANTI-CORN LAW LEAGUE

When the campaign against the New Poor Law became absorbed into the nascent Chartist movement in 1838, the same individuals remained to the fore and the gulf with mainstream Methodism, uniformly opposed to Chartism at connexional level, became even more pronounced. The Cleckheaton Chapel opened by William Smith and the seceding Wesleyan supporters of J.R. Stephens from the Halifax Wesleyan Circuit became a Chartist Church with visiting preachers such as Benjamin Rushton denouncing 'with fiery eloquence . . . the men who refused political justice to their neighbours'. So too did the Primitive Methodist Round Hill Chapel at Roper Lane, Northowram, with which William Thornton was associated, making 'a quiet schism' from Primitive Methodism in 1839; while the Methodist New Connexion Chapel at Ambler Thorn, having incurred the public disapprobation of the circuit quarterly meeting for making a collection at the chapel 'for the Chartist fund for the defence of the agitator J.R. Stephens', joined the Barkerite secession in 1841.[68]

Both Thornton and Rushton embarked on lecture tours for the Stephens Defence Fund and played a prominent role in the vast open-air Chartist meeting at Hartshead Moor in May 1839, which Thornton opened in prayer, prompting Feargus O'Connor to quip: 'when we get the People's Charter I will see that you are made the Archbishop of York'. At the same meeting, Abraham Hanson, seconding a vote of confidence in O'Connor in a speech which resulted in his expulsion from the Wesleyan society at Elland, urged the crowd to keep away from preachers who 'preach Christ and a crust, passive obedience and non-resistance' and 'go to those men who preach Christ and a full belly, Christ and a well-clothed back – Christ and a good house to live in – Christ and Universal Suffrage.'[69] William Thornton subsequently emigrated to America to escape prosecution and in March 1840, William Brooke, who had attended Elland Wesley Sunday School during the period 1829–37, was among those indicted and later convicted for riot and conspiracy at Bradford, no doubt strengthening further the resolve of orthodox Methodists to counter the influence of the movement.[70]

In 1839 the trustees of York Street Wesleyan Chapel in Todmorden complained that:

> . . . nearly all the inhabitants of this densely populated vale are radicals. Many of them instead of attending the Lord's house . . . despise all religion . . . and their Sabbaths are chiefly spent reading the *Northern Star*.[71]

In August, a body of Chartists, 'chiefly men and lads from the country', attempted to disrupt Sunday morning worship at Halifax Parish Church, taking 'possession of most of the pews' and obliging the regular occupiers 'to put up with other places or leave the church' but they failed to persuade the preacher, the Revd W. Gurney, to take a Chartist text.[72] Moreover, in 1842 the Todmorden Chartists were thwarted in their attempt 'to spoil the collection' at the Blackshaw Head Wesleyan Chapel anniversary by organizing a rival camp meeting nearby, when 'a multitude of scholars and other members of the chapel congregation . . . immediately commenced singing hymns and spiritual songs and never ceased till the meeting was entirely dispersed'.[73] The Chartists also suffered a more serious rebuff later in the year when the employees of the New Connexion Methodist, Jonathan Akroyd, refused to be drawn into the plug riots. During these disturbances, the most serious challenge to public order in the town during the Chartist era, local Methodists were called out of Sunday morning worship to be sworn in as special constables and some, such as the Wesleyan worsted machinery manufacturer Jabez Bunting Farrar, played a prominent role in the restoration of order.[74]

After the 1847 election, when the Chartist candidate Ernest Jones had been received enthusiastically by New Connexion Methodists such as James Millington and Primitive Methodists such as George Buckley, and with the emergence of municipal Chartism in 1848, New Connexion Methodists became more receptive to Chartist ideas. At a reform meeting called by the mayor, in June 1848, resolutions of no confidence in the House of Commons for 'the utter contempt shown for the petitions of the people' and calling for every member of the community 'to be fully represented according to the Charter' were moved by New Connexion Methodist Alderman Dennis and the Independent Francis Crossley.[75] Earlier that year, however, some New Connexion Methodists had withdrawn their names from a requisition initiated by Chartists calling a meeting to sympathize with the French Revolution and in June, at a local preachers' meeting at Todmorden, a charge was brought, though never substantiated, against a local preacher named Lea with Chartist sympathies for 'giving utterance in the pulpit to his political creed'.[76]

For most of the Chartist period Wesleyan and New Connexion Methodists were more willing to become associated with the predominantly middle-class Anti-Corn Law League, despite the official neutrality of the Wesleyan Conference on this issue. George Beaumont chaired the inaugural meeting of the Halifax Anti-Corn Law Association in February 1839 and Jonathan Akroyd, who later declared that the Corn Law was decidedly opposed to that religion which proclaimed 'peace on earth and good will to man', was also prominent in the leadership of the movement. Other leading Methodist supporters of the League included New Connexion Methodists James Akroyd, William Birtwhistle, John Styring, Daniel Ramsden and John Holt and Wesleyans William Hatton, Samuel Denton, John Jackson and John Dennison.[77]

OWENITE SOCIALISM

Old and New Connexion Methodists alike reacted strongly to the growth of Owenite Socialism during the 1830s and early 1840s. To the Wesleyans, socialism was synonymous with infidelity; to Methodists of the New Connexion it was full of 'loathsome rottenness'.[78] An Owenite branch had been established in Halifax by 1837 and during 1838 anti-socialist lectures were delivered by the Revd Peter Duncan, a Wesleyan minister, and P.K. Holden, a New Connexion Methodist. In March 1838, the *Halifax Guardian*, whose Wesleyan proprietor, J.U. Walker, spearheaded the attack on socialism in the town, alleged that socialists had infiltrated the Halifax Temperance Society, which had a broader basis of Methodist support in the 1830s than in the 1840s, following the proscription of the movement by the Wesleyan Conference in 1841.[79] These allegations were, however, strenuously denied by James Millington, one of the leading Methodist New Connexion supporters of the temperance movement, and the onslaught on socialism was resumed when John Brindley, the self-appointed crusader against socialism, was invited to give a series of lectures at the Northgate Hotel in December 1839 and January 1840. The meetings, chaired by the Wesleyans A.G. Suter and the Revd F.A. West, resulted in an 'extensively signed' petition being forwarded to Parliament and the formation of the Halifax Association for the Refutation of Infidelity and Suppression of Blasphemy which aimed to disseminate 'the principles of Divine Truth in opposition to infidelity and especially to socialism, without reference to the peculiar views of any body of Christians'. No fewer than 14 of its 41-member executive committee were Wesleyans, in addition to A.G. Suter and J.U. Walker, who acted as treasurer and secretary respectively.[80]

Moreover, in April 1840, the Revd Joseph Barker, who had previously served in Halifax as a Methodist New Connexion minister, returned to the town to give a series of anti-socialist lectures at the Oddfellows Hall to audiences estimated on each occasion at around 2,000, which concluded with the formal adoption of a resolution:

> . . . that the religion of Christ is calculated . . . to eradicate the evils of society and make mankind truly happy; and that, on the contrary, the system of Robert Owen . . . is calculated to increase the evils of society and make mankind vicious and miserable.[81]

The campaign against Owenite Socialism, with its challenge to conventional Christian theology and morality, was one which Methodists in general and Wesleyans in particular could support wholeheartedly. Wesleyan alarm at the socialist presence in the town, based in premises formerly occupied by the Wesleyan seceders, was intensified by their attempt to secrete socialist literature in Wesleyan tracts in 1839. Moreover, one of the leading protagonists of the socialist case at Brindley's meetings was a former Methodist. For the Wesleyans, socialism, like anti-Sabbatarianism, Unitarianism and Roman Catholicism, all of which provoked them into bursts of political agitation in the 1830s and 1840s, posed a threat which could be clearly identified and challenged without the compromising of principles which might be involved in the support of other forms of extra-parliamentary protest in an age of revolution. To a large degree, this attitude was shared by the major offshoots of Wesleyanism, the Methodist New Connexion and Primitive Methodism, though not by the more radical Stephenite and Chartist factions which seceded in the 1830s and 1840s.[82]

CONCLUSION

The relationship between evangelicalism and the politics of extra-parliamentary protest in Halifax during the period from the American Revolution of 1775 to the French Revolution of 1848 was multi-faceted and dynamic, shaped by changing economic, social and political contexts. Evangelical businessmen who had felt intimidated by Luddism and stood alongside Dr Henry William Coulthurst and the Revd Jabez Bunting in condemning the disturbances of 1812, found the prospect of enfranchisement in 1832 more appealing, and were prepared to engage in the political excitement of the Reform crisis to ensure the passage of the Whig Reform Bill. Thereafter, many became increasingly willing to support political agitation on issues of principle that concerned them in the 1830s and 1840s such as the campaigns against colonial slavery, the educational clauses of Sir James Graham's Factory Bill, the Maynooth grant and the Corn Laws.

Most Halifax Evangelicals throughout the period, however, remained determined to adhere to the advice of Dr Henry William Coulthurst to abhor 'French principles and French conduct' and the 'revolutionary experiments' that had plunged the continent of Europe into a protracted and costly war during the period from 1792 to 1815. Indeed, in January 1848, with France moving towards the overthrow of the July monarchy of Louis Philippe, the priority for many Halifax Evangelicals was the establishment of a branch of the Evangelical Alliance in the town to end 'the great sin of divisions' within the Christian Church so that it might be better equipped for its primary task of evangelism and mission. The meeting convened for this purpose, attended almost entirely by Wesleyan and Independent ministers and laymen, brought together on the platform the Wesleyan superintendent minister, the Revd Amos Learoyd, and the minister of Zion Independent Chapel, the Revd James Pridie, and leading Wesleyan and Independent laymen such as William Heap, E.M. Wavell, William Hatton, John Crossley and John Baldwin.[83]

However, a minority of local radicals, some of whose political convictions remained rooted in their Evangelical Nonconformity, but whose increasingly tenuous links with organized religion had now been severed, would have shared the aspirations of the former Wesleyan local preacher, Abraham Hanson of Elland, at a Chartist meeting at the Oddfellows Hall in Halifax convened to sympathize with the French Revolution in February 1848, when he proclaimed:

. . . the principles of the French Revolution would not stop in France; already they were beginning to make the thrones of despots tremble . . . whether [the middle classes] came to their help or not, or whether the government moved itself or not, a revolution would take place.

Indeed, Benjamin Rushton, the former Halifax Methodist New Connexion local preacher, addressing the same meeting in language which combined revolutionary ideology with biblical imagery, expressed the hope that 'French principles would inoculate all Europe and liberty, friendship and brotherhood would extend from the rivers unto the ends of the sea'.[84]

Notes

1   Bradford Local Studies Library, Federer Collection, A sermon preached in the parish church of Halifax before the volunteer corps of infantry of the town and parish of Halifax, 29 January 1804, pp. 12–15. I am grateful to Dr D.W. Bebbington of the University of Stirling, Dr E. Royle of the University of York and Professor K. Laybourn of the University of Huddersfield for commenting on a preliminary draft of this chapter.

2   J.U. Walker, *A History of Wesleyan Methodism in Halifax* (Halifax, Hartley and Walker, 1836), pp. 192–3. For a fuller discussion of evangelicalism during this period see D.W. Bebbington, *Evangelicalism in Modern Britain* (London, Unwin Hyman, 1989); M.R. Watts, *The Dissenters, II, The Expansion of Evangelical Nonconformity 1791–1859* (Oxford, Clarendon Press, 1995); D. Lovegrove, 'English Evangelical Dissent and the European Conflict 1789–1815', in W.J. Sheils (ed.), *The Church and War* (Oxford, Basil Blackwell, 1983), pp. 263–76 and J.A. Hargreaves, 'Religion and Society in the Parish of Halifax, *c.* 1740–1914' (unpublished PhD thesis, Huddersfield Polytechnic, 1991).

3   J. Mayhall, *Annals of Yorkshire* (Leeds, Joseph Johnson, 1861), p. 152. For the origins of the provincial reform movement see D.G. Wright, *Popular Radicalism. The Working-Class Experience 1780–1880* (London, Longman, 1988), pp. 23, 27, 29, 30–31 and E. Royle and J. Walvin, *English Radicals and Reformers, 1760–1848* (Brighton, Harvester Press, 1982), chapters 1–2.

4   Wright, *Popular Radicalism*, pp. 37, 39; J.A. Hargreaves, *Factory Kings and Slaves: South Pennine Social Movements, 1780–1840* (Hebden Bridge, Pennine Heritage, 1982), p. 6.

5   C. Emsley, *British Society and the French Wars, 1793–1815* (London, Macmillan, 1979), p. 26; C.D. Webster, 'Robert Parker, Attorney', *Transactions of the Halifax Antiquarian Society (THAS)* (Halifax, 1966), pp. 79–82; West Yorkshire Archive Service (WYAS), Calderdale District Archives (CDA), Duke of Portland to Robert Parker, 20 November 1795, RP: 3/372.

6   H.T. Dickinson, *British Radicalism and the French Revolution, 1789–1815* (Oxford, Basil Blackwell 1985), pp. 76–7; Public Record Office (PRO), Home Office Papers, HO 42/157, 42/196; J. Liddington, *Presenting the Past. Anne Lister of Halifax* (Hebden Bridge, Pennine Pens, 1994), pp. 32, 36; S. Maccoby, *English Radicalism, 1786–1832* (London, Allen and Unwin, 1955), p. 359, n. 1.

7   C. Hall, 'Domestic Harmony, Public Virtue', in L.M. Smith (ed.), *The Age of Revolution* (London, Macmillan, 1987), p. 79.

8 PRO, Home Office Papers, Address of the gentry, clergy, merchants and manufacturers and other inhabitants of the town and neighbourhood of Halifax, 3 November 1775, HO 55/12/3.

9 T.W. Hanson, 'Corn Market', *THAS*, (1945), pp. 31–32.

10 WYAS, CDA, Resolutions of a meeting at the Talbot Inn, 22 December 1792, MISC: 8/116/19.

11 Cited in Webster, *THAS*, (1966), p. 81.

12 WYAS, CDA, Manuscript of sermon preached at Halifax Parish Church, 12 December 1790, MAC: 46/18.

13 Calderdale Central Library (CCL), A sermon preached before the University of Cambridge, 25 October 1796; CCL, Horsfall Turner Collection.

14 Anon., *Itinerary of Halifax* (Halifax, 1875).

15 Sheffield City Library (SCL), Wentworth Woodhouse Muniments (WWM), Fitzwilliam Papers, Dr Coulthurst to Earl Fitzwilliam, 22 June 1812, F46/127. I am grateful to Olive, Countess Fitzwilliam's Wentworth Settlement Trustees and the Director of Sheffield City Libraries for access to this collection.

16 Ibid., A list of those Luddites who had taken the oaths before Dr Coulthurst at Halifax, 10 February 1813, F46/127.

17 PRO, Home Office Papers, Halifax Declaration, 27 January 1817, 42/157.

18 H. Whitbread (ed.), *I Know My Own Heart* (London, Virago, 1988), p. 214.

19 Anon., *An Account of the Life, Ministry and Writings of the Reverend John Fawcett* (Halifax, P.K. Holden, 1818), p. 379.

20 J. Cockin, *Memoirs of Joseph Cockin* (Idle, 2nd edn, 1841), pp. 193–4.

21 SCL, WWM, Fitzwilliam Papers, Sir Francis Wood to Earl Fitzwilliam, 11 August 1812, F46/40.

22 N. Ascherson (ed.), *The Times Reports the French Revolution* (London, Times Books, 1975), pp. 7–11.

23 H. Rack, *Reasonable Enthusiast. John Wesley and the Rise of Methodism* (London, Epworth, 1989), pp. 317, 374–80, 487–91.

24 Cited in Walker, *Wesleyan Methodism in Halifax*, p. 178.

25 Ibid., p. 179.

26 J.C. Bowmer and J.A. Vickers (eds), *Letters of John Pawson, 1* (Peterborough, Methodist Publishing House, 1994), p. 134.

27 Ibid., pp. 108, 130.

28 Walker, *Wesleyan Methodism in Halifax*, pp. 217–18.

29 F. Peel, *The Risings of the Luddites, Chartists and Plug-Drawers* (Brighouse, 3rd edition, 1895), p. 102. Fuller treatment of the relationship between Methodism and Luddism is provided in J.A. Hargreaves, 'Halifax and the Yorkshire Luddite Disturbances of 1812', *THAS*, (1986) and 'Methodism and Luddism in Yorkshire, 1812–13', *Northern History (NH)*, XXVI, (1990), pp. 160–85.

30 *Leeds Mercury*, 18 April 1812; WYAS, CDA, Halifax Circuit Directory, MISC. 546; Burial and Grave Register, South Parade Wesleyan Chapel, Halifax, MISC. 486/14.

31 D. Hempton, *Methodism and Politics in British Society 1750–1850* (London, Hutchinson, 1984), pp. 99–104; John Rylands University Library Manchester (JRULM), Methodist Church Archives (MCA), J. Bunting to T. Lessey, 31 May 1811, PLP 18.6.3.

32 T.P. Bunting, *The Life of the Revd Dr Jabez Bunting* (London, 1887), p. 370; Walker, *Wesleyan Methodism in Halifax*, p. 255.

33 JRULM, MCA, J. Ashworth to J. Bunting, 22 March 1811, PLP 18.6.1; Halifax Circuit Plan, 5 January to 14 June 1812; F.A. West, *Memoirs of Jonathan Saville* (London, 1843), pp. 31–2; Bunting, *Jabez Bunting*, p. 371; Walker, *Wesleyan Methodism in Halifax*, p. 255.

34 SCL, WWM, Fitzwilliam Papers, Information of Thomas Broughton of Barnsley, 26 August 1812, F46/122B.

35 *Report of the Proceedings under Commissions of Oyer and Terminer and Gaol Delivery for the County of York* (York, 1813), p. xi.; WYAS, LDA, Radcliffe MSS, Colonel Norton to J. Radcliffe, January 1813, 126/114; N.C. Smith (ed.), *Selected Letters of Sydney Smith* (Oxford, Oxford University Press, 1981), p. 66.

36 Peel, *Rising of Luddites*, p. 263; C. Robertshaw, *History of Elland Wesley* (Elland, 1974), p. 9; Bunting, *Jabez Bunting*, p. 371.

37 JRULM, MCA, J. Bunting to G. Marsden, 28 January 1813, PLP 18.6.9; WYAS, CDA, MISC. 546; T. Shillitoe, *Journal*, *I* (1839), 192; J. Wood, Diaries, 1813 (I am grateful to Mr J. Knight for access to this unpublished manuscript.)

38 T. Jackson, *Recollections of My Own Life and Times* (London, 1873), p. 137.

39 WYAS, Leeds District Archives, Radcliffe MSS, Address to Joseph Radcliffe from the town of Halifax, June 1813, metal canister.

40 E.P. Thompson, *The Making of the English Working Class* (Harmondsworth, Penguin, 2nd edn, 1968), p. 13; Bunting, *Jabez Bunting*, p. 371.

41 JRULM, MCA, PLP 18.6.9.

42 ibid.

43 Robertshaw, *Elland Wesley*, p. 9.

44 Hempton, *Methodism and Politics*, pp. 12–14; JRULM, MCA, PLP 18.6.9.

45 WYAS, CDA, Halifax Wesleyan Local Preachers' Meeting Minute Book, 1805–24, MISC. 481.2, 16 December 1816, January 1817.

46 T. Cheetham, *An Account of the Life of Thomas Cheetham of Ripponden, near Halifax, Written by Himself* (Bradford, 1825), pp. 17, 19.

47 Hargreaves, thesis, pp. 208–10; *Huddersfield and Halifax Express*, 8 October 1831, 19 May 1832.

48 Robertshaw, *Elland Wesley*, p. 14.

49 *Huddersfield and Halifax Express*, 26 February 1831.

50 Ibid., 8 October 1831; Robertshaw, *Elland Wesley*, p. 14.

51 *Huddersfield and Halifax Express*, 12 February 1831.

52 Ibid., 12 March 1831, 16 July 1831.

53 WYAS, CDA, Halifax North (Salem) MNC Circuit Local Preachers' Meeting Minute Book, 1829–51, 13 April 1829, 11 January 1830, MR. 74.

54 J. Horobin in *Halifax Guardian Almanack* (Halifax, 1920), pp. 49–51; E.V. Chapman, *John Wesley and Co.* (Halifax, 1952), pp. 44, 61; Thompson, *English Working Class*, p. 435.

55 E. Yeo, 'Christianity in Chartist Class Struggle, 1838–42', *Past and Present*, 91, 1981, p. 116.

56 *Huddersfield and Halifax Express*, 1 October 1831, 22 October 1831, 12 November 1831.

57 Ibid., 19 May 1832.

58 Watts, *Dissenters*, p. 446; E. Halévy, *The Triumph of Reform* (London, Ernest Benn, 3rd edn, 1961), p. 115 n. 1.

59 *Huddersfield and Halifax Express*, 17 September 1831, 13 April 1833, 7 August 1834, 17 February

1838, 28 April 1838, 26 May 1838; *Halifax Guardian*, 26 January 1833, 2 February 1833, 27 July 1833, 18 July 1837.

60 Ibid., 17 September 1831; 28 April 1838.

61 J.T. Ward, *The Factory Movement* (London, Macmillan, 1962), pp. 50, 56, 85, 294; C. Driver, *Tory Radical: The Life of Richard Oastler* (New York, Octagon, 1946), pp. 137–9; M.S. Edwards, *Purge This Realm. A Life of Joseph Rayner Stephens* (London, Epworth, 1994).

62 Driver, *Tory Radical*, pp. 65–6, 547–50.

63 *Halifax Guardian*, 10 March 1842, 22 April 1843, 13 April 1844, 20 April 1844; *Huddersfield and Halifax Express*, 10 March 1842, 2 June 1832.

64 Hempton, *Methodism and Politics*, pp. 164–71.

65 K. Tiller, 'Late Chartism: Halifax 1847–58' in J. Epstein and D. Thompson (eds), *The Chartist Experience* (London, Macmillan, 1982), pp. 312–13; M.S. Edwards, 'Methodism and the Chartist Movement', *London Quarterly and Holborn Review (LQHR)*, (1966), p. 304; G.B.A.M. Finlayson, *England in the Eighteen Thirties* (London, Edward Arnold, 1969), p. 81; Halévy, *Triumph of Reform*, p. 154.

66 *Halifax Guardian*, 12 April 1834, 19 April 1834; WYAS, CDA, MISC. 481, 3, 1, 29 September 1834; H.W. Harwood, *History of Methodism in Midgley*, 1933, p. 32.

67 *Halifax Guardian*, 1 April 1837.

68 *Halifax Guardian*, 23 January 1838, 4 March 1838; Thompson, *English Working Class*, p. 439; Yeo, *Past and Present*, 91, (1981), 117.

69 *Huddersfield and Halifax Express*, 13 April 1839; *Northern Star*, 20 April 1839.

70 Chapman, *John Wesley and Co.*, p. 58.

71 WYAS, CDA, York Street Wesleyan Chapel, Todmorden, Trustees minute book, 18 April 1839, TM 2/1.

72 *Huddersfield and Halifax Express*, 24 August 1839.

73 *Halifax Guardian*, 18 June 1842.

74 G.R. Dalby, 'The Chartist Movement in Halifax and District', *THAS* (1956), pp. 100–1; *Halifax Courier*, 25 November 1893.

75 *Halifax Guardian*, 28 August 1847, 24 June 1848.

76 WYAS, CDA, Todmorden Wesleyan Local Preachers' Meeting Minute Book, 28 June 1848, TM 188.

77 Halévy, *Triumph of Reform*, p. 335; *Halifax Guardian*, 2 February 1839, 9 March 1839, 11 January 1840, 25 January 1840, 18 April 1840, 3 December 1842, 16 December 1843.

78 E. Royle, *Victorian Infidels* (Manchester, Manchester University Press, 1974), pp. 49, 296; Edwards, *LQHR* (1966), p. 305.

79 *Halifax Guardian*, 20 March 1838, 27 March 1838, 8 December 1838; Taylor, *Methodism and Politics*, pp. 140–1.

80 *Halifax Guardian*, 14 December 1839, 1 February 1840, 29 February 1840.

81 *Halifax Guardian*, 11 April 1840.

82 *Halifax Guardian*, 1 June 1844, 12 April 1845; Halévy, *Triumph of Reform*, p. 153; F.C. Mather, *Chartism and Society* (London, Bell and Hyman, 1980), pp. 290–3.

83 *Halifax Guardian*, 22 January 1848.

84 Ibid., 18 March 1848.

4

John Stuart Mill on War

William Stafford

Perspectives

No issue raises more urgent and more agonizing questions in moral philosophy than war. John Stuart Mill was one of the most important, perhaps *the* most important, moral philosopher of the nineteenth century; and though he wrote only one short essay, 'A Few Words on Non-Intervention' (1859), devoted exclusively to the morality of war, reflections on that topic crop up in many of his writings. Teasing out his stance on this issue ought therefore to be fruitful.[1] But because of the scattered and unsystematic nature of his thoughts, it might be useful to begin by establishing a framework of perspectives from which to question the texts.

First, we might come to them with a set of expectations about what a central liberal of the first three-quarters of the nineteenth century would be likely to say. We might expect such a person to be, if not a pacifist, at least, in Ceadel's terms, a 'pacific-ist',[2] one who thinks that war is a relic of the ages of savagery and barbarism, destined to pass into history with the onward march of humanity. For the liberal puts his faith in reason, free discussion and compromise. Bentham, one of the mentors of Mill's youth, thought that enlightened legislation and institutions could and would put a stop to war. Nations should unite in confederations to deter aggression, and there should be a kind of united nations, to comment on the doings of states, to engage in arbitration and, ideally, to co-ordinate international policing. There should be disarmament treaties, and perhaps a European Union.[3] Some of these ideas were endorsed by Mill's father.[4] These continued to be liberal aspirations and they were combined with the belief which was embodied in the peace settlement of 1918 that, whereas military autocracies and aristocracies were obviously belligerent, liberal democracies would be pacific.[5] All of this was further buttressed by free-trade pacific-ism, 'the bag-man's millennium',[6] associated especially with Cobden, but something of a cliché among liberal political economists of the period. According to this doctrine, not only was free trade maximally beneficial to all countries: it also drew them into peaceful co-operation and interdependence, teaching them that war could bring no gains and would bring certain losses. Bentham, Cobden and Goldwyn Smith drew the corollary that empires were of no benefit to the imperial power and therefore there was no sense in imperial rivalries: empires cost money to maintain and defend, and they brought no economic advantages which could not better be secured by free trade.[7] Of course, there was a widespread liberal hostility to standing armies, which propped up despotism, and to impressment and conscription which violated the freedom of the individual. Liberal individualism is anti-war at a deeper level. For Bentham, collectivities such as states are fictitious entities. The so-called national interest is simply the sum of the interests of all the individuals living in a certain territory. To go to war for the sake of 'national honour' is absurd. Our duties are to individuals – to all individuals, irrespective of nationality, hence this kind of liberalism leaps from the individual straight to cosmopolitanism.[8] The later utilitarian Sidgwick, writing at the height of imperialist nationalism, thinks similarly that cosmopolitanism is the way of the future.[9] In all of these ways liberalism may be anti-war, or as its enemies might say, soft on war. Was Mill soft on war?

It is, however, possible for liberalism to go the other way, and this brings me to my second perspective. A familiar narrative of warfare tells of the recurrence of 'crusading' war, referring obviously to the crusades but also, for example, to the wars of religion of the sixteenth and seventeenth centuries.[10] It is generally thought that crusading wars, wars for a cause, are especially bitter and destructive: those who feel that religious or moral right is on their side will fight more enthusiastically, and will feel justified in wreaking terrible vengeance on their irreligious and unrighteous enemies. It was against this background that Vitoria in the sixteenth century and Grotius in the seventeenth challenged the justice of religious wars; the eighteenth century saw a reaction against crusading zeal, and eighteenth-century wars, sovereigns' wars for bits of territory, are thought to have been more limited, less bloody. But the French Revolution brought back crusading, as nations fought for principles, for and against liberty, equality and fraternity, and mass slaughter returned.[11] Liberalism became implicated in this resurgence of crusading warfare, because alongside the individualists and cosmopolitans were the Mazzinis and Garibaldis, those who were ready to fight for freedom and national independence. Did Mill advocate crusading warfare?

A third perspective derives from the history of just war theory. There is a well-known and powerful Western tradition of reflection about the morality of war.[12] Theologians such as Augustine and Aquinas have contributed to it, so have Natural and International lawyers of the sixteenth through the eighteenth centuries such as Grotius, Vitoria and Vattel. There has been an input from the practitioners of war also: from the codes of chivalry and from manuals of military discipline such as that of Gustavus Adolphus. The point and purpose of the tradition of just war theory is to prevent or contain the destructiveness of war, to limit war. It has been argued that this tradition – which has been powerfully recuperated since 1945[13] – failed in the nineteenth century, that philosophers and lawyers paid too little attention to it. Because they failed to keep it alive and develop it, it has been said, therefore the world was that much less well prepared for the horrific potential of twentieth-century warfare.[14] No doubt the power of moral preaching is limited, and helpless against regimes committed to ideologies which regard morality in politics as a form of weakness, but it is not everywhere and entirely powerless. If this narrative is correct, then the remote possibility opens up that a vigorous tradition of just war theory would have prevented the horrors of Hamburg and Hiroshima. The narrative is, I think, questionable. Influential books on international law were published in the nineteenth century, and there was further development of codes of military discipline.[15] A formally agreed code regulating war began to develop through international treaties and conventions – the Geneva Convention of 1864, the Hague Conferences of 1899 and 1907.[16] But it is still worth posing this question in relation to our subject: did Mill fail in this vital task of philosophy?

A fourth, and final, perspective arises from recent philosophical debate about utilitarianism and the morality of war. It can be argued that a utilitarian approach to war leads to conclusions which are morally unacceptable. Classic just war theory – before the utilitarianism of Bentham, Paley, Mill and Sidgwick – was not overtly or systematically utilitarian. It revolved around a set of rules, divided into two categories: the rules of *jus ad bellum* (the right to war) and the rules of *jus in bello* (right in war).[17] The rules of *jus ad bellum* state the conditions which justify going to war – for example, a war may only be waged to right a specific wrong, if there is a good chance of winning, and if all other means short of war have first been tried. In the late twentieth century, moralists are increasingly concluding that the only wrongs which can justify resort to war are attack or the threat of attack.[18] One of the rules happens to be essentially utilitarian: it states that war is only justified if the good likely to be achieved outweighs the harm likely to be caused.[19] If that rule is interpreted in accordance with the classic utilitarianism of Bentham, for which 'good' means pleasure and 'harm' means pain or the loss of pleasure, then one is forced to ask how many wars have ever been justified: unless the attacker was bent on genocide or cruel oppression, surely in many cases it would have been rational, as Bentham insisted, simply to surrender when attacked.[20] For many pleasures would still be available under foreign domination, whereas death means the end of all pleasure. But surely, many people would find this conclusion unacceptable. Utilitarian liberalism, once more, looks 'soft' on war. Utilitarianism has an opposite problem with the rules of *jus in bello*. These rules are concerned with justice in the manner of waging war, and the most important of them is the rule of non-combatant immunity. Non-combatant men, women and children are innocent, to kill them intentionally is murder. But utilitarianism will not necessarily conclude that killing them is wrong. To a utilitarian, if it is right to go to war, it may be right to use the most efficient means of winning *no matter what those means are.* If burning babies to death in Dresden or Tokyo shortens the war and on balance saves lives, then burning babies may be the right thing to do. Some people find this unacceptable also, and think that it shows utilitarianism to be deeply flawed. They take a 'moral absolutist' position which insists that certain acts – for example the murder of innocents – are wrong no matter how beneficial their consequences.[21] Does Mill's utilitarian approach to war avoid or respond to these problems? I will now consider his writings in the light of these four perspectives.

PHILOSOPHIC RADICAL OPTIMISM

In the period of his youthful radicalism, Mill's attitude to war was largely Benthamite, and a good measure of this liberal optimism persisted throughout his life. We find the seventeen-year-old proclaiming the uselessness of colonies in 1823,[22] and in 1824 deploring the *Edinburgh Review*'s pessimistic assertion that the progress of enlightenment would not reduce war. In his debating speeches of these years, strong anti-war sentiments are expressed: 'I have as little respect . . . for a fighting nation as I have for a fighting individual, and I am by no means anxious that my country should be considered the Tom Cribb [a famous pugilist of the day] of Europe.'[23] In classic radical mode he blames war on corrupt, idle aristocracies who favour large armies in order to keep the people down and themselves in jobs.[24] They get the glory and the people pay the price:

> I grudge nobody his glory, if he would pay for it himself. I have a great respect for Sir Arthur Wellesley, [the Duke of Wellington] and *ceteris paribus* I would much rather that he should be . . . a hero and a duke, than not: but when I consider that every feather in his cap has cost the nation more than he and his whole lineage would fetch if they were sold for lumber, I own that I much regret the solid pudding which we threw away in order that he might obtain empty praise.[25]

In 1833 he maintained that, because England was an island and a naval power, she needed scarcely any army at all.[26] In the following year he frankly confessed 'to all the wickedness of an earnest desire for peace, which we would not forego till some greater evil seemed likely to attend it than is certain in war'.[27] Similar utilitarian calculations led him to condemn a war for national honour in 1840: 'A nation can show itself offended without threatening a vengeance out of all proportion to the affront and which would involve millions that never offended them with units that did.'[28] Like Bentham and Cobden, he thought in his youth that nations were not rivals for wealth, but rather that each nation had an interest in the prosperity of every other: free trade and international commerce were the truest guarantee against war.[29] He reiterated these sentiments to the Cobden Club in 1869.[30]

Throughout his life Mill was an opponent of the maxim, 'my country, right or wrong', and he always detested the jingoism of politicians such as 'that shallow and senseless coxcomb Palmerston',[31] to see whose hanging Mill would have been ready to walk twenty miles.[32] To care only for one's own countrymen was a token of barbarism: civilized human beings would recognize that justice between nations was the same as justice between individuals: 'We know not why it should be less shameful in a nation than in an individual, to care about nothing but its own interest.'[33] For example, even if it were the case that a canal at Suez would threaten British imperial interests, Mill thought it would be wrong for Britain to oppose the building of a canal if that waterway would benefit mankind as a whole; nations have duties towards the weal of the human race.[34]

Mill's optimistic moralism in international affairs rested upon a grand narrative. He thought in standard enlightenment terms of three stages of savagery, barbarism and civilization. The earlier stages were characterized by brutishness and the rule of force: civilization was marked by reason and the rule of law and as it spread, wars would cease. The Middle Ages, a period of arbitrary rulers and a military aristocracy, was an epoch of barbarism and incessant war, which the more advanced clergy attempted in vain to restrain by the Truce of God.[35] Mill thought his own age was much better; for example the abolition of the slave trade demonstrated an immense step in the progress of mankind.[36] When in 1848 he wrote his *Principles of Political Economy* he thought that wars had come to be confined for the most part to those places on the globe where civilization came into contact with savages.[37] Subsequent events rather dented this optimism, but Mill continued to believe that the onward march of democracy and the end of military monarchies would curb aggression – especially if the enfranchised subjects kept a vigilant watch on government in relation to foreign policy and military expenditure.[38] He thought that the great experimental democracy of the United States did not have ambitions for territorial gains, and consistently spoke and wrote in favour of friendship between Great Britain and that country, 'the only two first-rate Powers who are also free nations'.[39] Freedom and peace would join hands.

Like Bentham, Mill looked to international action and the creation of international institutions in order to prevent war. Just as the state of nature, with all its violence, was left behind as individuals put themselves under government and the rule of law, so the next step was for states to submit themselves to an international tribunal. Such a tribunal would regulate the nations of the world in much the same way as the Supreme Court regulated the states of the American Union.[40] It would treat states impartially and equally, just as the civil law accorded equal treatment to individuals.[41] Mill thought that the London Conference of 1830, between Britain, France, Austria, Russia and Prussia, which put a stop to the war between Belgium and Holland and which recognized Belgian independence, was the first step towards a 'federative system of police for the European commonwealth', 'a sign and precursor of a great advancement of civilization, gradually, but surely preparing'.[42] In 1864 he was pleased that Britain had protested against the seizure of Schleswig-Holstein by Prussia, thinking that it was 'the inauguration of the practice of bringing international political wrongs under a moral police', and he looked forward to a time when such wrongs would be repressed by a sharper mode of international interference.[43] In 1868, he thought that the peaceful settlement of the *Alabama* dispute was a further step in the process of defining and ratifying international law.[44] In 1870 he was insisting that international action should have been taken to protect Belgium during the Franco-Prussian war:

> If war between nations is ever to be put an end to, it can only be as war between individuals has been checked in civilised societies – by the generation of a police & an impartial umpire to settle quarrels. To create such a system it is necessary that all courageous and right feeling men sh^d be ready to suffer in protecting the weak in politics as they ought to be in civil life.[45]

Indeed he thought that Gladstone could and should have stopped the war by declaring that the English navy would aid whichever of the two powers was attacked by the other.[46]

It was perfectly consistent with this that he should favour federal unions which reduced the number of states in the world: this would help to eliminate war, both by reconciling those states thus united, and also by making them strong enough in their unity to deter any would-be aggressor.[47] His instincts were cosmopolitan: 'Whatever really tends to the admixture of nationalities, and the blending of their attributes and peculiarities in a common union, is a benefit to the human race.' Accordingly, though usually a supporter of national independence from foreign rule, Mill did not relish the prospect of states breaking up into ever smaller units. It was better for the Bretons to participate in French civilization, than to sulk on their own rocks as half-savage relics of former times.[48] He was not prepared to accept the argument that the American south was entitled to recognition as a separate nation simply because its rebel government demanded it:[49] that would be like arguing that the Isle of Wight would be morally entitled to independence if the inhabitants of Parkhurst Prison seized it and declared it a separate state.[50] More controversially, in 1862 he asserted that England would not be morally obliged to let Ireland and Scotland go without a fight.[51]

PHILOSOPHIC RADICALISM REVISED

If Mill was ever a Benthamite optimist about the prospects of a rapidly pacified world, then that optimism did not last. Europe, he thought, would continue to be a dangerous place as long as it contained despotic military monarchies such as Austria and Russia. He was inclined to be optimistic about Prussia, as a modernizing state well on the way to freedom.[52] This optimism took a setback when Prussia defeated Austria in 1866: Mill ruefully remarked that an expiring feudality had been overcome by a powerful Caesarism.[53] But he consistently and wrongly saw Prussia as an innocent party, waging a war of self-defence against France in 1870.

Mill's optimism was dented above all by events in France and Great Britain. He had a youthful enthusiasm for France as, since her great Revolution, the country where a better future was being prepared. But by 1840 he was depressed by the warlike propensities of Thiers in France and Palmerston in Britain. In 1842 we find him deploring the blustering bellicosity of the popular parties in England, America and France and as a result questioning the radical grand narrative, according to which war was the game of kings, destined to pass away with the advance of parliamentary liberalism.[54] Mill's thought about foreign affairs and war was always shadowed by the memory of the Napoleonic wars, and he was greatly troubled by the accession of Napoleon III after 1848. He saw Napoleon as the greatest enemy of humanity, and in 1859 was afraid that England would be crushed between the two great military despotisms of France and Russia: in that event, freedom would have to take refuge in America and Australia.[55] As a friend of liberty, it galled him that he was forced to hope that Austria would defeat France: but in 1859 he judged France under Napoleon III to be more regressive and dangerous even than Austria.[56]

Mill remained torn between hope and gloom. This is reflected in an important House of Commons speech in 1867, in which he commented that the mid-century belief that war in Europe was drawing to a close had faded:

> We were mistaken; but the light which led us astray was light from heaven. We have since had opportunities of learning a sadder wisdom . . . seen the Continental Powers outvying one another in converting all the flower of their youth into standing armies, ready at any moment to draw the sword, not only in defence, but in aggression.[57]

Not only monarchs, but the people too, were ready to go to war for national self-assertion or aggrandizement, or even for mere excitement.[58] These anxieties were focused by the Franco-Prussian war of 1870. At the outset he feared that if Napoleon III won, then England's turn would be next and her national existence at stake. He blamed not only the emperor, but also the politicians and intellectuals of France in general: but he still held to the faith that the French peasantry, the people, had not wanted war.[59] By 1871, however, he was shocked to observe that the leaders of the English working classes, hitherto zealous for peace, were loudly demanding war with Germany on behalf of France.[60]

For these, and perhaps for other reasons, Mill made an intellectual journey where international politics and war were concerned parallel to that which he made in relation to domestic politics: that is to say, away from the black-and-white simplicities of Benthamite philosophic radicalism, towards a more complex and cautious position. He did not give up all hope of international action to establish a regime of peace, nor of the confederation of states into larger units, but he came to feel that such developments were a long way off. From the 1830s onwards he was convinced that British imperial federation was impossible, because of the distances involved, because of differences of interest between Britain and her colonies, and because of the absence of any tradition of equal political cooperation.[61] (Bentham of course would never have favoured this form of federation – he wanted to do away with empires altogether.) Where Europe was concerned, he thought that the Cobden club was naïve in believing that war could be prevented in the world as it was.[62] Like other philanthropists he looked forward to universal peace, but did not think that European federation, nor an international court of arbitration, would be possible until there had been a considerable advance in intelligence and morality, and until the political institutions of the European states had become more closely assimilated, presumably on a basis of liberty and democracy.[63]

On empire, Mill disagreed quite fundamentally with Bentham, Cobden and Goldwyn Smith. Bentham had gone so far in his hostility as to advise Britain to give up her possessions in India; he did not believe that a foreign power would govern another people in their own best interests.[64] It is scarcely to be expected that Mill or his father, both employees of the East India Company, would agree with that. Mill's approach to this issue was grounded upon the 'standard of civilization'.[65] As we have seen, he thought that the community of nations should be a republic of equals, governed by international law. But savages and barbarians could not be admitted to that community and need not be treated as equals before the law.[66] Savages have not yet learnt the first lesson of civilization, that of obedience, and barbarians lack the foresight and self-restraint which would enable them reliably to keep agreements and to observe rules. Wherever a civilized country has barbarous neighbours, it may have no choice but to conquer them, and this was the situation of the British in India.[67]

But this, Mill thinks, can be for the good of the conquered. To be ruled by a more advanced people may help them to progress more rapidly towards civilization: empire is therefore as justified as any other mode of government if its aim is to train up the subject peoples for eventual self-rule.[68] Not only did Mill view British rule in India in this light: he also thought that English rule in Ireland was similarly justifiable in theory, if not in practice. In the 1830s he was inclined to describe the Irish as savages, needing to be governed by a good stout despotism, like India.[69] He continued to think that for many reasons, including the good of the Irish themselves, it would be better if Ireland remained under English rule – but only if the Irish could be reconciled to it.[70]

Mill also thought that there were economic advantages in setting up white settler colonies. He followed Edward Gibbon Wakefield in arguing that the problems resulting from overpopulation, such as low wages and low profits, could be alleviated by helping surplus labourers to settle overseas.[71] They should pay back the costs of their passage, so as not to diminish the capital of the mother country, and they should not be allowed to scatter as subsistence farmers over the new territory. In order to maximize productivity, population in the colony should be sufficiently concentrated to encourage commerce, industry and the division of labour.[72] Such colonies ought to thrive up to self-government.[73] But unlike Goldwyn Smith, who could see no advantage in a continuing imperial or commonwealth relationship, Mill thought that a slight bond ought to be retained as long as possible. It rendered war impossible between the members, and was a step towards international cooperation and universal peace. It protected the members from conquest by a despot. And finally it strengthened the influence in the world of Great Britain, a power, Mill thought, than which no other was more committed to liberty.[74]

Mill has considerable disagreements, then, with liberal pacific-ists such as Bentham and Cobden. We have yet to measure the full extent of the difference, which has to do with fundamental attitudes and orientation. For the essential point is that that Mill was, in certain situations, an enthusiast for war. The most striking instance of this was the American Civil War: Mill was passionate about, as he saw it, the North's struggle against slavery. It was about this that he wrote:

> For these reasons I cannot join with those who cry Peace, peace. . . . War, in a good cause, is not the greatest evil which a nation can suffer. War is an ugly thing, but not the ugliest of things: the decayed and degraded state of moral and patriotic feeling which thinks nothing *worth* a war is worse.[75]

Writing to the Peace Society in 1847, he insisted that though progress would put an end to war, 'I regard war as an infinitely less evil than systematic submission to injustice.'[76] It was cowardice for a nation to submit to injury or even to insult.[77] There was no question for him that nations have a right of self-defence, and high-spirited nations have other rights which they are entitled to enforce.[78]

As remarked in the introductory section, an endorsement, even a welcoming, of war like this is problematic for utilitarianism: how often could it conceivably promote the greatest happiness? Mill's stance on this relates to a broader acceptance of violence in political life.[79] He was not against revolution for the sake of political progress if it had the support to succeed, and indeed insisted that 'I have sympathized more or less ardently with most of the rebellions, successful and unsuccessful, which have taken place in my time.'[80] So why did Mill, as a utilitarian, think that war could be justified?

To answer this question we need to return to Mill's grand narrative of history, his account of progress from savagery through barbarism to civilization. War mattered to Mill, because war played a crucial part in advancing or retarding that progress. Mill did not think that progress depended solely or even primarily on vast impersonal forces, whether economic or mental. Progress – and therefore the happiness of humanity – had to be fought for. So, while Bentham deplored the literature of classical Greece and Rome because of its emphasis on drums and trumpets,[81] Mill was all his life excited by that literature and convinced that the battles it narrated were central in humanity's struggle towards the light. The triumph of the Greeks over the Persian empire, and of Athens over Sparta, were victories of civilization over barbarism, and if the hegemony of Athens had not been secured, enlightenment and liberty might never have dawned. If the Greeks had not defeated the Persians at Marathon, then by 1066 'the Britons and the Saxons might still have been wandering in the woods'.[82] The eclipse of Athens by Macedonia and Rome marked a return to barbarism. The fall of Athens was secured by the failure of her expedition to conquer Sicily, and Mill wrote to his wife from Syracuse, the scene of the Athenian defeat:

> That event decided the fate of the world, most calamitously . . . Perhaps the world would have been now a thousand years further advanced if freedom had thus been kept standing in the only place where it ever was or could then be powerful. I thought & felt this as I approached the town till I could have cried with regret and sympathy.[83]

This is an epic conception of classical history, and Mill conceived the history of his own time in the same manner, as a struggle between civilization and barbarism, liberty and tyranny: 'The absorption of Greece by Macedonia was one of the greatest misfortunes which ever happened to the world: that of any of the principal countries of Europe by Russia would be a similar one.'[84] He was glad of the Crimean war with Russia.[85] Especially as he became disillusioned with France after the *coup d'état* of Napoleon III, he increasingly saw Great Britain as the Athens of the modern world. It was Britain which forced the end of the slave trade, Britain was the nation most governed by moral principle in its dealing with foreigners, Britain was the European bastion of liberty. The security and influence of Great Britain was in the interests of humanity as a whole. Therefore it would be wrong for Britain to disarm in the face of the military despotisms, wrong for her to allow her naval power to be weakened.[86]

Mill likewise saw the American Civil War as a conflict between civilization and barbarism. Not only that: on more than one occasion he wrote of that war as having therapeutic value, a struggle which would regenerate the nation and its democracy, saving it from stagnation: 'A man who has nothing which he is willing to fight for, nothing which he cares more about than he does about his personal safety, is a miserable creature who has no chance of being free.'[87] A fascinating insight into the way in which Mill could reconcile war and utility is provided by his remarks on the assassination of President Lincoln. Coming at the time of the North's victory over the South and slavery, Mill saw it as a noble martyrdom, the crown of a noble life, and also as the ultimate happiness for Lincoln himself.[88] This reveals Mill's distance from Bentham, and the extent to which he had modified Benthamite utilitarianism. Lincoln could only be thought of as finding happiness in death, if happiness meant something other than pleasurable sensations, only if he found his happiness in the forwarding of ideal ends, ends which might not be achieved during his lifetime. Having made this move, it was easier for Mill to justify not only war, but also fighting to the death. It was right, he insisted, that 'a people inferior in strength should fight to the death against the attempt of a foreign despot to reduce it to slavery' – for if despots knew this would happen, if they knew they could not count on an easy victory, then they would be reluctant to attack.[89] This too makes sense if we suppose individuals finding their happiness in devotion to an ideal, in this case the independence of small nations.

To complete this account of Mill the warrior, it should be noted that at the time of the Franco-Prussian war he was ready to stand on a platform advocating universal, compulsory military service. At a time when war between liberty and despotism threatened, Britain needed a large army, but a large professional standing army could itself become an instrument of despotism. Therefore a popular militia was the answer, after the Swiss model: a few months of service, with periodic refreshers of a fortnight or so, would suffice, and would have the further benefit of making young men more steady and vigorous in the ordinary pursuits of life.[90]

WAS MILL A LIBERAL CRUSADER?

In the light of all this, would it be correct to classify Mill as a crusading warrior, someone ready to fight not merely in self-defence against aggression, but also for the sake of principles – to put it in the most pejorative way, in order to impose his principles on other peoples, bringing back bloody wars of religion in secular guise? There are passages which appear to support such an interpretation. In the aftermath of the French revolution of 1848, Lamartine declared the right of the French republic to come to the aid of nations attempting to free themselves from a foreign yoke. Lord Brougham attacked him, and Mill came to Lamartine's defence. In the course of his argument, he likened his own age to the era of the Reformation: 'What religious sympathies were then, political ones are now; and every liberal government or people has a right to assist struggling liberalism, by mediation, by money, or by arms, wherever it can prudently do so.'[91]

Mill was even prepared to say that if the Confederate South succeeded in establishing itself as an independent power, a 'barbarous and barbarizing Power', then a general crusade of civilized Europe might be necessary to extinguish it.[92] Because of its character the South could not be admitted to the community of nations, with equal rights: it ought to be crushed immediately as a pest,[93] and the Northerners who fought against it were heroes.[94] He had earlier contended that Britain and France ought to enforce the abolition of the slave trade on Portugal and Brazil, searching every vessel that entered the ports of the 'contemptible little powers' if necessary.[95] Implicitly also, he accepted as war aims not merely the repulsion of aggression, but also punishment and the enforcement of reparation; as he saw it the Prussians were entitled to inflict these on the French in 1870.[96] A victor would be entitled at least temporarily to impose a certain form of government – presumably Mill means a liberal representative one – on a defeated enemy.[97]

But remarks like these need to be read in the setting of Mill's thought as a whole; and when this is done, it becomes clear that he cannot be classified as a crusader. With very few exceptions, the only wars he is prepared to justify are defensive ones. This is the message of his most important single statement on international relations, his essay 'A Few Words on Non-Intervention' of 1859.[98] The argument of that essay is that one nation should not impose liberal institutions upon another, nor intervene in a struggle between progressives and reactionaries in another nation. This looks like the extension of Mill's celebrated liberty principle from individuals to nations. That principle states that individuals may never be interfered with, even for their own good, when their considered actions harm no-one but themselves. Where nations are concerned, Mill elaborates the maxim of non-interference in the following way. If the progressive forces in a country are not strong enough to obtain liberal institutions without foreign help, then that country is not ripe for such institutions. Either the majority are not in favour, or the will, the earnest desire is lacking which would enable the people to defend and operate them: 'Their good government would last no longer than the freedom of a people usually lasts who have been liberated by foreign arms without their co-operation'.[99] As Luban and Walzer have insisted, this is not a very persuasive argument; the history of the twentieth century has led us to doubt that majorities longing for freedom will always overcome cruel tyrannies.[100]

There are just two types of situation when Mill is prepared to contemplate intervention. An example of the first would be where a reactionary power had already intervened in the internal struggle for freedom in order to prop up despotism – as Russia crushed the liberal forces in Hungary after the revolution of 1848. In such a case it would have been legitimate for Britain and France to weigh in on the side of freedom, to threaten or declare war on Russia.[101] What Mill was advocating here was neither aggression nor crusading. Rather it would be *resisting* aggression, a war of defence against Russian aggression. Essentially it would be a matter of enforcing the principle of non-intervention itself, against a power, Russia, which had violated it. Arguably Mill was entirely consistent in his adherence to this principle. In his defence of Lamartine against Brougham mentioned above he wrote that 'Assistance against foreigners, not against native rulers, was the only assistance of which the smallest mention was made.'[102] And the crusade which he thought might be necessary against the barbarizing slave power of the Confederacy was described by him as a *defensive* crusade. Following Cairns's analysis of the economics of slavery, Mill thought that it was a system of agriculture which quickly exhausted the soil, and which therefore was impelled to aggression and territorial expansion.[103]

The other type of situation is where there is a conflict between evenly matched forces, which has been going on for a long time and of which no prospect of resolution is discernible. In such a case a power or powers would be justified in intervening to put an end to the conflict, for the sake of peace and humanity, as the European powers intervened to end the struggle between Holland and Belgium in 1830.[104]

Mill's doctrine of non-intervention, classically formulated in 1859, was already formed in 1830. His earlier statements reveal an important aspect of the genesis of the doctrine, and help us to understand, in the face of the criticism of Luban and Walzer mentioned above, why Mill was so uncompromising in his insistence that a people should be left to forge its own destiny. In 1830 and 1831, French newspapers and politicians were demanding a war for liberty:

> The French may be assured, that the English people will approve of their *enforcing* the principle of non-intervention against the despotic powers, but will disapprove of their *violating* that principle, in order to crusade in support of the subjects of other states against their governments, however just the resistance of such subjects may be, or however certain their destruction, if not aided from abroad.[105]

What preoccupied Mill and formed his thinking was the history of the Directory and of the Empire of Napoleon I, when a crusade for liberty turned into a rage for victory and conquest, plunging Europe into a quarter of a century of war. Mill was afraid that such crusading would return, 'enslaving foreign countries under the forms of liberty', putting a stop for a long period to the progress of civilization, and even throwing it back.[106] His fears were revived after 1848, when Napoleon III seized power and intervened in the struggle for Italian independence. The memory of Napoleon and an enduring fear of French ambitions led Mill to his doctrine of non-intervention and to an insistence that only defensive wars could be justified.

DID MILL FAIL AS A MORALIST OF WAR?

We come now to the last and most important question. Was Mill lamentably inattentive to the range of issues raised by the morality of war, issues which were to become so pressing in the century after his death? The previous sections make it apparent that no hasty condemnation of Mill would be warranted. Maybe it is to be regretted that he did not write a major essay on the subject, pulling together his scattered thoughts; but those scattered thoughts are numerous and substantial, revealing a continuing preoccupation with international morality. Mill wrote and spoke on empire and colonies, on treaty obligations, on the rights of neutrals and on extradition, on international institutions and conventions and on national struggles for independence and liberty. Above all in his essay on non-intervention he addressed the issue of *jus ad bellum* and argued that only defensive warfare could be justified.

It could be said, however, that Mill would have done better if he had paid more attention to and sought to develop the tradition of just war theory, for that tradition had a richness and fullness, for instance on questions of *jus ad bellum*, which utilitarian speculation about war does not match. Benthamite utilitarianism loudly proclaimed its break with earlier moral thinking, for example with the doctrine of natural law out of which the just war tradition grew. Earlier moralities, to Bentham, were unscientific, lacking in objectivity. It is clear that Mill at least began by sharing this attitude to the tradition of international law. So we find him in 1849 proclaiming his disagreement with Pufendorf, Burlamaqui and Vattel, and insisting with his teacher Austin that to refer to international law is to misuse the word law. There is only international custom, which may be based upon nothing more than opinion or prejudice, and 'are international usages the only kind of customs which, in an age of progress, are to be subject to no improvement?'[107] In due course he came to take a more positive view of international customs and conventions, and by the time of his inaugural address as Rector of St Andrews University in 1867 he was recommending that all educated persons should study international law.[108] Still we may say that he never really engaged with the tradition.

Finally, did Mill fail to address the issues of *jus in bello*, those issues so catastrophically raised by the massacre of civilians in the twentieth century? In attempting to tease out his thought on this, it really is a matter of piecing together scattered hints. He does not provide as much in the way of coherent utilitarian discussion as Sidgwick or even Paley. In general it can be said that he is not guilty of utilitarian opportunism, of thinking that the end justifies cruel and arbitrary means. He recognizes the 'law of necessity' – that nations may for the sake of self-preservation do things not normally allowable. But nations should abide by the rules of law and morality wherever possible, and necessity should be invoked only with extreme reluctance and caution, in the direst of emergencies;[109] in essence this seems akin to Michael Walzer's position in *Just and Unjust Wars*, which attempts to reconcile utilitarianism with a respect for human rights.[110] Mill appears to be in favour of the rule of non-combatant immunity, but he nowhere explicitly addresses this issue. He does not explore the difficult question, which has exercised twentieth-century philosophers, of how such a rule could be derived from utility.[111] Moreover, he did not think through the implications of blockading as a war strategy. He regarded it as an essential weapon for a naval power like Britain, and was inclined to justify naval power as defensive rather than offensive.[112] But blockades, like sieges, harm civilians as much as combatants, and if prolonged can cause civilian deaths, as happened in Germany at the end of the First World War.[113] In contravention of his usual insistence upon the rule of law he was prepared also, at the end of the American Civil War, to advocate extensive confiscation in order to break the power of the slaveholding oligarchy.[114] General Sherman's march through Georgia and burning of Atlanta provided a foretaste of twentieth-century war against civilians: if Mill knew of it, he made no comment.

Perhaps we should not blame him for failing to foresee twentieth-century developments. As an advocate of reason and law, as a consistent opponent of the doctrine of racial inequality, he could not have anticipated the Social–Darwinist and will-to-power philosophies which legitimated aggressive and exterminative warfare in the first half of the twentieth century. Nor did he envisage how powerful and dangerous militant nationalism would become as a mass phenomenon, and how much hatred of the foreigner it would generate. Mill continued to think, in eighteenth-century fashion, that a major problem was the strength of private interest and the consequent neglect of the public good. From Coleridge and others he had learnt that patriotic sentiment could help to solve this problem, and so he tended to regard national feelings as good, worthy of being fostered. If anything he feared that national spirit would grow too slowly, or be too weak.[115]

Above all, Mill failed to address the issues of *jus in bello* because of the grand narrative to which he subscribed. It lulled him into a false sense of security, leading him to think that war crimes were increasingly a thing of the past. Cruelty to enemies was a characteristic of savagery. The Middle Ages were stained with torture and murder, chivalry was a cheat which barely mitigated the butchery that went on: but medieval knights were bored and cowardly savages, and their day was over. Modern soldiers were disciplined, brave and civilized; the mild and respectful treatment of prisoners was universal in modern Europe:

We continue to talk of the continence of Scipio; yet, what mighty matter did this continence amount to? He did not ravish a beautiful woman, whom the fortune of war had thrown into his hands. Now, if this be greatness, what subaltern officer, we were going to say, common soldier, in the British army, is not as great a man as Scipio?[116]

Mill thought that, under the influence of women and the controlling discipline of public opinion, ferocity was dying out in modern Europe.[117] In 1857 we find him appalled at massacres in China; but the lesson he draws is that the Chinese, unlike the Europeans, are barbarians who recognize no laws of war and fail to come up to the standard of civilization.[118] Mill was inclined to disbelieve stories of modern European and American commanders giving their troops licence to pillage, burn and rape; and even if they *were* true:

> If any English commander at the present time were to do the like, he never could show his face again in English society even if he escaped being broken by a court martial; & I think we are entitled to blame in others what none of us, of the present generation at least, would be capable of perpetrating.[119]

Mill was aware of events and developments which told against this optimism; but he gave them little weight, or regarded them as exceptions which proved the rule. The bloodiness of modern warfare results in great part from the mechanization of warfare, the cheap mass production of weapons, and more destructive weapons. These developments were anticipated in Mill's lifetime, in both the American Civil War and the Franco-Prussian War.[120] Mill knew that modern science and industry were girding themselves to the work of destruction, and 'bringing forth every year more and more terrific engines for blasting hosts of human beings into atoms, together with the defences by which they vainly seek to shelter themselves'.[121]

He knew that white settlers, in India or New Zealand, would oppress 'inferior races' if they could, but had faith that this would be stopped by enlightened imperial administration; he always thought of his employer, the East India Company, as the protector of the natives.[122] He was disgusted by the inhuman and ferocious repression of the Indian mutiny, but did not lose his faith in civilization as a result: he hopefully suggested that many of the military men on the spot were restrained by their professional code and discipline from such atrocities.[123] He campaigned tirelessly to bring Governor Eyre to trial for murder on account of his brutal and illegal stamping out of a small rising in Jamaica. He thought that the great majority of the English people were on his side – 'Were I not so convinced I sh[d] be ashamed of my country.'[124] Mill had faith in the decency of the common people of Great Britain, who would not tolerate holding Ireland by force, would not be prepared to perpetrate Jamaican horrors.[125] He blamed British support for American slavery, and for the brutal repressions of the Indian mutiny and the Jamaica rebellion, on the class sympathy of the upper sections of society with privilege and established power. Social and political equality would put a stop to such evils.[126]

We might conclude, then, by observing in sadness a salient difference between Mill and us. Mill did not properly address the problem of *jus in bello*, because he thought it was no longer a problem; civilized states were less and less likely to commit war crimes. He thought this because of the optimistic grand narrative to which he subscribed. We of this century have been sickened by war crimes on an appalling scale, and as a result have recovered and developed the just war tradition in philosophy and law. But the other consequence of this experience is that we no longer have faith in any grand narrative of progress.

Notes

1   I am indebted to the excellent article by K.E. Miller, 'John Stuart Mill's Theory of International Relations' (1961) reprinted in J.C. Wood (ed.) *John Stuart Mill Critical Assessments* (London, Routledge, 1991), vol. 4, pp. 169–87; see also S. Grader, 'John Stuart Mill's Theory of Nationality: A Liberal Dilemma in the Field of International Relations', *Millennium: Journal of International Studies*, 14:2, 1985, pp. 207–16 and P. Smart, 'Mill and Nationalism. National Character, Social Progress and the Spirit of Achievement', *Journal of the History of European Ideas*, 15, 1992, pp. 527–34.

2   M. Ceadel, *Thinking about Peace and War* (Oxford, Oxford University Press, 1987), pp. 5, 102 ff.

3   J. Bentham, 'Principles of International Law', *The Works of Jeremy Bentham*, ed. J. Bowring, (Edinburgh, William Tait, 1843), vol. 2, pp. 547, 552–4.

4   James Mill, *Essays on Government, Jurisprudence, Liberty of the Press, and Law of Nations* (London, J. Innes, 1825).

5   Ceadel, *Peace and War*, p. 118; T. Nardin and D.R. Mapel (eds), *Traditions of International Ethics* (Cambridge University Press, 1992), p. 210.

6   H. Sidgwick, *The Elements of Politics* (London, Macmillan, 1891), p. 293.

7   Bentham, 'International Law', pp. 557, 559; Miller, 'John Stuart Mill's Theory' p. 169; J.C. Wood, *British Economists and the Empire* (London, Croom Helm, 1983), p. 35.

8   Bentham, 'International Law', pp. 538, 544.

9   Sidgwick, *Elements of Politics*, pp. 287, 296.

10   J.T. Johnson, *Can Modern War be Just?* (New Haven CT, Yale University Press, 1984), p. 177.

11   J.T. Johnson, *Just War Tradition and the Restraint of War* (Princeton, NJ, Princeton University Press, 1981), pp. 192–6, 304.

12   Johnson, *Can Modern War be Just?*; Johnson, *Just War Tradition*.

13   Johnson, *Just War Tradition*, p. 329. I have found the following especially useful: M. Walzer, *Just and Unjust Wars* (London, Allen Lane, 1978); C.R. Beitz, M. Cohen, T. Scanlon and A.J. Simmons (eds), *International Ethics: A Philosophy and Public Affairs Reader* (Princeton University Press, 1985) is excellent, and has a running commentary on Mill on non-intervention; R. Norman, *Ethics, Killing and War* (Cambridge, Cambridge University Press, 1995).

14 Johnson, *Can Modern War be Just?*, p. 16.

15 Ibid., p. 14; G.W. Gong, *The Standard of 'Civilization' in International Society* (Oxford University Press, 1984), p. 26.

16 Johnson, *Just War Tradition*, pp. 59–60.

17 Johnson, *Can Modern War be Just?*, p. 3.

18 Ibid., p. 21; Ceadel, *Peace and War*, pp. 10–13; R.L. Holmes, *On War and Morality* (Princeton University Press, 1989), pp. 159–61.

19 I here use the word 'utilitarian' loosely, as equivalent to 'consequentialist': utilitarianism judges an action right if the good consequences outweigh the bad.

20 J. Glover, *Causing Death and Saving Lives* (Harmondsworth, Penguin, 1977), p. 284; T. Nagel, 'War and Massacre', in Beitz *et al.* (eds), *International Ethics*, p. 55.

21 Ibid., pp. 60–71.

22 References to Mill are to the *Collected Works of John Stuart Mill*, ed. J.M. Robson and others (33 vols, University of Toronto Press, 1962–1991) (hereafter *CW*): *CW*, vol. 20, pp. 26–7.

23 *CW*, vol. 26, p. 373.

24 Ibid., pp. 267, 330, 373.

25 Ibid., p. 373.

26 *CW*, vol. 23, p. 615.

27 Ibid., p. 665.

28 *CW*, vol. 13, p. 454.

29 *CW*, vol. 18, p. 220; vol. 26, p. 316.

30 *CW*, vol. 29, p. 372.

31 *CW*, vol. 13, p. 456.

32 Ibid., p. 460.

33 *CW*, vol. 23, p. 466: see also vol. 16, p. 1108; vol. 19, p. 564; vol. 20, p. 347.

34 *CW*, vol. 21, pp. 116–17.

35 *CW*, vol. 20, pp. 20, 32–3, 241.

36 *CW*, vol. 23, p. 348.

37 *CW*, vol. 3, p. 707.

38 *CW*, vol. 17, pp. 1637, 1760, 1762, 1774–5.

39 *CW*, vol. 19, p. 560; vol. 21, p. 127.

40 *CW*, vol. 19, pp. 557–8.

41 *CW*, vol. 17, p. 1762.

42 *CW*, vol. 23, p. 632.

43 *CW*, vol. 25, p. 1206.

44 *CW*, vol. 18, p. 246. Great Britain eventually agreed to pay compensation for the damage inflicted on Northern American shipping by the *Alabama*, a Southern American warship built and fitted out in Britain.

45 *CW*, vol. 17, p. 1760.

46 Ibid., p. 1767.

47 Ibid., pp. 559–60.

48 *CW*, vol. 19, p. 549.

49 *CW*, vol. 15, p. 752; vol. 21, p. 160.

50 *CW*, vol. 21, p. 137.

51 Ibid., p. 160–1.

52 *CW*, vol. 23, p. 728; vol. 15, p. 598; vol. 24, pp. 1079–82.

53 *CW*, vol. 16, p. 1197.

54 *CW*, vol. 24, p. 831.

55 *CW*, vol. 15, pp. 610, 619.

56 Ibid., p. 611.

57 *CW*, vol. 18, p. 222.

58 Ibid., p. 224.

59 *CW*, vol. 17, pp. 1754, 1774–5.

60 Ibid., p. 1798.

61 *CW*, vol. 23, pp. 404–5; vol. 13, p. 393; vol. 19, pp. 564–5; vol. 17, p. 1685; vol. 32, p. 233; Wood, *British Economists*, pp. 33–4.

62 *CW*, vol. 32, p. 224.

63 *CW*, vol. 17, pp. 1798–1800.

64 Bentham 'International Law', p. 548.

65 Gong, *Standard of Civilization*, pp. 14–15.

66 *CW*, vol. 21, p. 346.

67 *CW*, vol. 19, p. 415; vol. 21, pp. 118–19. For a critique of Mill see Smart, 'Mill and Nationalism'.

68 *CW*, vol. 19, pp. 550, 567–8; vol. 21, p. 119.

69 *CW*, vol. 6, p. 217; vol. 12, p. 365.

70 *CW*, vol. 16, pp. 1328–9; vol. 6, pp. 520–3.

71 R.N. Ghosh, 'John Stuart Mill on Colonies and Colonisation', in Wood, (ed.), *John Stuart Mill Critical Assessments*, vol. 4, pp. 354–67.

72 *CW*, vol. 22, pp. 270–3; vol. 23, pp. 735–42.

73 *CW*, vol. 25, p. 1099.

74 *CW*, vol. 19, p. 565; vol. 32, pp. 145, 233; vol. 15, p. 784; vol. 17, p. 1685.

75 *CW*, vol. 21, p. 141.

76 *CW*, vol. 13, p. 729.

77 *CW*, vol. 24, p. 834.

78 *CW*, vol. 21, pp. 114, 347.

79 G. Williams, 'J.S. Mill and Political Violence', *Utilitas*, 1, 1989, pp. 102–11.

80 *CW*, vol. 21, p. 137; vol. 18, p. 166; vol. 25, p. 1203.

81 Bentham, 'International Law', p. 544.

82 *CW*, vol. 11, pp. 273–4, 313, 321; vol. 24, p. 1086.

83 *CW*, vol. 14, p. 384.

84 *CW*, vol. 19, p. 550.

85 *CW*, vol. 14, pp. 163–4.

86 *CW*, vol. 19, pp. 551, 565; vol. 18, p. 223; vol. 21, pp. 111, 115; vol. 25, p. 1097; vol. 16, pp. 1034, 1109.

87 *CW*, vol. 21, pp. 135, 142; vol. 15, p. 835; vol. 16, p. 993; c.f. Ceadel, *Peace and War*, p. 26.

88 *CW*, vol. 16, pp. 1044, 1051.

89 *CW*, vol. 15, p. 854.

90 *CW*, vol. 29, p. 413; vol. 17, pp. 1760, 1792, 1806.

91 *CW*, vol. 20, p. 346.

92 *CW*, vol. 21, p. 141.

93 *CW*, vol. 15, p. 752.

94 *CW*, vol. 32, p. 201.

95 *CW*, vol. 23, p. 349.

96 *CW*, vol. 17, pp. 1764–5.

97 *CW*, vol. 21, pp. 123, 346.

98 Ibid., pp. 111ff.

99 *CW*, vol. 19, p. 403.

100 D. Luban, 'Just War and Human Rights', in Beitz *et al.* (eds), *International Ethics*, p. 215; Walzer, *Just and Unjust Wars*, p. 101.

101 *CW*, vol. 21, p. 124.

102 *CW*, vol. 20, p. 342.

103 *CW*, vol. 21, pp. 149, 151, 157.

104 *CW*, vol. 23, p. 632.

105 *CW*, vol. 22, p. 284.

106 Ibid., pp. 259, 215, 299–300; cf. 'Just War and Human Rights', pp. 199–200.

107 *CW*, vol. 20, p. 345.

108 *CW*, vol. 21, pp. 246–7.

109 *CW*, vol. 15, p. 756; vol. 21, p. 131 n.

110 J. Teichman, *Pacifism and the Just War* (Oxford, Blackwell, 1986), p. 109; Walzer, *Just and Unjust Wars*, p. 231.

111 Ibid., pp. 132–3; G.L. Mavrodes, 'Conventions and the Morality of War', in Beitz *et al.* (eds), *International Ethics*, pp. 83–5; R.B. Brandt, 'Utilitarianism and the Rules of War', *Philosophy and Public Affairs*, 1, 1972, p. 93.

112 *CW*, vol. 18, pp. 223–4; vol. 21, p. 138.

113 Walzer, *Just and Unjust Wars*, pp. 172–3.

114 *CW*, vol. 16, pp. 1066, 1100.

115 *CW*, vol. 24, p. 1079; vol. 13, p. 536.

116 *CW*, vol. 20, pp. 20, 28–9, 32–41; vol. 19, p. 548.

117 *CW*, vol. 20, p. 42; vol. 21, p. 330; vol. 17, p. 1864.

118 *CW*, vol. 15, p. 528.

119 *CW*, vol. 15, p. 804.

120 Johnson, *Just War Tradition*, pp. xi, 33.

121 *CW*, vol. 18, p. 222.

122 *CW*, vol. 16, p. 1136.

123 *CW*, vol. 18, p. 189.

124 *CW*, vol. 16, p. 1411.

125 *CW*, vol. 6, p. 520.

126 *CW*, vol. 16, pp. 1205–6, 1208–9.

5

THE ETHICS OF WAR: THE EARL OF ELGIN AND THE WAR WITH CHINA, 1857–60

J.A.G. Roberts

THE ETHICS OF WAR

The idea that the conduct of war should be subject to rules and restrictions can be traced far back in the history of the West. Herodotus, writing in the fifth century BC, and describing the war between Greece and Persia, indicated what was deemed appropriate in the treatment of prisoners of war and of cities which had been captured. The chivalric code of medieval Europe assumed that knights shared a common culture and mores with regard to sparing women and being magnanimous to a defeated enemy. References to the 'law of arms' argue the existence in the Middle Ages of 'some sort of prototype of the Geneva convention, a branch of international law governing the conduct of war'.[1] That such rules of war might be flouted even by those who should have shown the greatest respect for them was shown in Shakespeare's *King Henry the Fifth*. In the course of the battle of Agincourt the king ordered his soldiers to kill their French prisoners, an action which was denounced by the Welsh soldier Fluellen as 'expressly against the law of arms'.[2]

The expectation that conduct in war should accord with ethical principles is less evident in the history of China. Both Confucius (traditional dates 551–479 BC), and his follower Mencius (*c.*370–*c.*300 BC) rejected the use of war to further the interests of the state, and because of this general condemnation neither suggested that the practice of war should be subject to an ethical code. Sunzi, the reputed author of the fourth-century Chinese manual *The Art of War*, a text which was to influence greatly Mao Zedong's military thinking, made no mention of the ethics of warfare. 'All warfare,' he wrote, 'is based upon deception.' However, the *Zuozhuan*, a commentary on the chronicle known as the *Spring and Autumn Annals*, which is dated between the fourth and early second centuries BC, refers to some conventions of war, for example agreement over the burial of the dead after a battle. By this time the Legalists – the name given to the followers of the ideas of Han Feizi (d. 233 BC) – openly advocated war as a means of strengthening the state. Some suggestion that there were expectations of standards of behaviour in combat may be discerned in early

Chinese fiction, for example in *Water Margin*, a fourteenth-century romanticized version of the adventures of an eleventh-century band of outlaws. These principles can scarcely be called ethics of war, for the massacres of the entire population of villages, collective acts of sadistic punishment, are presented without any moral condemnation.[3]

The first systematic attempt to define *jus in bello*, that is the law concerning the conduct of war, was made by the *philosophes* of the European Enlightenment. Emmerich de Vattel, in *Le droit des gens, ou, principes de la loi naturelle, appliquée à la conduite et aux affaires des nations et des souverains*, published in 1758, attempted to define the 'enemy', that is who should be regarded as a combatant as opposed to a non-combatant, and to determine the laws of war with respect to public and private property. Surprisingly Vattel suggested that in his day war was often carried out with 'a high degree of courtesy'.[4] However, in *Candide* Voltaire satirized the behaviour of the French and Prussian soldiers in the Seven Years' War, accusing both sides of burning villages and raping and killing the inhabitants 'in accordance with the rules of international law'.[5] Half a century later Tolstoy, in *War and Peace*, was equally sceptical, for he had Prince Andrew Bolkhonsky declare 'War is not courtesy but the most horrible thing in life; and we ought to understand that, and not play at war.'[6]

In the first half of the nineteenth century, the argument of 'military necessity', which declared that although there are rules of war breaches of them may be justified, continued to be cited to justify actions which were contrary to the spirit of those rules. In 1801 the British navy destroyed the naval fleet of Denmark, a neutral state, and justified the deed on the grounds that Britain would be seriously endangered if the Danish navy should support Napoleon. Six years later Britain landed troops at Copenhagen and destroyed naval stores to prevent the Danish fleet from sailing. Incidents like this demonstrated that 'military necessity' could be invoked under most circumstances provided that the action had popular and governmental support. In the War of 1812 between Great Britain and the United States of America, British commanders set aside conventions relating to avoiding unnecessary damage to the property of non-combatants and threatened that buildings would be destroyed unless their owners paid a ransom for their preservation.

At the philosophical level the 'law of military necessity' may be related to the utilitarian view of ethics, that is the view that ethical judgements should be based on the principle of maximizing good and minimizing evil. In the circumstances of war this implied choosing to commit a lesser evil in order to prevent the commission of a greater evil. The application of such a principle would appear to suspend, but not overthrow, the principles of *jus in bello*. Modern formulations of the rules of war anticipate this situation and argue that rules may not be set aside on the grounds of military necessity, because such considerations were taken into account when the rules were framed.[7]

In the mid-nineteenth century the first attempts were made to codify the rules of war and to support them through international agreements. An early example of this tendency was the Declaration of Paris on Maritime Commercial Warfare of 1856. In 1863 Henri Dunant, a Swiss philanthropist who had been shocked by the suffering caused by the Franco-Austrian war of 1859, published *Souvenirs de Solférino*, and in 1864 played a leading part in the founding the Red Cross. The American Civil War, which pitted the two sides of a supposedly civilized nation against each other, was notable for the issue in 1863 of *United States Army General Order No. 100*, otherwise known as Francis Lieber's Code. The order set out the current state of the laws of war for the benefit of the Union side. In the following year the first Geneva Convention agreed on the *Convention for the Amelioration of the Wounded in Time of War*. This was ratified at that time by twelve states, including France but excluding Great Britain. The Franco-Prussian war of 1870 inspired further agreements – not perhaps because of a greater humanitarianism, but because the war demonstrated only too cruelly the progress that had been made in the production of weapons of mass destruction and the willingness of the participants to extend the scope of war through the use of economic weapons. In 1874 the Brussels Declaration on the Rules of Military Warfare, which was to remain unratified, attempted to define the laws and customs of land warfare. In 1880 the Institute of International Law produced a manual of the laws of war on land, and its ideas were publicized by the Swiss international lawyer Johann Caspar Bluntschli. Further Conventions, held at The Hague and Geneva between 1899 and 1929, extended the range of agreements; for example, the second Hague Convention prescribed rules relating to naval bombardments of civilian targets. In 1949 a further Geneva Convention consolidated previous agreements and set out rules governing the treatment of prisoners of war and the protection of civilians in time of war, including the unjustified destruction of property.

When formulating the rules of war, distinguishing between soldier and civilian is crucial. In regular warfare the fighting is done by soldiers who are separated from the mass of the population by their uniform and their weapons, and because they are subject to military discipline. This distinction breaks down in irregular warfare where soldiers may be faced by guerrillas or militia, supported by the civilian population and often indistinguishable from civilians. Irregular conflict becomes common when, because of the inadequacies of the regular troops, volunteer forces are formed to defend the locality or the country, in which case they may be inspired by a sense of national consciousness. The war of American Independence provided an early example of this sort of conflict. In the French Revolution it took the form of the *levée en masse* and in the Peninsular War the term 'guerrilla' came into use, and the tactics of popular resistance to foreign invasion took shape.

The years in which *jus in bello* was being formalized coincided not only with European wars fought between states which shared a common cultural heritage, but also with wars fought between European powers, in particular Great Britain, and countries which had a different cultural background. Europeans were often quick to accuse the peoples of these states of barbarity because they failed to observe Western rules of war. In China, where resistance to the West was a forerunner of later wars of national liberation, the popular response at the time of the first Opium War (1839–42) to the presence of foreign soldiers on Chinese soil was to raise village militia, or 'braves', to oppose the 'barbarians' who were stereotyped as lewd and profit-seeking.

The event which was to have the strongest and most immediate impact on the handling of the crisis in China was the Indian Mutiny or uprising which broke out in early 1857. In May Indian soldiers seized Delhi and murdered European women and children living there. Other massacres of Europeans occurred at Jhansi in June and Cawnpore in July. To British eyes these events were mutiny, not war, and they defied humanitarian standards, because they involved the killing of defenceless European women and children. These features justified the suspension of the rules of war and the application of the most severe reprisals.

ELGIN'S FIRST MISSION TO CHINA

Since the first Opium War (1839–42) the view had been held in some quarters in Britain that a second war would be needed before China fully implemented the terms of the Treaty of Nanjing (Nanking)[8] which according to the British permitted foreign trade and residence at the southern port of Guangzhou (Canton). In 1849, when the Governor of Xianggang (Hong Kong) had decided against enforcing the right of entry into Guangzhou, Palmerston had scribbled an infamous note:

> . . . the Time is fast coming when we shall be obliged to strike another Blow in China. . . . These half-civilized Governments, such as those of China, Portugal, Spanish America, all require a Dressing every eight or Ten years to keep them in order.[9]

In 1856, an incident involving a small boat called the *Arrow* led to a limited conflict between the two countries. The *Arrow* had been seized by Chinese officials who had lowered the Blue Peter ensign the ship was flying. The Governor-General, Ye Mingchen, asserted that the ship was Chinese and that it was engaged in piracy, and he refused to apologize for the alleged insult to the British flag. In retaliation Admiral Seymour, the commander of the British naval forces, captured the forts guarding the access to Guangzhou, and began slow firing, with a single gun, at the Governor-General's *yamen* or administrative compound. As neither side had at hand the force necessary to resolve the issue, the situation soon reached a stalemate. The level of bitterness between the two communities increased with three incidents, all of which were suspected by the British to have been carried out with the collusion of the provincial government, and all of which were considered by them to contravene the rules of civilized behaviour. The first was the burning of the foreign warehouses in Guangzhou on 14 December, and the second the offering of thirty taels in silver in head-money for every Englishman killed or captured. The last straw was an attempt on 14 January 1857 to poison the European population of Xianggang by putting arsenic in the bread supply. A Chinese baker resident in the colony was named as the person immediately responsible, but it was alleged that evidence implicated the Chinese authorities. The American and French envoys and the Portuguese governor of Aomen (Macao) added their names to the protest to the Chinese authorities, describing what had happened as a 'barbarous method of conducting war'.[10] Ye Mingchen, responding to Dr Peter Parker, the American commissioner, agreed that the deed should be condemned, 'to poison people in this underhand manner is an act worthy of detestation', but he insisted that it had been provoked by the 'unnumbered evils which have been inflicted upon the Chinese by the English'.[11]

It was at this point that James Bruce, the 8th Earl of Elgin (son of the 'Elgin Marbles' Bruce), was called upon to head a mission to China to settle outstanding issues between the two countries. Elgin came from an aristocratic but impoverished Scottish family. He had a strong academic background, having obtained a first in Classics from Oxford and having been elected a Fellow of Merton College[12] When a student he had been influenced by the intense high Anglicanism prevailing in Oxford at the time and he had responded to Coleridge's call 'for a self-sacrificing and cultured élite: the "clerisy", men who would be equal to the crisis of their times'.[13]

After a short period as a Member of Parliament, Elgin succeeded to his father's title and decided on a career in the public service. In 1842 he was appointed Governor of Jamaica, where he dealt with the issue of negro emancipation, and came to believe firmly in the value of introducing British political institutions into colonial territories.[14] Between 1847 and 1854 Elgin was Governor-General of Canada, where he handled the complex issue of introducing responsible government while reconciling the interests of ethnic groups. This experience led him to opine that his function as Governor-General was to act as 'moderator between parties' and as 'the representative of the interests which are common to all the inhabitants of the country'. Whereas there were those who would have gladly seen the severities of the law practised upon those from whom they believed they had suffered, according to Elgin, 'my business is to humanise – not to harden'.[15]

Elgin was a professional diplomat, not a soldier, but his position as British plenipotentiary (alongside Baron Gros, the French representative) empowered him to decide when force should be used, though the conduct of campaigns was the responsibility of his and Baron Gros's military commanders. Even before he had embarked on his mission, Elgin had expressed his resentment that he had not been given discretionary authority over the military as well as over the diplomatic proceedings and this tension was to be apparent throughout his first mission.[16]

Elgin arrived in Xianggang at the beginning of July 1857 and six days later he was presented with an address signed by 'a large number of influential persons connected with the trade with China'. In it the Xianggang merchant community gave its outspoken advice on the 'Guangzhou difficulty':

> . . . we would take this the earliest opportunity of recording our opinion – an opinion founded upon long and reluctant, and, we may add, traditional experience – that any compromise of it, or any sort of settlement which shall stop short of the complete humiliation of the Guangzhouese, which shall fail to teach them a wholesome respect for the obligations of their own Government in its relations with independent Powers, and a more hospitable reception of the foreigner who resorts to their shores for the peaceable purposes of trade, will only result in further suffering to themselves, and further disastrous interruptions to us.[17]

Apart from the wishes of the British government and those of the Xianggang merchants, Elgin was under pressure to act vigorously from other quarters. Some British officials in China were notably eager to take the offensive. These included Sir John Bowring, the Governor-General of Xianggang and author of the hymn 'In the Cross of Christ I glory'. Another proponent of decisive action was the young British Consul at Guangzhou, Harry Parkes, who had been in China since the age of thirteen, and who was described by journalist George Wingrove Cooke as one of 'the "twenty-years-in-the-country-and-speak-the-language" men'.[18] His experience implied that Elgin lacked sufficient knowledge of local conditions and would need advice if he was to make sound judgements on the appropriate course of action. Parkes was notoriously overbearing in his treatment of the Chinese. Most of the military commanders in China – who were well aware that European forces, and in particular Western ships, now held an absolute military superiority over the Chinese forces – were keen to cut a dash. Even some missionaries lent their support to the use of military force.

Elgin had to carry out his task while subject to unprecedented attention from the media. *The Times* sent a special correspondent to cover the campaign and an artist drew sketches for the *Illustrated London News*. This was the first Chinese campaign to be photographed officially. A.M. Rossier took photographs of French troops in Guangzhou in 1858, and these formed part of a stereo series issued by Negretti and Zambra in 1859, which detailed the sights of Guangzhou after its capture by the Anglo-French expeditionary force.[19]

While *en route* to China Elgin heard of the trouble at Meerut which marked the beginning of the Indian Mutiny. When he reached Singapore, he received an urgent message from Charles John Canning, Earl Canning, a former fellow-student at Christ Church, Oxford, and now Governor-General of India, asking that Elgin should divert troops from the Chinese expeditionary force to Calcutta to assist in the suppression of the mutiny. At that time Elgin had no troops with him, but he sent orders that the transports carrying his troops should divert to India. Elgin continued to Xianggang, where on 14 July a steamer arrived bringing further letters from Canning which gave a very gloomy appraisal of the situation in India and which brought news of the massacre at Cawnpore. Elgin, noting that he had no further resources he could send to Canning, and concluding that without the expeditionary force there was nothing that he could achieve in China, decided to go to India himself with the few troops and the warship which he had at his disposal.

When staying in Calcutta with Canning in August 1857 Elgin heard in full detail of the progress of the insurrection and of the response which the British authorities had made or were contemplating making. In June Colonel James Neill had marched to the relief of the Cawnpore garrison and had carried out his notorious 'cleansing' of the area around Benares. He had declared:

> I wish to show the natives of India that the punishment inflicted by us for such deeds will be the heaviest, the most revolting to their feelings, and what they must ever remember. . . . Who could be merciful to one concerned? Severity of the first is mercy in the end.

After Cawnpore had been recovered in July, Neill forced Indian soldiers accused of mutiny to lick up traces of the blood of the British victims and then hanged them.

Elgin agreed that most of the crew of his ship the *Shannon* should be formed into a naval brigade, which would march with some of the ship's guns on Delhi. The *Shannon* itself, with a skeleton crew, remained in the river opposite Calcutta, 'able, if the need were, to knock all the city to bits'.[20] This threat to bring down retribution on a city was not an idle one. In April 1858, when General Sir Hugh Rose captured Jhansi, an eye-witness remarked 'No maudlin clemency was to mark the fall of the city.'[21] Some five thousand of its inhabitants died in the subsequent reprisals. George Canning, the viceroy of India, who attempted to moderate the severity of these punishments, was castigated as 'Clemency Canning'.

Elgin's sympathies were not entirely on the side of the British. After only a few weeks in China, and an even briefer stay in India, he had formed a poor opinion of the attitude Europeans displayed towards indigenous peoples. On 21 August 1857 he noted in his journal:

It is a terrible business, however, this living among inferior races. I have seldom from man or woman since I came to the East heard a sentence which was reconcilable with the hypothesis that Christianity had ever come into the world. Detestation, contempt, ferocity, vengeance, whether Chinamen or Indians be the object. There are some three or four hundred servants in this house. When one first passes by their *salaaming* one feels a little awkward. But the feeling soon wears off, and one moves among them with perfect indifference, treating them, not as dogs, because in that case one would whistle to them and pat them, but as machines with which one can have no communion or sympathy.[22]

When in China Elgin maintained his serene confidence in European and particularly British racial superiority. However his patrician sense led him to disdain what he regarded as the crude and dangerous manifestation of that feeling by those whom he considered to be his social inferiors, a category which perhaps included all the white colonial population of Xianggang.

THE CAPTURE AND OCCUPATION OF GUANGZHOU

After frustrating attempts at negotiation with the Chinese authorities, on 12 December 1857 Elgin and Baron Gros sent an ultimatum to Ye Mingchen ordering him to surrender Guangzhou. At the time Elgin's main concern was that he did not have sufficient force at his disposal to deal humanely with the situation if Ye refused:

My greatest difficulty arises from my fear that we shall be led to attack Guangzhou before we have all our force, and led therefore to destroy, if there is any resistance, both life and property to a greater extent than would otherwise be necessary.[23]

Ten days later he took a gun-boat to within pistol shot of the walls of Guangzhou, now threatened by British ships. Later he recorded his feelings:

I never felt so ashamed of myself in my life, and Elliot [the British naval commander] remarked that the trip seemed to have made me sad. There we were, accumulating the means of destruction under the very eyes, and within reach, of a population of about 1,000,000 people, against whom these means of destruction were to be employed! 'Yes,' I said to Elliot, 'I am sad, because when I look at that town, I feel that I am earning for myself a place in the Litany, immediately after "plague, pestilence and famine."'[24]

As there was no reply from Ye Mingchen to the ultimatum, bombardment of
the city commenced on 27 December 1857 and continued in slow time for 27
hours. The principal objective of the shelling was to breach the massive city
walls, but 24-pound rockets were also fired and parts of the city were set alight.[25]
Elgin remained very sensitive about attacking a civilian target. He noted
privately 'I hate the thing so much, that I cannot trust myself to write about it.'[26]
But when the bombardment was over, and the city had been occupied, Elgin
observed that the damage was less than he expected:

> I am on the whole, therefore, disposed to think that the measure proved to be
> a good one, as the terror which it has excited in the minds of the
> Guangzhouese is more than in proportion to the injury inflicted. . . .[27]

Elgin now had to decide on the city's future treatment. His immediate concern
was for the inhabitants, how 'to prevent the wretched Guangzhouese from being
plundered and bullied' by the occupying force. He noted that the allied troops
evinced a 'very low standard of morality in regard to stealing from the Chinese'.

The governor-general, Ye Mingchen, had refused to surrender and had
disappeared. He was captured in person by Harry Parkes and then interrogated.
It was not clear whether he was being treated as a prisoner-of-war or as a war
criminal – the accusation that he was the latter arose because he was believed to
have ordered the execution of 60,000–70,000 rebels in the course of the
suppression of the recent Red Turban rebellion. Western descriptions of Ye
Mingchen in captivity stressed his corpulence, his unhygienic habits and the
crudeness of his manners. During his interrogation, when he laughed loudly in
response to a question about a missing English resident, the antipathy of his
captors towards him was so great that 'if the audience could have decided the
matter, Ye would have been taken out and hanged'.[28] Ye himself admitted later
that he expected to be put to death. Elgin dismissed that idea, but as it was
considered that Ye's presence in Guangzhou, or even in China, was liable to
cause further disturbances, he was taken as a prisoner to Calcutta, where he died.

With other matters outstanding in China, Elgin could not just withdraw from
Guangzhou, the possession of which he regarded as a 'material guarantee' to be
used when reaching a settlement with the Chinese government. Against hard-line
advice he decided against a purely military occupation, concluding that for the
proper administration of the city he would have to come to an agreement with
those Chinese authorities who remained in post. As a consequence a novel
administrative structure was created, a 'mixed government', composed on the
allied side of three commissioners, the British consul, Harry Parkes and Thomas
Holloway and Captain Martineau representing the French, and on the Chinese
side of Bogui, the governor of the province of Guangdong and the city officials of
Guangzhou. Initially martial law was imposed and the commissioners were told

that they would receive instructions from the commanders-in-chief for their guidance. However, Elgin declared that he was 'personally responsible for the policy which has subjected, and still subjects, Guangzhou to martial law' and that it was only by Parkes keeping him fully acquainted with the situation that he could decide whether he should persevere in that policy. Elgin formalized the arrangements he had made with the provincial government. Bogui, the Governor of Guangdong, and his officials were recognized at a ceremony at which Elgin and Gros were present. The 'mixed government' was ignored by the emperor in Beijing and was to undergo constant sniping from local Chinese interests, and in time from London.

Elgin had been urged to use the opportunity provided by his capture of Guangzhou to punish its inhabitants as a reprisal for their previous breaches of the rules of war and of what was deemed to be uncivilized behaviour. However he chose to use the opportunity to present the Chinese with an example of just and efficient administration. In his journal he wrote 'No human power shall induce me to accept the office of oppressor of the feeble'.[29] The three commissioners took over the yamen of the Tartar General as their headquarters and scheduled a daily meeting at 8 a.m. to discuss the affairs of the city, after which one of them would see Bogui to discuss any matters requiring his attention. Arrangements were made to raise a police force from the battalions occupying the city, originally to be composed of forty English and twenty French soldiers. Its members would receive extra pay, and would carry out regular patrols through the streets. This force was supplemented by 700 Chinese soldiers and 600 braves, presumably militia, the former to police the city and the latter the suburbs. Steps were taken to inform the inhabitants of the arrangements which had been made and to encourage them to return to their homes and to resume their normal activities. Particular emphasis was placed on ensuring the good conduct of the allied forces. The Chinese were forbidden to sell spirits to soldiers and accusations of looting were taken seriously. Nevertheless, it soon became apparent that the misbehaviour of the British and French troops continued to cause apprehension among the inhabitants.

That the Commission was intent on enforcing the law was made plain on 13 January when a marine who the previous day had been seized in the act of robbing a Chinese was put on trial before the Commissioners, an event which attracted the attention of many Chinese. The Commissioners found him guilty and sent him to the commander-in-chief, who decided on the punishment to be inflicted. This was fixed at four dozen lashes, and the sentence was carried out in the courtyard of the governor's yamen.[30] On 19 February 1858 a proclamation was issued advising any Chinese who had suffered intrusion from foreign troops to report the matter immediately to the nearest patrol. On 25 January the British commissioners issued detailed instructions to the English police, which called for them to direct their attention:

. . . to the condition of the streets, the closing or opening of shops, the demeanour of Chinese towards foreigners; and they will take careful note of those places where they finds heaps of filth, or unburied coffins, deposited, and will direct the linguist of the station to require the Tepaou of the ward to see to their removal; when this is not done, the neglect of the Tepaou will be reported to the Commissioners.

And they added optimistically:

If during the occupation of Guangzhou the affairs of the city, in so far as the allies are concerned, be wisely, temperately, and firmly administered, I am not without hope that the people at its close may regret our departure. In that event a result will have been achieved of great importance, which will confer credit on all who have a share in bringing it about.[31]

Despite his involvement in these arrangements, Parkes was critical of Elgin's decision to reinstall Bogui and to administer Guangzhou through a mixed government, and of other examples of what he regarded as weakness, and he wrote privately to Edmund Hammond, the Permanent Secretary at the Foreign Office, expressing these misgivings:

The Guangzhou people appear completely perplexed; not less with the policy of their own Government than that of the Allies. That a city should be captured then at once given back into the hands of its former Government is a circumstance wholly without precedent in their annals, and they scarcely know how to regard the fact. I doubt whether they consider it a mark of strength on our part.[32]

In a letter to his brother-in-law, the missionary Dr W. Lockhart, Parkes criticized Elgin and the arrangements that he had sanctioned:

The chief thing that disconcerts me is our China policy. Generally it is a weak one, and gives no promise of any great success. Lord Elgin I do not consider a *great man*. He may be a man that suits the Government well, very cautious, having ever before him Europe, Parliament, the World, the Public, etc. It is with him, What will these parties say to this or that? and not What is best suited to the emergency? Conciliation, mildness, etc., etc., is with him therefore the order of the day: it will quiet the House, it will satisfy the British Public, etc., etc.; and in truth, seeing how poor Sir John Bowring caught it by the said public and his Parliamentary friends for doing the best thing he ever did do (next to the Siamese Treaty), and acting vigorously, a public man has not much encouragement in these parts. . . .

Here we have a slippery customer in Bogui, and the good that should have resulted to us from the capture of the city is negatived in no small degree by what has occurred since. He is playing off the 'braves' and the villagers against us as of old, and the consequence is that no one is safe a mile from the city. And how do you think that this is met by *Plenipotentiaries*? *By ordering that no one should go a mile from the city*! and by directing that a savage attack on a party of thirty-five officers and men which took place in a village six miles from Guangzhou shall be passed unnoticed!! Oh for the time when one may be able to bid adieu to official life, and take to growing cabbages![33]

In March Elgin sailed north to bring direct pressure on the government in Beijing. Around Guangzhou, with the secret approval of the emperor, gentry leaders formed the Guangdong Central Militia Bureau and started a resistance movement which harassed the foreign occupying forces and the complicit civilian population of the city. In July the movement made an unsuccessful attempt at recapturing Guangzhou.[34] The activities of the gentry gave support to those who had argued that Elgin's treatment of Guangzhou had been too lenient. In July 1858 the Earl of Malmesbury, the new Secretary of State for Foreign Affairs, stated bluntly that the 'mixed government' of Guangzhou was 'wholly inefficient for all objects of administration and policy' and he ordered that it should be replaced by 'a military government acting according to the rules of martial law'. Four months later Elgin replied that the mixed government was merely an expedient to enable the commanders-in-chief to govern a vast population 'with whose manners and language they are of course wholly unacquainted'.[35] In fact the commissioners' administration of the city created what has been described as a 'social protectorate', which not only attempted to introduce the principles of sound urban administration, but also broke up the coolie trade and stopped the oppressive taxation of Guangzhou shopkeepers.[36]

Two other steps taken by Elgin touch on aspects of the ethics of war. One was the imposition of a naval blockade of the trade of Guangzhou. The principles associated with this type of commercial warfare had been defined as recently as 1856 in the Declaration of Paris, which permitted blockades but which also declared that blockades, 'in order to be binding, must be effective'.[37] The allies clearly did not have enough ships to achieve this and trade was never entirely suppressed. Elgin soon lifted the blockade of the river, a step which was greeted with greater enthusiasm by the commercial interests than by the commanders of the armed forces.[38]

On 31 January, in the interests of investigating the whereabouts of missing Europeans, Elgin visited two of the Guangzhou prisons. He was shocked and disgusted by what he saw, but concluded that the squalor and maltreatment of prisoners was the result of neglect rather than cruelty.[39] When news of the conditions of the Guangzhou prisons reached England, Elgin, who had initiated the visit, was criticized for allowing such conditions to persist in a city under allied control. Malmesbury, the new Secretary of State for Foreign Affairs, was supplied with a report on the state of the prisons compiled by a missionary named Lobschied. He wrote to Elgin saying that 'it will be a disgrace to the allied Powers not to avail themselves of the present opportunity to liberate, or, at all events, to alleviate the position of, the unfortunate creatures confined in these prisons'.[40]

As Elgin moved north he called at the treaty ports along the coast and stopped for some time at Shanghai. He had proposed to Baron Gros that they should rendezvous with their forces at the mouth of the Bei river which gave access to Tianjin and the approaches to Beijing. On 15 April the Dagu forts controlling the estuary were silenced and the expedition moved up river. The Chinese government now felt compelled to negotiate and in the ensuing dealings Elgin assumed the character of the 'uncontrollably fierce barbarian', treating the Chinese envoys in a peremptory fashion and bullying them until the terms of a treaty, the Treaty of Tianjin, had been agreed.

ELGIN'S SECOND MISSION AND THE BURNING OF THE SUMMER PALACE

When the British and French diplomats returned to north China the following year to ratify the Treaty of Tianjin, they were driven back at the Dagu forts. The Chinese action was denounced in the British parliament as perfidy and as further proof of the treacherous nature of the Chinese. The repulse led to the dispatch of a much larger expedition in 1860 to force the Chinese to accept the settlement.

When Elgin reluctantly agreed to head this second mission to China, he was aware that the slightest suspicion of weakness on his part would be seized upon by his critics. On his return to Xianggang in June 1860 he received Harry Parkes, who was still acting as Commissioner in Guangzhou. Parkes recorded telling Elgin that the 'Chinese questions' were promising to give greater trouble than ever before and that our 'mild undecided policy' had had much to do with this. He thought that Elgin must feel that matters must 'now be promptly arranged' or they would become very serious.[41]

With these thoughts still in his mind, Elgin, accompanied by Gros, landed near Tianjin at the end of July 1860. The large forces at their disposal captured the town of Beitang and outflanked and seized the Dagu forts. Almost immediately the Chinese began negotiations and agreed to a treaty which gave the Western powers additional concessions. At the same time discussions were held about how the Treaty of Tianjin should be ratified, an event which was to take place in Beijing.

As the expeditionary force advanced towards Tongzhou, thirty miles east of Beijing, a group of British and French diplomats, including Harry Parkes and a journalist for *The Times*, and escorted by some British and French soldiers and twenty Indian cavalrymen, was cut off from the main force by a large detachment of Chinese troops. On 18 September Parkes, Henry Loch, Elgin's private secretary, and a Sikh soldier, displaying a white flag, went ahead to secure the safe passage of the main group, but they were seized and taken to the Chinese commander-in-chief, the famous Mongol soldier Prince Senggelinqin. The rest of the party was made prisoner later. According to Parkes' account members of his group were buffeted and kicked, even though he had pointed out to Senggelinqin that he should pay the same respect to an English flag of truce that the English had always paid to those so repeatedly sent in by the Chinese.[42] The members of the party were now made prisoners and taken to Beijing, where they were clapped into irons and subjected to further abuse. Those who survived were released three weeks later.

In the meantime, the collapse of negotiations had prompted Elgin to take further military action. He had warned the Chinese authorities that if any harm befell the prisoners, severe punishment would be imposed. The Chinese government replied that any onward move would be the signal for the prisoners' execution. Elgin concluded that the only chance of saving the prisoners' lives was to concentrate on the main objective of the campaign, and he informed the Chinese authorities that he would sign no convention with the Imperial Commissioners except within the walls of Beijing, and that if the prisoners were put to death, he would destroy that city.[43] The allied forces advanced on Beijing and threatened to storm the walls if the imperial authorities did not open the gates.

On 6 October 1860 the Allied troops took up quarters in the Old Summer Palace, an eighty-square-mile park some two miles north-west of Beijing. Those Westerners who in the past had visited the palace had been entranced by the beauty of its buildings and the harmony of its setting. It had originally been laid out in the twelfth century, but in the eighteenth century it had been transformed by Jesuit missionaries into a 'miniature Versailles'. At first the allied commanders tried to prevent looting – a restraint which only lasted a few hours. Subsequent charges and counter-charges were laid on whether it was the French or the British troops who had started to plunder. When Elgin and Gros, the French plenipotentiary, arrived they condemned what had occurred. Elgin said 'I would like a great many things the Palace contains, but I am not a thief.'[44] But the looting had to be sanctioned and it was regularized by arranging an auction of the plundered goods and distributing the proceeds among the soldiers.

Twenty days after their capture the surviving prisoners were released. As soon as possible they were asked to report on the treatment they had received and the fate of the prisoners who had succumbed. Henry Loch produced his report on 9 October. His ill-treatment had been confined to the day of his capture and his account was therefore somewhat restrained. Furthermore, he was in relatively good health. However, on 13 October Elgin received reports from two Indian soldiers of Fane's Horse. One of them, Jowalla Sing [sic], described the treatment that he himself had received, and he also gave details of the manner of the death of his European officer, Lieutenant Anderson. Like the others, on capture Anderson had been tightly bound and given scarcely any food:

> After the first day at the second place [outside the king's palace, about three miles from Beijing], Lieutenant Anderson became delirious and remained so, with a few lucid intervals, until his death, which occurred on the ninth day of his imprisonment. Two days before his death his nails and fingers burst from the tightness of the cords, and mortification set in, and the bones of his wrist were exposed. While he was alive worms were generated in his wounds, and eat [sic] into and crawled over his body. They left the body there three days and then took it away.[45]

In time it was established that twenty-one of the thirty-nine prisoners had died in captivity. Further details about what had happened were supplied by Harry Parkes, whose lengthy report was widely circulated, appearing, for example, in the *Illustrated London News*.

By now the military campaign was nearly completed and the plenipotentiaries' next task was to reach, or to impose, a diplomatic settlement. However, the gross breach of diplomatic protocol with regard to the seizure of Parkes and his party while displaying a flag of truce, and the explicit reports about the abuse the captives had suffered, ensured that Elgin could not fail to make a severe response. He suspected that the Chinese court might have regarded the arrest of the prisoners as a successful measure, in that it had paralysed the movement of the allies and had gratified the resentment of the emperor, without entailing any specific penalty. This suspicion led Elgin to remark that:

> Low as is the standard of morals which now obtains in China on such points, we should in my opinion have still further lowered it if we had not treated the act in question as a high crime calling for severe retribution.[46]

Elgin now had to decide on the form the reprisal should take, while bearing in mind that preferably it should be acceptable to Baron Gros. Elgin had been advised by his military commanders that the campaign should be wound up within two weeks, as it was not deemed practical to keep an allied force in the vicinity of Beijing through the impending winter. The retribution had therefore to be sufficiently severe to produce the required effect, yet capable of rapid execution, so as not to delay the conclusion of the peace treaties beyond 1 November. He considered greatly increasing the indemnity imposed on China under the treaty, but decided that, as it had already been increased, a further indemnity would cripple the imperial revenues of China and place an additional burden on the Chinese people, who were not responsible for what had happened.

There was the possibility of demanding further territorial concessions, but if a concession were to be obtained, this might lead to international complications. Elgin weighed up the arguments for demanding the surrender and punishment of the individuals guilty of the violation of the flag of truce and the cruelty to the prisoners, but concluded that if the Chinese were presented with a general demand they would merely send 'some miserable subordinates'. They would never surrender the truly guilty persons, that is to say Senggelinqin and the Prince of Yi, without a degree of compulsion which was not available. Moreover Elgin considered that the Chinese practice of throwing responsibility for the acts of government onto individuals too closely resembled the Chinese mode of conducting war.[47] It had been suggested to Elgin that he should burn Beijing itself, but he rejected that option on the grounds that the inhabitants had done nothing wrong. The destruction of the Forbidden City, the emperor's palace within the city, was embargoed because the safety of public buildings in the capital had been guaranteed under the terms agreed when the allies had entered Beijing. Elgin suggested the erection of a monument to commemorate the act of treachery which the Chinese had committed, but Gros objected. The only punishment the two representatives did agree upon was the payment of an indemnity to the prisoners who had survived and to the families of those who had died. This was fixed at 300,000 taels for the twenty-six English and 200,000 taels for the thirteen French.

It was only after having rejected other courses of action that Elgin decided upon the destruction of the Summer Palace. He justified this decision on various grounds. As Elgin believed that the emperor was 'clearly responsible for the crime committed' and the Summer Palace was the emperor's favourite residence, he considered that to destroy it would be particularly hurtful both to his pride and to his feelings. Elgin had been told that De Normann, the attaché to his brother the Hon. Frederick Bruce, and some other prisoners, had been taken in the first instance to the Summer Palace, where the ill-treatment began which resulted in their deaths. Some articles of their clothing had been found in the rooms adjoining the Hall of Audience, and their horses and saddles had been recovered from the stables.[48] The palace had already been looted and, as most of the valuables had already been removed, the army would go there 'not to pillage, but to mark, by a solemn act of retribution, the horror and indignation with which we were inspired by the perpetration of a great crime'.

However, when Elgin indicated that his choice was to destroy the Summer Palace, he found that Baron Gros, the French plenipotentiary, objected on the grounds that the building had no strategic importance. Gros's preference was the destruction of the Forbidden City, but said that that should be contingent on the failure of negotiations. The British and French military commanders, whose troops would be called upon to carry out the destruction, echoed the views of their plenipotentiaries. General Montauban, the French military commander, characterized the proposal as an act of vandalism unlikely to produce the result intended. As a result the French contingent distanced itself from the action. On the other hand, General Hope Grant, the British commander, reiterated that the destruction of the Forbidden City would contravene the agreement which had been reached when the allies entered Beijing. He therefore favoured the alternative plan of destroying the Summer Palace. This view was echoed by Harry Parkes, who observed that the Manchu court had lately spent two-thirds of its time at the Summer Palace and that his countrymen had been put to the torture there by direction of the court itself.[49] The argument that it would be 'a ruthless act to destroy so much that was rare, beautiful, and valuable' was countered on the British side by claiming that the palace had already been looted and that there was nothing kept there which was unique in the shape of books and manuscripts.

The order therefore was given for the systematic destruction by fire of the 200-odd buildings which made up the Summer Palace. Lord Elgin wrote to Prince Gong, who now represented the Chinese government, informing him of the decision, and he caused proclamations in Chinese to be displayed which declared:

> That no individual, however exalted, could escape from the responsibility and punishment which must always follow the commission of acts of falsehood and deceit; that [the Summer Palace] would be burnt on the 18th, as a punishment inflicted on the Emperor for the violation of his word, and the act of treachery to a flag of truce; that as the people were not concerned in these acts no harm would befall them, but the Imperial Government alone would be held responsible.[50]

The Revd M'Ghee, the chaplain to the British forces, who condoned the decision and witnessed its execution, reflected:

> It was a sacrifice of all that was most ancient and beautiful, but it was offered to the manes of the true, the honest, and the valiant, and it was not too costly, oh, no! one of such lives was worth it all. It is gone, but I do not know how to tear myself from it. I love to linger over the recollection and to picture to myself, but I cannot make you see it. A man must be a poet, a painter, an historian, a virtuoso, A Chinese scholar, and I don't know how many other things besides, to give you even an idea of it, and I am not an approach to any one of them. But whenever I think of beauty and taste, of skill and antiquity, while I live, I shall see before my mind's eye some scene from those grounds, those palaces, and ever regret the stern but just necessity which laid them in ashes.[51]

On 24 October 1860 Elgin entered Beijing accompanied by a strong escort and with the streets lined with British troops. There he signed the British version of the Convention of Beijing. The following day Baron Gros repeated the entry and signed the French version of the same convention. The two agreements contained articles added in response to the seizure and mistreatment of British and French subjects. The British convention provided for the cession in perpetuity of the Jiulong (Kowloon) peninsula opposite Xianggang. The French convention, in its French version, provided for the return of the property of Christian establishments which had been confiscated during the period of persecution. To the Chinese version was attached an additional clause which made it lawful for French missionaries to buy land or build houses in the interior of China. The Chinese authorities always insisted that this clause had been added surreptitiously[52]

When news of Elgin's action in burning the Summer Palace reached Europe, it was greeted with a mixed reaction. In France it was criticized as an act of vandalism, and criticisms were also voiced in the British press and regrets were expressed by members of the Cabinet. However, Palmerston, now Prime Minister, gave Elgin his robust support. He wrote:

> I am heartily glad that Elgin and Grant determined to burn down the Summer Palace, and that the blackness of the ashes shall mark where it stood. . . . [it was] absolutely necessary to stamp by some permanent record our indignation at the treachery and brutality of these Tartars, for Chinese they are not.[53]

When Elgin returned to London, he fulfilled a number of public engagements, including being the guest of honour at the annual dinner of the Royal Academy, on which occasion Sir Hope Grant, his commander-in-chief in China, was also present. When Elgin spoke after the dinner he began by thanking the academicians for drinking his health and added:

> I trust I may infer from it that in your judgment Sir, and in that of this company, I am not so incorrigibly barbarous as to be incapable of feeling the humanising influences which fall upon us from the noble works of art by which we are surrounded.

He then approached the 'burning question', asserting:

> . . . no one regretted more sincerely than I did the destruction of that collection of summer-houses and kiosks, already, and previously to any act of mine, rifled of their contents, which was dignified by the title of Summer Palace of the Chinese Emperor. But when I had satisfied myself that in no

other way, except, indeed, by inflicting on this country and on China, the calamity of another year of war, could I mark the sense which I entertained, which the British army entertained . . . and which, moreover, I make bold in the presence of this company to say, the people of this country entertained – of an atrocious crime, which, if it had passed unpunished, would have placed in jeopardy the life of every European in China, I felt that the time had come when I must choose between the indulgence of a not unnatural sensibility and the performance of a painful duty.[54]

CONCLUSION: THE ETHICS OF WAR

Elgin's dilemmas over the capture of Guangzhou and the burning of the Summer Palace came at a time when the issue of the ethics of war was beginning to be debated in Europe. They also came soon after the Indian Mutiny had encouraged a strident racism which justified discriminatory treatment of those who belonged to what Elgin himself called the 'inferior races'.

Elgin was certainly aware of the ethical issues raised during his missions to China, and in particular over the capture of Guangzhou and the burning of the Summer Palace, two incidents which he admitted had placed him in a moral dilemma. The decisions he took on each occasion were shaped by a variety of pressures, which included the need to satisfy his Christian conscience and to fulfil what he regarded as his public duty. It was important that he should retain the confidence of the armed forces and continue to cooperate with the French. Matters of expediency and military necessity could not be ignored. From the time of his arrival in Guangzhou he had been made aware of the strength of the demand from the European community for vigorous action, implying the setting aside of ethical considerations in favour of teaching the Chinese a lesson. The advice of China-Coast experts, the attentions of the press, instructions from London, all encouraged him to choose severity rather than lenity. Western views of the character of the Chinese and the trustworthiness of the Manchu court, views which he ignored at his peril, were almost entirely negative. It might be argued that Elgin's desire to pursue an ethical policy, most evident during his first mission, was influenced by these pressures and that on the second mission he became less patient, more determined to take decisive action, hoping thereby to complete his task swiftly and return home promptly.

Nevertheless, Elgin did feel it necessary to justify his actions, and his sensitivity to the ethical issues which were being raised is clear enough. With regard to the occupation of Guangzhou, it appears that he rejected advice to use terror to intimidate the population, and instead chose to try to win over the inhabitants of the city through a demonstration of principled administration. When it came to the burning of the Summer Palace, his calculations were utilitarian.

No direct link is suggested between what he said and did on those occasions and the attempt to define the law concerning the conduct of war which followed soon after. However, his actions were widely reported in the European press and those who were to initiate the process of formalizing international agreements on the ethics of war would have been aware of them.[55]

Notes

1   M.H. Keen, *The Laws of War in the Late Middle Ages* (London, Routledge & Kegan Paul, 1965), p. 2.

2   William Shakespeare, *King Henry the Fifth*, Act IV, Scenes vi–vii.

3   C.T. Hsia, *The Classic Chinese Novel* (Bloomington, Indiana University Press, 1980), p. 96.

4   Quoted in Geoffrey Best, *Humanity in Warfare: The Modern History of the International Law of Armed Conflicts* (London, Methuen, 1983), p. 36.

5   Voltaire (François Marie Arouet), *Candide or Optimism* (tr. John Butt) (Harmondsworth, Penguin Books, 1956), pp. 25–6.

6   Quoted in Best, *Humanity in Warfare*, p. 13.

7   R.B. Brandt, 'Utilitarianism and the Rules of War', in Marshall Cohen *et al.* (eds), *War and Moral Responsibility* (Princeton, NJ, Princeton University Press, 1974), pp. 25–45.

8   Chinese names are given in *pinyin*, but the more familiar form of the name is given in brackets when used for the first time.

9   W.C. Costin, *Great Britain and China, 1833–60* (Oxford, Oxford University Press, 1937, repr. 1968), pp. 149–50.

10 Hosea Ballou Morse, *The International Relations of the Chinese Empire* (3 vols, New York, Longmans, Green Co., 1910–18, repr. New York, Paragon Book Gallery, no date), vol. 1, p. 436.

11 Quoted in Harley Farnsworth MacNair (ed.), *Modern Chinese History: Selected Readings* (1923, Paragon Book Reprint, New York, 1967), p. 250.

12 Theodore Walrond (ed.), *Letters and Journals of James, Eighth Earl of Elgin* (London, John Murray, 1873), pp. 2–6.

13 Jack Beeching, *The Chinese Opium Wars* (London, Hutchinson, 1975), p. 238.

14 Walrond (ed.), *Letters and Journals*, p. 26.

15 Ibid., p. 96.

16 Laurence Oliphant, *Narrative of the Earl of Elgin's Mission to China and Japan in the Years 1857, '58, '59* (2 vols, Edinburgh, William Blackwood and Sons, 1859) repr. with an introduction by J.J. Gerson (London, Oxford University Press, 1979), vol. 1, p. vii.

17 British Parliamentary Papers, *Correspondence Relative to the Earl of Elgin's Special Missions to China and Japan, 1857–1859*, Address to the Earl of Elgin from Jardine, Matheson & Co. and 85 others, 8 July 1857.

18 George Wingrove Cooke, *China: Being 'The Times' Special Correspondence from China in the Years 1857–58* (London, G. Routledge & Co., 1858), p. 389.

19 C. Worswick and J. Spence, *Imperial China: Photographs 1850–1912* (London, 1979), p. 84.

20 Walrond (ed.), *Letters and Journals*, p. 199.

21 Michael Edwardes, *Red Year: The Indian Rebellion of 1857* (London, Hamish Hamilton, 1973), p. 121.

22 Walrond (ed.), *Letters and Journals*, p. 199.

23 Ibid., p. 210.

24 Ibid., p. 212.

25 Cooke, *China*, pp. 310–9.

26 Walrond (ed.), *Letters and Journals*, p. 214.

27 Ibid., p. 215.

28 Cooke, *China*, p. 345.

29 Walrond (ed.), *Letters and Journals*, p. 220.

30 *Correspondence, 1857–1859*, Minute of the Commissioners, enclosed in the Earl of Elgin to the Earl of Clarendon, 13 January 1859.

31 *Correspondence, 1857–1859*, Consul Parkes to the Earl of Elgin, 27 January 1858; General Orders for the English Police, 25 January 1858, enclosed in the Earl of Elgin to the Earl of Clarendon, 27 January 1858.

32 Stanley Lane-Poole, *Sir Harry Parkes in China* (London, Methuen, 1901, repr. Paragon Book Gallery Ltd, New York, no date), p. 177.

33 Lane-Poole, *Sir Harry Parkes*, p. 177.

34 Frederic Wakeman, Jr., *Strangers at the Gate: Social Disorder in South China, 1839–1861* (Berkeley, University of California Press, 1966), pp. 164–72.

35 *Correspondence, 1857–1859*, the Earl of Malmesbury to the Earl of Elgin, 2 July 1858; the Earl of Elgin to the Earl of Malmesbury, 5 November 1858.

36 Wakeman, *Strangers at the Gate*, p. 174.

37 Best, *Humanity in Warfare*, p. 213.

38 Alexander Michie, *The Englishman in China During the Victorian Era: As Illustrated in the Life of Sir Rutherford Alcock, K.C.B., D.C.L.* (2 vols, London, 1900, Taipei, 1966), vol 1, pp. 322–3.

39 Walrond (ed.), *Letters and Journals*, p. 223.

40 *Correspondence, 1857–1859*, the Earl of Malmesbury to the Earl of Elgin, 14 June 1858.

41 Lane-Poole, *Sir Harry Parkes*, pp. 204–5.

42 This failure to respect a white flag was, in British eyes, a *prima facie* breach of the rules of war. The use of a white flag to indicate that the bearer came forward to negotiate, not to fight, was a well-established convention, which had been used frequently during the revolutionary and Napoleonic wars. Best, *Humanity in Warfare*, p. 124.

43 Henry Brougham Loch, *Personal Narrative of Occurrences During Lord Elgin's Second Embassy to China, 1860* (London, John Murray, 1869), pp. 245–6.

44 Beeching, *Chinese Opium Wars*, p. 318.

45 British Parliamentary Papers, *Correspondence Respecting Affairs in China, 1859–60*, the Earl of Elgin to Lord J. Russell, 13 October 1860.

46 *Correspondence, 1859–1860*, the Earl of Elgin to Lord J. Russell, 25 October 1860.

47 After the Boxer uprising, the Allied powers demanded the surrender of senior officials held responsible for encouraging the Boxers to attack westerners. As a result a number of officials were executed or forced to commit suicide and others were banished or degraded. Immanuel C.Y. Hsü, 'Late Ch'ing foreign relations, 1866–1905', in Denis Twitchett and John K. Fairbank (eds), *The Cambridge History of China*, 11 (Cambridge, Cambridge University Press, 1980), pp. 70–141.

48 Loch, *Personal Narrative*, p. 268.

49 Lane-Poole, *Sir Harry Parkes*, p. 251.

50 Loch, *Personal Narrative*, pp. 271–2.

51 Revd R. Th. M'Ghee, *How We Got to Pekin* (London, 1862), quoted in MacNair, *Modern Chinese History*, p. 317.

52 Morse, *International Relations*, vol. 1, pp. 615–16.

53 Palmerston to Sidney Herbert, 20 December 1860, quoted in Jasper Ridley, *Lord Palmerston*, (London, Panther Books Limited, 1970), p. 723.

54 Walrond (ed.), *Letters and Journals*, pp. 391–2.

55 As an example of how such influence might be exerted, see the suggestion made by H.B. Loch that Lord Napier's conduct with reference to the release of prisoners during the Abyssinian campaign of 1867 might have been influenced by his experience in China, when he served as second-in-command to General Hope Grant. Loch, *Personal Narrative*, p. 246.

6

Conservative Electoral Strategy, Creating Political Stability and the Advent of Mass Democracy, 1914–18

Andrew Taylor

In happy states, the Conservative party must rule upon the whole a much longer time than their adversaries. In well-framed polities, innovation – great innovation that is – can only be occasional. If you are always altering your house, it is a sign that you have a bad house, or that you have an excessively restless disposition – there is something wrong somewhere.

W. Bagehot, *The Chances for a Long Conservative Régime in England* (1874)

The Architecture of Political Stability

The Conservative attitude to mass democracy was not altered fundamentally by the First World War. The Conservatives' traditional response of delay remained in place but the circumstances in which it was conducted were far more complex than before August 1914. It was perhaps fortunate that politicians were accustomed to dealing with a crisis of the state and the disruption of the party system as both were features of pre-war politics. The political consequences of the war for domestic politics can be overstated even though the Fourth Reform Act of 1918 transformed electoral politics. The electorate exploded from 7.6 million (1910) to 21.7 million; from 28 per cent of the population, the franchise increased to 78 per cent, of whom 40 per cent were women and 20 per cent men who would not have had the vote before 1914. Pre-1914 domestic politics were concerned with finding a new equilibrium; post-1914 politics were also concerned with preserving the *status quo* and winning the war. The war was a catalyst which accelerated the pace of some changes but in many respects 'the war had a conservative or even reactionary effect which nullified changes which might otherwise have occurred.'[1]

The political structure devised to maintain equilibrium and win the war – the Lloyd George Coalition – proved untenable, which meant that the only structures available for the management of mass democracy were those of mass democracy itself. The beneficiary of these changes was not Lloyd George, nor even the Labour Party, but the Conservative Party as the supreme expression of party government and executive dominance, the twin buttresses of political stability.[2]

War represents the greatest test a political system can face. The 1914–1918 conflict raised doubts about the viability of British political institutions but this was not the first time this had occurred in British political history and the period covered by this chapter can be compared with 1689–1715. This was a period of instability from which emerged stability. The growth of a large political nation and frequent general elections in a concentrated period reflected a nation in flux and 'whatever their personal ambitions or intentions, politicians had to try to dominate a majority of that active voting political nation. This could only be done by the attitudes, ideas, and organization of party.' In both these periods Britain was embroiled in a continental war which 'called into being an executive far larger than England had ever known; an executive, moreover, that was inextricably linked with the legislative, and the growth of a large executive is as important to the political history of the period as the existence of a large electorate.'[3]

Political stability is 'the acceptance by a society of its institutions, and of those classes of men or officials who control them'. Political stability does not simply emerge; it 'becomes actual through the actions and decisions of men, as does revolution. Political stability, when it comes, often happens to a society quite quickly, as suddenly as water turns to ice.'[4] The creation of political stability is, therefore, the process whereby a society comes 'to accept a pattern of political authority and the institutions that are required for its translation into government'. In early eighteenth- and early twentieth-century Britain the same factors underpinned the growth of political stability: single-party government, a legislature firmly under control of the executive, and a common sense of identity between the governing élites. If united élites underpin political stability, it can be lost when institutions and élites under stress begin to fragment which means stability has to be renegotiated. Political stability is not a final end-state as politics is dynamic and the environment of British politics after 1906 was very stressful. Stability had to be renegotiated more or less continuously in a dynamic, liberal, democratic political system constantly interacting with a stressful environment.[5]

After 1906 Conservatives feared they were finally confronting the realities of mass democracy which encouraged some of them to urge the party to make a positive appeal to the working class to marginalize an independent working-class consciousness. The party did the opposite, becoming embroiled in bitter constitutional struggles. This Conservative failure to adapt has been ascribed to inept leadership, the social composition of the party and political irrationality. That the Conservatives *should* have made a positive appeal to the 'new democracy' is an assertion that has gone largely unchallenged.

This chapter has four sections. The first examines the 'new politics' thesis, the second the argument that for Conservatives to change their political strategy would have been an act of political irrationality; the third section examines the reassertion of the executive after 1916, and the fourth considers the impact of the war on Conservative electoral strategy. It also explores the Conservative Party's successful adaptation to a rapidly changing political environment and concludes that the main reason for this adaptation was a willingness to reassess established positions with little interference from ideology.

A DESTABILIZING POLITY?

The scale of defeat in 1906 convinced many Conservatives that a sea-change had occurred in British politics. Balfour wrote to Edward VII's private secretary that the election was much more 'than the swing of the pendulum'. He feared, 'We are face to face (no doubt in a milder form) with the Socialist difficulties which loom so large on the Continent. Unless I am greatly mistaken, the Election of 1906 inaugurates a new era.'[6] Defeat threw into sharp relief the exhaustion of Salisburian conservatism, an exhaustion revealed in the conflict over the Workmen's Compensation Act (1897) which expressed the tension within the party over social reform and conservatism's relationship with mass democracy.[7] Salisbury and Balfour have been blamed for not responding positively to the new politics: Salisbury's delaying tactics and Balfour's failure to reverse the Taff Vale decision have been interpreted as major political errors.[8] Salisbury and Balfour in refusing to bid for working-class votes contrasted with Disraeli or Lord Randolph Churchill who 'might have been alive to the significance of the new movements, and might have been skilful enough to demonstrate to the working classes that their true and permanent interests lay in not attempting to wreck the capitalist system, but in taking advantage of its immense underdeveloped possibilities'.[9]

Did ideological and political indolence prevent conservatism adapting to the new mass class-based politics? The National Union's Organization Committee agreement to mount a national campaign against Lloyd George's budget and Sir Robert Herman-Hodge's urging that the party concentrate the campaign on the industrial areas stressing how all classes would be affected by increased taxation has been seen as an example of the party seeking to break out of the electoral laager of late nineteenth-century conservatism.[10] Conservative organizations in industrial areas had a difficult job reconciling traditional Conservative issues with the demands of the 'new' politics. Yorkshire Conservatives, for example, noted that since 1906 'the Government have attacked all Classes of property, Capital has left the Country, the value of property has been diminished, and enormous burdens have been placed on industrial and landed interests.' As a result, 'Antagonism has been stirred up between Class and Class.' The Conservative appeal was 'to all those who value a United Kingdom, the sanctity of religious endowments and the welfare of the Working Classes'.[11] When a serious attempt was made to respond to 'new politics' after 1903 with tariff reform, the party split.

After 1906 socialism was the enemy but 'the stumbling block of Unionism, radical or conservative, throughout the Edwardian period was its relationship with organized labour, as distinct from the various vague appeals to "the working-class" or Tory Democracy'.[12] Despite a proven ability to win working-class votes the 1906 election suggested Conservatism was increasingly vulnerable as the electorate 'had at last become conscious of themselves and their powers, and had begun to organise themselves in trade unions and in labour representation committees. . . . They had begun, too, to formulate demands that lay outside the programme of both the old parties.'[13] Many Conservatives believed that if the party was 'ever to regain its former position . . . it must reconstitute itself more in harmony with the 20th century requirements of a thoroughly up-to-date Democracy'. The electorate was 'no longer dependent on what it [was] told by the publican over a mug of beer' so Conservatives must 'drop the entire fiscal bogey, and seek to re-unite the party on a strong policy of social reform'.[14] There was, critics of the leadership argued, no inevitable link between social reform and socialism: judicious reform would unite the nation and strangle socialism.

Conservatives had grounds for concern. In 1900 the Labour Representation Committee (LRC) polled 63,304 (1.8 per cent of the total votes cast) but in 1903 Liberal–Labour cooperation was enshrined in the Gladstone–MacDonald Pact. This helped Labour increase its vote to 329,748 (5.9 per cent of the total vote) electing 30 MPs in the 1905/06 general election; in February 1910 this increased to 505,657 votes (7.6 per cent) and 40 MPs; and although its vote fell to 371,772 (7.1 per cent) in December it secured 2 more MPs. Despite Labour's dependence on cooperation with the Liberal Party and its relatively small number of MPs many Conservatives saw these results as a portent. This increase in the strength of parliamentary socialism was all the more threatening because of union domination of the Parliamentary Labour Party (PLP). One year after the founding of the LRC on the initiative of the TUC 41 unions with a total membership of 353,000 were affiliated, in 1906 the figures were 158 unions with 904,000 members. After 1906 an increasing number of unions (including the miners in 1909) were affiliating to the Labour Party and by 1910 151 unions with 1,394,000 members were affiliated. In 1910 39 of the PLP's 42 MPs (92.8 per cent) were union sponsored.

Conservatives had long believed that the organization and mobilization of working-class political power would influence public policy. Between 1906 and 1914 the Liberal government passed eleven major statutes which stemmed directly from 'the condition of England question' as well as the Parliament Act (1911) that instituted salaries for MPs of which working-class MPs were the obvious beneficiaries. This legislation also increased the size of the state bureaucracy which at the lower levels drew on trade union expertise. Between 1906 and 1912 the Board of Trade, for example, employed 117 union members, 124 joined the National Insurance Department, 48 the Home Office, and 85 were employed in other parts of the civil service. In 1912 Bonar Law charged the Liberals with using state patronage to win working-class support and curry favour with the unions.[15]

The trade unions had long been perceived as a political threat but the scale of labour unrest seemed to presage Salisbury's fear of a trade union despotism. Union membership grew from 1.9 million to 2.02 million (1900–2), declining to 1.6 million (1906), and then it recovered to 2.4/2.5 million by 1910, expanding dramatically from 2.5 million to 4.1 million (1911–14). The number of union members affiliated to the TUC grew by 982,000 (43.9 per cent) between 1900 and 1914 while the number of union members grew by 2.2 million (53.6 per cent). This differential is important because TUC-affiliated unions were regarded as the most moderate, so union growth outside the TUC implied the emergence of a more militant trade unionism. Fourteen major strikes between 1911 and 1914 accounted for 51 million out of 71 million working days lost and one (the coal strike of February to April 1912) involved 1 million workers and cost 30.8 million working days. Strikes seemed to be becoming increasingly national, threatening entire industries and designed to coerce the state.

There were sections within Conservative ranks who supported making a positive appeal for working-class votes.[16] A major obstacle to such an appeal was the party's social composition and internal power structure. Despite frequent urgings that the party select working-class MPs, nothing was done and Central Office could do nothing to promote working-class candidates given the constituency associations' autonomy. The Conservatives also resisted the state payment of MPs which would directly benefit working-class political representation. Even if there had been any desire on the part of the leadership to democratize the party as a whole or widen the social composition of the parliamentary party (which there was not), Balfour was far more concerned with maintaining unity in the conflict resulting from tariff reform and resisting Lloyd George. An effective response, Dutton argues, could have been provided by a programme of moderate social reform easily justified by an appeal to Disraelian politics (so calming internal party fears), but Balfour remained 'curiously unresponsive'. The Conservative failure to formulate a positive response inevitably led it, by default, to *laissez-faire* and obstructionism. Milner's judgement was that 'The Unionist Party, with *The Times*, I am sorry to say, at the head, were all "rushing violently down a steep place" into the bog of a purely Conservative narrow middle-class and negative policy'.[17]

Historians have tended to assume, therefore, that the party's lack of interest in social reform was a serious and avoidable political error.[18] Is this in fact the case? Conservatives developed a distinctive approach to social policy which had an impact on the *Campaign Guide* prepared for the 1915 General Election, while the Unionist Social Reform Committee (USRC), an unofficial policy study group founded in 1911, produced several reports on social questions. The USRC was a diverse group united by a desire to professionalize and modernize Conservative social politics and policy and after 1910 many Conservative MPs were attracted by a distinctive brand of Tory social reformism clearly different from both Lloyd Georgism and socialism.[19] The USRC justified its approach by reference to Disraeli and Tory democracy but was also influenced by Fabian socialism and state intervention. Neither Fabianism nor state intervention was likely to recommend the USRC to the party, neither was the Committee's desire to conciliate the unions likely to be welcomed at a time of industrial unrest. Not surprisingly the USRC aroused considerable disquiet in the party.[20]

The behaviour of the party leadership in these years is often couched in terms which accuse Bonar Law of irrationality. Blake sees the party's attitude as a reaction to the feeling that British politics were teetering on the brink of revolution and that 'it was their duty, through the House of Lords, to preserve the public from the consequences of its own folly till it came to its senses' and Jenkins portrays the Conservative motivation as an overwhelming drive to win power at any cost.[21] Dutton concludes that 'adaptation . . . was imperative . . . the Unionist party needed to cultivate a positive and popular appeal based on a forward policy'.[22] But is this so? Did adaptation to a new political environment require a 'forward' policy? Why then did the Conservatives not try to compete with the Liberals? Was the failure to adopt a social-Toryism politically irrational? The Conservative Party had in the past shown itself able to win working-class votes without a social reform programme. The strains of maintaining party unity proved too great and Balfour was in effect forced from the leadership and was replaced in 1911 by Andrew Bonar Law. If Balfour was 'curiously unresponsive' why was he succeeded by an even less responsive leader? Were the Conservatives behaving perversely, or was Bonar Law's succession a rational political response to the post-1910 political environment?

CONSERVATISM AND THE POLITICS OF ANTI-SOCIALISM

Andrew Bonar Law is an important figure in the development of the modern Conservative Party and has been described as 'the most formidable giant-killer of the century'.[23] A dour Scots-Canadian whose oratorical style was compared to the hammering of rivets, he had made his fortune in the Glasgow iron trade and was, in terms of Edwardian conservatism, a relative outsider. He has been justly described as 'The Unknown Prime Minister' and was said to care about only two political issues (tariff reform and Ulster), but this belies his importance.

In his study of Bonar Law's opposition to Home Rule, Smith rejects interpretations which attribute his behaviour to inexperience, miscalculation, opportunism, or irresponsibility and argues he pursued a sophisticated, effective political strategy intended to win the next election.[24] He had been elected leader unopposed after the withdrawal of Walter Long and Austen Chamberlain in the interests of party unity, and he maintained Balfour's strategy of resistance. The crucial difference was style: 'this melancholy teetotal widower . . . *met the needs of a demoralised party* better than Balfour. It was a matter of style not policy – bluntness, vigour and invective, instead of dialectic, urbanity and subtlety.' Balfour's resignation and Bonar Law's selection had an immediately beneficial effect on party morale. After the 13 November meeting at the Carlton Club, Bridgeman wrote 'we all parted with the feeling that "we are jolly good fellows" and so we really are'.[25] Bonar Law's concern was to position the Conservative Party so that it could benefit from the political climate which developed after the 1910 elections. When analysing Conservative strategy we should always remember that 1914 had no special significance for politicians or anyone else. Politicians had no idea that war would break out and they focused their attentions on 1915.[26]

Bonar Law's strategy derived from his conviction that 'for the Conservatives social reform was not on the whole a profitable line to pursue. If the country wanted more and better social reform it would not vote Conservative.'[27] This was a sentiment which commended itself to the party but what about the electorate? Although a tariff reformer, Bonar Law recognized that tariff reform (intended by Chamberlain as a positive appeal to the working class) had not only failed to win over the working class, it had cost votes and split the party. Bonar Law, none the less, was reluctant to abandon tariff reform entirely and confessed to Salisbury his 'real belief that in the troubles ahead of us connected with labour we are moving very fast in the direction of revolution'. He could see no clear means of averting this but still believed 'that it is by means of Tariff Reform that we might, so to speak, get the train for a time at least shifted on to other lines'.[28] Surveys established that constitutional issues and Ulster, which were of fundamental importance to the Conservative Party, held little electoral attraction except where anti-Catholic/anti-Irish sentiment was strong but they found considerable disquiet among Liberals of all classes with the Liberal government's policies and labour unrest.[29] Nearly thirty years ago Pelling demonstrated that social reform was not a major concern of working-class voters. Indeed, there was considerable popular suspicion of state intervention. This did not ease the Conservative difficulty. Bridgeman, for example, noted the National Insurance Bill 'is full of iniquities, and yet to vote against it will stop even the good part of it taking place and can of course be painted as a black crime of oppression of the poor by the rich in Lloyd George's best style'.[30]

Social historians have identified traits within the working class (and which permeated the class structure) that can be described as pro-Conservative. These traits were 'opposition to big capital and to big labour; the appeal from principle to common sense; hostility to the state; attachment to the close and familiar, whether in the context of neighbourhood, family, class, religion or moral values; an acceptance of the political *status quo*, coupled with a distrust of those who maintain it'.[31] It was therefore rational for Bonar Law to conclude that a positive appeal to working-class voters would antagonize the party and potential supporters without producing any significant gains. Bonar Law, however, did not deduce from this that the Conservative Party was on the verge of electoral marginalization.

Political developments after 1910 pointed to a Conservative revival, not decline, as Conservative losses of 1906 were recouped in the 1910 elections.[32] It was increasingly clear that the Labour and Liberal parties were neither natural nor inevitable allies, and that there were elements in both parties deeply hostile to the other, while Labour's MPs were of course swamped by the masses of Liberal MPs of whom only a small number could be described as 'advanced'.[33] Political reality and the party balance in the Commons meant that Labour had little option other than to cooperate with the Liberals as it could expect no concessions from a Conservative government. Dependence on the Liberals and by-election failures when faced with Liberal opposition pointed to Labour's inability to achieve electoral take-off. Conservative by-election gains in this period were substantial. Between the December 1910 general election and the outbreak of war there were twenty by-elections. In December 1910 these constituencies elected fifteen Liberals, three Labour and two Conservative MPs but the by-election results reveal an almost complete Conservative clean sweep. The Conservatives made fourteen gains from the Liberals, losing just one to them. Labour defended four seats and lost them all, three to the Liberals and one to the Conservatives. In one a Conservative was defeated by an Independent Conservative. The by-election evidence is that the Conservatives were winning the electoral battle and this makes Dutton's description of Conservative gains as a 'dead end' inexplicable.[34] As we shall see later, it was the Conservatives who were gaining ground at the municipal level and the fading of industrial unrest also increased Bonar Law's room for manoeuvre.[35] The failure of the London Dock Strike and the resolution of the miners' Minimum Wage Strike in 1912 marked the end of a cycle of industrial unrest. While the unrest strengthened Conservative suspicion of the unions, its fading eased the pressure on Bonar Law to 'do something' about the unions, enabling him to concentrate on Ulster and Home Rule. Industrial relations had stabilized so there was no need for a specifically Conservative response.

Bonar Law had secured the leadership as the unity candidate and recognized social reform was not acceptable to the bulk of the party. Smith points out that the Conservative Party in 1912 was not a happy party. It had suffered three election defeats and six years of radical legislation (with Home Rule and land reform about to follow) and it had forced Balfour's resignation. There was no clear alternative policy to resistance over Ulster which would unite the party: tariff reform had been shelved as utterly divisive and social reform would cause similar internal problems, so only Ulster remained as an issue capable of uniting Conservatives. When appointed a Whip in June 1911 Bridgeman felt the

Conservatives needed, above all else, a clear lead as 'we have a leader who does not appear to lead, and a lot of dissatisfied private members, each of whom have ideas of what our policy ought to be, but all of them different from each other'.[36] Bonar Law was temperamentally suited to providing a clear lead and defence of the Union provided his basic platform. Until he established his authority Bonar Law could do nothing to antagonize his party, hence his staunch defence of core Conservative issues which, of course, he found personally congenial. The Conservatives had recovered from the disaster of 1906 without a positive appeal and the 1910 elections demonstrated the existence of a considerable number of voters who were dismayed by events and might be lured towards conservatism.

Bonar Law's conviction that neither his strategy nor political developments were hostile to Conservative interests also influenced the overhaul of the party organization conducted by Arthur Steel-Maitland, although the process was initiated by Balfour. This had two purposes: first, it was designed to rationalize party structures so that the Conservatives could function as the focal point for anti-progressivism in British politics; and second, it was intended to recreate the efficiency of the 'Middleton Machine' which had proved crucial in securing and maintaining Salisbury's hegemony between 1886 and 1902.[37] Steel-Maitland's reforms were designed to improve the party's efficiency within the political *status quo*. Short-term campaigning would not win a secure Conservative vote; this required long-term propaganda – 'The socialists do not push matters just before an election, they keep digging at the people all the year round.'[38] The traditional tasks of party organization (voter registration and mobilization) were augmented with an emphasis on political education, propaganda and intelligence which was new to British politics.[39] These reforms further reflect Bonar Law's conviction that there was no need for the Conservatives to democratize and popularize.

The electoral potential of anti-socialism can be seen in Conservative successes in local government. Socialism in local politics posed a more immediate threat to Conservatives than socialism in national politics. London municipal politics provide an illustration. The London Municipal Society (LMS) took control of the London County Council (LCC) in 1907 using an aggressive anti-progressive propaganda campaign attacking high rates, financial mismanagement and municipal socialism. The LMS was also able to exploit changes in the composition of the electorate and patterns of party allegiance at a time when the loyalty of the London working class to Liberalism was weakening. Thus 'whenever Conservatives could be persuaded to turn out and vote for the LMS candidates at the LCC elections, they would provide a natural majority for Municipal Reform'.[40] Effective propaganda and voter mobilization required grass-roots organization, hence the vital importance of Steel-Maitland's organizational reforms. The Conservative local government effort inside and outside London was based on anti-socialism and an enormous amount of effort was devoted to placing this message before the electorate. By 1914 there was evidence that 'opposition to all forms of municipal "extravagance" began to earn electoral dividends' and there was no reason why this strategy should not work in national politics.[41]

It is true that the Conservative Party recognized it 'needed to show awareness of a mass working-class electorate'.[42] Virtually every section of the Conservative Party, from the 'wets' to 'radicals' such as Lord Willoughby de Broke, revealed such an awareness but the question that really matters is, what effect did this have on party policy? In her study of the USRC, Ridley notes that Bonar Law controlled closely the official policy-making machinery and the USRC was an unofficial body created to keep younger Conservative MPs occupied.[43] The USRC was, and remained, unofficial and as party leader, with the final say over policy, Bonar Law could pay as much or as little attention to it as he wished. The *Campaign Guide* did contain elements of a moderate social reform package but this was kept under wraps by Bonar Law. The reason why he did this is obvious: an early revelation of the contents of the *Campaign Guide* would have provoked internal controversy as well as a response from the Liberals perhaps forcing the leadership either to tone down its proposals or make changes. Political developments did not require the publication of such a programme and Bonar Law was well aware of the problems posed by a substantial working-class electorate but did not conclude that this dictated a Conservative social reform programme.

The dominance of Home Rule, it has been argued, meant that 'this positive and constructive side of Unionism was not really the overall party image presented to the outside world in the years immediately before the Great War'.[44] In terms of the analysis presented here, this is precisely what we should expect. Studies of Conservative politics are influenced by the assumption that social reform was a more 'real' political issue than Ulster but this assumption is anachronistic and a-historical as it derives from a perspective in which 'normal' politics are perceived to be dominated by socio-economic issues and controversies. These issues were certainly predominant in Edwardian politics but so were others and some of these had a greater immediate resonance in Conservative politics. This point is conceded by Dutton, for example, who refers to a number of younger Conservative MPs who wrote to Bonar Law at the end of 1913 calling for a positive policy on land reform but who none the less 'accepted the priority of Ulster in Conservative policy'.[45]

Many historians assume the Conservative Party ought to have adopted a social reform package and that it failed to do so is considered a glaring defect. This ignores the evidence presented here that the party strategy after 1911 was effective without such a policy. Even those historians who concede the Conservatives staged a recovery feel compelled to identify the absence of social reform from the Conservative agenda as a weakness. Stubbs, for example, describes the Conservative revival as 'by no means an entirely healthy recovery' because of the lack of a social programme.[46] Politically this is meaningless; from Bonar Law's point of view what mattered was recovery and recovery was *de facto* healthy.

Managing a Democracy at War

In August 1914 the Conservatives had a sustainable political strategy based on three elements: that there was no pressing need for a social reform programme, a deep suspicion of the Liberals and Labour, and opposition to politically motivated trade unionism. This can be described as parliamentary anti-socialism. In the wider political context the bases of political stability were under threat, for while the Liberals formed a single-party government they had to rely on non-Liberal votes for their parliamentary majority: non-Liberal votes which supported causes opposed by the Conservatives. With the outbreak of war these problems were eased but not resolved and were supplemented by a growing perception that the executive was incapable of responding to the demands of war.

Initially the Conservatives seemed to have nothing to lose by adopting a stance of 'patriotic opposition' and there was no pressure from within the party for a coalition. On 28 August 1914 the three major parties concluded an electoral truce (renewable annually) to avoid contested by-elections and Liberals remained the sole possessors of office. Nevertheless, peacetime disputes spilled over into wartime politics. On 15 September Bonar Law and his supporters walked out of the Commons chamber in protest at the continuation of the Welsh Disestablishment and Home Rule Bills and a Conservative whip complained, 'It is unnatural in an Opposition not to criticize freely, & indeed I think it is [our] duty to do so at any rate in cases where mistakes have been made which might be repeated if attention is not called to them.'[47] Cameron Hazlehurst gives the Conservatives three strategies – seek greater consultation with the government, increased opposition, or coalition – though all had significant drawbacks. Furthermore these strategies were still within the boundaries of pre-1914 politics as understood by its practitioners, but the war (which showed no signs of ending quickly) raised the possibility of a seismic political shift forced by the growing importance of organized labour and mass consent for the war effort.[48] The Conservative sense of grievance was heightened by Asquith's failings as a wartime chief executive which led directly to the crisis of May 1915.

May 1915 reveals the degree to which the already stressed pre-1914 bases of political stability had broken down under the impact of war. Conservative resentment was fuelled by the party truce because while 'they undertook to suspend their own machinery and propaganda work in the country, the government went on with its programme of controversial domestic legislation'.[49] This added to the problems in prosecuting the war and Bonar Law's patriotic opposition created a political vacuum on the Conservative backbenches which was filled by W.A.S. Hewins' Unionist Business Committee (UBC) formed early in 1915 which increased significantly the potential for parliamentary rebellion.

By May 1915 there were unmistakable signs of a governability crisis: a failing executive, a legislature escaping from control, the erosion of party government and growing intra-élite conflict.[50] The crisis exploded with the shell scandal and Fisher's resignation as First Sea Lord and, despite Bonar Law persuading the UBC to hold its fire, it was clear that power was slipping away from the executive back to the House of Commons, a reversal of the flow since 1867. The beneficiary was the Conservative backbench. This loss of executive control was central to Bonar Law's prime concern that:

> . . . the hold of the Government on the country and to some extent on the House of Commons was weakening and that in consequence – for in a democratic country patience is a difficult virtue and people judge mainly by results – the Government would get steadily weaker at the very time that the greatest possible strength would be required.

Bonar Law's patriotic opposition policy could not contain the tensions generated and 'nothing would prevent full-blooded debate in the House and I looked with absolute dismay at the prospect of ordinary party warfare at such a time.'[51]

The first Coalition (May 1915–December 1916) resolved the immediate political crisis but solved nothing fundamental. Asquith remained Prime Minister, all but one of the senior posts went to Liberals (Bonar Law received the Colonial Office) and the Conservative backbench remained deeply discontented. May 1915 did allow the parliamentary leadership – Liberal and Conservative – to retain the political initiative so preserving the distribution of power. Given Bonar Law's known hostility to coalition his acceptance of one on such unfavourable terms is explicable only in terms of an overriding need to preserve the established bases of politics. Five months after the crisis Bridgeman commented on the 'general feeling of unrest in the House, indescribable but one feels it by instinct'.[52] This continued unrest was politically very serious as 'The first Coalition was indeed made by parliamentary pressure but it was created to thwart this pressure, not to satisfy it', but Taylor is wrong in his view that 'the party leaders were more in control than ever'.[53] The August 1914 truce and the first Coalition were the continuation of pre-war political orthodoxy and May 1915 to December 1916 can be seen as the expiring gasp of nineteenth-century politics or, alternatively, the birth pangs of modern British politics.

In terms of the architecture of political stability and the problems of managing the war, the re-establishment of executive authority was the first objective. This meant the assertion of prime ministerial authority and control over the House of Commons. The assertion of prime ministerial power was essential for the coordination of the war effort and this lay at the heart of the crisis of December 1916. Cabinet government might, as Bagehot decreed, have been the efficient secret of the British constitution but while the war had preserved its secrecy, it

had raised serious doubts about its efficiency and that of its chairman. Leo
Amery found Edward Carson, for example, was 'very depressed about the
hopelessness of the present system of governing by 22 gabblers round a table with
an old procrastinator in the chair'.[54] By the autumn of 1915 Lloyd George's
mistress described the situation as 'very ominous' because Asquith 'pooh-poohed'
Lloyd George's attempts to inject a sense of urgency into the prosecution of the
war as the Prime Minister was 'of the opinion that the war will be over in
3 weeks'. The Conservative members of the Cabinet 'are sick of his "wait-and-
see" methods and the whole country is getting tired'. This lack of push and go
was important as the labour situation was deteriorating rapidly. The alternative –
based on the Dardanelles Committee – was composed of six to eight members '&
decides the important matters, while the bigger Cabinet simply talks and wastes
time . . . "Well, what did you decide today?" I said to D. [David Lloyd George]
after the big Cabinet meeting yesterday. "Nothing", he replied – "We never
do".'[55]

Party discipline held to the extent that there was no realistic possibility of the
disenchanted appealing directly to public opinion over the heads of their party
leaders. Bridgeman noted the level of hostility to Asquith in the summer of 1916
but he 'regard[ed] the breaking up of the Coalition as a disaster of sufficient
magnitude to outweigh all other considerations, even broken pledges'.[56] There
was, however, a sufficient level of discontent in parliament to provoke a major
Conservative rebellion over the sale of enemy property in Nigeria (directed at
Bonar Law as Colonial Secretary) to seriously destabilize relations between and
within the governing élites. The November 1916 Conservative rebellion on the
sale of enemy property expressed an overwhelming desire to find a Prime
Minister who would win the war. On 1 December 1916, Lloyd George proposed
a three-man War Council excluding the Prime Minister and two days later
(despite Conservative hostility) Bonar Law declared his support for Lloyd
George. This infuriated Liberal ministers and led Asquith to withdraw his
agreement to the War Council. On 5 December both Lloyd George and Asquith
resigned; George V sent for Bonar Law but Asquith (understandably) refused to
serve under Bonar Law who urged the King to send for Lloyd George. On 7
December Lloyd George appealed for the Labour Party's support and Bonar
Law delivered a suspicious Conservative backbench on the grounds that Lloyd
George was the only man capable of winning victory. Lloyd George became
Prime Minister.

On 7 December 1916 the modern British core executive based on a
dominant Prime Minister was established. This development was noted by
contemporary observers.[57] In terms of the development of the political system
the immediate and long-term consequences of Lloyd George's arrival must be
distinguished. The first Coalition 'had been conceived within an orthodox
party framework; Lloyd George's, formed when the war crisis was far more

desperate, was defined in terms of policies and personalities'.[58] Lloyd George became Prime Minister because he was the only man capable of organizing victory which required an augmented core executive which, in turn, would reinforce the Prime Minister's power. The Lloyd George Coalition was war dependant and therefore unstable (it collapsed in 1922) but its long-term consequences were to boost executive authority and put the Conservative Party in power more or less continuously until July 1945. Although Lloyd George was Prime Minister of a multi-party coalition his position depended on Conservative votes. The second Coalition was a product of parliamentary, and especially Conservative, backbench discontent and was a throwback to the parliamentary politics of 1832–67 when the House of Commons could make or break ministries. The House of Commons could only do this because of the erosion of executive authority and a disciplined majority under the impact of the Edwardian and wartime political crises.[59]

RESPONDING TO MASS ELECTORAL POLITICS

Politicians recognized early on in the war that it would most likely produce a much larger electorate. Thirty years ago Trevor Wilson set the psephological ball rolling by comparing the war to a 'rampant omnibus' which swept away a stable party system, splitting the Liberal Party and thereby creating political space for the Labour Party to expand.[60] The weakness of this theory is that pre-war politics were not stable but the core of the debate is whether or not class was replacing religion as the basis of mass political loyalties.

Post-1910 politics confirmed Bonar Law's judgement that the Conservatives had little to gain and much to lose from social reform. If his judgement was correct, this casts doubt on the strength of the upsurge in class politics. Research on the development of class politics in early twentieth-century Britain confirms the rationality of Bonar Law's decision not to make a positive appeal to the new democracy. Wald's pioneering study argues religion remained the most potent influence on pre-1918 electoral behaviour. Using multivariate analysis Wald regresses class and sectarianism against the Conservative vote and finds that the proportion of Nonconformists in a population predicts more variance in the vote than class-derived factors (Table 6.1). In pre-1918 elections, he argues, 'religious factors were clearly dominant' but after 1918 'class clearly gained ascendancy in structuring the vote'. Table 6.1 gives the main bases of voter alignment and the key point is the growing strength of class as a determinant of voting behaviour from 1910 onwards with class becoming the most powerful influence from 1918 onwards. Wald concludes that his analysis 'sustains the traditional view of a dramatic alteration of cleavage bases between 1910 and 1918, a movement of the vote from a confessional to a class alignment'.[61]

Table 6.1: Patterns of Voter Alignment, 1885–1929

Election	Anglican	Non-Conformist	Catholic	Agriculture	1951 Class	Multiple r2
1885	0.31	−0.27	0.35	−0.16	0.23	0.25
1886	0.29	−0.33	0.21	−0.18	0.39	0.21
1892	0.24	−0.36	0.08	−0.09	0.01	0.14
1895	0.07	−0.37	0.22	0.07	0.15	0.14
1900	−0.03	−0.02	0.45	−0.04	−0.04	0.21
1906	0.23	−0.38	0.10	0.20	0.09	0.20
1910 (J)	0.26	−0.49	0.20	0.20	0.18	0.30
1910 (D)	0.44	−0.39	0.22	−0.05	0.27	0.32
1918	0.47	−0.28	0.03	−0.56	0.65	0.43
1922	0.32	−0.40	0.07	−0.17	0.70	0.46
1923	0.49	−0.33	0.07	−0.14	0.67	0.53
1924	0.34	−0.30	0.10	0.15	0.66	0.49
1929	0.52	−0.29	0.11	−0.37	0.68	0.58

Source: K.D. Wald, *Crosses on the Ballot. Patterns of British Voter Alignment since 1885* (Princeton University Press, 1985), Table 8.3, p. 214.

Table 6.2: Predictors of the Conservative Vote in the General Election of 1918

Predictor	Beta	Predictor	Beta
Coupon in Favour	0.30	Metal workers	0.09
Professionals	0.19	London Seat	−0.10
Electrical Workers	0.17	Working-Class Seat	−0.11
Women Electors	0.16	Established Labour Candidate	−0.12
Catholic Priests	0.11	Sitting Liberal MP	−0.14
Middle-Class Seat	0.11	Mining Seat	−0.19

Source: Turner, *British Politics and the Great War*, Table 5b, p. 417.

The implications of Wald's work for Conservative political strategy are obvious: the First World War was critical for the emergence of class politics. Class politics might have emerged without the 1914–18 war but it, and the massive extension of the franchise in 1918, ensured class politics developed far faster than if the conflict had not taken place. As Conservative politicians could not foresee the war they could not take the shift from religion to class into account in their strategy and, in any case, there was little evidence that class was becoming the determinant of mass electoral behaviour. If class politics was a weak growth and the class party (Labour) was not achieving electoral take-off, why should Conservatives try to appeal directly to the working class as a class before 1914? If Wald is correct and the traditional bases of mass electoral behaviour were not altering significantly the Conservative Party would, by adopting a class strategy, have been antagonizing its core supporters and encouraging internal conflict for no gain.

A related point is the restricted nature of the pre-1918 franchise which, it has been argued, neutralized a considerable amount of non-Conservative electoral support. In December 1910 the electorate numbered 7.7 million and only 58 per cent of the adult male population had the vote.[62] Lord Selbourne argued that difficulties derived not from extending the franchise *per se* but from to whom the vote was given and on what criteria. Extending the vote to more men and some women, he argued, should be confined to tax- and ratepayers who would be most likely to vote Conservative and there was no evidence that these new voters would vote either as a class or as a sex. Selbourne believed 'they will be divided all through' and that Bonar Law 'underestimated the support our party gets from the manual workers': as the Conservatives polled as many votes as the Liberals, Selbourne thought 'that the addition of the wives as voters will tend to increase the general Conservatism of the class of manual workers not its Radicalism'. He concluded by noting that 'The grant of the franchise to a lower class has always tended to make those who had the franchise previously more Conservative'.[63] Conservatives could be forgiven, none the less, for being alarmed by Pease's 1912 franchise bill which would have created an electorate of 9.5 million based on virtually universal male suffrage subject to minimal residence qualifications. The bill passed its second reading undamaged but Bonar Law successfully protested that including women's franchise clauses at the Committee stage would render the bill different to that approved by the House of Commons. The Speaker agreed and declared the bill invalid.[64] With Pease's bill disposed of and the restricted franchise preserved there was again no reason for Bonar Law to alter his strategy, but did the Fourth Reform Act transform this environment?

Matthew, McKibbin and McKay argue that the war *per se* actually did very little to alter Labour's position in the party and political system but that the 1918 Act did have a dramatic effect in boosting Labour's electoral chances. By enfranchising those who before 1914 did not (for whatever reason) have the vote but who were more likely to vote Labour, the 1918 Act laid the foundation for Labour's growth. Turner argues this only works if the pre-1918 franchise was hostile to Labour and that the stresses of war did not affect significantly the social bases of electoral support. Turner's analysis of the psephological consequences of the war concluded: 'Working-class political choices begin to make sense only when they are treated not as a passive translation of social characteristics, but as an active response to events.'[65] The First World War could not compress a sufficient range of social change to account for Labour's rise nor could the extent of social change before 1914 account for Labour's rise and what appeared to be (by 1914) Labour's stagnation.

Turner's analysis of the impact of the 1918 Act focuses on the Coupon issued by Lloyd George and Bonar Law to Conservative, Liberal and Labour MPs who pledged their support to the Coalition. It is not possible to identify clearly the determinants of the Conservative vote in 1918 because Conservatives fought as part of a coalition but this does not obscure the purpose of the underlying strategy. The 1918 election 'was a deliberate and largely successful effort to hold back the advance of the Labour Party . . . and it is impossible to tell for certain whether Conservatism or the Coalition was the appeal which lured potential Labour or Liberal voters away'.[66] Turner's data supports the broad trend of Wald's analysis but with some key differences. The most powerful class predictor in 1918 was the proportion of miners in a constituency but the strongest predictor of a Conservative vote (Table 6.2) was an organizational factor, the Coupon, followed by professional worker status and (if it is not too anachronistic a term) the 'new' working class. Women constituted two-thirds of the new electorate and there is a strong relationship between the percentage of women in a constituency and Conservative voting, which Turner interprets as an indicator of a constituency's class structure since in 1918 middle-class constituencies tended to have a higher proportion of women voters.[67] Also, a large proportion of men were away and less likely to vote; this means the 1918 election was more middle-class and more female which was important as women were more likely to vote for the Coalition. This suggests an emerging complex gender/class-based electoral politics. Religiosity was important in those areas where politics (for example, Liverpool, Clydeside, parts of Lancashire) were influenced by a Green–Orange split. Class and party predictors point to the strength of class as an influence on electoral behaviour and these increased their influence in the 1922 general election.

The Conservatives were ambivalent towards Lloyd George. While his determination to win the war could not be doubted, the long-term consequences of his apparent rapport with organized labour and his enthusiasm for state power worried many Conservatives. Nevertheless, Lloyd George remained an indispensable asset to the governing élites and while the war lasted he and the Coalition were impregnable. Lloyd George had no party until May 1918 when he created a Coalition Liberal organization which, along with his reputation, he used to achieve a favourable allocation of seats in the electoral agreement of July 1918. The Conservative objective after 1916 was to create a party system which would underpin postwar stability. For Conservatives, the key issue was the role of the state, and party attitudes coalesced around pre-war assumptions. The main threat to this was organized labour, although the governing élites never really lost the political initiative despite the need to recognize and consult (albeit temporarily) the organized working class and their organizations.[68] The ejection of Arthur Henderson from the Coalition and the abandonment of reconstruction demonstrates that the fundamentals of politics were not significantly changed by the war and that the Conservative-based Coalition was a very effective barrier to political change.

Growing labour unrest in 1917 led many Conservatives to doubt that Lloyd George could handle the unions and the working class. By the Armistice there was a deep Conservative distrust of Lloyd George but, as one Conservative noted, 'Unity seems to me so essential if the orderly elements are to prevail against the forces of disorder'.[69] Popular support for the war seemed to offer an opportunity for marginalizing working-class political consciousness and isolating socialism. Prominent in the emergence of patriotic labour was Lord Milner, who had been frustrated by what he regarded as conservatism's pre-1914 negativity. The war had created a group of patriotic socialists and trade unionists with whom Conservatives could cooperate and the patriotic labour movement seemed to be a valuable auxiliary as well as providing an opportunity to split the Labour Party and trade unions.[70] Patriotic labour emerged in 1916 as the British Workers' League (BWL) – later renamed the National Democratic Labour Party (NDLP) – and although initially critical of all established parties it was drawn to the Conservatives because of a common rejection of class war and hostility to Germany. Amery actively promoted patriotic labour on the grounds that 'the conflict of the future was between those who had the national and patriotic and those who had the international point of view, and that [I] was prepared to endorse and back any programme that was patriotic, even if I disagreed with its details, providing it secured the adhesion of the working-classes to the national and imperial idea'.[71] The difficulty was that patriotic labour's policy preferences were uncomfortably socialist.

By the end of 1916 negotiations were under way on a programme to harmonize relations between capital and labour and translate this into postwar politics. Discussions began in April 1917 on an electoral agreement covering thirty constituencies but difficulties developed, the BWL's importance increased with the Russian Revolution and the domestic industrial unrest of 1917, and throughout 1917 Steel-Maitland and the BWL negotiated a common programme. The Conservative Party was careful, however, to give these talks no official status.[72] By late 1917/early 1918 it was increasingly difficult to reconcile patriotic labour with the Conservative Party. The constituencies would not accept their candidates without the leadership's endorsement but this might make patriotic labour seem more of a creature of the Conservative Party.[73] Ironically, the fear was that patriotic labour might cost the party working-class votes. Nevertheless, Bonar Law insisted the Conservatives must work with patriotic labour.[74] These difficulties were smoothed over by the Coupon and the NDLP fielded twenty-seven candidates of whom ten were elected. Patriotic labour was a creation of the war; once the war ended so did its political rationale and it was wiped out in 1922.

The patriotic upsurge of the war years and the leftwards drift of Labour politics prompted the question of what, if any, direct link the Conservative Party ought to have with the working class. Traditionally, the Conservatives feared the consequences of a party within a party, and class linkages both violated the One Nation self-image and limited the leadership's room for manoeuvre. The Unionist Labour Movement and the Labour Sub-Committee, though founded in 1919 on the initiative of Lancashire Conservative trade unionists, emerged from the strains of wartime politics. Their purpose was to organize pro-Conservative trade unionists against socialism and industrial militancy in support of king, constitution and empire and help secure the election of Conservative trade unionists to union office, public bodies, and the House of Commons.[75] The aim was not 'fight trade unions [or] trade unionists, but . . . that small and determined body which dominates the present Labour Party . . . the men who would shake hands with Bolshevists and would upset the whole fabric upon which the Constitution of the country had been built'. In industry it sought 'a readjustment of the ideas between employers and the employed, whereby they might have industrial peace and goodwill among men'.[76] Conservative trade unionists and voters could not, however, create an autonomous political base in the labour movement to challenge the Labour Party–trade union link, and the Unionist Labour Movement was a failure.[77]

The Coalition's manifesto declared that 'The principal concern of every Government is and must be the condition of the great mass of the people who live by manual toil'. Central to the Coalition's policy in war and peace was Labour's marginalization. By early 1918 ministers began to marginalize the unions, the Labour Party's marginality was demonstrated by Henderson's removal from the Cabinet and Labour was swamped (in terms of seats) in the 1918 election. The Coalition had a vested interest in portraying the Labour Party, reborn as a socialist party, as extremist. The electorate (women were a particular target) were warned that voting Labour would lead to 'A Republic in this Country, Civil War and Revolution, Lenin, Trotsky and Up with Bolshevism and Communism' and 'The "Labour" Party stands for Waste, Bankruptcy, Ruin for All. For Bolshevism! For Unemployment! For Revolution!'[78] This was for mass consumption only. In private, politicians knew that whatever threat Labour posed it was not a revolutionary threat, but a connection had to be established (and was established) in the electorate's mind between Labour and extremism. Between 1918 and 1922 Conservatives contemplated various schemes to limit the impact of the new electorate, such as proportional representation, reform of the House of Lords and Coalition. By 1922 the party had abandoned any attempt to place structural or institutional obstacles in the path of mass democracy.[79] This meant it had to rely on obstacles provided by liberal democracy itself. Conservative strategy was based on two premises: that mass democracy was a *fait accompli* and that the Conservative Party had to educate the electorate into an appreciation of the legitimate (i.e. limited) role of government. As J.C.C. Davidson expressed it, 'Before the war it was possible with a limited and highly expert electorate to put forward Party programmes of a restricted and well-defined character, but nowadays I am quite sure that while not departing from the principles of our Party we must endeavour to gain the confidence not of our own voters but of the mugwump vote.'[80] This strategy was helped by the distortions of the electoral system and the emergence of a two-and-a-bit party system in which the only alternative to voting Labour (outside the Celtic fringe) was voting Conservative. The institutions of parliamentary democracy became, therefore, an effective barrier to mass democracy. In the inter-war period the Conservatives won a majority of the votes cast in 1931 and 1935 (technically as part of a coalition) and never a majority of the electorate but won a majority of seats in 1922, 1924, 1931 and 1935. The Conservatives were able to dominate British politics with an average of 45 per cent of the votes cast and 33 per cent of the electorate; furthermore, it took fewer votes to elect a Conservative MP than a Labour or Liberal.

Liberal/Conservative cooperation during and after the First World War fatally undermined the Liberal Party. It became caught in a classic two-party squeeze and a spiral of declining organizational vitality and financial viability. The last substantial Liberal electoral challenge (before 1974) came in 1929 so the destination of the votes released by Liberal decline (a major consequence of war-time politics) is a major factor in modern British politics. Evidence gathered in the early 1960s concluded that while 'the Labour Party succeeded to the Liberals' place as the Conservatives' main opponent in the British party system, only a minority of historical Liberal support went to Labour'.[81] The flow of the Liberal vote to the Conservative and Labour parties is seen by Butler and Stokes as a further indicator of the rise of class with Liberal voters identifying Labour as responsible for Liberal decline and socialism as antithetical to core Liberal ideas. Particularly important was the Conservative appeal to the children of working-class liberals which helped broaden Conservative working-class support.[82]

The year 1918 was a watershed in British politics. Despite the difficulties inherent in the methodology of historical psephology the evidence of Wald and Turner points to a substantial increase in class voting as a determinant of mass political behaviour. So was 1918–22 a transitional period from one type of mass behaviour to another? The 1918 Act enfranchised large numbers of new voters and the First World War fractured the historic Liberal Party; these new voters were more likely to go against a Labour Party whose support was based on long-term political and industrial patterns derived from union membership, a party whose base was heavily dependent on the mining areas.[83] This isolation would change over time. This supports Cowling's analysis of Conservative strategy: 'Between 1920 and 1924 the Conservative Party made three long-term decisions. The first was to remove Lloyd George from office. The second was to take up the role of "defender of the social order". The third was to make Labour the chief party of opposition. These decisions were attempts to contain the upheaval caused by the Labour Party's arrival as a major force and to gain whatever advantage could be gained from it.'[84] The advantage gained was Conservative hegemony.

WAR, PARTY GOVERNMENT AND THE STABILIZATION OF POLITICS

This chapter challenges the assumption that the Edwardian Conservative Party ought to have had an explicit social policy and that in not having such a policy the Conservatives were committing a serious political blunder for which their leaders were responsible. This interpretation only makes sense if the political landscape was being transformed by the rise of class politics.

At first sight political developments after 1906 indicated that a realignment to class politics was under way but closer inspection of the evidence points to a different conclusion. The psephological evidence points to the maintenance of the traditional bases of mass political preferences supplemented by class politics. Consequently, Bonar Law's well-attested hostility towards social reform was not a case of ideology or prejudice overcoming political realities, nor was it the result of inexperience; rather it expressed an important political truth – there were few votes for the Conservatives in social reform. This remained true even after the outbreak of war. Steel-Maitland's organizational reforms were intended to enhance the party's electoral position by mobilizing its maximum support. These reforms were not an attempt to reorient the party towards the mass electorate and class politics but to maximize Conservative support within the contours of existing politics. They could, however, be easily redirected to meet the needs of postwar politics. Conservatives were able to win mass support without making an appeal to the working class.

Clearly the war posed a major threat to the bases of politics. Intra-élite conflict, coalition politics, the rise of labour, and the problem of running the war provoked two major crises (May 1915 and December 1916) which revealed that power was slipping away from the executive. The first Coalition was an inadequate response but the second represented a major shift in the conduct of politics by establishing the modern core executive. Conservatives feared that under democracy the House of Commons would become the plaything of radical party caucuses faithfully reflecting the wishes of an electorate manipulated by demagogues. Their fears were misplaced. The House of Commons and party organization became dominated by the party leadership and, since the Conservatives were from 1918 the dominant party, they were dominated by the Conservative leadership. The fall of the Coalition, the fragmentation of the opposition, and the distortions of the electoral system ensured the Conservatives could rule on a minority of the popular vote. What mattered above all was preserving the unity of the party in the country and the Commons.

This was facilitated by the emergence of mass politics in the late nineteenth century, especially the growth of political parties whose purpose was to elect MPs and sustain a government. True, this required the alignment of parties with popular sentiment but popular sentiment was malleable. MPs were elected on a party label and were identified with and committed to a party whose political success and grass-roots organization ensured their election. The concomitant was disciplined parties in the House of Commons under the control of the party whips and party leaders which placed parliamentary sovereignty under the control of party leaders and the whips' office. Legislative power was at the disposal of party leaders who controlled a disciplined majority and this helped to isolate government from direct mass pressure under all but the most extreme circumstances. This relative autonomy was further enhanced by the reorganization and centralization of government via the Cabinet Secretariat and the central role of the Treasury, and the chief beneficiary of this process was the Prime Minister who became the focal point of the party and governmental system.

The First World War and the 1918 election did not lead directly to the emergence of a simple class-based pattern of electoral behaviour in the inter-war period but to a model that emphasized continued turmoil. The implication of this for Conservative political strategy was the adoption of different strategies for different political circumstances: Bonar Law's parliamentary socialism, the Lloyd George Coalition, and Baldwin's promotion of non-partisan Conservative politics as a response to Labour's replacement of the Liberal Party. It was pragmatism not class, social reform or ideology which drove Conservative politics in this decade.

Notes

1 J. Turner, *British Politics and the Great War. Coalition and Conflict 1915–1918* (New Haven CT, Yale University Press, 1992), p. 2.

2 Party government has three characteristics: first, all major decisions are taken by individuals chosen in elections conducted along party lines or by individuals appointed by and/or responsible to such individuals. Second, policy is decided within the governing party or in negotiations between parties in a coalition. Third, cabinet ministers and the Prime Minister are selected from within their parties and are responsible to the people via these parties. R.S. Katz, 'Party Government: A Rationalist Conception', in R. Wildermann (ed.), *The Future of Party Government* (de Gruyter, 1986), p. 43.

3 J.H. Plumb, *The Growth of Political Stability in England, 1675–1725* (London, Peregrine Books 1969), pp. 11, 12.

4 Plumb, *The Growth of Political Stability in England*, p. 13.

5 K. Middlemas, *Politics in Industrial Society. The British Experience since 1911* (London, André Deutsch, 1979) describes this negotiating process.

6 Quoted in E. Halévy, *A History of the English People in the 19th Century, Volume 6, The Rule of Democracy, 1905–1914* (London, Ernest Benn, 1970), p. 92. Wald argued the elections of 1886 and 1906 were not realigning elections in that there was no surge in mass participation, no marked increase in electoral instability and no fundamental change in the social bases of party support and electoral behaviour. See K.D. Wald, 'Realignment Theory and the British Party Development: A Critique', *Political Studies* 30: 2, 1982, pp. 207–20.

7 P. Marsh, *The Discipline of Popular Government, Lord Salisbury's Domestic Statecraft, 1886–1902* (Brighton, Harvester Press, 1978), pp. 265–70.

8   R. Blake, *The Conservative Party from Peel to Thatcher* (London, Fontana, 1985), p. 175.

9   F.J.C. Hearnshaw, *Conservatism in England* (London, Macmillan, 1933), p. 245.

10 Proceedings of the Conservative Party *Central Council Minutes*, 14 May 1909 (Brighton, Harvester Microform) and Middlemas, *Politics in Industrial Society*, p. 39. In January 1911 the Central Council did discuss social reform but its records give no account of the discussion.

11 *Yorkshire Provincial Area Records*, Finance and General Purposes Committee's Minutes, 6 May, 1912 held at the Yorkshire Conservative Offices, Leeds.

12 A. Sykes. *Tariff Reform in British Politics* (Oxford, Clarendon Press, 1979), p. 194.

13 Hearnshaw, *Conservatism in England*, p. 245.

14 D.A. Cosby, 'The Conservative Disaster, and What It Signifies', *Westminster Review*, 165: 3 March 1906, p. 237.

15 Halévy, *The Rule of Democracy*, pp. 446–7.

16 This was not confined to the 'left' of the party. Lord Willoughby de Broke's concept of National Toryism envisaged a social contract between the working class and the Tory élite in the interests of national regeneration. See, for example, his 'National Toryism', *National Review* 59, 1912, pp. 413–27. For the radical right as a whole, see G.D. Phillips, *The Diehards, Aristocratic Society and Politics in Edwardian England* (Cambridge MA, Harvard University Press, 1979).

17 J. Barnes and D. Nicholson (eds), *The Leo Amery Diaries Volume 1: 1896–1929* (London, Hutchinson, 1980), Milner to Amery 27 December 1907, p. 62. D.S. Dutton, 'The Unionist Party and Social Policy, 1906–1914', *Historical Journal* 24: 4, 1981, pp. 875–7.

18 For example, M. Pugh, *The Making of Modern British Politics* (Oxford, Blackwell, 1982), pp. 106–7, Sykes, *Tariff Reform in British Politics*, chapter 9.

19 J. Ridley, 'The Unionist Social Reform Committee, 1911–1914: Wets Before the Deluge', *Historical Journal*, 30: 2, 1987, p. 391.

20 Ridley, 'The Unionist Social Reform Committee', pp. 408–9.

21 Blake, *The Conservative Party from Peel to Churchill*, p. 190, and R. Jenkins, *Asquith* (London, Collins, 1964), p. 275.

22 Dutton, 'The Unionist Party and Social Reform', p. 872.

23 A.J.P. Taylor, *English History 1914–1945* (Harmondsworth, Penguin, 1975), p. 42.

24 J. Smith, 'Bluff, Bluster and Brinkmanship: Andrew Bonar Law and the Third Home Rule Bill', *The Historical Journal* 36: 1, 1993, pp. 161–78.

25 Blake, *The Conservative Party from Peel to Thatcher*, p. 194, and P. Williamson (ed.), *The Modernisation of Conservative Politics. The Diaries and Letters of William Bridgeman, 1904–1935* (London, The Historian's Press, 1988), entry for 13 November 1911, p. 54, hereafter, Bridgeman Papers.

26 Bentley, *Politics without Democracy*, p. 346.

27 R. Blake, *The Unknown Prime Minister* (London, Eyre & Spottiswoode, 1955), p. 140.

28 Bonar Law Papers (House of Lords Record Office) *BL 33/4/34*, Bonar Law to Salisbury, 3 May 1912, hereafter BL.

29 *BL 26/1/76*, Walter Long to BL, November, February and March 1911–12, Constituency Survey.

30 H. Pelling, *Popular Politics and Society in Late Victorian Britain* (London, Macmillan, 1968), pp. 1–18, and *Bridgeman Papers*, W. Bridgeman to C. Bridgeman, 26 November 1911, p. 57.

31 A.J. Lee, 'Conservatism, Traditionalism and the British Working Class', in D. Martin and D. Rubinstein (eds), *Ideology and the Labour Movement* (London, Croom Helm, 1979), p. 96.

32 N. Blewett, *The Peers, the Parties and the People. The General Elections of 1910* (London, Macmillan, 1972), pp. 399 *et seq.* and *Bridgeman Papers*, entry for 20 February 1914, p. 73, for the Conservative revival.

33 Bentley, *Politics without Democracy*, p. 347.

34 Dutton, 'The Unionist Party and Social Reform', p. 879.

35 D. Rubinstein, 'Trade Unions, Politicians and Public Opinion 1906–1914', in B. Pimlott and C. Cook (eds), *Trade Unions and British Politics, The First 250 Years*, 2nd edn (London, Longman, 1991), pp. 48–68.

36 Smith, 'Bluff, Bluster and Brinkmanship', p. 163, and *Bridgeman Papers* entry for 1911, p. 40.

37 Marsh, *The Discipline of Popular Government*, chapter 6.

38 *BL 24/5/159*, A. Stringer to Bonar Law, 27 December 1911.

39 J. Ramsden, *The Conservative Party in the Age of Balfour and Baldwin* (London, Longman, 1978), chapters 4 and 5 for details. In April 1912 the Central Office Lecture Department employed 125 permanent staff (costing £320) and 443 casuals (costing £592). A 13-week van campaign in Lancashire, for example, held 184 meetings and reached 56,399 people, 62 street corner meetings reached 22,595 people, and a 4-week seaside resort campaign held 495 meetings which 19,840 attended.

40 K. Young, *Local Politics and the Rise of Party. The London Municipal Society and the Conservative Intervention in Local Elections, 1894–1963* (Leicester University Press, 1975), pp. 96–7.

41 Young, *Local Politics and the Rise of Party*, pp. 104–12.

42 Dutton, 'The Unionist Party and Social Policy', p. 877.

43 Ridley, 'The Wets before the Deluge', p. 409.

44 Dutton, 'The Unionist Party and Social Policy', p. 881.

45 Ibid., p. 882.

46 J. Stubbs, 'The Impact of the Great War on the Conservative Party', in C. Cook and G. Peele (eds), *The Politics of Reappraisal* (London, Macmillan, 1975). Bridgeman noted in his diary the growing disarray of the Liberal Cabinet, the poor morale of its supporters, the slowness of its legislative programme and 'their doubt as to desirability of an election before they become still more unpopular': *Bridgeman Papers*, entry for April–August 1912, p. 59.

47 *Bridgeman Papers*, diary 29 November [1914], pp. 81–2.

48 C. Hazlehurst, *Politicians at War July 1914 to May 1915. A Prologue to the Triumph of Lloyd George* (London, Jonathan Cape, 1971), p. 158.

49 K.O. Morgan, '1902–1924', in D. Butler (ed.), *Coalitions in British Politics* (London, Macmillan, 1978), p. 31.

50 *Bridgeman Papers*, diary May 1915, p. 83.

51 Bonar Law's own account of May 1915 was sent to Lord Buxton (Governor-General in South Africa) on 17 June 1915, quoted in R. Rhodes James, *Memoirs of a Conservative. J.C.C. Davidson's Memoirs and Papers 1910–37* (London, Weidenfeld and Nicolson, 1969), pp. 24–5.

52 *Bridgeman Papers*, Bridgeman to C. Bridgeman, 14 October 1915, p. 89, and S. Koss, 'The Destruction of Britain's Last Liberal Government', *Journal of Modern History* XL: 2, June 1968, pp. 257–77.

53 A.J.P. Taylor, 'Politics in the First World War', in his *Essays in English History* (Harmondsworth, Penguin, 1976), p. 228.

54 Amery to his wife (21 July 1915) in *Amery Diaries*, p. 123.

55 A.J.P. Taylor (ed.), *Lloyd George. A Diary by Frances Stevenson* (London, Hutchinson, 1971), September 2nd and October 5th 1915, pp. 56–7.

56 *Bridgeman Papers*, diary 27 June 1916, p. 105.

57 *Amery Diaries*, letter to W.M. Hughes, Prime Minister of Australia, 8 January 1917, p. 138; and Lord Curzon in the House of Lords (19 July 1918), quoted in H.J. Hanham, *The Nineteenth-Century Constitution. Documents and Commentary* (Cambridge University Press, 1969), pp. 83–4.

58 Morgan, '1902–1924', p. 33.

59 Taylor, 'Politics in the First World War', p. 242.

60 T. Wilson, *The Downfall of the Liberal Party* (London, Collins, 1966).

61 K.D. Wald, *Crosses on the Ballot. Patterns of British Voter Alignment Since 1885* (Princeton, NJ, Princeton University Press, 1983), p. 214. In a letter to Bonar Law, Bridgeman regretted Steel-Maitland's and Central Office's failure to give greater prominence to religious issues, calculating there were some 50 seats which might be won 'by the votes of Liberal and Socialist Churchmen'. He claimed Welsh Disestablishment had cost Charles Masterman the Bethnal Green by-election, a seat which Bridgeman knew well. *Bridgeman Papers*, Bridgeman to Bonar Law, 28 February 1914, p. 73.

62 H.C.G. Matthew, R.I. McKibbin and J.A. Kay, 'The Franchise Factor in the Rise of the Labour Party', *English Historical Review*, 61, 1976, pp. 723–52.

63 *BL 25/3/26*, Lord Selbourne to Bonar Law, 12 March 1912.

64 M. Pugh, *Electoral Reform in Peace and War* (London, Routledge, 1978), p. 36.

65 Turner, *British Politics and the Great War*, p. 395.

66 Ibid., p. 434.

67 For surveys of the link between women and the Conservative Party, see B. Campbell, *The Iron Ladies. Why Do Women Vote Tory?* (London, Virago, 1987) and J. Lovenduski, P. Norris and C. Burness, 'The Party and Women', in A. Seldon and S. Ball (eds), *The Conservative Century. The Conservative Party since 1900* (Oxford University Press, 1994), pp. 611–35.

68 See the work of C.J. Wrigley, 'Trade Unions and Politics in the First World War', in Pimlott and Cook (eds), *Trade Unions in British Politics*, pp. 69–87, and at greater length his *David Lloyd George and the British Labour Movement in Peace and War* (Brighton, Harvester Press, 1976) and *Lloyd George and the Challenge of Labour. The postwar Coalition 1918–1922* (Hemel Hempstead, Harvester Wheatsheaf, 1990).

69 *Bridgeman Papers*, Bridgeman to C. Bridgeman, 24 November 1918.

70 R. Douglas, 'The National Democratic Labour Party and the British Workers' League', *Historical Journal* 15: 3, 1972, pp. 533–52, and J. Stubbs, 'Lord Milner and Patriotic Labour', *English Historical Review* 87 (October) 1972, pp. 717–54.

71 *Amery Diaries*, 8 November 1918.

72 Stubbs, 'Lord Milner and Patriotic Labour', pp. 741–2.

73 Conservative Party Archives (CPA) *NUA 2/1/35*, Special Conference on the Representation of the People Bill, 30 November 1917, p. 8.

74 *The Times*, 2 November 1917.

75 Archives of the British Conservative Party Series 3. Pamphlets and Leaflets 1915–1925 *NUA Pam 1982* (1920/42), *The Why and Wherefore of the Unionist Labour Committee, or, The Labour Wing of the Unionist Party* (Brighton, Harvester Microform, 1984).

76 *NUA Pam 1976* (March 1920), *The Labour Committee National Unionist Conference at Southport*, pp. 5, 8.

77 CPA (Bodleian Library, Oxford) *NUA 6/1/1–3* Report of the Principal Agent, July 1924.

78 *NUA Pam 1951* (1920/1), *What the 'Labour' Party Wants*, and *NUA Pam 1948* (1920/7), *What the 'Labour' Party Has Done*.

79 For example, D.H. Close, 'The Collapse of Resistance to Democracy: Conservatives and Second Chamber Reform, 1911–1928', *Historical Journal* 20: 4, 1977, pp. 898, 904–5.

80 *Davidson Papers*, (House of Lords Record Office), Davidson to Baldwin, 14 January 1929.

81 D. Butler and D. Stokes, *Political Change in Britain. The Evolution of Electoral Choice*, 2nd edn (London, Macmillan, 1974), pp. 167–8.

82 Ibid., p. 170.

83 D. Tanner, 'The Labour Party and Electoral Politics in the Coalfields', in A. Campbell, N. Fishman and D. Howell (eds), *Miners, Unions and Politics 1910–1947* (Aldershot, Scolar Press, 1996), pp. 59–92.

84 M. Cowling, *The Impact of Labour, 1920–1924. The Beginning of Modern British Politics* (Cambridge University Press, 1971), p. 1.

7

THE BRADFORD INDEPENDENT LABOUR PARTY AND THE FIRST WORLD WAR

Tony Jowitt and Keith Laybourn

Considering how bravely our manhood is serving the state in Flanders, if these demagogues (ILP) lack the spine to fight the least they should do would be to remain silent and inactive while others do the nation's work.[1]

Dear Mr Jowett,
As 'one of the Boys' kindly allow me to thank you personally for your efforts for Peace during the past four years. I am quite sure that when 'the Boys' come home they will tell you the TRUTH, re the terrible wastage of lives, inhuman conditions, filth and immoral environment, and thus you will live in the memories of YOUNG men as being a MAN of whom one can be justly proud. I hope too that you will be returned at the head of the poll on the 14th December.

A Boy from France[2]

Bradford, in 1914, was widely recognized as one of the great industrial cities in the United Kingdom where it was said that five-sixths of the wool consumed in the country passed through its factories at some stage in production and marketing.[3] At the same time it had a powerful reputation as a progressive city during the late Victorian and Edwardian period. As J.B. Priestley, with possibly a hint of overenthusiasm for his home town, wrote: 'In those pre-1914 days Bradford was considered the most progressive place in the United Kingdom.'[4] That reputation was largely founded on the role of the Independent Labour Party and the social welfare reforms that it had introduced. However, in addition it had a reputation for cultural progressivism through a curious amalgam of the European merchants who played a powerful role in the mercantile, cultural and philanthropic life of the city with the more stolid local Yorkshire culture. It made Bradford:

. . . one of the most provincial and yet one of the most cosmopolitan of English provincial cities . . . there was . . . this odd mixture of pre-war Bradford. A dash of the Rhine and the Oder found its way into our grim runnes – t' mucky beck. Bradford was determinedly Yorkshire and provincial, yet some of its suburbs reached for as far as Frankfurt or Leipzig.[5]

It has long been recognized that the First World War had a dramatic impact on British society, not least in the area of political history. This chapter attempts to look at its impact on the Independent Labour Party in Bradford, within a wider community setting. In particular it aims to elucidate the differences within the party and within the local trade union movement, recognizing that the simplistic division between a pro-war trade union movement and an anti-war Independent Labour Party fails to recognize the complexity of the division that characterized the labour movement in Bradford.

In April 1914 the Annual Conference of the Independent Labour Party (ILP) was held in Bradford. Since the Inaugural Conference, also held in Bradford in 1893, the party had grown rapidly, with the Bradford branch being probably the largest in the country. With an excess of local pride, J.H. Palin stated in his welcoming address:

Bradford has no really historic traditions: in Domesday Book it is described as a waste, and nine hundred years of capitalist administration has not improved it. Indeed the only improvement effected in Bradford since its establishment has been caused by the work of the Independent Labour Party. As a matter of fact the history of Bradford would be very largely the history of the Independent Labour Party.[6]

He went on to describe the rise of the party locally, with its 1,600 paid up members, 'which probably neither of the orthodox political parties could boast'. At the previous municipal elections the party had polled 43.1 per cent of the votes cast, had 20 members on the City Council, 3 members on the Board of Guardians, 1 Member of Parliament and:

. . . they would see that the ILP was not only the political party of the future, but that, so far as Bradford was concerned, it was the political party of the present . . . and there was no danger of the Bradford branch going wrong and if they would follow its lead the party would go on, and would eventually become the dominant party in British politics.

Table 7.1. The Growth of the Labour-Socialist Vote in Bradford between 1891 and 1913[7]

Year	Liberal %	Tory %	Labour %
1891	47.4	47.3	5.3
1892	41.0	42.3	16.7
1893	38.1	39.5	22.4
1894	40.3	37.3	22.4
1895	44.5	43.7	11.8
1896	44.7	46.1	9.2
1897	39.5	45.7	14.8
1898	41.1	41.9	17.0
1899	43.2	44.0	12.8
1900	36.0	45.2	18.8
1901	41.2	42.1	16.7
1902	36.0	47.2	16.8
1903	46.5	44.7	8.8
1904	42.8	42.0	15.2
1905	34.6	43.4	22.0
1906	26.3	47.0	26.7
1907	35.9	33.6	30.5
1908	31.8	38.2	30.0
1909	30.2	39.0	30.8
1910	31.5	33.3	35.2
1911	33.6	35.4	31.0
1912	32.2	36.1	31.7
1913	29.7	27.2	43.1

Although best known for its involvement with socio-economic issues such as school feeding, child welfare measures and municipal housing, the party had always been concerned with the wider issues of the relationships between individuals and the state and between states. However, for much of its existence the ILP had shown only a limited concern with international affairs with the passing of a few rhetorical motions about the international solidarity of the working classes. In the immediate pre-war years it began to show an increasing concern. In 1912 the Bradford Trades Council resolved to express its approval:

> . . . of the proposal for a general stoppage of work in all countries about to engage in war, and further we urge upon all workers the necessity for making preparations for a simultaneous stoppage of work in those countries, where war is threatened.[8]

Throughout 1912, 1913 and 1914 there was an increasing number of articles in the *Bradford Pioneer*, the local ILP newspaper, about the Armaments Trust, secret diplomacy and the need to foster international unity. What characterized the vast majority of these contributions was a wordy rhetoric about peace and internationalism rather than the development of any practical policies to confront war.

The most frequent writer in the *Bradford Pioneer* on the peace issue was the Revd R. Roberts, a Congregational Minister who had had a somewhat stormy relationship with the ILP over the previous twenty years.[9] Roberts reflected one important strand within the ILP, a strand whose primary concern was with individual and national ethicalism, continually stressing overall moral rather than economic issues. Dominating this perspective was the fervent belief that war was immoral and that the ILP must lead a propaganda fight against militarism. As Roberts wrote in early 1914:

> Alone among the parties in Great Britain the Labour Party is pledged against militarism. . . . We must take up the Fiery Cross and carry it to the remotest hamlet in the country, call every man and woman to the colours. 'Down with militarism'. That is our cry – as it is also the cry of our comrades all over Europe. Blazon it on the banners. Write it on the pavements. Sing it in the streets.[10]

The outbreak of war in 1914 came with startling suddenness. As late as 1 August 1914 continental socialist leaders were still not convinced that war was even a likely possibility. As Haupt suggests, they were the captives of their own myths about their ability to prevent war and unaware of the depths of national chauvinism.[11] They were caught short by the events, pushed on to the defensive and literally became disorientated spectators, waiting to be submerged by the gathering wave of nationalism.

In Bradford, in the midst of the period of national ultimatums, the ILP called a mass meeting on 2 August which deplored the threatened war but did not advocate immediate working-class action to prevent it. In his speech to this meeting, Fred Jowett, ILP MP for Bradford West, referred to war as a crime against humanity but made no demands for strikes or mass demonstrations to oppose the outbreak of war. Rather he closed his speech with a note of resignation: 'Let us who are socialists keep our minds calm, our hearts free from hate, and one purpose always before us – to bring peace as soon as possible on a basis that will endure.'[12]

Such unanimity of purpose evaporated with the declaration of war. The Bradford ILP fractured into pro-war and anti-war factions, but within these two basic divisions there were further sub-divisions. First, there were pacifists who were opposed to war *per se*. A second group felt the need to protect Britain and to defend Belgium while vigorously opposing the secret treaties which led to war and supporting a call for peace. Third were those who felt that the need for the prosecution of the war was essential to the defence of the country and temporarily transcended socialist objectives. Fourthly, and closely allied to this third group, were those who felt that Prussianism was a real danger to the world and had to be defeated come what may.

Contrary to the general impression given by the local Tory and Liberal press, there were very few members of the ILP who adopted an outright pacifist stand. At the national level the main advocates of pacifism were Bruce Glasier, Clifford Allen, Arthur Salter and Fenner Brockway, with Philip Snowden on the edge of this group though he was never a fully committed pacifist.[13] There was a professional, middle-class temper to this group which was composed largely of writers, journalists, academics and doctors. They took a pure pacifist line that all war was wrong, and some of them supplemented their hostility to war by forming the No-Conscription Fellowship and working with the Union of Democratic Control.[14] Although there was some welling of support for this group when they managed to gain some measure of control at the National Conference of the ILP in 1917, it was never a significant force in the politics of the Bradford ILP. Pacifism attracted only a few middle-class members of the ILP, most prominently, the Quaker, Arthur Priestman, and William Leach.[15]

The leading ILP pacifist in Bradford was William Leach, an employer who had joined the party in the 1890s. For more than fifty years he remained one of the leading political figures in the local ILP and Labour movement, being returned as a city councillor before the First World War and as ILP and Labour MP for Bradford Central constituency between 1922 and 1924, 1929 and 1931, and 1935 and 1945. His importance to the local Labour movement was immeasurably increased by the fact that he was also a prolific writer on socialist issues. He was a frequent contributor to the *Bradford Labour Echo*, the Bradford ILP paper of the late 1890s, and became editor of another such paper, *Forward*, between 1904 and 1909. It was through *Forward* that he mounted the publicity campaign which ultimately helped to win municipal school feeding – which meant school dinners in Bradford. During the First World War his major contribution was to act as editor of the *Bradford Pioneer*, taking over from the increasingly pro-war Joseph Burgess.[16] From this point the paper moved decisively towards an anti-war stance. In October 1915, Leach articulated the paper's policy:

> We hate all war, especially the present one. This is a pacifist or peace journal conducted among other purposes, with the object of stating as well as we can, the ILP position on the hideous tragedy now being enacted in Europe. . . . Human life is the most sacred thing we know, and its preservation, its development, its best welfare, must therefore be our religion on this earth.[17]

There was a changed atmosphere within the local ILP. Instead of confidence about the continued growth of the party and the movement, the pacifists saw themselves as a beleaguered minority led by Leach. However, they made up for their small numbers with an increasing fervour for pacifism. For some like Snowden it brought them back into the mainstream of the party, reviving the ethical/moral dimension of the party which had been largely submerged in the immediate pre-war years. The *Bradford Pioneer* reported extensively on the work of the No-Conscription Fellowship and the Union of Democratic Control, and provided full coverage to the speeches of the many opponents of the war who lectured at the ILP's New Picture House in Morley Street. It referred to Bertrand Russell, an ex-Liberal, as 'a recent and very valuable acquisition to the ILP.'[18] When E.D. Morel lectured at the Picture House he was described as 'that distinguished jail bird . . . now a member of the ILP and of the Bradford Branch.'[19]

At the heart of the pacifist case was a clear perspective on the dignity of human life, which was reinforced in Bradford by the treatment of the local German merchant community. At the outset of the war the *Bradford Daily Telegraph* had perceived different perspectives on the war as being possible: 'We may have our differences as to the necessity of Great Britain participating in the War, but there will be none of the bitterness displayed during the Boer War, when the opprobrious epithet "Pro-Boer" was hurled at those who were in the minority.'[20] However, very rapidly, opponents of the war were being abused in the local press and by local Nonconformist ministers from their pulpits. The mood changed within a matter of weeks and can be most clearly seen in the changed attitude to the German merchant community. Throughout August Germans and German premises were attacked and during 1914 and 1915 many members of the community were taken into custody, with a small number being interned for the duration of the war.[21] William Leach pointed to the hypocrisy of the situation in his article 'What Germany has done for Bradford' where he wrote:

> Let us therefore remember that Bradford is probably the most Germanized town in Great Britain. It is very likely that no town has availed itself so freely of the service of public-spirited Germans as Bradford has done . . . I shall not hate the Germans. I shall continue to like them, to respect them and to be glad I know so many of them. The German waiters, pork butchers, musicians, chemists, electricity experts, doctors, teachers, merchants and the like have served Bradford exceedingly well.[22]

At the end of the war, William Leach stood for Bradford Central, where he was comprehensively defeated by the Coalition Conservative candidate, who obtained almost 4,800 votes more than he did, although he did have the comfort of being more than 3,300 votes ahead of Sir James Hill, the sitting Liberal candidate.[23] Reflecting upon his defeat, he strongly reiterated his commitment to pacifism:

I have never felt so pugnaciously right in my life. I still disbelieve in war. As long as I am in public life I will not support bloodshed for any cause, whether that cause appears right or does not. It looks as if this victory fervour has swept us out. But it will pass. Liberalism is defunct, Socialism is deferred, and the Coalition will be deflated.[24]

But such pacifist sentiments were not shared by the majority of the leadership of the Bradford ILP, nor many of the contributors to the *Bradford Pioneer*, for the dominant strand within the anti-war section of the Bradford ILP was not pacifism.

The majority of the anti-war section of the party appear to have followed the lead of Fred Jowett who was never an outright pacifist, but accepted the need for 'National Defence'. Jowett, who had been returned as Bradford's first ILP MP in 1906, was the dominant figure in the Bradford Labour ranks during the First World War. Throughout the First World War he tried to articulate a viewpoint of what caused the war and how wars could be eradicated in the future. As he argued in his Chairman's speech to the 1915 ILP Conference at Norwich 'Now is the time to speak and ensure that never again shall the witches' cauldron of secret diplomacy brew the war broth of Hell for mankind'.[25] In an important article in the *Bradford Pioneer* in June 1916 he explained that:

I believe that the war would never have arisen if the government had carried out an open and honest foreign policy and disclosed to the people who had most to lose the relations between themselves and foreign governments with whom they were acting in collusion.[26]

His constant theme throughout the war was that it had been caused by the secret treaties which had been arranged, though frequently denied, by the British government. 'His fad', as the *Standard* said of Jowett, 'is the democratic control of foreign affairs'.[27] In connection with this Jowett also demanded that the government should specify its war aims and should be forced towards the negotiating table.

To Jowett, then, the war was caused by the secret treaties arranged by the British government and should be settled as quickly as possible. But on numerous occasions he declared that he was in favour of a British victory over 'Prussianism' and that he could not agree to the settlement of the war without 'the restoration of Belgium to complete sovereignty'.[28] He constantly maintained that a nation had a right to defend itself and frequently paid homage to those who had given their lives in the First World War.[29] In many respects Jowett's policy closely resembled the views expressed by Keir Hardie in his famous article 'We must see the War through, but denounce Secret Diplomacy'.[30] Although Jowett's position on the war, as with the stance adopted by Hardie, often appeared ambiguous and at odds with the ILP's declared opposition to the war, he was categorical in his wish to see the war speedily concluded in favour of the allies. On his attitude towards the anti-war resolution passed by the 1916 ILP Conference, of which he was Chairman, he reminded one critic that:

> The ILP resolution to which you refer only expressed the view that Socialist Parties as organised bodies should support no war. It did not attempt to lay down such a policy for individuals. If it did I should be opposed to it in principle.[31]

Such a distinction between the actions of individuals within a party and the policy of a party was confusing to many critics of the ILP and permitted Jowett to both support and oppose the war in different guises. Here was a classic case of having one's cake and eating it. But in many respects, his position was clearly understood by many members of the Bradford ILP and offered some common ground between the warring factions within the local party.

The fact is that a substantial proportion of the membership of the Bradford ILP was committed to the war effort either on the negative grounds of the need for 'National Defence' or on the more positive ground that Prussianism needed to be destroyed. Both shades of opinion, though by no means exclusive to the pro-war position, were evident in Bradford. By the middle of August 1914 the Revd R. Roberts had totally changed his stance and accepted the necessity of war:

> . . . the hour of reckoning has come. This legend of 'blood and iron' has to be shattered. Either it must be smashed or civilisation must go under. Its victory would be the enthronement of the War God in the centre of European civilisation and the crushing of Socialism for generations.[32]

For these groups conversion to the acceptance of war was total and as they had argued in a totally committed way previously about the immorality of war they now argued for an absolute commitment to the active prosecution of the war and the total necessity for an Allied victory. Again Roberts wrote:

> Through 40 years of public life, I have preached . . . I have never believed humanity would so far break down as to make it necessary to pay the extreme price of waging a war to preserve the peace. Yet for my sins, I have lived to see that . . . We are threatened with the ruin of civilised society. The success of Prussia in the awful tussle for life means that humanity will sink in smoking ruin. In the first place what is our duty as a British people? We must fight the battle to a triumphant finish. At whatever cost of life and treasure we must fight (I cannot tell the pain it cost me to write that sentence. I never thought I should live to do it) . . . Better to die than to be Prussianised. Better to be

wiped off the face of the earth than to exist squealing and squirming under the Prussian jack boots.[33]

It is quite clear that a substantial group of trade union members of the ILP supported the war effort. Their views were clearly presented by Jessie Cockerline, the regular trade union correspondent for the *Bradford Pioneer* who, in an article 'My Country – Right or Wrong', wrote:

> War is upon us and whatever we may think about the management or mismanagement, the civilisation or lack of civilisation which makes war possible, we must put it away for the present and realise to the full that the angel of death reigns as goddess, and her best servitors will prevail. We must realise, and act upon the knowledge, that it is far better to be among the victorious than among the vanquished and for this reason alone the cry must be 'My Country Right or Wrong'.[34]

There were other examples of a similar acceptance among the trade unionists in the party; J.H. Palin and Councillor A.W. Brown being to the fore.

Palin is, perhaps, the most interesting of these ILP trade unionists who supported the war effort. A prominent member of the Amalgamated Society of Railway Servants, having been the chairman of the ASRS at the time when the union was involved in the Taff Vale dispute, and a leading public figure in Bradford, as an ILP councillor and alderman up to and during the war, Palin was easily the most important pro-war Socialist who remained within the Bradford ILP. Until early 1917 he was the trade union correspondent of the *Bradford Pioneer*, having taken over from Jessie Cockerline, and prominently displayed his support for the war. At first, in 1914 and 1915, his views were tolerated in the confusion of opinion over the war within the ILP ranks, but he became an increasing embarrassment to Leach and the anti-war *Bradford Pioneer*, and was obviously out of step with resolutions passed by the Bradford ILP. This difference of opinion was sharply indicated at the 1916 ILP Conference when, despite being mandated to support a resolution committing all Socialist parties of all nations to refuse to support every war entered into by any government, Palin cut across the comparative equanimity of the meeting and bluntly stated that:

> We do not want the Germans here. Assume that the workers of this country had carried out this resolution at the beginning of the war, and the Socialists of other countries had not, and had rallied or been forced to join the army, where at the moment would Great Britain have been? At any rate, it seems to me that more time is required to get a considered opinion to start afresh after the war.[35]

Although he was reprimanded by T.W. Stamford, President of the Bradford ILP, Palin remained unrepentant and subsequently went to France to help with war transportation.[36] Yet the fact is that despite the preponderance of anti-war sentiments within the Bradford ILP there was a substantial proportion of the membership which supported the Palin line.

When the *Bradford Daily Telegraph* attacked the ILP's resistance to the war effort and its inability to 'raise a single finger to help the country to prosecute the war successfully', Jowett replied that 'In proportion to its membership the ILP has more adherents serving in the army and navy by far than either of the two other political parties.'[37] Censuses of the Bradford ILP membership confirm this impression. A census in February 1916 indicated that of the 461 young men in the local party membership of 1,473, 113 were in the trenches, 4 had been killed, 1 was missing, 9 had been wounded, 3 were prisoners of war, 118 were in training in England, 6 were in the Navy and 207 were attested under the Derby scheme as necessary home workers.[38] A similar survey in 1918 found that of the 492 members liable for service, 351 were serving in the forces while 48 were conscientious objectors or were on national work.[39]

Such fragmentation of opinion was also evident in the Bradford Trades Council, which had been closely connected with the activities of the Bradford ILP since the early 1890s. The pro-war and anti-war factions were fairly equally divided until 1916, when the latter group gained the upper hand after the introduction of military conscription.

The 'Anglo-German War', or 'European War', caught the Trades Council in a quandary. On the one hand, in November 1912, it had passed a resolution calling for a general stoppage in the event of an outbreak of war.[40] On the other hand it was evident from the outset that many members of the Trades Council were smitten by patriotic sentiments when the First World War began. As a result of this imbroglio the Trades Council permitted itself to drift with events. Its commitments to international peace and the International Socialist Bureau were forgotten. It generally followed the Labour Party Policy of working with the Government and the authorities to encourage recruitment, although there were occasional decorous statements from its officials and delegates about the need to secure a peace as quickly as possible. In general, the Trades Council spent the early years of the war dealing with the practical realities of living under war conditions. In 1914 and 1915 the main activity of the Council was to check up on the price and shortages of foodstuffs. This activity later gave way to Anti-Rent-Raising campaigns, to the raising of money through the Lord Mayor's Relief Fund, and to involvement in the activities of the Joint Food Vigilance Committee, alongside the ILP, the British Socialist Party and the Workers' Municipal Federation. Perhaps the Council's most emotive campaign of the practical type was its attempt to force the Government to accept responsibility for providing pensions to war widows and weekly relief and benefits to soldiers and sailors injured in the fighting. All these campaigns reflect the day-to-day functioning of the Trades Council.[41] But the Trades Council was also a litmus-paper to the changing mood of the Bradford working class to the war. From the start of the war there was a sizeable minority of delegates to the Trades Council who opposed war. The leaders of this group were George Licence, Charlie Glyde and J.W. Ormandroyd. The anti-war sentiments of Fred Jowett, expressed in the *Year Book* for 1914, also tugged the heartstrings of many delegates, although he was more equivocal about the war in subsequent statements.[42] On the other hand the silent majority gave their tacit approval to the war, and activists, such as Alderman J.H. Palin, went to fight in France alongside several hundred Bradford ILPers and thousands of Bradford trade unionists.[43] By 1916 and 1917, however, the attitude of the Council was beginning to change.

The threat of military and industrial conscription, raised in 1915, was pivotal in changing the attitude of the Trades Council, although several other issues conflated to compound the shift in thinking. In June 1915, the Trades Council passed a resolution opposing conscription:

> . . . believing conscription in any form to be a violation of the principles of civic freedom hitherto prized as one of the chief heritages of British liberty, and that its adoption would constitute a grave menace to the progress of the nation; it believes that a recourse to a compulsory system is uncalled for in view of the enormous roll of enlistments since the war began and further; it is impossible to reconcile a national service in industry with private profit-making, and further protests against those employers who are dismissing men because they are of military age. It therefore urges Parliament to offer their utmost opposition to any proposal to impose upon the British people a yoke which is one of the chief concerns of Prussian militarism.[44]

The concern expressed here was just as much about the Munitions Act of 1915, which had suspended Trade Union rights and prevented vital workers from moving from job to job without a certificate of approval from the employer, as it was about military conscription. The Trades Council delegates began to drift away from supporting the TUC Parliamentary Committee's circular calling for trade union help in army recruitment and, in a series of votes and a ballot in 1915 and 1916, indicated its withdrawal from army recruitment campaigns. A vote of delegates towards the end of 1915 produced an equal number of votes for and against the recruiting campaign.[45] A circular to affiliated trade unions in December 1915, requesting the opinions of societies to the recruiting campaign, was voted on by just over a third of the societies and produced a result of 19 societies for and 11 against, though those in favour represented only 6,757 members compared to the 11,157 against. Many small societies did not vote on the issue and three abstained.[46] Although the vote was inconclusive the introduction of conscription in 1916 led to the Trades Council's withdrawal from direct involvement in helping army recruitment.

The anti-war section within the Trades Council drew strongly from the opposition to conscription, although opposition to conscription did not in itself signify opposition to the war. The Trades Council pressured the Yorkshire Federation of Trades Councils to hold a No-Conscription Conference at the Textile Hall, Bradford in December 1915 and, in January 1916, it sent delegates to an ILP No-Conscription Conference at Leeds.[47] As the 1916 Annual Report indicates, there were still 'differences of opinion on the War', but it is also clear that the anti-war position was burgeoning in the Council's meetings.

William Leach, editor of the *Bradford Pioneer*, was permitted to present the views of the Union of Democratic Control to the Trades Council, and in September 1915 the Council affiliated to the movement.[48] By 1916 it was possible to organize a Peace Conference under Trades Council auspices. That Conference decisively condemned the Labour MPs for joining the Government and pushed strongly for peace negotiations.[49] The Trades Council also sent delegates to the Leeds Conference of June 1917, at which the Workers' and Soldiers' Council was formed in the hope of forcing forward the demand for international peace negotiations.[50]

By 1917 the Trades Council was increasingly being dominated by what Palin dubbed 'militant pacifists'.[51] The 'peace movement' was prevalent within the Trades Council, though there was still a sizeable commitment to the war effort by some of the affiliated unions. Many of those who became committed to the Peace Campaign of 1917 were not so much pacifists, or opponents of the war, as opponents of the government's military conscription policy. The imprisonment as a conscientious objector of Revis Barber, the son of Walter Barber who was secretary of the Trades Council, did much to win trade union support for the 'peace movement'.[52] Thus, by 1917 and 1918, Bradford became one of the centres of the anti-war movement and the Trades Council had become one of its chief supporters. Although there was a substantial minority of trade unionists who supported the war this was by no means as prevalent a mood within the Bradford trade union movement as it would appear to have been within the national trade union movement. If the Bradford ILP was divided on the issue of the war so was the Bradford Trades Council and the Bradford trade union movement at large.

The emphasis placed upon the 'Peace' movement by the hostile Tory and Liberal press in Bradford has served to conceal the fact that there were substantial differences of opinion within the ILP and the Trades Council over the war issue. The press broadcast the view that Bradford was a hotbed of such anti-war activities. Prominent ex-Bradford ILP members added to the illusion by offering an informed tarring of all members of the ILP and the Trades Council with the same brush. The leading ex-ILP critics of the Bradford ILP were Joseph

Burgess and Edward R. Hartley. Joseph Burgess had had a long association with the ILP. It was his paper, *The Workman's Times*, which had called together delegates from Labour societies to meet at the Bradford Conference in 1893. As an editor of Labour newspapers, and as a supporter of the activities of the Socialist Sunday School movement, he had established for himself great respect within the Labour movement.[53] He worked in Lancashire and London for many years but came to live in Bradford before the First World War, and edited the *Bradford Pioneer* until the summer of 1915 and was elected President of the Bradford ILP in 1915. A critic of the war at its outset, proclaiming that 'We have no quarrel with Germany. . . . Stand firm workers, in reaction to the seduction of those who will appeal to you in the name of patriotism', he had quickly changed his position by the summer of 1915.[54] He joined the Socialist National Defence Committee in June 1915 and was threatening to stand as parliamentary candidate for the National Socialist Party for Blackburn at the next general election, although he never did so.[55] The pages of the *Bradford Pioneer* are full of the letters of Burgess and the comments of the Bradford ILP in what one headline referred to as 'The Burgess Comedy'.[56] The Bradford ILP was very sensitive to the antics of a man who had so recently been at the centre of its activities. It was equally sensitive to, and disparaging of, the attacks levelled against it by Hartley.

Hartley, a butcher by trade, had been a member of the ILP from the mid-1890s and a member of the Social Democratic Federation, later to become the British Socialist Party, since 1902. He had represented the Bradford ILP on the City Council and had stood as the 'Socialist' candidate in the Bradford East parliamentary elections of 1906 and 1910.[57] It was his activities with the SDF in connection with the Dewsbury parliamentary by-election of 1913 which threw him into conflict with both the ILP and the Labour Representation Committee. Yet he still maintained some support in the Bradford Moor ward of the city where his activities as a councillor, lecturer and singer had won him considerable local respect. At the beginning of the war he very quickly adopted a pro-war stance, anticipated the introduction of military conscription, and became the organizing representative of the pro-war British Workers' League in the Bradford area.[58] His main pro-war activity in Bradford began in July 1917, when the 'Peace Campaign' was beginning to reach its zenith and in the wake of the Leeds Conference of June 1917. Both the Bradford ILP and the Bradford Trades Council were represented at this Conference, as was befitting a centre of peace agitation.[59] In response the British Workers' League held its inaugural meeting at which Hartley was the main speaker. The *Bradford Pioneer* sent a reporter to the meeting and suggested that about three-quarters of the 1,000 people present were opposed to the 'anti-ILP tone' of the meeting.[60] The British Workers' League continued to berate the Bradford ILP throughout 1917 and 1918. A. Howarth of the League said that 'Bradford had disgraced itself more than any other town in the country.'[61] Victor Fisher, secretary of the BWL, said to a Bradford audience that 'Sinister pacifism is more rampant in your midst than in any other part of the United Kingdom with the exception perhaps of the Clyde and South Wales.'[62] But such strictures against the Bradford ILP and the Bradford 'pacifists' were of limited impact, especially after the death of Hartley in early 1918.[63]

One of the major questions facing historians is why did the ILP and trade unions begin to go their separate ways after the First World War? This question is particularly important in the case of Bradford, which, as Reynolds and Laybourn have argued, maintained its preponderance within the national ILP movement due to the early establishment of a link between the Bradford Labour Union/ILP and the Trades Council.[64] In Bradford the war served to fragment both the ILP and the Trades Council, and fractured the Bradford Labour Movement with the preponderant role played within it by the ILP. It is clear that trade union members of the ILP began to go their own way and that the war had been a major cause of the rupture. Men such as J.H. Palin and Michael Conway, pre-war ILP stalwarts, turned their attention to the newly-formed Labour Party. In addition the ILP took in a significant number of anti-war ex-Liberals during the war who once more by their very presence brought about an increasing divorce with the working classes. Some of the '1917' and '1918' Liberals had more in common with the middle-class pacifist strand of the Bradford ILP's thinking than with the average working-class trade union member of the party.[65] This dichotomy was undoubtedly hardened with the return of many young male members of the ILP from the war.

The First World War had profound consequences for the Bradford ILP and served to disturb the long-established relationship between the ILP and the trade union movement, though perhaps not in the blunt manner which has often been suggested by historians. The war had an unsettling effect on the alliance rather than an immediate catastrophic impact. It would appear that other factors played upon the loosening effect of the war. In particular, the debate over the new Labour Party Constitution of 1918, which was to give power to the trade union movement at the expense of socialist societies such as the ILP, served to put a gap between local trade unionists and the local ILP. R. McKibbin has amply demonstrated the tensions which resulted from the ILP's opposition to the 1918 Constitution and has indicated the way in which the Constitution paved the way for the formation of new labour parties throughout the country to which local trades councils became affiliated.[66] The creation of the Bradford Labour Party in April 1919 certainly did much to undermine the position of the Bradford ILP.

The ILP had run Labour politics in Bradford since the 1890s. In the 1890s it had dominated the political activities of the Labour movement in connection with the Trades Council. From 1902 onwards it had shared the control of Bradford Labour politics with the Trades Council and the Workers' Municipal

Federation, a body which had been formed in order to bring non-Socialist trade unionists more directly into Labour politics.[67] From 1907 onwards the Joint Committee of the ILP and WMF made local political arrangements for the Bradford Labour movement.[68] But in 1918 the basis of the alliance was altered. Bradford was to be reorganized into four parliamentary divisions, instead of three, under the Representation of the People's Act, and a local Labour Conference was held in November 1917 to discuss the changes.[69] At this Conference representatives of the ILP, trade unions and cooperative societies agreed to contest all the seats at the next election and formed a committee of twelve representatives to discuss the selection of candidates. However, also out of this committee, and its deliberations throughout 1918, sprang the decision to hold a Conference on the Formation of a Central Labour Party for Bradford in September 1918.[70] A further committee of eleven representatives was set up to draft a constitution and the Bradford Labour Party officially came into existence on 5 April 1919, formally uniting the ILP, Trades Council and the WMF into one Labour organization for the first time.[71] It was a move which was to prove the undoing of the Bradford ILP whose importance within local politics began to diminish in the 1920s as the Bradford Labour Party increasingly became the focus of Labour politics.

The Bradford ILP never fully recovered from the traumas imposed by the First World War and the developments within the wider Labour movement during and after the war. It was already conscious that its prominence with the national ILP organization was under threat well before the end of the war. It launched the 'Bradford ILP Forward Movement' in 1918, pointing to the countrywide growth of the ILP and the tremendous step forward which had been made in Leicester and Scotland.[72] By implication, Bradford was lagging behind in these encouraging developments and was mindful of the need to protect its 'great reputation' and 'unique position' in the party. But events overtook it, allegiances changed and the divorce of the ILP from working-class opinion in Bradford finally occurred when the ILP disaffiliated from the Labour Party in 1932. The decision as taken at Jowett Hall in Bradford might have been expected to produce a large-scale defection from the local Labour Party, but this did not happen: only one of the twenty-nine Labour councillors and eight aldermen on Bradford City Council opted to remain in the ILP and Bradford ILP candidates obtained only derisory support in municipal elections during the late 1930s.[73]

Clearly, in 1914 the Bradford Labour movement was dominated by the ILP. It is equally obvious that the war started the process that led to the Bradford ILP's sorry state in the 1930s. But the loss of ILP support was more subtle than the conventional view that it resulted from an impasse between socialist opposition to the war and trade union patriotism. The war deeply divided both the Bradford ILP and the Bradford trade union movement and other factors, more to do with the developments within the Labour Party than to tensions within ILP support, helped to define the new relations within the Labour movement after the war. However, it is overwhelmingly clear that trade union, and thus working-class, support switched from the ILP to the Labour Party between 1914 and 1920. The end product, as R. McKibbin stressed almost twenty-five years ago, is that 'class loyalty drove out socialist doctrine' within the Labour Party. The anguish which both the national and Bradford ILP organizations faced over whether or not to continue as separate organizations from the Labour Party are indicative that the ILP had recognized the fundamental switch of allegiances that had occurred. The war provided an important, if not necessarily vital, part in explaining why the trade union movement and the ILP began to veer apart. Such a separation of the ILP and trade unionism ultimately proved terminal to the Bradford ILP which had always relied heavily on trade union support. The Labour Party, not the ILP, was to be seen as the liberating force for the working class in the future and the ILP was left to dwell upon the role of Socialists inside, and outside, the Labour Party.

Notes

1 *Bradford Weekly Telegraph*, 23 July 1915.

2 *Bradford Pioneer*, 20 December 1918.

3 'Bradford and the Yorkshire Manufacture: An American's Observations at Worstedopolis' in *Bulletin of the National Association of Wool Manufacturers* (1895).

4 F. Brockway, *Socialism and Sixty Years: the Life of Jowett of Bradford 1864–1944* (London, 1946), preface by J.B. Priestley, p. 8.

5 J.B. Priestley, *English Journey* (London, 1934), pp. 158–60.

6 *Yorkshire Observer Budget*, 13 April 1914, though different papers provide marginally different accounts of Palin's speech.

7 Bradford Trades and Labour Council, *Year Book*, for 1913 and 1914.

8 Bradford Trades and Labour Council Minutes, 7 November 1912.

9 He had joined the ILP in the mid-1890s and had been returned as an ILP member of the School Board alongside Margaret McMillan in 1897. He left the ILP in 1903 due to its unwillingness to cooperate with the Liberals but drifted back into its ranks before the First World War.

10 *Bradford Pioneer*, 9 January 1914.

11 G. Haupt, *Socialism and the Great War: The Collapse of the Second International* (London, 1973), particularly pp. 195–215.

12 *Bradford Pioneer*, 7 August 1914.

13 See C. Cross, *Philip Snowden* (London, Benn, 1966), p. 129 and J.A. Jowitt, 'Philip Snowden and the First World War', in K. Laybourn and D. James (eds), *Philip Snowden, the First Labour Chancellor of the Exchequer* (Bradford, Bradford Metro, 1981), pp. 39–57.

14 Fenner Brockway was particularly prominent in this respect, and Snowden was on the Executive of the Union of Democratic Control alongside Liberal pacifists such as E.D. Morel, also on the Executive, and Bertrand Russell, who was on its General Council. Not all ILP members of the UDC were necessarily pacifist, for F. Jowett was also on the Executive. For the Executive and General

Council of the Union of Democratic Control see the *Bradford Pioneer*, 8 November 1915. It is interesting how many of the Liberal members of this organization formed the '1917' and '1918' Liberals who moved over to the ILP and the Labour Party.

15 Arthur Priestman was a leading Bradford businessman from a prominent Quaker industrial family. For details of his career see the *Bradford Labour Echo*, 23 November 1895, *Bradford Daily Telegraph*, 4 October 1912 and his obituary in the *Bradford Pioneer*, 25 January 1918.

16 Joseph Burgess was editor of the *Bradford Pioneer* until June 1915 when Leach took over. See *Bradford Pioneer*, 29 December 1916.

17 *Bradford Pioneer*, 22 October 1915.

18 Ibid., 26 October 1917.

19 Ibid., 19 April 1918.

20 *Bradford Daily Telegraph*, 4 August 1914.

21 See reports in the *Bradford Daily Telegraph*, 7 and 31 August 1914 and 30 July 1915.

22 *Bradford Pioneer*, 23 December 1914.

23 *Bradford Daily Telegraph*, 30 December 1918.

24 Ibid.

25 *Bradford Pioneer*, 9 April 1915.

26 Ibid., 2 June 1916.

27 Cited in F. Brockway, *Socialism over Sixty Years: The Life of Jowett of Bradford 1864–1944* (London, George Allen & Unwin, 1946), p. 152.

28 *Bradford Pioneer*, 2 June 1916.

29 Ibid., 2 June 1916 and 13 April 1916.

30 Republished from the *Merthyr Pioneer* in the *Bradford Pioneer*, 21 April 1916.

31 *Bradford Pioneer*, 2 June 1916.

32 Ibid., 14 August 1914.

33 Ibid., 16 October 1914.

34 Ibid., 14 August 1914.

35 Ibid., 28 April 1916.

36 Bradford Trades and Labour Council, Minutes, 8 February 1917. He took up his duties in France on 12 February 1917.

37 *Bradford Pioneer*, 21 May 1915.

38 Ibid., 25 February 1916.

39 Ibid., 1 March 1918.

40 Bradford Trades and Labour Council, Minutes, 7 November 1912.

41 Ibid., 12 January, 13 February and 8 November 1915.

42 Bradford Trades and Labour Council, *Year Book*, 1914 (Bradford, 1915).

43 See note 33. Also, Dr H. Munro, a prominent member of the Bradford ILP before the war, took the first Volunteer Motor Ambulance Corps to the front, and a Dr Munro fund was formed in order to provide financial help for this unit: *Bradford Pioneer*, 8 January and 15 March 1915.

44 Bradford Trades and Labour Council, Minutes, 17 June 1915.

45 Ibid., Minutes, Letter of 5 November 1915.

46 Ibid., Minutes, Letter and Circular, 10 December 1915.

47 Ibid., Minutes, 8 November and 9 December 1915 and 3 January 1916.

48 Ibid., Minutes, 9 September 1915.

49 Ibid., Minutes, 7 December 1916 for leaflet on Conference and 9 January 1917 for a report on Conference.

50 Ibid., Minutes for May and June 1917.

51 M. Ashraf, *Bradford Trades Council 1872–1972* (Bradford, Bradford Trades Council, 1972), p. 94.

52 Bradford Trades and Labour Council, Minutes, 29 November 1917.

53 Joseph Burgess is examined in H. Pelling, *Origins of the Labour Party* (London, 1954). He produced his autobiography *A Potential Poet* (Burgess, Ilford) in 1927.

54 *Bradford Pioneer*, 7 August 1914, 30 July and 29 December 1916.

55 Cross, *Philip Snowden*, p. 106.

56 *Bradford Pioneer*, 20 July 1917.

57 See K. Laybourn and J. Saville, 'Edward Hartley 1855–1918', in J. Bellamy and J. Saville, *Dictionary of Labour Biography*, Vol III (London, Macmillan, 1976), pp. 97–9.

58 *Bradford Pioneer*, 20 July 1917.

59 Ibid., throughout May and June 1917.

60 Ibid., 27 July 1917.

61 *Bradford Weekly Telegraph*, 9 November 1917.

62 *Bradford Pioneer*, 13 July 1917.

63 Ibid., 25 January 1918.

64 J. Reynolds and K. Laybourn, 'The Emergence of the Independent Labour Party in Bradford', *International Review of Social History*, XX, 1975, part 3, pp. 313–46.

65 B. Barker, 'Anatomy of Reform: The Social and Political Ideas of the Labour Leadership in Yorkshire', *International Review of Social History*, XVII, 1973.

66 R. McKibbin, *The Evolution of the Labour Party 1910–1924* (Oxford, Oxford University Press, 1974), particularly pp. 91–106.

67 Workers' Municipal Federation Minute Books, 1902–1916 in the Bradford Trades and Labour Council collection in the West Yorkshire Archive Service, Bradford.

68 Ibid., Minutes, 4 March 1907.

69 Bradford Trades and Labour Council, Minutes, 15 November 1917.

70 Ibid., Minutes, 14 September 1918.

71 *Bradford Pioneer*, 11 April 1919.

72 Ibid., 29 March 1918.

73 M. Le Lohe, 'A Study of Local Elections in Bradford County Borough 1937–1967', unpublished PhD Thesis, University of Leeds, 1972, p. 141.

8

A COMMUNITY OF RESISTANCE: THE ANTI-WAR MOVEMENT IN HUDDERSFIELD, 1914–18

Cyril Pearce[1]

PREAMBLE

At the outbreak of war in 1914 Britain was unique among the combatant nations in being unable to call upon a conscript army. Until 1916 its war effort relied upon voluntary enlistment. That Britain was able to feed the war's enormous appetite in this way with willing recruits has been taken as evidence of the strength of the appeal to patriotism in British culture at that time. It is a view which has seldom been subjected to detailed analysis since the weight of evidence in its favour has seemed so overwhelming. It has, therefore, continued to be taken as an unquestioned assumption. For that reason it is also assumed that opposition to the war was barely tolerated and that those who opposed the war were in a very small, ineffectual and poorly organized minority of individuals acting for conscience's sake.[2]

The broad intention of this chapter is to suggest that the evidence for Huddersfield presents a number of alternative views. It will argue first, that enthusiasm for the war was less complete and more equivocal; second, that it was possible for anti-war views to be tolerated; third, that the anti-war community was broad based, extensive and well organized; and finally, that conscientious objectors (COs) were more than just individual prisoners of conscience.

CONTEXT AND RATIONALE

Since 1918, the general view of British attitudes to the war has combined two unchanging assumptions: first, that it is possible to speak of a 'national' mood, and second, that the mood reflected the war's general popularity. The only significant way in which that view has been modified since it was first advanced is the acceptance that, by 1917, the war's popularity had begun to wane.

If this is true for the more general accounts, those dealing with opposition to the war have also changed very little. They are equally prone to dealing with events at the national level and from a largely metropolitan perspective. The work of James Hinton and Sheila Rowbotham forms notable exceptions.[3] Added to this however, there are two debilitating tendencies: the first is to diminish specific anti-war opinion by incorporating it as part of an even grander process to chart the history of pacifism or to describe the growth of the Labour Party.[4] The second, to which historians sympathetic to the war's opponents often fall victim, is to become pre-occupied with the conscientious objectors themselves and with their individual struggles to the extent that opposition to the war is seen only in those terms.[5]

Attempts to identify diversity in the popular mood tend to end up either as tokens within the national picture or merely exceptions which prove the general rule.[6] There is a very real need for local and regional studies to address this. Sadly, despite massive outpourings of scholarly work on Britain and the Great War, we are still largely ignorant of what was really going on where the people were in the towns and villages of Britain.[7]

HUDDERSFIELD – A SPECIAL PLACE?

The question of anti-war sentiment in Huddersfield during the 1914–18 war was first raised publicly in 1915 by John Hunter Watts, a patriotic socialist and War Office recruiting agent. He warned his first public meeting in Huddersfield that '. . . the War Office informed him that the most serious opposition to recruiting came from this district . . .' Will Thorne spoke of Huddersfield as '. . . a hotbed of pacifism . . .' and Cunninghame Graham, another pro-war veteran of the Labour movement, attacked Huddersfield's anti-war campaigners as '. . . skunks, scoundrels, cowards, pacifists, neuters, neither men nor women . . .'.[8] Many years later, Wilfrid Whiteley, one of the 'skunks', confirmed the view that opposition to the war was stronger in Huddersfield than in other towns. He also maintained that opposition was more genuinely tolerated there than anywhere else he knew.[9]

Huddersfield in 1914 was typical of the generality of English industrial towns. It had a population of more than 100,000 but it served an area of more than twice as many. It was almost entirely a product of the nineteenth-century processes of industrial revolution and urbanization, having had a population of only 7,268 in 1801. The economic engine for its growth was the wool textile trade which, by 1911, accounted for over 40 per cent of the town's employed population.[10]

From the beginning, it had been a radical town, or, at least, a player in most of the major political upheavals of the nineteenth century. The Luddites, Owenite socialists and cooperators, the Chartists, factory reformers and Poor Law resisters had all made their early marks there. Secularism had been strong as had republicanism but it was, by the turn of the century, primarily a Nonconformist town with the institutions and attitudes to match. Temperance, 'self-help' and the Protestant work ethic were still very much in evidence.

Politically, Huddersfield's traditions in 1914, although crumbling to both left and right, were overwhelmingly Liberal. It was a Liberalism which continued to proclaim the traditional virtues of liberal democracy and individual liberty and yet was itself dominated by a tight wealthy industrial and commercial élite joined by family ties, sectarian affinities and an extensive network of social and charitable organizations. Mouthpiece for that élite was the Woodhead family's *Huddersfield Examiner*. Since 1868 the Liberal party had dominated the Town Council and had pursued a vigorous policy of civic progress through municipal enterprise. By 1914, however, this always incomplete radicalism had almost run out of steam. Two years earlier, for the first time, the Liberals had lost overall control of the Council. At the parliamentary level, however, the Liberal tradition held fast. In 1914 Huddersfield was represented by Arthur Sherwell, a radical Liberal of the older kind, a temperance writer and campaigner and associate of Seebohm Rowntree.

In local politics, the principal beneficiaries of Liberalism's relative decline were the Conservatives. Labour, by comparison, had failed to achieve any lasting electoral success. Nevertheless, despite being handicapped by a persistent local weakness in trade union membership, it had established an active presence in Huddersfield's political life. A small and vigorous Trades and Labour Council dated from 1885, and socialist politics of the Independent Labour Party (ILP) variety had taken root there as early as 1891. By 1914 it had spawned an extensive sub-culture of clubs, Socialist Sunday Schools, socialist societies and a militant branch of the British Socialist Party (BSP); but the movement was fractious and divided.

In this setting the outbreak of war was met with enormous anxiety and little enthusiasm. There was no mass hysteria of the sort reported elsewhere. There was no great public show when war was declared and few occasions during the war when Huddersfield demonstrated any real pro-war fervour. Indeed, the *Examiner* made a virtue of it by suggesting that:

> . . . in place of the flag-waving militarism which sometimes manifests itself in such periods, there is a restraint which speaks of a quiet determination to 'see the business through' and, on the part of those who cannot give their services in the field, a desire to realise the spirit which MILTON observed when he wrote; 'THEY ALSO SERVE WHO ONLY STAND AND WAIT'.[11]

There were no anti-German riots and no sustained attempts to disrupt anti-war meetings. Even J. Bruce Glasier '. . . congratulated Huddersfield upon its admirable record since the war began in maintaining freedom of speech, and in sustaining public meetings . . .'.[12] Open-air meetings were occasionally attended by what the *Examiner* described as 'lively scenes', but there was only one recorded attempt to break up an anti-war meeting. In January 1917, half a dozen young men 'in the uniform of the Royal Flying Corps' trying to disrupt a meeting in the Victoria Hall, at which the principal speaker was Philip Snowden, were routed by the 'pacifists' and ejected from the hall.[13]

This reluctance to be carried away by the passions of wartime can also be seen in the town's response to the call for recruits. In the early months of the war young men from Huddersfield, like young men everywhere else, joined up in droves. But, when the promise of peace by Christmas was not fulfilled, that enthusiasm quickly disappeared. Huddersfield's recruiting performance in 1915 was poor and the cause of some alarm within the town's élite.[14]

Unfortunately the debate around the recruitment issue has persisted as a debate about the presence or absence of the proper patriotic impulse. The truth for Huddersfield, as elsewhere, is much more complex. The simplicities of 'patriotism', 'honour' and 'duty' are tender blooms when faced with practical considerations of work, family, food and comfort. The expanded job opportunities of the wartime economy offered secure work and income levels of the sort that many local workers had never before enjoyed.

Added to this, there were other aspects of the recruiting process which provoked hostility and helped foment cynicism. For example, from the early weeks of the war the appeal to patriotic altruism, which was the local recruiting committee's principal tactic, was supplemented by a growing process of more equivocal inducements. In the autumn of 1914 these were fairly benign. There were supplements to pay, jobs held open, and free rent for soldiers' families living on local landed estates. By 1915, however, some of these inducements took forms which challenged both the spirit and the letter of the voluntary principle. Employers were 'releasing' men of military service age to 'encourage' them to enlist and the local recruiting committee approached other employers to ask them to replace shop assistants and office workers with women so that men might be 'released' to 'volunteer'.

A circular from the Local Government Board in March 1915 even invited local authorities to explore the feasibility of 'releasing' eligible men. By mid-April Leeds Corporation had 'released' 500 but Huddersfield had refused. The Council set its face against such 'compulsory voluntaryism.'[15]

AN ANXIOUS BUT TOLERANT ELITE

There are numerous factors which contributed to the particular quality of Huddersfield's response to the 1914–18 war. Of these, three might be considered the most significant. First, the nature and behaviour of the local élite and, as a consequence, that of the local social and political establishment. Second, the character of the socialist, labour and trade union movement and third, the emergence of a distinctive community of resistance opposed to Britain's involvement in the war.

For Huddersfield's largely Liberal élite the war was unwelcome. As the crisis gathered during the summer of 1914 it argued for non-intervention. Once war had been declared the emphasis was switched to loyalty to Asquith and the Liberal government. Nevertheless, the switch could hardly be described as wholehearted and enthusiastic.[16] In common with much of the rest of the Liberal establishment, the *Examiner*'s stance throughout the war was loyal but critical. At times it was vigorous in its defence of long-held Liberal principles when these were seen to be threatened by military conscription and the Munitions Acts.[17] It was also remarkably tolerant of the war's opponents. The Liberal establishment was not alone in this. There were elements within local Conservatism which were part of the same consensus. Indeed, until its demise in 1916, the Conservative *Huddersfield Chronicle* noticeably refused to join the '. . . shrieking brotherhood of armchair patriots . . .'.[18]

If we take the Town Council as the formal expression of the élite view then the picture is confirmed. As has been shown, it resisted the pressure to 'release' its employees during 1915 on the grounds that this would compromise the voluntary principle. While other local authorities moved to prevent the anti-war campaigners from holding meetings in council premises or on council land Huddersfield maintained its commitment to free speech throughout the war.

That is not to say that the Council was unanimously or even consistently free from the taint of pro-war excess. There was a lobby of mainly Conservative councillors led by Alderman Ernest Beaumont who persistently argued the ultra-patriotic line. In 1916 it was the Council's policy towards its schoolteachers who were conscientious objectors that became the point at issue. Leeds City Council refused to employ known COs as teachers and by December 1916 had dismissed three of them and a school caretaker too for good measure. For Huddersfield the matter came to a head when two CO teachers, who had been directed to work of national importance away from the town, asked whether they would be able to return to their old jobs after the war.

For Alderman Beaumont there was no question: 'Boys taught by cowards compare unfavourably with boys taught by patriotic men . . .' and he spoke of '. . . purging the state of dangerous elements detrimental to the future of education . . .'.[19] The Council would have none of it. Beaumont's view was rejected by a combination of Liberal, Labour and Conservative members.

This tolerance extended to the work of the local police. In other parts of the country they were often accused of helping the jingoistic elements to attack anti-war meetings or, at least, of standing by and doing nothing. In Huddersfield however, even opponents of the war admitted '. . . the local police . . . have shown no sign of infection by the Prussian spirit, and, at all times carry out their difficult duties with tact and impartiality . . .'.[20]

Probably the defining moment for the Council and for the Liberal establishment came in June 1915. A resolution from the local recruiting committee called upon the Council to support a form of 'National Service'. The response was a debate which re-affirmed the Council's commitment to the voluntary principle. Elsewhere, the Huddersfield Women's Liberal Association weighed in on the side of Liberal principle and agreed unanimously that:

. . . all forms of compulsory military service . . . are contrary to the principles of individual liberty for which the Empire stands . . . [and that] . . . the voluntary system had more than justified itself, and [they] would deplore the introduction of Prussianism and the doctrine of slavery of the citizens of this country . . .[21]

With the Liberals shaken by the declaration of war, by the time this debate took place the cracks in the edifice of unity that the *Examiner* had been working hard to prevent or disguise had already widened. Arthur Sherwell, sharply critical of the formation of the Coalition government, had from the summer of 1915 sat in opposition as an Independent Liberal. Thereafter, he campaigned persistently against the government's every departure from the paths of traditional Liberal orthodoxy. In particular he campaigned against military conscription and in doing so showed scant respect for Asquith or his cabinet colleagues. For many Liberals Sherwell was articulating their deepest concerns but for others, probably a sizeable number of the Huddersfield Liberal Association, such public disloyalty was unforgivable. In February 1916, Huddersfield's Central Liberal Club struck his name off its list of Honorary Vice-Presidents. This was an unprecedented act and reflected the tensions which were, by that time, beginning to tear at Liberal unity.[22]

LABOUR AND SOCIALIST ANTI-WAR UNITY

If the pressure of wartime was undermining the traditional self-confidence of the Liberal élite and beginning a process of fragmentation, then, for the labour and socialist movement in Huddersfield it had the opposite effect.

For a number of years before 1914 the movement had been seriously divided. A vigorous, if small, Marxist group in the shape of the Huddersfield branch of the British Socialist Party (BSP) had conducted a running battle with the local movement's ILP-dominated leadership. This struggle was acted out on street corners, in the meetings of the Trades and Labour Council and in the columns of the movement's own newspaper, *The Worker*. It contributed to the left's persistent failure in local council elections just at the time when Labour was making significant advances elsewhere.[23]

Nationally, the labour and socialist movement's united opposition to the war melted away when war was declared. The majority of the Parliamentary Labour Party and the TUC fell in with the government. The ILP, on the whole, but with local variations, continued to oppose the war while the BSP was chronically divided. A vigorously pro-war BSP Executive, led by Blatchford and Hyndman, found itself at odds with a majority of local branches which took an unequivocal anti-war class position.[24] In Huddersfield, however, the outbreak of war set many of the pre-war differences to one side and the 'Socialist Unity' for which *The*

Worker and others had been campaigning was practically, if not formally, achieved. It was opposition to the war which now made it possible.

However, while the ILP line was consistent, the arguments which sustained it were not. Influences on ILP policy ranged from an ethical opposition to war and militarism in general to a neo-Marxist rejection of the war as a '. . . quarrel . . . between the ruling classes of Europe . . .'. The ILP in Huddersfield mirrored all of that. Significantly, as the dominant force in the local labour and socialist movement, it took both the Trades Council and the Labour and Socialist Election Committee (LSEC) along with it.[25]

For the members of Huddersfield's BSP branch there was no equivocation. Arthur Gardiner, one of its leading figures, later explained:

> . . . I took up the position as did most of the young fellows of the Huddersfield Socialist Party, of anti-war. It wasn't an anti-war movement from the viewpoint of a religion or even of pacifism – we were based definitely and soundly on the theory of the class struggle and that the 1914–18 war was merely a fight for foreign markets which we were not prepared to give our lives for.[26]

Untroubled by any concern for the niceties of party considerations in either the ILP or the BSP, *The Worker*'s editor, George Thomas, and his staff argued and campaigned for a determined resistance to the war. Their lively and largely Marxist analysis and persistent campaigning gave Huddersfield's labour and socialist movement a real intellectual force and cutting edge.

That is not to say that this anti-war line went entirely unchallenged. Huddersfield's senior Labour councillor, Alderman William Wheatley, broke the pattern. He worked for the local recruiting committee and worked to support the war effort.[27] Other ILP, Socialist Sunday School and Socialist Club members must have supported the war but they did not come out and say so. Many of them either voluntarily enlisted or went without protest when conscripted. George Hargrave, in 1914 an ordinary member of the Stonemasons' Society and *Clarion* reader, later recalled: 'I enlisted in the army because I was what we called a patriotic socialist, because I wanted to defend and preserve the British way of life as against the German way of life.'[28] How many more labour and socialist men and women in Huddersfield shared this view in the autumn of 1914 is difficult to judge.

The only significant challenge to the hegemony of this anti-war view appeared in the summer of 1915. It coincided with the appearance in West Yorkshire of John Hunter Watts, one of the British socialist movement's 'old guard'. A Londoner, he had been a prominent member of the Social Democratic Federation and BSP since the 1880s and was closely associated with its veteran leader H.M. Hyndman. He took Hyndman's patriotic socialist line at the outbreak of war and, when the anti-war elements took over the BSP in 1916, joined him in the formation of the National Socialist Party. In 1915 he was employed by the War office as a recruiting agent. His task would seem to have been to do what he could to undermine the anti-war domination of Huddersfield's labour and socialist movement.[29]

He quickly set about bringing together some of the scattered elements of pro-war or patriotic socialist opinion to create the Huddersfield Workers' Own Recruiting Committee (HWORC). His recruits were largely disaffected oddities and outsiders and notwithstanding two or three months of hectic activity made little headway. The purpose of the HWORC was overtaken by the advent of conscription. By November 1915 Hunter Watts had moved on and, without him and his War Office backing, the challenge to the anti-war consensus faded.[30]

A BROAD-BASED MOVEMENT

Had the position in Huddersfield been a combination of, on the one hand, Liberal establishment tolerance, uncertainty and division and, on the other, an apparently unassailable Labour and socialist opposition to the war, then the story would have been remarkable enough. But there was more than that. There was a substantial pre-war history of opposition to war and militarism which had united a number of the sections of the centre-left from radical Liberals to Marxist socialists.

Huddersfield's radical Liberalism and the local ILP's ethical brand of socialism arguably shared a common source. Those common threads had first combined to oppose the Boer War. The Huddersfield branch of the South African Conciliation Committee brought together members of the Trades Council and the ILP with members of the radical wing of the Liberal Association. This successful mobilization of local anti-war feeling had helped to define and mobilize a local constituency. Some of its key players were still active when war broke out in 1914.[31]

As the years before 1914 gave rise to questions of war and peace, empire, armaments and conscription, elements of the previous groupings re-appeared. It was less closely organized and fraught with new political problems; nevertheless, it was a group of radical Liberal and Labour town councillors who responded to a broad-based campaign and persuaded the Education Committee to re-name its 1914 Empire Day holiday for local schools 'Peace and Empire Day'.[32]

During 1913 both the Leeds Peace Congress and the newly-formed West Riding Peace Federation contained representatives of Huddersfield's radical Liberalism and the Trades Council. However, what stirred the anti-militarist alliance into action was the National Service League's 1913 campaign for a system of national service. In late December 1913 representatives of the Society of Friends, Huddersfield ILP, the Huddersfield Adult School Union, the Huddersfield Junior Liberal Association, the Free Church Council and the BSP branch formed the Huddersfield Committee against Compulsory Military Service. It was later joined by representatives of the Trades Council and the Labour and Socialist Election Committee. Three of the prime movers in the Committee were veterans of the Boer War campaign, Ben Riley of the ILP, Joshua Robson and his son John, both Quakers and Liberals. They were joined by Robert Hopkinson, heir to a prosperous engineering business and unattached left-of-centre radical. All four were to become deeply involved in the wartime anti-war movement.[33]

The plan was to organize a 'Great Peace Demonstration' to be addressed by local MPs and at which resolutions opposing military conscription and increases in military spending were to be put. Arthur Sherwell (Huddersfield) and Charles Trevelyan (Elland) were happy to support the resolutions against conscription but declined to oppose military spending. There was stalemate. The Trades Council, Labour and BSP representatives withdrew and the Liberals went ahead with the demonstration but with only the anti-conscription resolution in place. Nevertheless, the *Worker*'s editor, George Thomas, still saw it as '. . . a crushing counterblast to the . . . National Service League and a strong declaration against the policy of the Liberal government in piling up the expenditure on armaments.'[34] In a sense this was true, but the absence of the representatives of the labour and socialist movement gave the meeting less credibility. Nevertheless, what the previous month had demonstrated was the extent of the pre-war anti-militarist and anti-war constituency in the town. The influence of that constituency was much in evidence in the town's initial response to the threat of war in July 1914. However, once war had been declared, the centre of resistance shifted to the labour and socialist movement. It was not until 1915 that the pre-war anti-militarist alliance re-appeared.

It was the formation, in February 1915, of the Huddersfield branch of the Union of Democratic Control (UDC) which marked its return. As a national organization the UDC had been formed shortly after the outbreak of war. Its prime movers were, initially, Liberals, middle-class intellectuals, writers and campaigning journalists and, significantly, Labour's Ramsay MacDonald and Philip Snowden. They had both taken a principled stand against the war and had committed themselves to campaigning against it.

Its objectives were a negotiated peace and the replacement of Foreign Office secret diplomacy by the democratic control of foreign policy. Initially a metropolitan grouping, the UDC expanded rapidly into a national organization. By October 1915, its first annual meeting, it had sixty-one branches to which numerous other organizations were affiliated – among them forty-eight Trades Councils. The branches were spread throughout Britain but with a concentration in the industrial areas and particularly in those where support for both radical Liberalism and the ILP was traditionally strong.[35]

At the beginning the UDC was irredeemably middle class, Liberal and well-meaning. Fenner Brockway described its members as '. . . bourgeois to their finger-tips. They were suave, gracious, cultured. They might have been lifted out of any gathering of the gentlemen of England.'[36] Branch membership, however, was generally more varied. In Huddersfield it represented a genuine coming together of radical Liberals, trade unionists and members of the ILP. The eleven members of its first provisional committee came from different sections of the town's radical community. Five of them were from some branch of the labour and socialist movement: Ben Riley, ILP; Wilfrid Whiteley, ILP and Socialist Sunday Schools; Fred Wood, Postmen's Federation, Trades Council and LSEC; R.H. Yates, Shop Assistants' Union, Trades Council, LSEC and Law Taylor, Postmen's Federation, Trades Council and Labour Alderman. The two women members were both active suffragists and members of the Huddersfield branch of the National Union of Women's Suffrage Societies (NUWSS). One of the two, Julia Robson Glaisyer, was a Quaker and prominent member of the Women's Liberal Association. Her father and brother's work in the local anti-militarist cause has already been mentioned.[37]

The remaining four original members are not easily categorized. Robert A. Hopkinson who, with Ben Riley, had called the meeting had been associated with the pre-war Huddersfield Committee against Compulsory Military Service. He was a rich industrialist with a radical left-of-centre background.[38] Edgar Woodhead was also a wealthy man, divisional clerk to the West Riding Education Committee, a Liberal and active member of the congregation of Milton Independent Chapel but a Quaker sympathizer and close friend of the Robson family. Of Messrs H. Oxley and Stokes, the other members of the provisional committee, little is known except that in November 1917 Huddersfield's Military Service Tribunal gave a 'Mr. H. Oxley', a conscientious objector, exemption from military service in order to do work of national importance.[39]

Membership of the Huddersfield UDC was not extensive. Unlike the pre-war anti-militarist groupings, it did not have any prominent representation from mainstream Liberalism. Although Liberal party members, Julia Glaisyer and Edgar Woodhead were not among its leading figures. It was also undermined for a time by the BSP's suspicions that it was a 'side-tracking organization'. Nevertheless, it was important because it established continuity with the pre-war movement and announced the existence of an ethical community with a common critical position on the war which cut across party, class and gender divisions.

Two things galvanized and further unified the anti-war movement: the failed campaign to prevent the introduction of conscription and the working of the conscription process itself. Indeed, the advent of conscription in the spring of 1916 became a major benefit to the war's opponents. Confronting the machinery of compulsion reinforced the bonds between the anti-war movement's diverse elements. Military Service Tribunals (MST) were monitored, case notes recorded, COs identified, traced, advised and supported, leaflets distributed and meetings organized. A veritable bureaucracy of busy-ness was created within which many helpers could find a role. The occasional little victories at Tribunal hearings and the public displays of support for local COs cheered the faithful and gave reassurance. Above all, conscription gave the anti-war movement its own flesh and blood conflict. It was their Western Front in that it presented opportunities for acts of physical courage and stoic endurance. The enemy was militarism and the coercive state, the troops were the COs and the battlegrounds were the Tribunals, the magistrates' courts, the courts martial, prisons and work camps. It even gave the anti-war movement its own local heroes.

At the centre of this unfolding drama were the No-Conscription Fellowship (NCF) and the No-Conscription Councils (NCC). Formed by Fenner Brockway and his wife Lilla in November 1914, the NCF was initially a small propagandist group aiming to bring together young men of military age who opposed the war. By the autumn of 1915 Fenner Brockway had brought within its orbit many of the 'great and the good' who were already associated with the wider anti-war campaign.[40] Although much was claimed for its rate of expansion during 1915, there is little evidence of its impact in Huddersfield until the early months of 1916. A factor in this might have been that, like the UDC, it seems to have preferred to meet in the ethically sound but politically neutral premises of the Society of Friends. However, by the end of January 1916 it had moved its premises, and probably its membership, sharply to the left, by meeting in the BSP rooms in the centre of Huddersfield. Indeed, once the battle for the rights of the COs was thoroughly joined, the left with a mixture of ILP and BSP militants seems to have taken it over entirely.[41] So much so that Adams and Poirier's view of the NCF as a '. . . doughty group of religious and philosophical pacifists . . .' bears little relation to the Huddersfield reality.[42] It is probably an unreal view of the NCF branches in other places too.

The NCF branches, almost of necessity, remained small and representative primarily of potential COs. The force of a broad-based opposition to the war and to conscription found more tangible expression in the formation of the Huddersfield No-Conscription Council. A National Council against Conscription had been formed in London 'to mount an eleventh-hour campaign against conscription' and had among its members most of those nationally-prominent activists whose names were already well known.[43] Local branches of the Council against Conscription began to appear during January 1916. Manchester had established its No Compulsion Committee by the 11th and a week later Huddersfield's No-Conscription Council was formed.

The initiative in calling the inaugural meeting had been taken by the Trades Council. Attending were also representatives of all the local labour and socialist organizations, the Society of Friends, the NCF, the Fellowship of Reconciliation and the Brotherhood and Adult Schools. Although complete records of the NCC have not survived, we do know that during its first year its management committee at one time or another had members from across the whole range of the anti-war ethical and political community. This broad-based membership persisted to the end of the war. Despite changing its name to Huddersfield Council for Civil Liberties (HCCL) it became the hub of anti-conscription work in the town.[44]

CONSCIENTIOUS OBJECTORS

When the Military Service Act came into operation in February 1916, the anti-war movement was faced with new and immediate challenges. Its central commitments to repeal the act and end the war had to give way to the urgent need to respond to the practical and ethical imperatives of a new situation. Robbins is not wide of the mark when he suggests:

> Until this point, if one led a quiet life, being an 'opponent of the war' was largely a matter of private conviction without public significance. Now it became a matter of general concern to the state. For eligible men, a choice between fighting on the one hand and accepting or refusing the alternatives offered on the other, could not now be avoided.[45]

Assessing the numbers of potential war resisters now faced with this choice is crucial to a proper understanding of the strength or weakness of the anti-war constituency. Unfortunately, there are no reliable data on which such calculations can be made. The indicators are all flawed, partial and subject to varying interpretations. Where figures do exist, they deal only with those who came within the Tribunal system and not all the war's opponents did that.

An impression of the extent of the problem can be obtained by considering those occasions when a potential CO had to decide what to do. Considered in this way it can be suggested that official statistics will necessarily underestimate the anti-war constituency by a very wide margin indeed. The first decisive occasion for the potential CO was when he received his call-up papers. At this point there were at least five options:

- accept and report to barracks as required
- appeal to the MST for exemption on grounds of essential war work – usually requiring employer support – but without revealing his anti-war views
- appeal to the MST for exemption on grounds of conscience
- refuse to collaborate with the system at all and wait to be arrested
- run away

No figures can exist of the numbers of those who, rather than face Tribunals, prison, personal and social censure, or a life on the run chose to accept conscription. As Ken Weller has suggested, family reasons, the fact that even army pay would help wives and dependants, often weighed more heavily in the balance than conscience or political convictions.[46] All that we can be sure of is that they did exist. One such from Huddersfield was Tom Whitehead. He was a member of Paddock Socialist Club and a trade unionist. When he was killed in France in December 1917, the *Worker* obituary suggested, ' although a soldier through the Military Service Acts he still held his views '.[47]

In the same way figures of any kind on the numbers of those who went on the run and avoided capture are simply not possible. Sheila Rowbotham, Raymond Challinor and Ken Weller have all drawn attention to the existence of an underground network helping fugitives to escape conscription but have been unable to quantify its use.[48] There is evidence of a number of Huddersfield men who went on the run but only one of them, Arthur Crowe, a BSP member, successfully avoided capture.[49] The nature of the evidence dictates that the picture is fragmentary and unclear although it is probably safe to say that only a small proportion of the war's opponents were ever prepared to take such drastic action.

For COs who did not apply for exemption on grounds of conscience but because of the war-essential nature of their work there are no figures. On the other hand, for the other two options possible at this first stage there are manageable, if debatable, figures. This is largely because both came within the official orbit of either MSTs or magistrates' courts and therefore stood some chance of making a mark on the record. John Rae's figures of the number of people nationally appearing before Tribunals on grounds of conscience are potentially suspect. He suggests that the total number of CO appeals to Tribunals was about 13,700; David Bolton, quoting NCF sources, argues for 16,100, while calculations based on the Huddersfield evidence indicate a national figure of between 18,000 and 19,000.[50]

Once beyond that first decisive stage the permutations and opportunities for decisions about how to react become almost endless and were often a matter for the individual's sense of what he could or should endure. Arthur Gardiner, for example, Huddersfield's most celebrated CO, suffered a breakdown while in prison and accepted a work camp place in East Anglia rather than endure the rigours of the further imprisonment he thought would kill him. His close friend, Percy Ellis, however, as an 'absolutist' refused the Brace scheme and spent the rest of the war in prison.[51]

Accepting that the number of 'potential' COs is unquantifiable, two questions persist: first, how many COs were there and, second, who were they? Those statistics of Huddersfield's opposition to the war which can be produced tell slightly different stories although they can be re-worked in a number of different ways. Two will suffice here.

Based on a combination of MST reports and press accounts it is possible to identify some of the motives of those coming before the MST (Table 8.1).

Table 8.1. Huddersfield Conscientious Objectors 1916–1918. Appeals to the Military Service Tribunal for exemption on grounds of conscience

Description	Totals	Percentage
SOCIALISTS (Total)	(39)	(32.23%)
BSP	9	
ILP	8	
Socialist Sunday School	11	
'Socialist'	11	
RELIGIOUS (Total)	(49)	(40.5%)
Baptist	1	
Christadelphian	22	
Church of England	2	
Methodist	5	
Quaker	3	
Roman Catholic	2	
Salvation Army	1	
Spiritualist	2	
'Religious'	11	
MORAL/ETHICAL (Total)	(31)	(25.62%)
OTHERS (Total)	(2)	(1.65%)
Republican	1	
Vegetarian	1	

121

Sources: Primarily the local Huddersfield press accounts of the MST hearings. In the reports not all the COs were named but motives were mentioned in sufficient detail to permit the kind of analysis shown above.

On the other hand, these are just those who appeared before the MST, not including the fugitives or those who went straight to the magistrates' court. The only way to measure those cases is by tracking named individuals as they appear in the press and other accounts (Table 8.2). While providing a smaller number – 109 as opposed to 121 – each of these cases is documented. What they do suggest is that the majority of those who claimed exemption on grounds of conscience at the MST in Huddersfield were 'Religious' COs of which the largest single group were Christadelphians. This distorts the picture if the intention is to use these figures to gauge the extent of the town's active anti-war community. The Christadelphians for their own reasons would have nothing to do with society at large or politics in particular.[52] If they are then excluded from this rough indicator the balance between the 'Socialist' COs and the 'Religious' COs shifts towards the former. In Table 8.2 that shift is already in evidence because there are those included here who did not appear before the MST. Nevertheless, if the Christadelphians are excluded again that balance becomes even more marked in favour of the socialists.

Table 8.2. Huddersfield Conscientious Objectors 1916–1918: named and tracked COs.

Description		Totals	Percentage
SOCIALISTS (Total)		(48)	(44.0%)
BSP		13	
ILP		10	
Socialist Sunday School		9	
'Socialist'		16	
RELIGIOUS (Total)		(35)	(32.06%)
Christadelphians		22	
Church of England		1	
Methodists		3	
Quakers		4	
Spiritualists		1	
'Religious'		4	
MORAL/ETHICAL	(Total)	(2)	(1.83%)
NCF/UDC/NCC	(Total)	(4)	(3.76%)
NOT KNOWN	(Total)	(20)	(18.35%)
		109	

Source: As Table 8.1.

The conclusion is simple: notwithstanding John Rae's case for the importance of the religious COs, when it comes to analysing the detail for Huddersfield two features are evident. First, the political COs were overwhelmingly socialists of one form or another; and second, that if considered as reflections of the components of the active anti-war community (i.e. with the exclusion of the Christadelphians) then that community is represented, in the main, by men with socialist beliefs.

What this all might mean in terms of Huddersfield's standing as a 'hotbed of pacifism' is difficult to say without comparative studies. The impression is that the number of COs – however calculated – is a significant indicator of the existence of a resilient local anti-war community – and herein lies a further issue.

The received view is that, ultimately, whatever the ideological source of their motivation, COs were individuals making a stand for freedom of conscience. The NCF's own journal, the *Tribunal*, and the majority of subsequent sympathetic accounts all stress the part played by individuals. What has been ignored is the extent to which the COs represented and spoke for a collective or group consciousness. The Huddersfield evidence suggests that local COs, especially those from within the labour and socialist movement, can be better understood when seen in this light. They were representatives of both ethical and Marxist components within the local anti-war movement and they were supported by an extensive and vigorous local organization.

A COMMUNITY OF RESISTANCE

In sustaining the anti-war community the parts played by clubs and societies and by labour and socialist families were important, but equally if not more important were the roles assumed by women.

Historically Huddersfield's labour and socialist movement had been augmented by clubs and societies which expressed its broader and less formal sub-culture. As wartime dramatized the issues facing it, the movement's need for the warmth and support of that sub-culture was greater than ever. Paddock Socialist Club, for example, emerged as something of a centre for radical resistance to conscription. Six of its members were COs and two of them rejected all concessions to the conscription system. Huddersfield Central ILP club extended its premises and increased its services to members and non-members alike by adding games and catering facilities. The 'billiards and mash' strategy seems to have been successful. By September 1916 the Central ILP was claiming a big increase in membership. Bazaars, whist drives and socials to raise money for the COs and their families became part of wartime club life.[53]

Family and friendship networks extended that work further. In the BSP, for example, there were at least four inter-connected families which contributed at least twelve active members between them, of whom three became COs. The ILP and the Socialist Sunday Schools were also part of an extended network of political families. Family networks linked closely with neighbourhood and friendship networks. They also meant that some family members, relatively inactive in the normal course of events, were motivated to step up their level of political work especially when their young men went as COs. This led to the greater involvement of women. The BSP was particularly affected. It lost most of its principal figures as COs and, as a consequence, for the first time, in 1917 two women were elected to the branch committee. Within the ILP too, and the left generally, women activists had a higher profile during 1916–1918 than they had enjoyed before.[54]

CONCLUSION

In Huddersfield the opposition to war had various roots. For some opponents it was a simple matter of international class loyalty; for others, the source was a deeper and less easily identified mix of ethical antipathies to violence and to the denial of individual freedoms which were seen to be inherent in war and militarism. These ethical positions grew from roots in radical and Nonconformist Christianity which were shared with local Liberalism. That shared antipathy to war and militarism had been manifest in the combined local opposition to the Boer War and in the immediate pre-war agitation against the National Service League and increased arms spending. It was revived in wartime by some radical Liberals through their collaboration in the Huddersfield branches of the UDC, the NCF and the NCC.

Official Liberal opinion, the historically dominant element in Huddersfield politics, was divided, anxious and ambiguous. It had struggled to oppose Britain's entry into the war, and then accepted the need to fight. It agonized at the social consequences of conscription and then accepted. It worried about its MP, Arthur Sherwell, because his loyalty to principle was greater than his loyalty to the Liberal government. And yet it still clung tenaciously to some of the tattered remnants of its Liberal values through tolerance of opposition and a principled resistance to the worst excesses of wartime patriotism.

The 1918 general election results were good for the anti-war movement in the Huddersfield area. Labour candidates with anti-war pedigrees did well in Huddersfield (32.47 per cent), Dewsbury (30.12 per cent) and the Colne Valley (41.16 per cent).[55] Contrary to experiences elsewhere, in these three constituencies at least an anti-war pedigree was not a handicap. Too much might be read into these results but for Huddersfield at least they did confirm the strength of the town's labour and socialist movement's opposition to the war. Rather than dividing the movement the war had united it. The struggle to resist conscription and the support for local COs after 1916 strengthened the bonds. At the same time a strong local labour and socialist sub-culture supplemented by ties of family and friendship, and informed by the campaigning vigour of the *Worker*, reinforced and sustained the anti-war value system against pro-war propaganda. In such a context those who refused to be conscripted into military service rather than being lonely prisoners of conscience became the vanguard and representatives of a particular community of resistance.

Where does all this put the Huddersfield experience and what might it have to say about the bigger picture? Should we regard it as eccentric to the general experience or symptomatic of something more widespread? On the other hand, perhaps the evidence here suggests that we ought to start asking different questions.

Notes

1   This chapter is based closely on work supervised by David Wright between 1984 and 1988 which resulted in my M.Phil. thesis, C. Pearce 'The Anti-War Movement in Huddersfield, 1914–1918' (Huddersfield, Huddersfield Polytechnic, 1988).

2   The source material for the general view is extensive. Some of the major past and recent works are as follows: A.J.P. Taylor, *English History 1914–1945* (Oxford, Oxford University Press, 1965); J. Stevenson, *British Society 1914–45* (Harmondsworth, Penguin, 1984); T. Wilson, *The Myriad Faces of War: Britain and the Great War, 1914–1918* (Cambridge, Polity Press, 1986); B. Waites, *A Class Society at War: England 1914–1918* (Leamington Spa, Berg, 1987); W.J. Reader, *'At Duty's Call' A Study of Obsolete Patriotism* (Manchester University Press, 1988); J. Turner (ed.), *Britain and the First World War* (London, Unwin Hyman, 1988); G.J. DeGroot, *Blighty: British Society in the Era of the Great War* (Harlow, Longman, 1996).

3   J. Hinton, *The First Shop Stewards' Movement* (London, 1973); S. Rowbotham, *Friends of Alice Wheeldon* (London, Pluto Press, 1986).

4   Into this category fit M. Ceadel, *Pacifism in Britain 1914–1945: the Defining of a Faith* (London, 1980); D. Hayes, *Conscription Conflict: The Conflict of Ideas in the Struggle For and Against Military Conscription in Britain between 1901 and 1939* (1949); Fenner Brockway, *Inside the Left: Thirty Years of Platform, Press, Prison and Parliament* (London, George Allen and Unwin, 1942); W. Kendall, *The Revolutionary Movement in Britain 1900–1921: The Origins of British Communism* (1969); and practically all the standard works on the history of the British labour movement.

5   The standard works in order of publication remain: J.W. Graham, *Conscription and Conscience: A History 1916–1919* (London, George Allen and Unwin, 1922); Hayes, *Conscription Conflict*; D.A. Martin, *Pacifism: An Historical and Sociological Study* (London, Routledge and Kegan Paul, 1965); D. Boulton, *Objection Overruled* (MacGibbon and Kee, 1967); K. Robbins, *The Abolition of War: The 'Peace Movement' in Britain, 1914–1919* (Cardiff, University of Wales Press, 1976); Ceadel, *Pacifism in Britain*; F.L. Carsten, *War against War: British and German Radical Movements in the First World War* (London, Batsford Academic and Educational, 1982); F. Goodall, *A Question of Conscience: Conscientious Objection in the Two World Wars* (Stroud, Sutton, 1997).

6   Wilson, *Myriad Faces of War*, pp. 170–81.

7   R.K. Middlemas, *The Clydesiders: A Left Wing Struggle for Parliamentary Power* (London, Hutchinson, 1965); A.R. Mack, 'Conscription and Conscientious Objection in Leeds and York During the First World War', (M.Phil., York University, 1983); J.A. Jowitt and K. Laybourn, 'War and Socialism: The experience of the Bradford Independent Labour Party 1914–1918' *Journal of Regional and Local Studies*, 4, Part 2, Autumn, 1984, pp. 57–72; K. Weller, *Don't be a Soldier: The Radical Anti-War Movement in North London 1914–1918* (London, Journeyman Press, 1985); Pearce, 'Anti-war in Huddersfield'; A.J. Peacock, *York in the Great War 1914–1918* (York Settlement Trust, 1993).

8   *The Worker*, 18 September 1915 and 27 November 1915.

9   C. Pearce, 'An interview with Wilfrid Whiteley', *Bulletin of the Society for the Study of Labour History*, 18, Spring, 1969, p. 18; Other unpublished interviews with Arthur Gardiner, George Hargrave and Florence Shaw suggest a similar view.

10   Much of the evidence from which this brief account of Huddersfield on the eve of the 1914–18 war comes is drawn from the following: D.F.E. Sykes, *The History of Huddersfield and its Vicinity*

(Huddersfield, The Advertiser Press, 1898); R. Booke, *The Story of Huddersfield* (Huddersfield County Borough, 1968); Robert Perks, 'The New Liberalism and the Challenge of Labour in the West Riding of Yorkshire with special reference to Huddersfield' (Ph.D., Huddersfield Polytechnic, 1985); E.A.H. Haigh (ed.), *Huddersfield A Most Handsome Town: Aspects of the History and Culture of a West Yorkshire Town* (Huddersfield, Kirklees Cultural Services, 1992).

11 *Huddersfield Daily Examiner*, 10 August 1914.

12 *Worker*, 4 August 1917.

13 Ibid., 29 January 1917 and 3 February 1917.

14 Pearce, 'Anti-War in Huddersfield', pp. 161–74.

15 West Yorkshire Record Office 'General Union of Textile Workers (Huddersfield) Minute Book', 10 and 13 November 1915; *Worker*, 17 and 24 April 1915.

16 *Examiner*, July and August 1914 *passim*.

17 Ibid., 12 August 1914.

18 *Worker*, 3 February 1917.

19 Ibid., 14 October 1916; *Examiner*, 19 October 1916.

20 F.L. Carsten, 'War against War', pp. 171–2; *Worker*, 3 February 1917.

21 *Huddersfield Weekly Chronicle*, 19 June 1915; *Worker*, 19 June 1915; *Examiner*, 19 June 1915.

22 *Examiner*, 16 February 1916.

23 This theme is dealt with comprehensively by R. Perks, 'The New Liberalism'.

24 The ILP's position is explained in Fenner Brockway, *Inside the Left* and Boulton, *Objection Overruled*; the BSP crisis in C. Tsuzuki, *H.M. Hyndman and British Socialism* (Oxford University Press, 1961).

25 Pearce, 'Anti-War in Huddersfield', pp. 128–35.

26 C. Pearce, 'An Interview with Arthur Gardiner' (Unpublished, 31 October 1968).

27 *Worker*, 22 August 1914.

28 C. Pearce, 'An Interview with George Hargrave' (Unpublished, 16 February 1969).

29 Tsuzuki, *Hyndman*, pp. 227, 235; Kendall, *The Revolutionary Movement*, p. 89.

30 Pearce, 'Anti-War in Huddersfield', pp. 136–54.

31 R. Perks, 'New Liberalism', pp. 348–52.

32 *Worker*, 18 April 1914.

33 Pearce, 'Anti-War in Huddersfield', pp. 100–8.

34 *Worker*, 14 February 1914.

35 UDC Archive (Hull University) DDC/1 Minute Books, General Council, October 1915; M. Swartz, *The Union of Democratic Control in British Politics During the First World War* (Oxford, Oxford University Press, 1971), pp. 60–61.

36 Fenner Brockway, *Inside the Left*, p. 54.

37 Pearce, 'Anti-War in Huddersfield', pp. 188–92.

38 Perks, 'New Liberalism', pp. 284, 332; *Examiner* (Obituary), 22 November 1947.

39 Ibid., 27 May 1924, 12 November 1917.

40 Fenner Brockway, *Inside the Left*, Chapter 9; J. Rae, *Conscience and Politics: The British Government and Conscientious Objectors to Military Service 1916–1919* (Oxford University Press, 1970), pp. 10–11; see also *Catherine Marshall Collection*, D/Mar, Cumbria Record Office, Carlisle.

41 *Worker*, 22 January 1916.

42 R.J.Q. Adams and P.P. Poirier, *The Conscription Controversy in Great Britain, 1900–18* (MacMillan Press, 1987), p. 247.

43 Boulton, *Objection Overruled*, p. 119.

44 *Worker*, 22 January 1916.

45 Robbins, *The Abolition of War*, p. 79.

46 Weller, *Don't be a Soldier*, p. 50.

47 *Worker*, 22 December 1917.

48 Rowbotham, *Friends of Alice Wheeldon*, p. 38; Weller, *Don't be a Soldier*, pp. 49–51; R. Challinor, *John S. Clarke: Parliamentarian, Poet, Lion-Tamer* (London, Pluto Press, 1977), pp. 42–3.

49 Pearce, 'An Interview with Arthur Gardiner'.

50 Rae, *Conscience and Politics*, p. 131; Boulton, *Objection Overruled*, p. 139.

51 Pearce, 'An Interview with Arthur Gardiner'.

52 F.G. Jannaway, *Without the Camp: Being the Story of Why and How the Christadelphians were Exempted from Military Service* (London, 1917).

53 *Worker*, 23 September 1916.

54 Ibid., 3 February 1917.

55 Ibid., 4 January 1919.

9

'The Minstrel Boy to the War has Gone': Rifleman 3008, Patrick MacGill and a Soldier's Experience of the First World War

David Taylor

The minstrel boy to the war has gone. In the ranks of death you'll find him.
His father's sword he has girded on, and his wild harp slung behind him.
'Land of song' said the warrior-bard, 'Tho' all the world betrays thee,
One sword at least, thy rights shall guard, one faithful harp shall praise thee.'

The minstrel fell! but the foeman's chain could not bring his proud soul under.
The harp he loved never spoke again, for he tore its chords asunder.
And said 'No chains shall sully thee, thou soul of love and bravery.
Thy songs were made for the pure and free. They shall never sound in slavery.'

(Thomas Moore)

The First World War still commands a fascination for my generation, born less than thirty years after the ending of hostilities. Even now, eighty years on from the end of that war to end all wars, there is a peculiar interest in a conflict which has become a part of the distant past – to be placed alongside the dimly-remembered wars of the eighteenth and nineteenth centuries – among a new generation for whom even the Vietnam war is history. This fascination, shared by so many of my age, grew in large measure from the fact that survivors of the First World War were living individuals, otherwise ordinary members of the family. For some, like David Wright, it was a father who had been part of this awful but awe-inspiring phenomenon.[1] For others, such as the author of this chapter, there was a generational gap but the link was no less real for that. Thus, there was the incongruity of two brothers – my great-uncles – one of whom had fought a traditional war in a cavalry regiment, the other who had been at the forefront of military technology in submarines. Even more immediate, there was my grandfather, part of the poor bloody infantry, whose pistol remained a memento (not to be seen, let alone touched by the children!), kept alongside a few ribbons and medals. The simple physical presence of such people was a constant, living reminder of the First World War and yet, for all their presence, there was a gulf that separated past from present. For many 'ordinary' survivors there was an unwillingness, more than inability, to recount their experiences. The war was either relegated to the background (albeit reappearing in nightmares) or transformed into a sanitized, comically-safe experience that could be recounted to family and friends who had not been there. And yet despite often elaborate psychological defences memories of the war could not be totally excluded and, as noted elsewhere, this led me to the discovery of one combatant who did attempt to put into print his experience. That man was Patrick Macgill.[2]

Patrick Macgill, the author of *Songs of a Navvy* and *Songs of the Dead End*, was a well-known 'minstrel' who enlisted in the London Irish Rifles at the outbreak of war. A self-educated Irishman from Glenties, Donegal, he had come to Scotland as a boy to pick potatoes and had stayed on to navvy in a variety of places, including the huge Kinlochleven reservoir, before the publication of a number of his short sketches of navvy life in the press led to a dramatic change of career. His *Children of the Dead End*, which dramatically outsold James Joyce in 1914, established him as something of a literary celebrity, acquiring the sobriquet of the Navvy Poet by the time war was declared.[3] On joining the army Macgill did not stop writing. A number of articles appeared in the *Daily Mail* and *Pearson's Magazine* and, in addition, he wrote several poems which, like much of his wartime prose, were produced while he was on active service. These writings were transformed into book form and appeared in 1915 and 1916 as *The Amateur Army*, *The Red Horizon*, *The Great Push: An Episode of the Great War* and *Soldiers' Songs*.[4] Unlike Thomas Moore's 'Minstrel Boy', Macgill did not end his life among the 'ranks of dead' but his 'songs' provide a fascinating insight into a man and the unprecedented circumstances in which he found himself, especially after his arrival in France. The wartime writings of Macgill, an under-valued and largely unknown writer today, deserve a wider audience, not least because they provide a distinctive perspective – that of a self-educated, working-class Irishman – on a war whose image has been largely created by educated, middle- or upper-class Englishmen. The texts also raise interesting and important questions about the way in which combatants sought to find expression for their experiences and to construct a narrative that made sense of these experiences and about the way in which the reader seeks to find meaning in them.

Macgill set out his purpose in his introduction to *The Great Push*:

The battleline is a secret world, a world of curses. The guilty secrecy of war is shrouded in lies, and shielded by bloodstained swords; to know it you must be one of those who wage it, a party to dark and mysterious orgies of carnage. . . I have tried in this book to give, as far as I am allowed, an account of an attack

in which I took part. Practically the whole book was written in the scene of
action, and the chapter dealing with our night at Les Brebis, prior to the Big
Push, was written in the trench between midnight and dawn of September the
25th. [1915]; the concluding chapter in the hospital at Versailles two days
after I had been wounded at Loos.[5]

The precise extent to which Macgill's war writings were censored (or self-
censored) is difficult to establish. This is a serious, though not unfamiliar,
problem. There is also a less obvious problem which relates to the ability of
Macgill (and any other writer seeking to do the same) to relate his experiences to
readers who have had no experience of the battlefield. The inadequacy of words,
of tropes, to capture 'reality' has engendered considerable debate among
historians. Similarly, an awareness of the restrictive nature of available narratives
has raised critical questions about what can be told and what can be known. In
this chapter it will be argued that in Macgill's construction/depiction of his
experiences of war there are (or can be found) two narratives – one more a
romance, the other more a tragedy – in his prose writings and that similar
tensions also exist in his poetry. Further, it will be argued that by recognizing the
importance of the persistence of the romantic interpretation of the war, we gain a
fuller understanding of the soldier's experience of the First World War than that
provided simply by the dominant, tragic interpretation which is seen to be rooted
in the 'aesthetic of direct experience'.

Before examining Macgill's writings in some detail, it is important to note the
extent to which our understanding of the First World War is coloured by the
writing of predominantly middle- and upper-class Englishmen; the sense of shock
and horror that was felt as young men, imbued with a naive patriotism and
simplistic notions of 'playing the game', came face to face with the realities of
modern warfare. The works are almost too familiar to mention: the well-known
poetry of Owen and Rosenberg, the autobiographies of Blunden, Graves and
Sassoon as well as the lesser-known plays and novels of Aldington, Sheriff and
Bartlett, and Williamson.[6] In particular the poetry of Sassoon and Owen has
come to be seen as encapsulating an essential truth. Their works:

> . . . were the first such poems to be written by men who had fought, and to
> have the authority of direct experience . . . for the first time the soldiers who
> fought it were also the artists who rendered it.[7]

The horrors of war, the loss of innocence, the corruption of idealism and the
hypocrisy of the patriotic lie are such well-known parts of our cultural upbringing
that it seems banal to mention them. The seemingly pointless slaughter of a
generation of idealistic youth underpins a powerful interpretation of the First
World War as tragedy.[8] So powerful is this interpretation that it seems almost

heretical to challenge it, not least because it represents an 'aesthetic of direct experience'. Hynes, for example, argues that these artists were responsible for the 'creation of a new language of truth-telling about war, in poetry, prose and the visual arts.'[9] These writers are seen to speak with almost unchallengeable authenticity and authority for all who had experienced the realities of the trenches. By implication, other writers using an older idiom are seen to have failed, for whatever reason, to tell the 'truth'. This is a powerful but problematic argument. Notions of a single 'truth' or an unquestionable 'reality' are unsustainable. What is more, it is by no means clear, as Macgill's war writings reveal, that direct experience necessarily led to a tragic interpretation. None the less, there is a powerful sense in which this narrowly-defined 'aesthetic of direct experience' approach provides a framework not only for later interpretations of the First World War but also for the reading/re-reading of texts produced during the war itself.

There is much in the wartime writings of Macgill which conforms with this essentially tragic perspective. There is a distinct shift in tone as one moves from *An Amateur Army*, through *The Red Horizon* to the more sombre *Great Push* in which the once-proud rifleman had become a stretcher-bearer. The brave soldier now was wracked with fear and there was a growing concern about the very purpose of his actions. Still a rifleman, he noted in *The Red Horizon* how solitude brought questioning and self-doubt:

> We are lonely, nearly every man of us. For myself I felt isolated from the whole world . . . [asking myself] 'Who are we?' . . . [and] 'Who shall give an answer to the question?' [and discovering] you've found out you've been posing a little before. Alone you're really a coward.[10]

In *The Great Push* Macgill, now a stretcher-bearer, wrote openly of his revulsion to the grim realities of war. Writing of the eve of the battle of Loos, the one-time navvy who had experienced violence, privation and even death in his travels, made the following observations:

> My normal self revolted at the thought of the coming dawn; the experiences of my life had not prepared me for one day of savage and ruthless butchery. . . . The harrowing sight [of pieces of human bodies] was repellent, antagonistic to my mind. The tortured things lying at my feet were symbols of insecurity, ominous reminders of dangers from which no discretion could save a man.[11]

There was disillusionment as he 'came across the dead, dying and sorely wounded; lives maimed and finished, and all the romance and roving that makes up the life of a soldier gone for ever'.[12] Of the German enemy he knew 'very little' and could not pass judgement on, let alone hate, a nation whom he had experienced as 'distorted lumps of clothing and mangled flesh pounded into the muddy floor'.[13] Unaware of and increasingly unconcerned about the 'importance of the events in which we took part', Macgill, noting how 'the shapelessness of Destruction reigned', concluded that war was nothing more than 'an approved licence for brotherly mutilation'.[14] *The Great Push* finishes with a haunting description as Macgill recalls falling asleep after the battle of Loos, at which he was wounded:

> Sleep was heavy in my eyes and queer thoughts ran riot in my head. 'What is to be the end of this destruction and decay?' That is what it means, this war. Destruction, decay, degradation.[15]

He dreams of the symbolic soldier, the single figure who stood for all those 'lines of men marching up long, poplar-lined roads':

> Yes, there He is, hanging on the barbed wires. I shall go and speak to Him. . . . I knew the dark grey bulk, it was He; for days and nights He had hung there a huddled heap; the Futility of War. . . . I was with Him in a moment endeavouring to help Him. In the dawn He was not repulsive, He was almost beautiful, but His beauty was that of the mirage which allures to a more sure destruction. . . . I saw now that He was repulsive, abject, pitiful lying there, His face close to the wires, a thousand bullets in His head. Unable to resist the impulse I endeavoured to turn His face upward, but was unable; a barb had pierced His eye and stuck there, rusting in the socket from which the sight had gone. I turned and ran away from the thing into the bay of the trench. The glory of the dawn had vanished, my soul no longer swooned in ecstasy of it. . . . [W]hat is He and all with Him but the monstrous futility of war. . . ?[16]

Similar sentiments emerge in Macgill's poetry. There is a poignant sense of loss in the simply written *After Loos*:

> Was it only yesterday
> Lusty comrades marched away?
> Now they're covered up in clay.
>
> Seven glasses used to be
> Called for six good mates and me –
> Now we only call for three.
>
> Little crosses neat and white,
> Looking lonely every night,
> Tell of comrades killed in fight.

> Hearty fellows they have been,
> And no more will they be seen
> Drinking wine in Nouex les Mines
>
> Lithe and supple lads were they,
> Marching merrily away –
> Was it only yesterday?[17]

The physical and mental suffering of the wounded (including the threat to a powerful notion of masculinity encapsulated in the idea of 'playing the game') is caught in the last stanza of *The Everyday of War*, written in hospital in November 1915:

> The ward-fire burns in a cheery way,
> A vision in every flame,
> There are books to read and games to play
> But oh! for an old, old game,
> With glancing bayonet and trusty gun
> And wild blood, bursting free! –
> But an arm is crippled, a leg is gone,
> And the game's no more for me.[18]

In poetry, as in his prose, fear threatens the individual – 'they'll call me a coward if I return/but a hero if I fall'[19] – and destruction is dominant: 'it's death and not the fairies who is holding carnival'.[20] But there was no dignity in death and the true horrors could not be communicated to those back home. The last stanzas of *Letters* run:

> We'll write to her tomorrow and this is what we'll say,
> He breathed her name in dying; in peace he passed away –
> No words about his moaning, his anguish and his pain,
> When slowly, slowly dying. God! Fifteen hours in dying!
> He lay a maimed thing dying, alone upon the plain.
>
> We often write to mothers, to sweethearts and to wives,
> And tell them those who loved them have given up their lives;
> If we're not always truthful, our lies are always kind,
> Our letters lie to cheer them, to solace and to cheer them,
> Oh: anything to cheer them – the women left behind.[21]

There is, then, much in Macgill's construction of his wartime experiences that is pessimistic, even tragic. And yet there is an alternative reading in which there is an optimism which comes from a construction of war that owes more to romance than tragedy. Describing his early training days in *The Amateur Army*, Macgill wrote of his experiences in positive terms. While training at St Albans he discovered a sense of solidarity which contrasted with his outcast days as a navvy when he existed on the fringe of society proper, helping to create a world of which he and his fellow navvies of *The Children of the Dead End* were never truly a part. In language reminiscent of Robert Graves, he described the battalion, marching at night, as a:

> . . . silent monster . . . full of unrestrained power; resolute in its onward sweep, impervious to danger, it looks a menacing engine of destruction, steady to its goal and certain of its mission.[22]

Even off duty there was a sense of shared experience that transcended the divisions of civilian life. Describing a coffee shop in St Albans, he observed how:

> . . . all sorts and conditions of soldiers drift into the place and discuss various matters over coffee and mince pies; they are men of all classes who have been as far apart as the poles in civil life, and are now knit together in the common brotherhood of war, caste and estate seem to have been forgotten; all are engaged in a common business, full of similar risks and rewarded by a similar wage.[23]

Experience in France proved to be somewhat less idealistic. In the dedication to *Soldiers' Songs* he still spoke warmly of the 'beloved regiment' and the way in which 'the circumstances of war strengthen the *esprit de corps* of a soldier'.[24] And yet while noting that the members of his section, despite their differences in civilian life, still 'agree very well', he was forced to concede that:

> . . . the same does not hold good for the whole regiment; the public school clique and the board school clique live each in a separate world and the line of demarcation between them is sharply drawn.[25]

Indeed, Macgill was even more scathing in a passage from his article 'Out There' which appeared in *Pearson's Magazine* in September 1915, which was cut when he wrote *The Red Horizon*. Dismissing talk of the new army as a democratic institution, he concluded that:

> . . . the new army is a miniature pattern of the society that created it. . . it has its poor and its wealthy, the poor feed on bully beef and army stew from start to finish; the wealthy dine well when a local hotel is not out of bounds, and can always find an impoverished private ready to take up their extra duties and fatigues at the hourly rate of a few coppers.[26]

Class divisions had not been eradicated. Men could not speak directly to officers and the latter 'must be saluted, and failure to observe the latter ceremonial can get a private in for any amount of trouble'.[27] And yet even in the more pessimistic *The Great Push*, Macgill could still strike a heroic note and talk of the individual soldier as being 'submerged in his regiment' and part of:

> . . . the Army, the British Army, which will be remembered in days to come, not by a figurehead, as the fighters of Waterloo are remembered by Wellington, but as an army, mighty in deeds, prowess and endurance; an army which outshone its figureheads.[28]

Macgill also had a clear, and more enduring, sense of self-worth as his career as a soldier developed. Coming from the overwhelmingly masculine world of the navvy, Macgill put great value in physical strength and bravery, in cunning (including verbal dexterity) and especially in comradeship. It is not clear what beliefs about war and the soldier Macgill brought with him when he enlisted but he quickly adapted to, and took pride in, his new life-style in the army. He openly proclaimed himself to be one of the 'fighting men . . . trained to the trade and licensed to the profession' and took fierce pride in being a rifleman, a specialist within the greater entity of the army.[29] Macgill presents himself in positive terms as an active, even heroic individual. Soldiering is seen as being both manly and romantic. Macgill saw himself as being part of 'a great adventure, full of thrill and excitement . . . [as] we stood on the threshold of momentous events'.[30] In the opening chapter of *The Red Horizon* there is an openly-declared sense of mission which sets the tone of his description of events in France. 'I had never realised my mission as a rifleman so acutely before. "To the war! to the war," I said under my breath, "Out to France and the fighting." '[31] Superficial jollity masked underlying worries. His very manhood was to be put to the test. On the eve of embarkation he pondered:

> What will it be like but above all, how shall I conduct myself in the trenches? Maybe I shall be afraid – cowardly. But no! If I can't bear the discomforts and terrors which thousands endure daily I'm not much good. But I'll be alright. Vanity will carry me through where courage fails. It would be a grand thing to become conspicuous by personal daring. Suppose the men were wavering in an attack, and then I rushed out in front and shouted: 'Boys we've got to get this job through'.[32]

Macgill's belief in the 'romance of soldiering', as he termed it, persisted even in the face of the realities of war. As well as the 'thrill and excitement' there was also camaraderie, deep friendships forged in war:

Mervin, perspiring profusely, marched by my side. He and I had been great comrades, we have worked, eaten and slept together, and committed sin together against regimental regulations. . . . I know not where he lies, but one day, if the fates spare me, I shall pay a visit to the resting place of a true comrade and staunch friend.[33]

Despite the undoubted horrors of trench warfare and the banality of day-to-day life behind the front line, there is still something noble, even chivalric about Macgill's perception of the war. The British army is in France to free a country with its shell-torn landscape and the ruined churches, destroyed by the enemy. As a soldier he is there to protect the civilians, the old men and women, especially the women, who are trapped in and around the battlefields. Macgill is open in his admiration for their fortitude and resourcefulness but he sees himself as their protector and liberator. In the concluding chapter of *The Red Horizon*, reflecting upon his life in the trenches behind the lines, he talks of 'the young soldier . . . his heart stirred with the romance of his mission' and of 'the mystery, the enchantment and the glamour' to be found. The book concludes with the simple observation: 'there is romance, there is joy in the life of the soldier'.[34]

There is also a more specific (and predictable) emphasis on the centrality of physical strength, vigour and courage as determinants of his soldierly manliness. This is seen most clearly in his war poems which abound with references to 'brave lusty lads' and 'supple lads and clean' with 'eager eye and stout young heart'. These are the men, the 'brave lusty comrades' who play the 'old, old game/With glancing bayonet and trusty gun/And wild blood bursting free!' It is they who show 'a good stiff upper lip for the old pal's sake/And the old battalion's pride.'[35] However, to see Macgill simply in terms of an unquestioned military masculinity would be misleading. The heroic and optimistic Macgill who started his training in 1914 is gradually transformed as the realities of warfare force a reconsideration of his values. The ideal of the offensive warrior was thwarted by the inaction that characterized the Western Front for much of the time. There was too much 'everlastin' waitin'' on an 'everlastin' road' for a man who 'longed for action, for some adventure'.[36] Indeed, a soldier's life was often less than inspirational. It was 'rather a dull game, not that blood-curling, dashing and sabre-clashing thing that is seen in the pictures'.[37]

Heroism was still to be found – and Macgill describes with pride the actions of his fellow London Irish riflemen under fire – but increasingly through *The Great Push* emerges a more melancholy tone, a more sombre construction of war in which isolation, fear and futility cannot be denied. The older, more positive self-image never entirely disappears. Macgill still speaks of his 'grand courage' towards the end of *The Great Push* but the balance has changed. The confident young man, defined by a physical and moral masculinity, who had joined the army and set off to France with scarcely a doubt, had been gradually replaced by – or more accurately had come to coexist with – a newer, less sure and more fearful 'self'. The old beliefs were not lightly cast aside, nor relegated to the back of his mind. There remained, at the forefront, a deep-seated and tenaciously held belief in such concepts as comradeship, courage and self-sacrifice – that is, precisely those grand abstractions, faith in which was supposedly destroyed by the experience of war. Macgill, and others like him, retained these ideals, not because the 'old' was too deeply-rooted to be eradicated, nor because these men lacked the sensibility and style to express the 'new truths' about war, but because they were a necessary part of survival. It was necessary to call upon an identity cast in a more heroic mould to withstand the pressures of events and to preserve the newer, less secure identity that had emerged. Macgill makes a crucial observation towards the end of *The Great Push*:

> All men have some restraining influence to help them in hours of trial, some principle or some illusion. Duty, patriotism, vanity and dreams come to the help of the men in the trenches, all illusions probably, ephemeral and fleeting, but for a man as ephemeral and fleeting as his illusions are, he can lay his back against them and defy death and the terrors of the world. But let him stand naked and looking at the staring reality of the terrors that engirt him and he becomes a raving lunatic.[38]

Living through unprecedented horrors, which he set out to record at the time, Macgill was aware of his changing perceptions. But the growing sense of futility and tragedy never resulted in the rejection of his optimistic beliefs. Indeed, his psychological survival depended upon the constant reassertion of traditional images and values of war. Macgill – and he was not alone in this – was able to avoid that sense of dislocation which could (and did) destroy the very identity of individuals beset by the appalling experiences of an increasingly technological and destructive war for which they had not been (indeed could not have been) prepared. The phrases may have been platitudinous, the values illusory – and the individuals may very well have been aware of this – but they served a vital function: mental survival. Macgill could never escape the shadow of his wartime experiences but he did not become a 'raving lunatic'. Macgill's 'proud soul' was not 'brought under' by the experience of war and his 'songs' ensured his survival in the greatest of wars yet experienced by man.

Hynes, in the epilogue to his impressive study of the impact of the First World War on English culture and society, writes of the need to understand how 'men and women faced with the new and terrible realities of history [during the First World War], have striven to comprehend them by imagining them'.[39] This is undoubtedly correct but all too often our imagination is distorted by a one-dimensional perception of the First World War. As Charles Carrington wrote in 1929:

. . . a legend has grown up, propagated not by soldiers but by journalists, that these men who went gaily to fight in the mood of Rupert Brooke and Julian Grenfell, lost their faith amid the horrors of the trenches and returned in a mood of anger and despair.[40]

Rifleman 3008 Patrick Macgill would certainly have agreed. As his autobiographical writings, often drafted at the front, reveal, there were two sets of war experiences which not simply coexisted but were intimately related. In a number of important ways the First World War was destructive of the old and creative of new thinking, but, in focusing on the loss of innocence, historians and literary critics alike have not simply overlooked but failed to appreciate the significance of the continuity and strength of traditional values and motifs. Precisely because of the unprecedented destruction and change, it was essential for the likes of Rifleman Macgill to retain and restate the importance of those values which had given meaning to their lives in the past and were needed to preserve self-respect and sanity in the present. We will not come close to understanding the experiences of those who fought in the Great War – those ordinary fathers, grandfathers and other family members who peopled our early lives – unless we recognize the romance as well as the tragedy of what they experienced in those unprecedented and terrible years.

Notes

1   D.G. Wright, *The Great War: A Useless Slaughter?* (Huddersfield Pamphlets in History and Politics, HP13, The Polytechnic of Huddersfield, 1991). Coincidentally one of the themes in this short, but wide-ranging, essay follows a line of argument consistent with that advanced here. It is a matter of personal regret that I was unable to discuss these ideas with David.

2   See my 'A Little Man in a Great War: Patrick Macgill and the London Irish Rifles', in B. Taithe and T. Thornton (eds), *War: Identities in Conflict, 1300–2000* (Stroud, Sutton, 1998). My interest in Patrick Macgill stems from the simple fact that he and my maternal grandfather both fought in the same regiment.

3   It is a measure of Macgill's popularity that *Children of the Dead End* (London, Herbert Jenkins, 1914) priced at 6*s.*, sold 10,000 copies in a fortnight on its appearance in 1914. In the same year, and despite buying some 120 copies himself, James Joyce was unable to achieve 500 sales of *Dubliners*. Macgill also had an impact on popular culture when his *Songs of the Dead End* (London, Yearbook Press, 1913) were put to music by Charles Wood and appeared as *Home to Glenties* (London, Herbert Jenkins, 1922).

4   Macgill's war writings are: *The Amateur Army* (London, Herbert Jenkins, 1915), *The Red Horizon* (London, Herbert Jenkins, 1916), *The Great Push: An Episode in the Great War* (London, Herbert Jenkins, 1916), and *Soldiers' Songs* (London, Herbert Jenkins, 1916). Much of the material in these autobiographical works had previously appeared as articles but there are a number of differences, most notably in the sanitizing of material for *The Red Horizon*. With the exception of *The Amateur Army*, these works are available as reprints.

5   Macgill, *The Great Push*, Introduction, no page number.

6 I.M. Parson (ed.), *The Men Who March Away: Poems of the First World War* (London, Chatto & Windus, 1965) and J. Silkin (ed.), *First World War Poetry* (London, Penguin, 1979) are two of the better anthologies. B. Gardner, *Up the Line to Death: the War Poets, 1914–18* (London, Methuen, 1964) contains much familiar material but is organized on thematic lines and is one of the few anthologies to contain a poem, 'Before the Charge', by Macgill. Edmund Blunden, *Undertones of War* (London, Cobden-Sanderson, 1928); Robert Graves, *Goodbye to All That* (London, Jonathan Cape, 1929); Siegfried Sassoon, *Memoirs of a Fox-hunting Man* and *Memoirs of an Infantry Officer* (London, Faber & Faber, 1928 and 1930); Richard Aldington, *Death of a Hero* (London, Chatto & Windus, 1929); R.C. Sheriff and Vernon Bartlett, *Journey's End* (London, Gollancz, 1930); Henry Williamson, *The Patriot's Progress* (London, Geoffrey Bles, 1930). For later commentaries the two outstanding works are P. Fussell, *The Great War and Modern Memory* (Oxford, Oxford University Press, 1975), chapter 5, 'Oh! What a Literary War', and S. Hynes, *A War Imagined: the First World War and English Culture* (London, Pimlico, 1992).

7 Hynes, *A War Imagined* is a good example but see the critique of this interpretation in Jay Winter, *Sites of Memory, Sites of Mourning: the Great War in European Popular Culture* (Cambridge University Press, 1992).

8 This interpretation is not the sole preserve of literary critics. See also the historical interpretations of John Terraine, *The Western Front, 1914–1918* (London, Hutchinson, 1964) and A.J.P. Taylor, *The First World War* (London, Hamish Hamilton, 1964). Both, in their different ways, stress the useless slaughter of idealistic young men.

9 Quotation from Winter, *Sites of Memory*, p. 2.

10 Macgill, *Red Horizon*, pp. 87, 172.

11 Macgill, *Great Push*, pp. 69, 77.

12 Ibid., p. 81.

13 Ibid., p. 88.

14 Ibid., pp. 88, 159.

15 Ibid., p. 251.

16 Ibid., pp. 251–3.

17 'After Loos' in *Soldiers' Songs* in *The Navvy Poet: the Collected Poetry of Patrick Macgill* (London, Caliban, 1984), p. 23.

18 'The Everyday of War' in *Soldiers' Songs*, pp. 61–2.

19 'Lament' in *Soldiers' Songs*, p. 31.

20 'Death and the Fairies' in *Soldiers' Songs*, p. 89.

21 'Letters' in *Soldiers' Songs*, pp. 57–8; *Great Push*, p. 211.

22 Macgill, *Amateur Army*, p. 72. Graves described drill as 'beautiful . . . a single movement of one large creature': R. Graves, *Goodbye to All That* (Harmondsworth, Penguin, 1979), p. 156.

23 Macgill, *Amateur Army*, pp. 63–4.

24 Macgill, *Soldiers' Songs*, p. 8.

25 Macgill, *Red Horizon*, p. 91.

26 Macgill, 'Out There', *Pearson's Magazine*, September, 1915, p. 293.

27 Ibid., pp. 293–4.

28 Macgill, *Great Push*, p. 134.

29 Macgill, *Amateur Army*, p. 55. See also p. 58 and p. 71 for evidence of the pride he took in being a rifleman.

30 Macgill, *Red Horizon*, p. 26.

31 Ibid., p. 14.

32 Ibid., p. 17.

33 Ibid., pp. 51, 55; also references to Irish mates in particular are found scattered through Macgill, *Great Push*. The question of Macgill's sense of Irishness is considered in my 'A Little Man in a Great War'.

34 Macgill, *Red Horizon*, p. 306.

35 Macgill, 'The Everyday of War' in *Soldiers' Songs*, p. 59.

36 Macgill, *Red Horizon*, p. 130.

37 Ibid., p. 130.

38 Macgill, *Great Push*, p. 162.

39 Hynes, *A War Imagined*, p. 469.

40 C. Carrington, *A Subaltern's War* (London, Davies, 1929), pp. 192–3.

10

ENGLISHNESS: THE CASE OF H.V. MORTON (1892–1979)

Michael Bartholomew

The maturity of studies of what has become known as 'Englishness' was marked in 1986, when R. Colls and P. Dodd published a collection of essays under the title *Englishness: Politics and Culture 1880–1920*. The essayists' work grew from a long tradition of studies of the rural, anti-industrial impulse in English culture, a tradition that had a few years earlier been much invigorated by Martin Wiener's controversial and frequently-discussed *English Culture and the Decline of the Industrial Spirit* (1981) and by Patrick Wright's powerful *On Living in an Old Country* (1985), a study which gave the topic a sharp theoretical edge. What these and other studies[1] have established and explored is the vitality and durability of the myth that modern England is not, in essence, a thickly populated, dynamic, industrial and commercial country. Rather, the myth insists that England is essentially rural, agricultural, tranquil and unchanging. This essential England is disclosed typically in quiet corners of the shires. (I am using 'myth' here not in the sense of 'untruth', but of a potent, seductive story which helps make sense of the lives of its adherents).

The myth was especially seductive to the generation who served in or lived through the First World War. The bugles that Wilfred Owen made faintly to call for the slaughtered in his 'Anthem for Doomed Youth' sounded not from the industrial towns that were likely to have been the youths' homes, but from 'sad shires'. Industrial, modern England could not, it seems, supply images deemed to be worth fighting for. A remark that Paul Fussell makes about Edmund Blunden's writing can apply more generally: in *The Great War and Modern Memory*, Fussell writes that attention was constantly addressed by Blunden to 'pre-industrial England, the only repository of criteria for measuring fully the otherwise unspeakable grossness of the war'.[2] And in his later book, *Abroad*, Fussell suggests that a great deal of travel writing was released by the ending of the war: writers who had for years been cramped and desolated went south for the sun.[3] Other writers, with whom Fussell is less concerned, stayed at home, willing themselves deep into an English landscape untouched by slaughter and destruction. Their books found a ready market. Any second-hand bookshop yields dozens of titles. A typical trawl fetched up Major General J.E.B. Seeley's *Forever England* (1932), A. Bonnet Laird's *This Way Arcady* (1926), W.S. Shears's *This England: a Book of the Shires and Counties* (1936), and the Batsford anthology *The Legacy of England* (1935) (with a contribution from Edmund Blunden on 'The landscape').

H.V. Morton (1892–1979) fits this specification of the devotee and purveyor of the myth of England well. He served in the war and, on resuming his life as a journalist, published some of his newspaper travel pieces between hard covers. The success of these books turned him into a prolific travel writer. He published over thirty titles, starting with books about England, Wales, Scotland and Ireland, and moving on to books about Italy, Spain, the Middle East and South Africa. He has been picked up by recent scholars in studies both of the construction of Englishness, and of between-the-wars writers, but he has not been marked out for special attention. My aim in this chapter is to put him more firmly on the map of Englishness. Morton repays attention because first, he is in many ways the archetypal presenter of an enduring and popular Arcadian vision of England. But secondly, Morton is interesting because from time to time he breaks the conventions of this genre and presents a clashing vision of a troubled, depressed England, a vision which is closer to and, in my view, sometimes more penetrating than those of canonized writers like George Orwell or J.B. Priestley, whose observations, made as they travelled round the country during the 1930s, are supposed to have been particularly insightful. Because Morton has received little scholarly attention, what follows needs first to be frankly descriptive: we need to know the outlines of his prolific and highly successful publishing career. But at the same time, I hope to locate Morton both within the decades in which he wrote, and within the developing field of studies of Englishness.

There is rather more to Morton than the half-invention, half-discovery of England that his books embodied. First, although he was, for most of the time, mesmerizing himself and his readers into 'the deep, deep sleep of England' (to use Orwell's phrase),[4] there are moments of self-awareness in his writing. In places, he begins to identify what is now routinely known as 'the heritage industry' – the cultural and commercial forces that persuade us that we can take day trips to the past, a past signified by items whose original significance, however earnestly we may seek it, is effaced by the glamour that inescapably accompanies the designation 'heritage'.[5] For example, Morton connects the medieval Canterbury pilgrims, who made their way to the shrine of Thomas à Becket, with those modern-day pilgrims who trek to see 'the spot where Nelson fell, Shakespeare's cradle, the bed that Queen Elizabeth slept in and Jane Austen's pen-wiper'. Who is to say, he reflects, that the modern objects of pilgrimage are more absurd than the medieval? Both are the product of 'a longing to make contact with something outside normal experience', a longing that is compulsive, but illusory and rarely satisfied. Or again, in Wales, trudging off to visit a waterfall that has, he writes, 'been sanctified by centuries of sightseeing', he feels as if he is 'being bullied by Ruskin'.[6]

Secondly, although Morton's strong inclination is generally to seek out the picturesque, the rural, the archaic, and places associated with the the pageantry of history, he was by no means blind to aspects of England that could not easily be accommodated to this version of the nation's character. Traditionally, cities have tended to be characterized as sites of, on the one hand, alien industry and commerce, and, on the other, squalor and poverty. Morton did not avoid industrial towns and, as I show below, when he wrote about them he often ran against the grain of the Merrie England mode by presenting them as places which, despite the disgrace of their slums, were exhilarating. And his accounts of the slums are at least as penetrating as the later accounts written by Orwell and Priestley. Morton was studiously non-party political, but he was happy for the Labour Party to publish, in 1933, a twopenny pamphlet of articles on slum housing that he had originally written for the *Daily Herald*.[7]

Thirdly, the sheer popularity of his writings commands attention. Twenty-nine editions of *In Search of England* and twelve of the companion volume *The Call of England*, were in circulation by 1943. All of his books went through edition after edition (as the shelves of any second-hand bookshop will testify). Translations were common. Precise figures of the numbers of his books in circulation are hard to come by. The records of his publisher, Methuen, give no quantities, but one commentator asserts that over a million copies of *In Search of England* were sold in Britain alone.[8] It is likely, then, that Morton was among the most widely read inter-war writers and, therefore, was one of the more influential shapers of English peoples' image of themselves and their country. Furthermore, he started publishing in the mid-1920s, and went on issuing books on England right up to the middle of the Second World War. He therefore registers a number of modifications to the myth, and demonstrates how it was put to use when war broke out again.

Lastly, Morton is worth paying attention to simply because he is, in most respects, an absolutely standard practitioner in a genre which was pervasive between the wars. Critical interest obviously tends to follow the extraordinary and the innovatory, but it can be revealing to pay close attention to the commonplace, in order to inspect the formulae that governed the production and reception of so many books. This is not to say that Morton was merely a mass-producer of banalities about cottages and hedgerows: he was a painstaking researcher and an engaging writer. (Eyemouth, he writes, 'stands facing the sea like someone warding off a blow'; Birmingham is 'the city whose buttons hold up the trousers of the world'; Robert Burns was a poet 'whose songs have curled up like an old dog on the hearthstone'.[9])

Morton's best known book, and the one upon which his status as a Merrie England ruralist is founded, is *In Search of England* (1927). His first five books, however, were little collections of vignettes of London life. Morton presents himself in these books as a self-deprecating, vaguely patrician and modestly intrepid narrator who roves round the city, by day and by night, bringing back accounts of the people – cabmen, river policemen, office cleaners, Billingsgate porters, Kensington Gardens nannies, chorus girls, down-and-outs, Harley Street doctors, and dozens of others – and places – Petticoat Lane street market, the Royal Mint, a night club, a boxing match, a city church, a Bloomsbury boarding house, and so on.[10]

Morton does not attempt to combine all the observations in his London books into a single, integrated vision, projected from a clear moral viewpoint; he is content to leave them as an assortment of vignettes of a variegated, cosmopolitan city. His London is neither united by a particular set of characteristics, nor riven by social conflict – even though he is at pains to point out the dismal wages on which many of the people he writes about have to scrape along. Above all, for a writer who was later to become such a staunch promoter of a rural vision of England, the early books on London are a positive celebration of the variety and vitality of city life. No stereotypical version of England has emerged, and we are, by definition, save for one passage, a long way from the green shires.

The exception is the passage on the grave of the Unknown Warrior in Westminster Abbey. The Unknown Warrior, Morton writes, 'lies not only at the heart of London, but also at the heart of England'. Morton himself was twenty-two years old in 1914, and served during the war with the Warwickshire Yeomanry, although I do not know in what capacity. There are hardly any explicit autobiographical references in Morton's books to his own war years, but plainly, the war marked him. In his later travel books, he always comments, often in great and passionate detail, on the war memorials erected in the towns and villages he passes through. It is, therefore, perhaps not surprising that here in the London books, despite their general lack of symbolic, unifying images, Morton should have given especial significance to the grave of the Unknown Warrior. In identifying the 'heart of England' as this grave in Westminster Abbey, he is seemingly cutting himself off from the symbolic potential of the green shires, but he goes on to draw them in. The Unknown Soldier sleeps in:

> . . . the silence of a mighty church, a silence as deep and lovely as though he were lying in some green country graveyard steeped in peace, above him a twilight in which the stored centuries seem to whisper happily of good things done for England.[11]

Symbolically, then, the soldier is lying simultaneously in London and in a country graveyard. And he is calling forth echoes of *Henry V*.

The green shires themselves came into view when, a year or so after the publication of his books on London, Morton published *In Search of England* (1927). Morton's habitual rhetorical modes include the extravagantly emotional (as in the passage on the grave of the Unknown Warrior), the comic and self-deprecating, the patrician, and the ironic, but only rarely does he choose to express his views formally and bluntly. *In Search of England* opens with a short introduction which is in this blunt mode, and which makes plain the project that informed what Morton feared might be read simply as the record of a lighthearted jaunt through the highways and byways. Morton explicitly claims that his book, despite the seeming inconsequentiality of his tour, addresses the serious matter of the condition of England. He observes that 'never before have so many people been searching for England'. His identification of the cause of this search is unremarkable: people are alienated from the lives and homes assigned to them in an urban and industrial society and, despite their living nominally in a country called England, they feel an urge to go in search of a place that will be recognized and felt as the *real* England. He does not develop this distinction between the real and what must be in some sense an unreal, bogus, inauthentic England in which people are compelled to pass their lives. We are now thoroughly habituated to this supposed distinction between the real and the inauthentic. (Holiday firms routinely stake their whole claim on their ability to transport their customers to the real Provence, or the real Tuscany, in implied contrast to some other version of these places.) It is not at all an obvious distinction, but Morton, and writers like him, do not need to stop and reflect on it, so sure are they that their readers will unquestioningly recognize it.

Perhaps the most notable example of a writer effortlessly dropping into this mode is that of Stanley Baldwin, the Prime Minister at the time when Morton was writing *In Search of England*. In his address 'On England and the West', Baldwin said that 'the things that make England' are 'the tinkle of the hammer on the anvil in the country smithy, the corncrake on a dewy morning, the sound of a scythe against a whetstone, and the sight of a plough team coming over the brow of a hill'.[12]

Continuing his own introduction, which may owe something to Baldwin's rhetoric, Morton says that the search for the real England has lately been made easier, for cheap road transport now penetrates every part of the country, facilitating the instinctive search for the rural 'common racial heritage'. What will the searchers find, though? Is the rural heartland in good shape? It is not; 'behind the beauty of the English country is an economic and social cancer'. Old estates are being taxed out of existence and broken up, cheap imported food is undermining farmers. What is the solution? It is idle to think that the 'intellectual solitude in which the rustic evolved his shrewd wisdom' can be sustained: the radio, roads and newspapers are irreversibly bringing villages into a wider culture. But the nation as a whole will flourish only when attention is paid to the rebuilding of secure, prosperous and traditional agricultural communities, supporting 'a contented and flourishing peasantry', to which the town-bred searchers can go for spiritual and physical refreshment.[13]

Morton's is hardly a profound analysis. The 1920s and '30s were full of such jeremiads which, in turn, have a lineage that stretches back through the Edwardian and Victorian social critics to the earliest commentators on the social effects of the Industrial Revolution. What makes Morton interesting is the unreflecting way in which he can trundle out this routine analysis of the ills of England, shortly after having produced books about the vivid lives of Londoners. Cramped and hard as some of these London lives were, Morton had not presented them as inauthentic. Collectively, and even in the absence of any overt, formal authorial statements, Morton's London books testify to an exciting, authentic urban culture. Yet the Arcadian myth, with its stock formulations of the degenerate city contrasting with the wise and profound countryside, is waiting to sweep him (and dozens of writers like him) off in search of the eternal verities. No doubt the buoyancy of the market for the myth had a lot to do with it: *In Search of England* went through three editions *a year* in its first four years. No journalist – which is what Morton was – is likely to ignore a market like that. At a less commercial level, and, as I have suggested, it may be that the extraordinary market during the 1920s for books like Morton's was driven partly by a compulsion among readers to locate a realm of the enduring and beautiful, in the face of the dislocation, brutality and meaningless of the First World War.[14]

Morton never wrote about his own war years, but the opening paragraphs of chapter 1 of *In Search of England* are very much in the mode of the officer in the trenches dreaming of the English shires. Morton opens with a recollection of a moment in Palestine in 1923 when, ill and fearful of dying, he was stirred by a picture of England that arose in his mind:

> . . . a village street at dusk with a smell of wood smoke lying in the still air and, here and there, little red blinds shining in the dusk under the thatch. I remembered how the church bells ring at home, and how, at that time of year, the sun leaves a dull red bar low down in the west, and against it the elms grow blacker minute by minute. Then the bats start to flicker like little bits of burnt paper and you hear the slow jingle of a team coming home from the fields.

Morton goes on to recall that there and then he vowed to himself that if he survived, he would 'go home in search of England, and the little thatched cottages of England'. He hoped to 'lean over English bridges and lie on English grass, watching an English sky'. He says too that his vision is widely shared. 'A little London factory hand' whom he had met during the war had said 'when pressed, and after great mental difficulty', that the England he was fighting for was the England of Epping Forest, not the England of the streets in which he lived.[15]

In Search of England is nominally a record of the motor journey that Morton undertook when he had returned safely back to England. He later disarmingly confessed that on the journey he had 'deliberately shirked realities' by making 'wide and inconvenient circles to avoid modern towns and cities': he had devoted himself 'entirely to ancient towns and cathedral cities, to green fields and pretty things'.[16] The book opens with him heading south and west, away from London.[17] His first, supposedly chance encounter is in Berkshire, where he meets 'the last bowl-turner in England', who plies his craft on a primeval lathe in a tumble-down hut lost in a maze of muddy lanes. As the reader expects, the bowl-turner, in suitably rustic terms, rejects the cash nexus: ' "Money?" he said with a slow faun-like smile, "Money's only storing up trouble, I think. I like making bowls better than I like making money." '[18] And so it goes, as Morton drives in a great loop down to Land's End, up to Carlisle, across to Newcastle and down the East side of the country, through Lincolnshire, over to Warwickshire, and back to London. The citizens of village, market town and cathedral city step obligingly and generally deferentially forward, as if straight from Central Casting, to utter, in formulaic dialect, gems of traditional legend, custom and wisdom. Between these encounters, Morton keeps the momentum up by sketching in, very effectively, colourful romantic historical background, and by pausing to reflect sonorously on the especial spirit of the places he visits ('At night, especially under this witching moon, the streets of Shrewsbury take you back to Old England. Butcher Row at night is perfect. . . .'[19])

But this is not the whole story. Powerful and seductive as the myths of Arcady and Merrie England are, Morton is not entirely swept away by them. For example, at a tiny village in Cornwall, he is put up for the night by an old farming couple. He elaborately builds up a picture of a Cornish Eden. But the culmination of this taste of paradise is his being invited up the lane to hear a neighbour's new battery radio which, after much tuning, beams in an evening of dance-band music from the Savoy. The proud owner of the radio tells Morton how closely it had kept them in touch with news of the General Strike ('we liked that Mr Baldwin, for he wor as plain as if he wor in this room. . . .'). Morton's artful juxtaposition of the metropolitan sophistication of the Savoy, the placid timelessness of rural Cornwall, and the world of urgent political action, is left to do its own work. No doubt the reader is supposed to sigh over the intrusion into Eden of vulgar modernity and the brutal world of politics, but Morton does not step out of the narrative and deliver a personal castigation. He leaves it at the elegiac, but noncommital level of 'the new picture of rural England; old heads bent over the wireless set in the light of a paraffin lamp'.[20]

He is more direct when he reaches Wigan, a town that later, in Orwell's account, achieved symbolic status. Morton says that, feeling conscious of having avoided the industrial regions, he turned down a road to Wigan as a sort of penance. He is agreeably surprised, partly because he finds the town less ugly than he had imagined, but chiefly because it is remarkably easy to get out of it, into pleasant neighbouring fields. He does his rather condescending best with the town, and – high praise from Morton – notes that 'it has one of the few good war memorials I have seen in England'.[21]

Paul Fussell, in his book on travel writing between the wars, has drawn attention to the way in which travel books are shaped. They are not, he persuasively argues, artless chronicles of one incident after another, but careful constructions, with characters, and plots that have beginnings, climaxes and resolutions. The customary division between the supposedly truthful travel book and the frankly fictional novel is hard to sustain.[22] In Fussell's terms, Morton's plot starts to build toward its climax when he reaches Warwickshire, birthplace of Shakespeare and the region in which Morton spent his youth. He is recaptivated by Stratford. Shakespeare and England bond there. Morton gives a fanciful account of glimpsing Titania, Peaseblossom and the rude mechanicals from *A Midsummer Night's Dream* in a nearby wood, and declares the view of the river from the churchyard to be 'one of the supremely English views'. But here, when the most potent elements of Englishness are in play, Morton enters an ironic, deflating recollection. As a youth, he recalls, he had worshipped Frank Benson, the actor-manager who had been responsible for the annual Shakespeare festivals at Stratford from 1886 to 1919. Morton recalls hearing Benson proclaiming that:

> . . . only through Stratford, the common meeting-place of the English-speaking world, could we heal the pains of Industrialism and make England happy again. We were to make the whole world happy, apparently, by teaching it to morris-dance and sing folk-songs and to go to the Memorial Theatre. With the splendid faith of Youth we pilgrims believed that England could be made 'merrie' again by hand-looms and young women in Liberty gowns who played the harpsichord. Then, I seem to remember, shortly after that war was declared. However. . . . . .[23]

The culminating point of the book is Morton's account of another casual, though actually highly improbable, encounter, this time with the vicar of an unnamed hamlet, seemingly near Warwick. The incident is immaculately stage-managed. (Morton's journey started, *Canterbury Tales*-like, in April: now it is harvest time, although the events in the book can scarcely have occupied five or six months.) Morton encounters the vicar in the churchyard and, among the ancient graves, hears him ruminate on the continuity of village life. The vicar invites him to stay overnight. They drink old port from Georgian glasses. Their talk is of the ancient, naturally hierarchical tradition of the place, and the mournful prospect of the breakup of the local estate when death duties are demanded. In the morning, the vicar conducts the Harvest Festival service in the church, before a contented, ruddy-faced congregation. And finally, in a passage which would have qualified for three stars on the *Cold Comfort Farm* purple passage scale:

> I took up a handful of earth and felt it crumble and run through my fingers, thinking that as long as one English field lies against another there is something left in the world for a man to love. 'Well,' smiled the vicar, as he walked towards me between the yew trees, 'that, I am afraid, is all we have.' 'You have England,' I said.[24]

The England for which Morton has been searching has been found, and its unsurprising identifying features are: remoteness from industrial city and all traces of modernity, the palpable presence of ancient, benign landowning and church authority, a contented population of agricultural workers, and a tinge of Shakespeare. Open politics has no place in England, although a vaguely specified, but none the less fundamental sense of the rightness of the old order – the almost comically old, eighteenth century, or even Tudor social order – is built into its very foundations.

I said earlier that *In Search of England* is 'nominally' a record of a motor trip around the country. But it is not a guide book. It would be impossible for the reader faithfully to trace Morton's route. Indeed, in some passages – the passages recording the Berkshire bowl-turner and the Warwickshire harvest festival, for example – he is extremely evasive about precise location. What, then, is the purpose of the book, and how do we account for its extraordinary popularity? The 'search' motif is important, I think. We have to imagine a reader who is not so much looking for a guide book for a journey he or she is planning, but who wants reassurance that there is, somewhere out there, an essential England. Morton's book convinces the reader that such an England has been sought and found, even though the locations of its quintessential sites are not disclosed. The reassuring knowledge that England is there, and that Morton has found it and described it for us, is maybe all the reader needs. Morton works simultaneously in the realms of topography and the imagination.

A year later, with four editions of *In Search of England* comfortably in the bag, Morton published a companion volume, *The Call of England* (1928). The new book had two functions, or three if we speculate that Morton was just vigorously hacking away at the seam of gold that he had had the skill and good fortune to open up. But the two reasons Morton gives were to do with the redress he felt he needed to make to the north of England. First, he wanted to attend to the industrial areas, and secondly, he wanted to introduce his readers, who, like him, tended instinctively to turn south and west whenever they sought the real England, to great tracts of what he had delightedly discovered to be equally English country, north of the Trent. (Presumably, he had a preponderantly south-eastern readership in mind.) In practice, the two objectives work against each other, and, predictably enough, the rural north gets far more attention than the industrial north. It is the Yorkshire moors and ruined abbeys, the Northumberland coast, the cathedral cities of Durham and York, the ancient small towns like Clitheroe, Beverley and Ripon that call forth his most effusive praise: '. . . you feel in little places such as Ripon that you touch the sturdy roots of England firmly locked in a distant and important past'.[25]

But Morton does go to the big industrial centres. The interesting thing, though, is that somewhat inconsistently, he does not fly to the opposite extreme and picture them as affronts to the essential England. Instead, he responds rather affirmatively to their confident style and their enormous vitality. Manchester and Liverpool win him over completely. He does mention the expected black puddings, clogs and shawls, but his imagination is really caught by the glamour of the Manchester Cotton Exchange, the raffish pubs, Liverpool Pier Head and the Great Dock Road – 'a magnificent epic of commerce'. Even Sheffield, which, as a steel town, was overwhelmingly smoky and and grimy, impressed him: 'The hard ugliness is queerly grand'.[26] He was not entirely blind, however, to the sorts of miseries that were, a decade later, to dominate the imaginations of later travellers from the south like Orwell. Morton's description, for instance, of the desperate world of the Liverpool casual dockworker is forthright and stark. But overall, his response to the industrial cities – including, later, Birmingham which he evidently already knew well and loved – is positive, very much in the way that his earlier response to London had been positive. Indeed, for all the clogs and shawls and rolling moors aspects of the north, he will allow no absolute disjunction between south and north. He points out that desperate casual dock work is as much a feature of London as of Liverpool life. (He later wrote a piece about casual workers in the London docks who were recruited for the dangerous and filthy job of scraping out the sludge from oil-fired ships' fuel pumps.[27])

In *The Call of England*, then, Morton attempted to integrate north and south, industry and country, into a more comprehensive vision of England. The north–south integration is a success, but he was unable successfully to incorporate industry into the essential England. At the book's close, as at the close of his first England book, he is magnetically drawn to Stratford-upon-Avon in the Warwickshire heartland. He finds a seat, close to Shakespeare's tomb, and reviews his journey. The highlights that he recalls are not the industrial cities, but the ancient northern cathedrals and the moorland abbeys. The essential features of England were not, it seems, under serious threat of redefinition.

These two books on England set Morton off on highly successful searches for the rest of the British Isles. *In Search of Scotland* (1929), *In Search of Ireland* (1930), and *In Search of Wales* (1932) quickly followed. These books lie outside the scope of this chapter, but it is important to note that they are substantial books, not just dashed-off afterthoughts (and Scotland was soon, like England, given a companion volume – *In Scotland Again* (1933)). Morton emphatically did not regard Ireland, Scotland and Wales as insignificant, vaguely comic or romantic appendages to England. The books are informed by a vivid sense of the autonomous histories of the four countries (especially of Highland, Jacobite Scotland), but, like the books on England, are regulated by prior notions of the essences of the countries he is visiting. In the book on Wales, for example, there is a painstaking, detailed and entirely sympathetic account of the life and work of Glamorgan coal miners. Morton goes down a mine (which reminds him of being in the trenches), gets to know the miners and their wives, and makes as plain as he can what family life is like when short time working and layoffs are always just round the corner, and where the basic wage of just over £2 a week is anyway pitiful. Morton offers no political commentary, beyond tersely commenting 'it is, of course, all wrong',[28] but the important point, in this study of Morton and Englishness, is that he was far readier to see the Glamorgan miners as the embodiment of something essential to the entity called Wales than he was to see their English equivalents as embodying anything essentially English. Maybe a stereotype is being struck here: to the English, the real Wales *includes* coal miners, just as it includes Snowdon.

This brings us to the books Morton wrote about England during the 1930s and '40s, the decades that saw George Orwell and J.B. Priestley taking their own, more celebrated – though in my view often less searching – journeys to the industrial areas. Morton's descriptions of life in the slums are as acute as Orwell's, even though they are set within a comparatively weakly formulated political perspective. Morton's most trenchant publication started life as a series of pieces for the *Daily Herald*. The series was reprinted in 1933 by the Labour Party, with a forward by George Lansbury, as a little twopenny pamphlet called *What I Saw in the Slums*, with photographs by James Jarché. In his introduction, Morton declares that he is not a member of any political party, but that he wished urgently to present 'a perfectly frank account of a short journey through the slums of six great industrial cities of England'. Close-up descriptions of squalid housing are interleaved with grim public health statistics. Political analysis, however, is not entirely absent. Slums, he says, cannot be cleared away by the unregulated private enterprise that produced them in the first place. Civic intervention is necessary. Sheffield's Labour council is singled out for praise.

The relationship Morton assumes with the poor and wretched people he meets is, as in his other books, patrician; he evidently feels no awkwardness in intruding into their lives and homes. Indeed, he points out that he was positively welcomed when he made clear that he was there to expose the wickedness of slum landlords, about whom he is unreservedly contemptuous: 'In a perfect state of society they would be stripped to the waist and whipped squealing through their own kennels.' He presents the people who live in the slums as engaged in a desperately unequal battle to preserve decency and respectability, symbolized by the women's Sisyphean practice of forever whitening their front doorsteps. The women particularly impress him:

> What a ghastly life they lead in mean streets. Always washing. Always cooking minute quantities of food. Always cleaning something that cannot be cleaned. Always enriching the earth. Always worried about something. This waste of energy is awful.[29]

In this short pamphlet, Morton offers no reflections on the relationship between the slums that have so outraged him and the essential England that is the quest of his other books. Implicitly, though, he presents the slums as a particularly grim legacy of the aberrant Industrial Revolution that has blighted an essentially green and pleasant land.

Morton continued to publish throughout the Second World War. He evidently felt a real threat of defeat, and it wrung from him even more intense evocations of the England that stood in jeopardy. In the summer of 1939, certain that war was close, he set off on yet another tour of England, to capture what he thought might be a final vision of it. He published his findings as *I Saw Two Englands* – the two being England at peace and England at war. His tour took him first to Kent, where he progressed from stately home to stately home (Penshurst, Knole, Hever, Chevening), and then in a clockwise loop, ending at Peterborough, where he watched gas masks being issued and realized that war was only weeks away.

A dozen years had passed since his first tour of England, and he registers the difference by remarking on the mock Tudor houses that were springing up along the new bypasses. The fashion for the Tudor, he writes:

> . . . may be deplorable or amusing, and it is easy to make fun of it, but it seems to express a longing for something good and, above all, something English. In a better world, our rulers and our educationalists would seek out the meaning of it, and if they found, as I think they might, that it expresses a turning away from a pitilessly mechanised age which is even now thinking of tearing itself to bits, they would see what could be done to deepen that instinct, to develop it and save it from the speculator.[30]

Morton himself does not press forward with a response to his own challenge.

The second half of the book is the record of a tour in October 1939, plainly undertaken with a good deal of official help, in the form of petrol coupons and passes to government installations, to inspect and report on the war effort. His conclusion is that England is fundamentally as 'sound as a bell', but is waiting for a leader.[31] The book ends with a highly-wrought postscript, written in the dark days of 1940. It ranges once again over the question of the identity of the essential England. The postscript purports to describe two nights in the life of a rural Home Guard unit commanded by Morton, although I would guess that a great deal of invention has gone into the account. On the first night, Morton leads his men – some of them veterans of the trenches of the First World War, and all intimately familiar from youth with every hedge and tree in the locality – in a sweep across the moonlit harvest stubble fields in search of reported German parachutists. 'The combined local knowledge of farmer, poacher, and sportsman had been pooled for a moment in order to hunt the invader from our corner of England.' On the second night, Morton stands watch on the tower of his village church, and uses the quiet night to muse on what the war was doing to England. The slums, the industrial towns, the mock Tudor bypass houses do not invade his musings. The threat posed by Hitler has pushed all the troubling aspects of England aside and has revealed the underlying, enduring England:

> . . . it comes to me that one of the most remarkable things about this war is the quiet way England has ceased to be a country or even a county for many of us, and has become a parish. All over our land, villages once proclaimed dead and done for have awakened to arms . . . my parish has become England. . . . [The danger of war] has accomplished for the villages of England what musical young men from Oxford, with bells at their knees, and earnest women in Liberty silk gowns hoped to do a decade ago; it has made England almost 'merrie' again.[32]

Two years later, and still fearful of defeat, Morton published his one and only novel, *I James Blunt*. It takes the form of a diary by a James Blunt, a 61-year-old resident of a southern English market town, recording his experiences of life following the successful invasion of Britain by the Germans. A swastika flies over the town hall. Jews and trade unionists have been rounded up. His grandchildren are corrupted by Nazi propaganda at the village school. In the bar of his local pub, the sporting prints have been taken down from the wall and replaced by pictures of Hitler. The story ends with the writer of the diary breaking off half way through an entry as a sinister knock comes on the door in the dead of night. The novel has no literary pretensions (but went through three editions within a month of publication); it is pretty frankly a piece of propaganda designed to chill the complacent. Its significance for this study of Morton's sense of Englishness is that, unsurprisingly, when he wished to symbolize the beleaguered nation, he unhesitatingly reached for 'a peaceful English country town', where 'everything blends beautifully, as English things do', near Farnham, in Surrey.[33]

The final text to be surveyed is a little book Morton published in 1943, entitled *Atlantic Meeting*. Morton was evidently well-connected, for he was asked, at short notice, and under conditions of strict secrecy, to be one of only two journalists accompanying Churchill on his voyage across the Atlantic in August 1941, to confer with Roosevelt and, as Morton saw it, to persuade America to join the war. Morton observes Churchill at close quarters during the voyage and ventures a conclusion about what he considers to be his unique qualities of leadership. They derive, Morton says, from his being deeply rooted in a pre-industrial, pre-class, 'old, warm, emotional England'. (He notes that Churchill was not afraid to weep openly during affecting scenes in the commercial feature films that were shown in the destroyer's wardroom, and which Churchill relished.) According to Morton, Churchill calls forth a response from the English people – the Scots, Irish and Welsh are nowhere to be seen in this account – because he is not identified with sectional, class, regional or industrial interests; he rises above all the jarring elements of a potentially riven country, and speaks from, and on behalf of, the essential England:

> I have sometimes studied the effect of Churchill's voice and words upon an ordinary gathering of men in a public house. Why, I have wondered, should they have been so firmly held, so silent until the last word? And I have wondered if it may not be that he speaks with the voice of an older England, that we recognise the voice, not of an industrialist, but of one who speaks to us as if from the deck of the *Golden Hind*. Churchill's voice is also classless. He has no public school accent. Like the Elizabethans, he speaks not as an Etonian but as an Englishman.[34]

Morton made a highly successful career out of writing books whose chief object was to serve the insatiable market for the myth that over that horizon, round that bend in the lane, across that field, lies an authentic England, untouched by the

the Industrial Revolution, by suburbia, by the anxieties of modern life. The myth was extraordinarily appealing to Morton's generation. People clung to it during the incomprehensible slaughter of the First World War. They pursued it on foot, on bicycles and in cheap motorcars down the open roads of the 1920s and '30s, and clung to it once again in 1939 when fears of a German invasion revived. The myth generated a sub-genre of books on England, and within that sub-genre, Morton was the most successful author. In many passages of his hugely popular books he is absolutely archetypal, but he was not entirely consumed by the myths he served. He forced himself to become acquainted with features of English life that were distinctly un-merrie, and he described them fearlessly. But he never fully integrated his vision of England: his focus always, in the end, narrows to the parish, the rural, the Arcadian – to an England that can never actually be visited or lived in – to (in Housman's phrase) a 'land of lost content'.

Notes

1   R. Colls and P. Dodd (eds), *Englishness: Politics and Culture, 1880–1920* (London, Croom Helm, 1986); M.J. Wiener, *English Culture and the Decline of the Industrial Spirit, 1850–1980* (Cambridge, Cambridge University Press, 1981, repr. Penguin, 1985); P. Wright, *On Living in an Old Country* (London, Verso, 1985); V. Cunningham, *British Writers of the Thirties* (Oxford, Oxford University Press, 1988); J. Giles and T. Middleton (eds), *Writing Englishness* (London, Routledge, 1995); A. Calder, *The Myth of the Blitz* (London, Cape, 1991), ch. 9.

2   P. Fussell, *The Great War and Modern Memory* (Oxford, Oxford University Press, 1975) p. 268. See esp. ch. 7, 'Arcadian resources'.

3   P. Fussell, *Abroad: British Literary Travelling Between the Wars* (Oxford, Oxford University Press, 1980).

4   G. Orwell, *Homage to Calalonia* (1938, repr. Penguin, 1989), p. 187.

5   See Wright, *On Living in an Old Country*; R. Hewison, *The Heritage Industry* (London, Methuen, 1987); R. Lumley (ed.), *The Museum Time Machine* (London, Routledge, 1988).

6   H.V. Morton, *I Saw Two Englands* (London, Methuen, 1942), 2nd edn., pp. 82–3; H.V. Morton, *In Search of Wales* (London, Methuen, 1932), 8th edn., 1936, p. 122.

7   H.V. Morton, *What I Saw in the Slums* (London, Labour Party, 1933).

8   K. Fields, 'The Travel Books of H.V. Morton', *Book and Magazine Collector*, 58, January 1989, pp. 50–6, esp. p. 52. No source is given for the figures.

9   Did the Burns phrase originate with Morton, or is he quoting? H.V. Morton, *In Search of Scotland* (London, Methuen, 1929), 17th edn, 1932, p. 268.

10 H.V. Morton, *The Heart of London* (London, Methuen, 1925); *A London Year* (London, Methuen, 1926); *London* (London, Methuen, 1926); *The Spell of London* (London, Methuen, 1926); *The Nights of London* (London, Methuen, 1926). Save for *A London Year*, these books were reprinted together as *H.V. Morton's London* (London, Methuen, 1940).

11 Morton, *The Spell of London* (10th edn, 1932), p. 15, cf. his comments on the Cenotaph, 'that mass of national emotion frozen in stone', *H.V. Morton's London* (13th edn., 1945), p. 19. On war memorials and their significance in general, see S. Hynes, *A War Imagined: the First World War and English Culture* (London, Bodley Head, 1990), esp. p. 270 *et seq.*

12 S. Baldwin, address to the Royal Society of St George, 1924, repr. in *England and Other Essays* (London, Allan, 1926), p. 7. The endurance of this mode among Prince Ministers is indicated by John Major's rhapsody about cricket, elderly spinsters cycling to evensong, and warm beer. Baldwin came from a family of Midland ironmasters. John Major was brought up in Brixton.

13 H.V. Morton, *In Search of England* (London, Methuen, 1927), 12th edn, 1930, pp. vii–xi.

14 The suggestion is made, for example, by Hynes, *A War Imagined*.

15 Morton, *In Search of England*, pp. 1–3.

16 H.V. Morton, *The Call of England* (London, Methuen, 1928), 6th edn, 1930, p. vii.

17 Alan Howkins has argued that the essential England that was constructed in the early decades of the twentieth century was located in *southern* England. Non-southern features could be incorporated only if they conformed with the southern pattern of field, hedgerow, lane and thatch. Moors and mountains are not English. See A. Howkins, 'The Discovery of Rural England', in R. Colls and P. Dodd, *Englishness: Politics and Culture*, pp. 62–88. Morton initially fits in well with this model. He heads south and west, rather than north and east. But he is not finally trapped by the model, for he rhapsodizes over Yorkshire, Northumberland, Northampton, and (particularly) Warwickshire – where he was brought up.

18 Morton, *In Search of England*, p. 10.

19 Ibid., p. 180.

20 Ibid., pp. 78–85. Morton works exactly the same trick of a dance band coming over the airwaves into the remote countryside, in his account of a night spent in a remote bothy in the Cairngorms. See H.V. Morton, *In Scotland Again* (London, Methuen, 1933, 10th edn, 1944), pp. 304–6.

21 Morton, *In Search of England*, pp. 187–90.

22 Fussell, *Abroad*, p. 174.

23 Morton, *In Search of England*, pp. 255–60. Morton himself trails off with the suspension points at the end of the quoted paragraph.

24 Ibid., p. 280. Stella Gibbons's *Cold Comfort Farm* (1932) satirized earthy, ruralist books. She alerted readers to purple passages in her book by signifying them with one, two, or three stars, on the Baedeker principle.

25 Morton, *The Call of England*, p. 64.

26 Ibid., pp. 150, 172.

27 H.V. Morton, *Our Fellow Men* (London, Methuen, 1936), 2nd edn, 1936, pp. 66–9.

28 Morton, *In Search of Wales*, pp. 246–67.

29 Morton, *What I Saw in the Slums*, pp. 9, 29.

30 Morton, *I Saw Two Englands*, p. 65.

31 Ibid., p. 282.

32 Ibid., p. 288.

33 H.V. Morton, *I James Blunt* (London, Methuen, 1942), p. 8.

34 H.V. Morton, *Atlantic Meeting* (London, Methuen, 1943), pp. 80–1.

11

'About Turn': The Communist Party of Great Britain and the Second World War, 1939–41

Keith Laybourn

In the six years prior to the outbreak of the Second World War the Communist Party of Great Britain (CPGB) and the Comintern (Communist International) were determined opponents of fascism. On the instructions of the Comintern, following Hitler's rise to power in Germany, the CPGB attempted to form a united front against fascism with other socialist parties between 1933 and 1935. On the insistence of Georgi Dimitrov, at the Seventh Congress of the Comintern in July and August 1935, the united front was replaced by the policy of encouraging the creation of a popular front, uniting all those parties willing to oppose fascism.[1] In September 1936, the CPGB considered the need to form a British battalion of the International Brigade to fight for the Republican government in Spain against Franco's fascists. In fact, it had declared its commitment to such a policy on 10 October 1936, two days before the Comintern officially announced the formation of the International Brigade.[2] Throughout the 1930s, moreover, the party had campaigned against Japanese aggression in Manchuria. Thus it seemed logical for Harry Pollitt, the General Secretary of the party, to declare, on 2 September 1939, the CPGB's support for Chamberlain's impending declaration of war against Nazi Germany. Yet, dramatically, within a month the party had changed its mind and Pollitt had resigned from his post, eventually taking on a lesser role as party organizer in Lancashire and Cheshire before returning to the Politburo (Political Bureau of leading party officials) in 1940. It was not until 13 July 1941, following the German invasion of the Soviet Union on 22 June 1941, that the Comintern and the CPGB officially changed their line once again and fervently committed themselves to the British war effort and the fight against fascism.

By any standards, even those of a party which was often faced with changes in policy and direction, this about turn on the Second World War in 1939 was a traumatic event which threatened what limited support the CPGB generated throughout the country. The point was emphasized by the Labour Party's pamphlet *Stalin's Men: About Turn*, which dubbed the CPGB 'not only the slaves of Moscow but the allies of Hitler'.[3] Why had this change, which involved the resignation of a man who had been the General Secretary of the party for ten years, occurred? And why was this decision reversed within less than two years?

For many years it was assumed that the change of policy in October 1939 resulted from the obvious pressures imposed upon the CPGB by Stalin and the Comintern. This view was not seriously challenged in 1979 when a special conference of the Communist Party's old faithfuls discussed the painful episode of 1939 – although they were divided on why the change of policy had occurred.[4] Based upon the publication of a report on this conference, in the mid-1980s, Noreen Branson suggested that there had been a strong reaction against the war by the Communist Party membership in Britain, many of whom supported the Comintern in its decision to oppose the war.[5] The argument goes that the party was thus reverting to type in opposing both imperialism and war as it had done in the 1930s. The support for the British war effort in September, led by Pollitt, was seen to be against the wishes of the party membership. By the late 1980s, Kevin Morgan was also suggesting that there was more flexibility in the Communist Party position than has been normally admitted, and that there was much debate between those who opposed and those who supported the changes in attitude towards the war in September and October 1939. He argued that whatever the influence of Moscow, the views of CPGB members appear to have carried some influence.[6]

Yet these new assessments are based largely upon the differences of opinion expressed at the 1979 conference of the old party faithfuls where there was, in fact, much disagreement about the extent to which Communist members were pro-war or anti-war. Much of this so-called freedom of action of the CPGB has now been challenged by the even more recent discoveries of Monty Johnstone. He has gone a long way to debunking such ideas and has re-emphasized that Stalin, Russian foreign policy, and the Comintern were decisive in changing the CPGB policy on the Second World War in 1939. The Dimitrov diaries, which have only just become available, reveal that on 7 September 1939 Stalin gave Dimitrov instructions to change the line and for the British, and other, communist parties not to oppose Germany. Indeed, Johnstone states that 'I would claim that there is no longer any room for doubt as to the pre-eminence of the role of the Comintern in securing this change.'[7] Whether such evidence fully refutes the British evidence, used by Branson and Morgan, is open to question. Nevertheless, it does hint of the past influence of the Soviet Union and the Comintern in dictating the direction of CPGB policies in 1928 with 'Class Against Class', in 1933 with the united front against fascism, and in 1935 with the popular front against fascism. In other words, the war policy changes of 1939 follow a well-worn pattern of Comintern domination of CPGB policies. The idea that British Communists could act independently of Moscow's wishes is seductive but hardly squares with the facts.

Notwithstanding differences of emphasis, few historians doubt the importance of Soviet foreign policy in determining the actions of the Comintern and its affiliates. Whatever doubts Morgan harboured about the room for manoeuvre within the Communist Party, he emphasizes that the prime concern of the CPGB was to protect the Soviet Union from invasion. In so doing, it encouraged the formation of a series of alliances, including the possibility of an Anglo-Soviet alliance, to prevent the isolation and invasion of Soviet Russia. When this did not occur, and the German-Soviet Non-Aggression Pact was signed on 23 August 1939, committing the Soviets to 'benevolent neutrality', it became obvious that the Soviet Union would act, through the Comintern, to ensure that all its affiliated organizations would work to oppose the war. In Britain's case this also meant a commitment to oppose Chamberlain's National government. The only serious question is – did this Comintern line accord with the views of the majority of CPGB members?

The purpose of this chapter is to examine the changes in CPGB policy in 1939 and 1941 in the light of the new evidence that became available in the mid-1990s. Microfilm copies of the internal records of the CPGB, particularly those of the Politburo and the Central Committee for the 1930s, have been obtained from Moscow, supplementing the paltry supply of such material that could previously be found in the papers of Harry Pollitt, Rajani Palme Dutt and other leading members of the party.[8] Combined with other sources, such as Home Office records, they seem to suggest that the CPGB changed its attitude towards the war because of the pressure emerging from Stalin and the Comintern, even though there was a softening of CPGB attitudes towards Britain's policy following the fall of France in June 1940. It was, however, to the relief of much of the party that it was allowed to support the British prosecution of the war, following the announcement of an alliance between Britain and the Soviet Union on 13 July 1941, less than a month after the occurrence of Operation Barbarossa on 22 June 1941, when Germany invaded the Soviet Union. The fact is that because of the Soviet Union, and Comintern direction, the CPGB changed its policy towards the war twice, following its initial support for the British government's approach in September 1939, in October 1939 and again in July 1941. There was also the softening of attitude that occurred after the 'Fall of France' in June 1940.

THE MOVES TO WAR

In the years and months immediately preceding the outbreak of the Second World War it is clear that the CPGB was attempting to avert war, criticizing the National government for being a friend of the fascist cause and hoping, since there were democratic forces at play, that Britain would sign a pact with the Soviet Union.[9] Such policies, particularly the opposition to both the war and the National government, appeared contradictory and led to conflict and confusion within the party with different sections supporting different views. On the one hand, Willie Gallacher MP was congratulated by the party for his opposition to Neville Chamberlain's visit to Hitler in Munich over the situation of

Czechoslovakia.[10] On the other, the *Daily Worker* commented favourably upon the prospects for peace brought about by the Munich meeting. Indeed, Pollitt was even persuaded that Chamberlain was anti-fascist by September 1938 and it took all the efforts of Rajani Palme Dutt, a leading intellectual figure within the party and faithful follower of the Moscow line, to keep the 1938 CPGB Conference at Birmingham in line with his own critical stance on Chamberlain.[11]

Further to this, the international crisis was hotly disputed within the Central Committee in May 1939 when the issue focused upon the extent to which attacks should be levelled against the Chamberlain National government because of its refusal to be involved in pacts that would protect the interest of Czechoslovakia. Some, such as Dutt, wished to play down this conflict while others, including Pollitt, wished to condemn fully the National government.[12] At this stage it is clear that the views of the CPGB were fluctuating considerably between its leaders and from meeting to meeting. It appears that the party felt that the imperialist war was about to begin, even as it was arguing that the fight against fascism would prevent war.

When the threat of war approached more directly, and the Soviet Union signed the Soviet–German Non-Aggression Pact on 23 August 1939, it was clear that the CPGB accepted that the opportunity for an Anglo-Soviet Pact had been missed and that the Soviets had opted for the best available alternative. Although this came like a thunderclap and was a bitter blow to Pollitt, and his supporters, the CPGB quickly interpreted it as a masterstroke. In fact, it was Stalin merely protecting the position of the Soviet Union.[13] Over the next six weeks this Pact was to present the CPGB with one of the biggest crises of its existence.

THE OUTBREAK OF THE SECOND WORLD WAR AND THE CHANGE OF DIRECTION SEPTEMBER TO OCTOBER 1939

The outbreak of the Second World War on 3 September 1939 posed major problems for the CPGB. Although it had previously criticized the Chamberlain government as being the friend of fascism and demanded peace, Pollitt and his colleagues produced a manifesto, on 2 September, stating that 'We are in support of All necessary measures to secure the victory of democracy over Fascism'. This was followed by the issue of Pollitt's pamphlet *How to Win the War* on 7 September, which suggested that the failure to fight fascism would be a betrayal of everything that the Communist Party stood for.[14] Within a month, on 2 October 1939, the Central Committee had changed its line completely, criticizing both the war and the National government. This change was so painful that it was nearly forty years before the old party faithfuls conducted an airing of the events.[15] Even then there was disagreement about what had happened and whether the various policies were justified. There seems less justification for equivocation and doubt now.

Pollitt's immediate reaction had been to support the war against Nazi Germany. This seemed to be the natural progression of a policy of opposing fascism in Spain and advocating the Popular Front, even though a policy of international peace had been the declared policy of the Comintern and the CPGB for some time. The manifesto which Pollitt, and the CPGB, produced supported the Chamberlain government in the war against Germany. Yet it was to be a war on 'Two Fronts', against both fascism and the National government. The idea was to replace Chamberlain's National government with a people's government, 'For fascism will not be defeated by the Chamberlain Government' and the war was 'a just war'.[16] Yet this line changed quickly, especially once the Moscow broadcast of 14 September described the war as an imperial one.[17] Allegedly, on the same day a press telegram arrived from Moscow informing the CPGB of the Comintern's change of policy but Pollitt seems to have suppressed it.[18]

At this point Rajani Palme Dutt, always a faithful follower of Moscow and the Comintern line, began to press for the Moscow, or international Marxist, line and claimed some support at the Central Committee of the CPGB. If he had much support it seems to have disappeared by the beginning of the Central Committee meeting on 24 and 25 September 1939. At this meeting, Dutt offered the Moscow line stating that:

> This war means enormous issues for us. It is firstly the extreme stage of imperialism. . . . Further the Imperialists are divided, they have not succeeded in their plan against the Soviet Union. . . . . The Soviet Union is enormously strengthened. . . . It is not a war for peace against aggression. We have to recognize quite clearly that the British ruling class which determined this war is conducting it for its purpose. . . . It is the fight for the British Empire against a threatening Empire. . . . Our line, the international line, is absolutely definite. If we accept the analysis of the imperialist war, we have to face the conclusions.[19]

Therefore, Dutt decided that there was a need to attack both Chamberlain and the imperial elements. In consequence he argued that the main fight of the working class was against their own imperialist government: 'We do not ignore fascism. But we do direct the fight against the Government as the central fight, that only a people's government can defend the people against fascism. . . .' It was also suggested that 'the retention of Poland's independence is a reactionary slogan', referring to Britain's declaration of war on Germany over the Nazi invasion of Poland.

Pollitt reacted strongly against Dutt's views.[20] He emphasized the need to defend the British people against fascism, just as the Soviet government was defending the Soviet people, and favoured the slogan 'Britain for the British' and the 'fight on two fronts'. He thus maintained that the CPGB needed to support the war against fascism no matter what Dutt and Moscow were saying.

Yet, at the end of the meeting on 24 September David Frank Springhall arrived from Moscow with a clear statement of the Soviet line. It was a timely intervention. The next day, 25 September, Springhall expounded this before the Central Committee. He discussed the conversations which he had held with Georgi Dimitrov and Andrew Marty and referred to the telegram of 10 September which 'had reached all parties but not us'. Evidently, the Secretariat of the Comintern had met on 9 and 10 September and agreed to a short thesis which stated that it was necessary to characterize the war 'not just as a war, but as an out-and-out imperialist war, a war which the working class in no country can give support to'. It was also argued that while Poland was not an imperialist state it could become part of a bigger fascist state. Dimitrov, in a second talk with Springhall, also emphasized that there should be no unity with the 'Chamberlain Socialists', a phrase which Willie Gallacher and some other Central Committee members did not understand. Eventually, after much discussion the fourteen points of Springhall's speech – including the suggestion that this was not a just war and that the party should oppose British government legislation for war credits – were reiterated. The CPGB, which the previous day was almost fully behind Pollitt's support for the war effort, was now being ordered to withdraw that support.

Pollitt suggested that the Politburo should meet at once and it was agreed that the Central Committee should be adjourned until 3 October. It in fact met on 2 October. It was also felt that the matter should not be discussed in the district committees until the Central Committee had made its final decision. It is quite clear that there was going to be no consultation with the rank and file of the party and that its higher committees were going to decide policy. Evidently, democratic centralism meant nothing in the face of orders from Moscow.

Nevertheless, the CPGB adjusted its political stance quickly. Over the next two weeks the *Daily Worker* denounced the first war budget of the British government on 27 September and then, on 30 September, the Politiburo declared the war to be against the interests of the people of Europe.[21] At the end of September and in early October, Salme Dutt, the wife of Rajani, sent a number of letters to Pollitt suggesting that he should go to his 'Poplar Pals', in a clear, if inappropriate, reference to George Lansbury and the pacifist section of the Labour Party.[22] Finally, the Central Committee meeting of 2 and 3 October 1939 accepted the Moscow line with three dissenting voices – Harry Pollitt, James Campbell and Willie Gallacher – although Pollitt asked that Gallacher's name be withdrawn from opposition once the vote had been taken.

At this meeting, which began on 2 October, Dutt made a powerful speech in favour of the Moscow line, maintaining that the whole party was on trial. An angry and indignant Gallacher responded by stating that 'I have never at the Central Committee listened to a more unscrupulous and opportunist speech as the one which has just been delivered'. Campbell further pointed to the inconsistencies of the change of line in Dutt's speech:

> We started with the idea of support for the war, but fight for a new government to carry it on. We are now asked to go over, oppose the war and use the situation to smash capitalism. We started to demand democracy for the Colonies, we must now come away from that and actively support colonial insurrection. We started by saying that we had an interest in the defeat of the Nazis, we must now recognize that our prime interest is the defeat of France and Great Britain because that will furnish the suitable conditions for a revolution in the country. . . . We started out by proclaiming the defence of the British people from fascism, we are now told that the defence of the British people from fascism is imperialism, that there can be no defence from imperialism until there is a revolutionary government in this country. . . . We have to eat all we have said. . . . I am against presenting the Soviet Union as a universal Santa Claus.[23]

Pollitt, more diplomatically, suggested that 'I am a loyal supporter of the C. I. . . . I am opposed to this thesis, I believe that in the long run it will do the Party very grave harm.'[24] He also believed that the Soviet Union was not yet out of danger from Germany, objected to the overthrowing of the United Front and Popular Front approaches and reflected that, in talks with Dimitrov, he had been told that the CPGB did not know how to look after the national honour of Britain. Pollitt felt that it was now time for the party to protect that national honour.

Shortly after this meeting Pollitt resigned as General Secretary of the CPGB, his position being untenable, although he offered his continuing services to the party.[25] He received several letters of thanks for his work, including one from Comrade Rose, stating that it 'was a big mistake for us all to lose you'.[26] Such was his frustration with the reversal of policy that it was not until 18 November 1939 that he could force himself to 'unreservedly accept the policy of the Communist Party',[27] blaming his hatred of German fascism and 'the influence of the fascist war of invasion on Republican Spain' for his aberration. It was a symbolic gesture which hid his true feelings.

The party was now officially in favour of 'revolutionary defeatism', the belief that the home country should be defeated in the hope of achieving revolutionary change as a result. A new Manifesto was published on 7 October 1939, declaring that the CPGB was opposed to both the war and the National government.[28] It stated that:

> The truth about this war must be told. The war is not a war for democracy against Fascism. It is not a war for the liberties of small nations. It is not a war

for the defence of peace against aggression. This war is a fight between imperialist powers over profits, colonies and world domination.[29]

The Executive Committee of the Comintern reiterated the point on the twenty-second anniversary of the Russian Revolution on 6 November 1939, emphasizing that 'The ruling circles of England, France and Germany are waging war *for world supremacy*.'[30]

This change of policy led to much division within the party throughout the country. Some members, such as Bill Moore of Sheffield, were pleased that the CPGB had returned to its peace policy. Years later, Moore recalled that the change of line was not due to the intervention of the Communist International: 'When Joe turns we all turn; and I just don't believe it. It would not have had as I remember, total acceptance unless it corresponded with the experience that I think all the Party had over the previous ten years.'[31] Ernie Trory (Sussex District organizer) has also made similar points, maintaining that it was only on 12 [13] July 1941, when the alliance between Britain and the Soviet Union was signed, that he accepted the need to work with the government against fascism.[32] These two felt that the defence of the Soviet Union was all important and that the pre-war commitment to peace was being maintained. Others disagreed, feeling that the mood of the party members was with the Pollitt line of fighting the war on 'two fronts'. Jack Cohen maintained that ' I don't recollect any of the enthusiasm for the new line when it was adopted, and I certainly don't agree that it represented the logical culmination of ten years of political activity by the party.'[33] Others also believed that the party should support Britain in the war. Eventually, however, most British Communists accepted the new party line, even if their support was given in a grudging and equivocal manner.[34] As Kevin Morgan wrote: 'The fact is that Stalin had signed a pact with Germany and the CPGB had to adjust its lines accordingly.'[35] It may be that historians will never be able to measure the extent to which the CPGB membership truly accepted the change of line but there was clearly dissent, remarkably little support for the anti-war line until 25 September, and considerable enthusiasm once the line was changed to a pro-war stance in July 1941.

In the West Riding of Yorkshire similar confusion certainly prevailed. Geoff Hodgson of the Leeds CPGB related that the majority of the branch loyally supported the Pollitt line of war on 'Two Fronts' in September 1939 and the new Comintern line came as a shock.[36] In contrast, Ernie Benson, a senior figure in the Leeds CPGB and District Organizer between 1936 and 1938, recalled that 'As I saw it, and also the majority of the Party members, it was a war brought about by the clash of rival capitalist powers, and a hatred of the Soviet Union. . . . An unjust war was being waged and we could not support such a war.'[37]

THE WAR, OCTOBER 1939 TO JUNE 1940

Over the next twenty months the Communist Party preached revolutionary defeatism but seems to have applied this policy with great flexibility. The focus of much of its activity was not so much the defeat of Britain as the need to establish immediate peace with Hitler. The party also sought to improve the lot of the working classes. Indeed, the party's application forms at this time contained the statement that:

> The rulers of Britain are using this war to declare heavy blows against their own people – employers have launched a sweeping attack on the workers' standards and conditions. The workers must organise to resist the combined attacks of the employers and the Government. If you agree with this you will join the Communist Party today.[38]

The Communist Party attempted to connect almost every issue with working conditions and living standards. It took up the case of the Aircraft Shop Stewards' National Council (formed in 1933), through *The New Propeller*, for better conditions of employers. Similar action occurred in other trades. Apparently, according to the government, 'In industry the Communist Party is making determined efforts to improve its position. Already its representation among shop stewards is out of all proportion to its membership and every grievance is exploited by them.'[39]

The CPGB found some major problems in adopting a more aggressive trade union policy. The most obvious was that some Communist trade union leaders simply ignored the party line. Arthur Horner, the South Wales Miners' leader, returned to his controversial and divisive approach of the early 1930s, nicknamed at that time as 'Hornerism'. This was demonstrated in the South Wales Miners' Federation's (SWMF) wage negotiations in October 1939 in which Horner argued in favour of the unions accepting two-thirds of the offer that the employers were making in response to the miners' demands. He also supported a situation where the SWMF voted three to one in favour of the war effort 'so long as it is fought against Fascists' aggression and for the achievement of a permanent peace'. This action brought him into conflict with the official Communist line.[40] The Home Office noted, of Horner, that 'His position as President of the South Wales Miners' Federation brings a good deal of kudos to the party but he has recently shown considerable unwillingness to accept their instructions. . . .'[41]

There is, indeed, some suggestion that many Communist leaders were attempting to 'dilute' the new Comintern-inspired line. Recently, Nina Fishman has argued that Harry Pollitt, Jimmy Campbell and other CPGB leaders focused upon industrial matters in order to minimize the unpopularity of the CPGB's anti-war stance and build up its contact.[42] She has argued, further, that the relationship between the trade unions and the CPGB remained as it was before 1939: 'British trade union leaders did not exploit the opportunity presented by the party's anti-war position to instigate a general inquisition against party activists.'[43] Apparently, only the Amalgamated Engineering Union and the Miners' Federation of Great Britain appear to have tested the relationship between Communist anti-war sentiments and the official trade union movement, with its more pro-war sentiments, but even here they agreed to differ. Fishman even suggests that the development of the National People's Convention movement from January 1941, aimed at developing the people's democratic and trade union rights and at uniting both anti-war and pro-war Communist and Labour supporters, was allowed to fade away for fear of challenging the trade union movement.[44] These claims may have some validity. Pollitt was certainly using industrial work as a basis for maintaining the CPGB connection with the trade union movement it had nurtured since the Comintern had permitted him, through the January resolution of 1932, to work through trade unions, stating that 'It would be wrong to separate the work of unions from the work in the factories. They are both part of the same fight and process.'[45] It is less certain, however, that the National People's Convention movement, to be discussed later, was abandoned for fear of upsetting the trade unions. The German invasion of the Soviet Union had more to do with that decision.

There were also other CPGB concerns in the early months of the war, although they amounted to little. There was particular opposition to the possibility that Britain might support Finland in its war of independence against the Soviet Union. In the end, British support for Finland did not emerge but Dutt, at the height of the emergency, declared that 'The Finnish conflict means that within less than three months of the beginning of the imperial war, direct war on the Soviet Union had begun.'[46] This did not please John Strachey, one of the intellectuals of the party, who had only been persuaded to the new line in November 1939. To him the Soviet invasion of Finland was the last straw and, feeling that the *Daily Worker*'s treatment of the matter was revolting, he left the party in May 1940, arguing that the Comintern's action had increased the possibility of the subjection of Western Europe to Nazi control.[47] There were also more domestic electoral concerns. Pollitt was defeated at the West Ham Silvertown parliamentary by-election in February 1940 and Isobel Brown was defeated at Bow and Bromley in June 1940.

The signs of support for the CPGB were somewhat contradictory. There seems to have been no great surge of interest in the CPGB while at its May Day activities in 1940 Comintern policies were largely ignored.[48] Nevertheless, there had been a steady increase in Communist support. In January 1940 the CPGB had about 20,000 members, an increase of 2,000 in the previous fifteen months, and the Young Communist League membership had risen to about 6,000 members. The bulk of the increase had, apparently, occurred since the outbreak of the war.[49] The CPGB was also making attempts to win the support of anti-fascist refugees.[50]

The growth of the Communist Party, and its opposition to the war, certainly attracted the attention of the British government which kept detailed notes on all its public meetings. In London these were gathered together by Special Branch and a distilled report sent to the Home Secretary. Apart from the enormous detail, often verbatim, of the public meetings, an assessment of the Communist Party's position and threat was often provided. In addition, it is clear that the government had agents operating at the highest level in the CPGB. Indeed, a Special Branch Report on 15 February 1940 stated that 'The following is a copy of the notes used by [David] Frank Springhall [London Organizer of the CPGB] when addressing said meetings which are being held in various parts of the country and are attended by leading members only.'[51] There were also enquiries into whether or not the *Daily Worker* was receiving foreign subsidies, in which it was suggested that MI5 should check the accounts at the Westminster Bank.[52] In fact British Intelligence was very well aware that the CPGB had been receiving £2,000 to £3,000 per month, two-thirds of it for the *Daily Worker*, from the mid-1930s onwards.[53] The government was clearly keeping a close eye on the activities of the CPGB and was fully aware of the splits within it.

THE CPGB, THE WAR AND THE PEOPLE'S CONVENTION, JUNE 1940–JUNE 1941

The attitude of the CPGB towards the war began to change with the fall of France in June 1940 and with Britain's rejection of Hitler's offer of a peace settlement on 19 July 1940. By that time the party was no longer overtly rejecting the war against Hitler, largely because of the fear of Nazi invasion and the London Blitz.[54] At this point, Pollitt was also re-establishing himself within the party hierarchy although Michael Foot remembered him as 'a frequent frustrated, drinking companion of those wretched months' desperate to defeat Nazism and wishing to play his part.[55] Indeed, he was also one of the four Communist signatories for a 'call to action' in September 1940 when the invasion threat was at its height.[56]

In this threatening climate for the survival of Britain, negotiations were conducted between the government and the party, with Willie Gallacher sending a letter to R.A. Butler, the Under-Secretary for Foreign Affairs, regarding the need to work closely together and suggesting the possibility of sending Pollitt, Gallacher, Dutt and Kerrigan to the Soviet Union to promote a change of policy.[57] This seems to have been raised with Sir Stafford Cripps, Britain's Ambassador in Moscow, who sent a telegram to Butler on 16 July 1940, stating that:

I do not believe that any of those named can influence Soviet foreign policy any more than any other unofficial figures. . . I do not consider any harm would be done by Pollitt coming, for whose honesty and intelligence I have great respect. I should respect any of the other two [sic] coming.

Interestingly, there was a letter from Maclean, Senior Principal at the Foreign Office, opposing the trip since he saw 'every member of the Communist Party' as ' an agent of a foreign power'.[58] Nevertheless, there was also a meeting on 23 July 1940 between Butler and Gallacher at which Butler expressed the view that the CPGB should be anti-Hitler.[59]

Yet, while the CPGB was prepared to talk to Churchill's wartime government, it is clear that moves in this direction were slow and halting. Gallacher, Rust and Dutt were still critical of Churchill's wartime administration as still not to be trusted,[60] and matters did not improve when the *Daily Worker* was suppressed in January 1941, against the advice given to the Home Office. Although Sir Alexander Maxwell felt the Communist Party was becoming 'more actively hostile' and 'defeatist', Viscount Swindon argued that the suppression of the *Daily Worker* 'would be a mistake' even though the leading article of 9 September 1940 had praised three 'worthy strikes' which had taken place.[61]

In this less critical and more cooperative atmosphere, the CPGB became convinced of the need to develop the alternative strategy of forming a People's Convention. The idea was initially put forward by D.N. Pritt, Labour MP and Communist sympathizer. He had originally developed the idea in June 1940, when he wrote that 'I appeal for the widest support of the People's Convention. Only the people can save themselves.'[62] Dutt also stressed the need for a broad alliance of Labour interests to be brought together in a Socialist Labour Alliance. By August 1940 Dutt was thinking of the need for a People's Convention which would be a wider coming together and reorganization of mass elements. These moves coincided with the fact that in July 1940 the Hammersmith Labour Party and Trades Council set up a People's Vigilance Committee to mount a campaign on the demands of the Communist Party. Out of these efforts a People's Convention was called, and held, in London on 12 January 1941. A People's Convention Manifesto had been circulated before the meeting suggesting six main points: the defence of the people's living standards, the defence of the people's democratic rights, adequate air raid precautions, friendship with the Soviet Union, the formation of a people's government and a people's peace to get rid of the causes of war.

The People's Convention filled three halls, attracted 2,234 delegates and purported to represent the interests of 1,200,000 people. It extended its original six points to eight, including the need for Indian independence, and was attended by Krishna Menon and R. P. Dutt, as well as Pritt and the other leading spirits. Not surprisingly, it was dubbed the 'People's Reichstag' by the *Daily Herald*.[63]

Within a few months the movement had distributed 632,000 pamphlets and 1,336,000 leaflets and manifestos. These included W.J. Square's *The People's Convention Movement*, Edgar G. Young's *The People's Peace*, W. Swanson's *Industrial Problems*, Dudley Collard's *Civil Liberties* and D.N. Pritt's *Friendship with the USSR*. It also produced different leaflets to explain to different groups of workers why they must support the People's Convention. It committed itself to a recall conference in August 1941, but this never took place owing to the changed political circumstances of June and July 1941 and the movement for the People's Convention simply disbanded itself.[64]

THE CPGB ENTERS THE WAR

On 22 June 1941 Nazi Germany invaded the Soviet Union along an 1,800 mile front, seized thousands of square miles of land and surrounded much of the Russian army. News of this invasion, Operation Barbarossa, was broadcast on BBC Radio later that morning. Now that Germany was invading the Soviet Union there was no way that Communists could regard the war as an imperialist war. Nevertheless, there were, at first, British Communist fears that the attack was in some way connected with Rudolph Hess parachuting into Scotland on 10 May 1941. The Central Committee issued a statement on 22 June 1941 suggesting that the attack upon the Soviet Union was fascism's supreme aggression and demanding that there should be an 'immediate military and diplomatic agreement between Britain and the Soviet Union'.[65] None the less, there was the feeling that upper-class reactionaries in Britain and the United States were still hoping for an alliance with Hitler against the Soviet Union and it was stated that 'This attack is the sequel of the secret moves which have been taking place behind the curtain of the Hess mission', a view which David Frank Springhall had also declared on the same day.[66] There was also no confidence in Churchill's wartime Coalition government, whose Tory and Labour leaders were seen to be anti-Soviet, and the party continued to call for a people's government. Yet Churchill broadcast to the nation on 22 June, revealing his intention to help the Russian people in their battle against Nazi Germany.[67] The CPGB was thus forced to reassess its position.

On 26 June Willie Gallacher, Communist MP for West Fife, declared that the CPGB would support the government if it collaborated with the Soviet Union.[68] On the same day, Harry Pollitt announced the need to remove pro-fascist groups from the government, dropped his demand for a people's government, and sent his pamphlet *Smash Hitler Now* to the press. The Central Committee met on 4 July and issued a manifesto entitled *People's Victory over Fascism*, urging an alliance with the Soviet Union, the removal of fascist supporters from government, the organization of production and the mobilization of the entire people for victory. Pollitt was also reinstated as the General Secretary of the party. On 8 July the new manifesto was elaborated in a political letter signed by Pollitt and sent out to the branches. It suggested that the victory over Hitler was the supreme issue of the day.

Pollitt had been vindicated. He had resisted the change in line, the 'new line' of October 1939, on grounds of class and his hostility to fascism and had attempted to develop the industrial policy of the party as an alternative to its nationally unpopular anti-war stance. Pollitt's papers contain a criticism of R.P. Dutt's book *Crisis of the British People*, which was never published because of the CPGB's involvement in the people's war from July 1941. Pollitt's comments reflect his long-standing views on the Communist Party's anti-war policy between October 1939 and July 1941:

> How is the mistake of the Party treated in September 1939 – completely glossed over – Yet this was a mistake of great consequence & over which there will always be endless discussion. . . .
>
> L[e]t R. P. D. read what he is writing now about Hitlerism & what he wrote in Nov. 1939.
>
> Dishonest to pose as leading Marxist in Europe and not to give attention to a political mistake of such importance in a book purporting to prove we have always been right.
>
> Can see value of such comprehensive sweep of world events in peace time, but not in the war . . . when aim of everything we write is mobilise for victory over fascism, over Hitlerite Germany. When no Soviet leader goes over past only in order to whip up anti-fascist feeling, when fundamentals of Communism are not touched upon. . . .
>
> God knows we have had enough battles of Quotations – Dare we afford another one now, when Party got its feet on the ground & when masses not interested in past, but only in the terrible present & future.[69]

In this passage, Pollitt had caught Dutt's essential style. Here was a man who would justify whatever twist or turn Moscow and the Comintern made, justify it with quotations and overlook the political somersaults that had been undertaken to achieve it. Dutt's intellectual commitment to Moscow contrasted with Pollitt's more working-class gut reaction which was prepared to accept that the CPGB was wrong in opposing the war in October 1939.

CONCLUSION

The vital lesson to be learned from the CPGB's approach to the Second World War is that the final and vital decisions were made by Stalin, the Communist Party of the Soviet Union and the Comintern – not by the CPGB. While the rank and file members and some of the leaders of the CPGB might express dismay and dissent, they did, in the end, pay homage to the official international

Marxist line because they recognized that the Soviet Union must be defended if international communism was to survive. The change of line to a pro-war position in June 1941, favoured by many British communists, was entirely a product of that need to continue to protect the Soviet Union. Pollitt's re-emergence as the leading member of the CPGB owed everything to that need. It was only the end of the Comintern in 1943, because of the recognition that Communist parties in different countries faced different problems, and the CPGB's omission from Cominform (Communist Information Bureau) when it was formed in September 1947 that permitted the greater freedom of the post 1950s era of the CPGB. Nevertheless, the Comintern and Soviet Union's decision to fight Hitler in 1941 permitted Pollitt and the CPGB to enter the war effort as the greatest of all patriots, campaigning for the increasing of industrial production and the opening of the Second Front in Europe to relieve the pressure of the German attack upon the Soviet Union. Pollitt campaigned tirelessly, produced numerous pamphlets such as *Into Battle* and *Smash Hitler Now*, and addressed many Trafalgar Square demonstrations in support of the war. Not surprisingly, the CPGB reached its apogee, with over 56,000 members by the end of 1942. Such success was fleeting and after 1947, with the emergence of the Cold War, the CPGB's opponents were all too ready to remember the way in which Moscow had dominated the CPGB in the past, even though such domination became much less evident as the postwar years continued. In the end, the Communist Party of Great Britain suffered greatly as a result of its domination by Moscow and the Comintern and the wartime episode of September 1939 to July 1941 does much to endorse the view that it was Moscow, not King Street, that determined the broad lines of CPGB policy until well after the end of the Second World War.[70]

Notes

1   J. Degras, *The Communist International, 1919–1943*, vol. 3 (London, Frank Cass, 1971); K. McDermott and J. Agnew, *A History of International Communism from Lenin to Stalin* (London, Macmillan, 1996).

2   Central Committee (of the CPGB), Minutes, 10 October 1936 to be found in the National Museum of Labour History, 103 Princess Street, Manchester.

3   Labour Party, *Stalin's Men: About Turn*, London, 1940, p. 3.

4   J. Attfield and S. Williams, *1939: The Communist Party and the War* (London, Lawrence & Wishart, 1984), particularly pp. 54–5.

5   N. Branson, *History of the Communist Party of Great Britain, 1927–1941* (London, Lawrence & Wishart, 1985) pp. 270–3.

6   K. Morgan, *Against Fascism and War: Ruptures and Continuities in British Communist Politics 1935–1941* (Manchester, Manchester University Press, 1989), pp. 92–5.

7   Monty Johnstone, 'The CPGB, the Comintern and the War, 1939–1941: Filling in the Black Spots', *Science and Society*, Special Issue on Communism in Britain and the British Empire, 61: 1, spring 1997, p. 28.

8   See n. 2.

9   Political Bureau, Minutes, 16 May 1939, comments of Comrade Shield, National Museum of Labour History.

10 Ibid., 19 March 1939, in comments made by Comrade Cornforth, National Museum of Labour History.

11 Morgan, *Against Fascism and War*, pp. 70–3.

12 Political Bureau, Minutes, 21 May 1939.

13 *Daily Worker*, 23 August 1939.

14 Attfield and Williams, *1939*, pp. 149–52 contains a copy of the Manifesto. This collection is based upon a conference held on 21 April 1979 organized by the Communist History Group which brought together surviving Communist participants to discuss the events of 1939.

15 Attfield and Williams, *1939*.

16 H. Pollitt, *How to Win the War*, (London, CPGB, 1939).

17 Morgan, *Against Fascism and War*, p. 89.

18 Ibid., p. 108.

19 Central Committee, Minutes, 24 September 1939.

20 CPGB, extra reel 6, September–December 1939, Central Committee, Minutes, 23, 24 and 25 September 1939.

21 Central Committee, Minutes, 30 September 1939.

22 Pollitt Papers, CP/IND/POLL/2/7, letter, 1 October 1939, in the National Museum of Labour History.

23 Central Committee, Minutes, 2 October 1939.

24 Ibid.

25 *Daily Worker*, 12 October 1939.

26 Pollitt Papers, CP/IND/POLL/2/7, letter from Comrade Rose to Pollitt dated 7 October 1939.

27 Letter of Harry Pollitt to Central Committee, dated 18 November 1939.

28 *Daily Worker*, 7 October 1939.

29 Attfield and Williams, *1939*, p. 170.

30 Ibid., pp. 175–6.

31 Ibid., p. 54.

32 Ibid., pp. 59–60.

33 Ibid., pp. 71.

34 Ibid., pp. 93–9.

35 Morgan, *Against Fascism and War*, p. 91.

36 Taped interview with Dylan Murphy, 12 December 1996.

37 E. Benson, *The Struggle is to Live* (People's Publications, 1980), pp. 195–6.

38 Ibid., p. 122.

39 PRO, HO/45. 25549 IECP Activities and Meetings 1940.

40 Morgan, *Against Fascism and War*, p. 140.

41 PRO, HO/45. 25549 IECP Activities and Meetings 1940.

42 N. Fishman, *The British Communist Party and the Trade Unions, 1933–1945* (Aldershot, Scolar Press, 1995), p. 259.

43 Ibid., p. 261.

44 Ibid., pp. 271–2.

45 Central Committee, Minutes, 16 January 1932; 'Immediate Tasks before the Party and the Working Class: Resolution of the Central Committee, CPGB, January 1932', *Communist Review*, February 1932, pp. 55–69.

46 Political Bureau and Central Committee, Minutes, December 1939 and with similar statements up to March 1940.

47 CP/IND/DUTT/06/02 in the National Museum of Labour History.

48 Morgan, *Against Fascism and War*, pp. 140–2.

49 PRO, HO 45/25549, IE CP Activities and meetings 1940.

50 Ibid., 8/2/1940 Special Branch Report regarding a 5/2/40.

51 Ibid., Special Branch Report, 15 February 1940.

52 Ibid., Special Branch Report, 15 March 1940.

53 PRO, HW 17, 17–21, for example 2727/UK, 2 April 1935.

54 Morgan, *Against Fascism and War*, p. 32.

55 K. Morgan, *Harry Pollitt* (Manchester, Manchester University Press, 1993), p. 116.

56 *World News and Views*, 28 September 1940, pp. 538–9.

57 PRO, FO 371/24856.

58 Ibid.

59 Attfield and Williams, *1939*, p. 32.

60 W. Gallacher, article in *World News and Views*, 3 August 1940 and W. Rust, 'Imperialism and Counter-Revolution', *Labour Monthly*, November 1940, pp. 606–7.

61 PRO, HO 45/25552 1940–1, letter from Sir Alexander Maxwell, July 1940, and letter from Lord Swindon to Dr John Anderson, 17 September 1940.

62 *Labour Monthly*, June 1940, p. 335. Also look at D.N. Pritt, *Forward to a People's Government* (London, 1940) p. 16.

63 *Daily Herald*, 14 January 1941.

64 There is a small collection of pamphlets and leaflets produced by the People's Convention movement in the British Library of Political and Economic Science, London School of Economics.

65 Central Committee, Minutes, 22 June 1941.

66 PRO, HO 45/25552 1940–1, report on a London District of the Communist Party meeting held just after the news on Operation Barbarossa broke.

67 *The Times*, 23 June 1941.

68 *Industrial and General Information*, 27 June 1941.

69 Pollitt, 'Points on R.P.D. book' in Pollitt Papers, National Museum of Labour History and also quoted in Morgan, *Pollitt*, p. 117.

70 16 King Street, London, was the headquarters of the CPGB. In postwar years its address became 16 John's Street, London.

12

THE SECOND WORLD WAR AND THE REFORM OF FURTHER EDUCATION IN BRITAIN

Brendan Evans

Historians contest whether war can be a source of positive social change, but it is evident that in twentieth-century Britain, war produced major educational reforms, in 1902, 1918 and 1944. In 1988 and 1993 two further pieces of educational legislation were established, but only after forty-four years of social change, during which the framework of the education system had been determined by the arrangements put in place in 1944. Whether or not a general thesis linking war to progressive reform can be sustained, it is apparent that the reform of 1944 was a direct consequence of war, as this analysis concerning the legislative development of further education in Britain reveals.

Undoubtedly the presence of further education in the provisions of the 1944 Education Act was partly the result of the context of the war in which the country was engaged. The 1944 Act defined further education as encompassing technical, continued, and adult education, and it is apparent that the case for all three was stimulated by the circumstances of the war. Further education was not the central thrust of the Act, which was centrally concerned with secondary education for all, the raising of the school-leaving age, resolving the relationship between church and state schools, removing obsolete units of educational administration, replacing a Board of Education with a Ministry and a President with a Minister, and increasing the capacity of the central state to steer the provision of education in Britain. The Act did ensure, however, that further education became a permanent feature on the postwar political agenda, although the advances which it secured were tentative and ambiguous. There are three sections to this analysis: first, a discussion of the debate about the impact of war and a description of the way in which war stimulated educational reform after 1940; second, an analysis of the pressure group politics which promoted technical and continued education; and third, an examination of the somewhat different campaign to promote adult education. The conclusion draws together the discussion on pressure-group politics and tests the validity of 'network' theories of policy-making; and considers whether the 1944 Act was sufficiently progressive to sustain the hypothesis that war promotes significant political change.

WAR AND SOCIAL CHANGE

The two world wars obtrude so evidently into twentieth-century British history that it is natural that historians relate them to historical developments. Marxists have confidently described war as an agent of social change. Marx suggested that war puts a nation to the test and Trotsky saw war as the 'locomotive of history'.

Yet there is little agreement among historians who argue a connection between war and social change as to how the process operates; or as to the precise nature of the changes which occur. Andrzjewski advanced 'the military participation ratio'.[1] This proposition is that the extent of social change generated by war depends directly upon the proportion of the population involved in the war effort. The bomber does not discriminate socially so all who contribute to the war effort seek recompense from the state. It is unlikely that the relationship between war and change is as simple as Andrzjewski claims, yet this does not invalidate the existence of some relationship. Bowley linked the experience of war to a reduction of class distance in society, the improvement of the position of women, and even 'socialistic legislation'.[2] Tawney asserted that the pressure for social change after the First World War was more than a desire to modify capitalism.[3] Marwick supports the argument, although he distinguishes 'guided' political change from 'unguided' social change. He cited the Education Act of 1918 as an example of 'collectivist social action' stemming from the 1914–18 war.[4] Titmuss undertook an analysis of the Second World War, concluding that the war exposed weaknesses ruthlessly and brutally, creating the demand for revolutionary economic and social change.[5]

Barnett subscribes to the thesis in a perverse way. Acknowledging that the war generated a reformist spirit among the British 'establishment', he regards it as an entirely negative phenomenon. So besotted were political leaders by the chimera of a 'New Jerusalem' that they took damaging decisions. The Coalition government failed, therefore, 'across the whole field of industrial and educational policy to evolve coherent medium or long-term strategies capable of transforming Britain's obsolete industrial culture. . . . Instead all the boldness of vision, all the radical planning, all the lavishing of resources, had gone towards working the social miracle of New Jerusalem'.[6]

Some historians contest the view which links war to progressive social change. Toynbee insists on the incompatibility of war and progress.[7] Havighurst argues that the changes produced by war were limited and that their form had already been determined.[8] Abrams maintains that the 1914–18 war merely advanced the cause of 'middle-aged propertied women'.[9] Millward points out that tax evasion developed during the Second World War.[10]

Calder presents a measured interpretation of the impact of the 1939–45 war. He points to the widespread public demand for postwar reform so that government had to make concessions, but balances this with the observation that 'the forces of wealth, bureaucracy and privilege survived with little inconvenience, recovered from their shock, and proceeded with the old business of manoeuvre, concession and studied betrayal'.[11]

It is likely that the 'military participation ratio' is too schematic. Change results from a variety of factors: war converts 'outsider' pressure groups to those whose voice is heard; new attitudes emerge among the privileged classes who recognize the shared hazards of war; the process of war exposes defects crying out for reform; and the need for the better management of resources and the more efficient deployment of the military and labour force of the country becomes obvious. At the very least war disturbs the *status quo*.

War revived the spirit of educational reform. Even the official civil servants at the Board of Education, encouraged by the President of the Board, Herwald Ramsbotham, responded to the demand. When it looked as if reform could founder on the rocks of Churchillian and die-hard Conservative opposition, R.A. Butler, who succeeded Ramsbotham in 1941, manoeuvred the politics of the wartime Coalition government to ensure that the impulse for reform would be consummated by legislation. If war placed the reform of education on the political agenda, were it not for the efforts of pressure groups the Education Act of 1944 might have been even more cautious and would have ignored further education altogether. It is also probable that but for Butler's persistence in building on the work of Ramsbotham and his officials, and his own skill in mobilizing supporters in the government, reform would not have occurred. The Act became known as the 'Butler Act' after Sir Edward Campbell, the Conservative MP for Bromley, stated during the third reading debate on the Act that as 'we called the old Act, the Fisher Act [after H.A.L. Fisher who was credited with steering the 1918 Act on to the statute book as President of the Board]. How are we going to remember this Bill? Shall we not call it the Butler Act'?[12] This interpretation filtered through to subsequent accounts and Butler encouraged the perception that it was his Act.[13] Yet it is apparent that one historical myth needs correction: the origins of the 1944 Act go further back than is often supposed. The so-called 'Butler' Education Act was set in motion by the work of Herwald Ramsbotham and his officials at the Board.

The Board's officials wanted to capture the initiative rather than allow the mounting pressures to take control of the reform agenda out of their hands. As the Permanent Secretary, Maurice Holmes expressed it, 'it is clear that other persons and bodies have ideas on postwar educational reconstruction, and I think this is a matter on which the Board should lead rather than follow'.[14] For Holmes, the possibility that the Government might set up a committee to recommend postwar education policy in response to public demand did not 'absolve us from forming our own views as to the educational changes which we would like to see in a postwar world'.[15] Holmes also considered that, 'the war is moving us more and more in the direction of Labour ideas'.[16] He also wanted the Board to retrieve the powers it had relinquished to the local authorities, to cease its tendency to react to the proposals of local authorities and teachers' organizations, and to become the lead body in educational policy-making.[17] Radical solutions driven either by the general public, sundry left-wingers, or even the Board's own acknowledged partners among the local authorities and the teachers' unions was not a fate a leading civil servant could regard with equanimity.

Board officials began to prepare a document outlining their ideas about educational reconstruction in 1940, and it was evident that they wished to confine discussion to themselves and, later, to their partners in public education. As Holmes informed the War Cabinet, officials were anxious that teachers and local authorities should not go off in 'unsound' directions, so discussions about reform should be informal and tentative.[18]

The War Cabinet was becoming involved in postwar planning in 1940 because it discerned 'that it was impossible, if Britain was victorious, to go back to the stagnant, class-ridden depressing society of the 1930s'.[19] It set up a war aims committee to prevent the topic getting into the hands of 'professors and propagandists'. Yet some early documents produced for the committee were written by intellectuals such as Arnold Toynbee and Harold Nicholson, who explicitly portrayed educational reconstruction as crucial.[20] From mid-1940 there was a steady stream of papers from the War Cabinet concerned with both Britain's anticipated postwar economic difficulties and systematic thought about the shape of society once the war was over.

It was as if there existed 'an implied contract between government and people; the people refused none of the sacrifices that the government demanded from them for winning the war; in return, they expected that the government should show imagination and seriousness in preparing for the restoration and improvement of Britain's well-being when the war had been won'.[21] At the end of 1940, a Minister without Portfolio was appointed, charged with devising the steps for the postwar reconstruction.[22]

The experience which assisted education in being a candidate for reform was evacuation which 'killed the old order in education'.[23] Reports from reception areas claimed that 'the state of the children was such that the school had to be fumigated after the reception', that 'children did not undress to go to bed, but put night clothes over their day clothes', and that 'children returned home as soon as a hot bath was suggested'.[24] More directly relevant was the shock expressed by a leading Conservative minister in the government, Oliver Lyttleton, who received evacuees in his house. He wrote, 'I had little dreamt that English children could be so completely ignorant of the simplest rules of hygiene, and that they would regard the floors and carpets as suitable places upon which to relieve themselves.'[25] Yet these deprived children were 'the products of free institutions of which Britons are bidden to think with pride'.[26] Even to win the war, policy-makers appreciated that the living standards of the population had to be raised.

The war briefly diminished social divisions and evacuation held a mirror up to society[27] so even that organ of the 'establishment', *The Times*, recognized that the experience of war warranted radical solutions and proclaimed that the 'answer to Hitler' was 'a new Britain involving planned consumption, abolition of un-employment and poverty, drastic educational reform, and family allowances'.[28]

The Times Educational Supplement, under its indefatigable campaigner for educational reform, H.C. Dent, kept up a barrage of demands. Herwald Ramsbotham admitted that the war made existing educational machinery obsolete and that 'something more than educational tinkering will be required'.[29] J. Chuter Ede, the Labour Parliamentary Secretary under both Ramsbotham and later Butler, implicitly supported both the theory that war presented tests to society, in this case through evacuation, and even the 'military participation ratio', when he argued that war gave youth the chance to show its worth to the nation.[30] If Butler ever appeared to be capitulating in the face of the opposition of reluctant Conservatives, Chuter Ede maintained the impetus. There are several examples of Conservative reluctance to countenance reform. Sir H. Williams (Croydon South), for example, asked for an assurance that the school-leaving age and the pension qualifying age should not become identical.[31] The attitudes of some other leading Conservatives had more resemblance to fascism than reformism. They demanded that schools should teach the virtues of obligation, duty, discipline, and pride in Britain's colonizing and missionary world role.[32] Alert to these threats, as well as to the 'dead hand of the Treasury', Chuter Ede welcomed Butler's attempts to persuade his Conservative colleagues in government that reforming education could cost £100 million while the Beveridge Report would cost £650 million. Yet he added that 'the Labour Party were getting suspicious that the 1918 trick would be worked on them again; they sensed a feeling among the Tories that we should be kept in the government until victory was assured and that then we should be pushed out and the world made safe for 1939 standards'.[33]

By the end of 1941 the reformers sensed victory, and urged the reform of particular aspects of the education system. To ensure that reform would not be too timid, however, in 1942 the Council for Educational Advance (CEA) was formed, embracing the Trades Union Congress (TUC), the Co-operative Union, the National Union of Teachers (NUT), and the Workers' Educational Association (WEA).[34] It sought comprehensive educational reform but specifically included further education.

When it appeared, shortly after Butler's appointment as President, that Churchill would not countenance an Education Act, Holmes seemed ready to capitulate. He acknowledged the probability that 'educational legislation is to be shelved till the war is over'.[35] An exaggerated view has grown up that Churchill intended to insult Butler by appointing him to the education portfolio.[36] The more convincing view is that Churchill had to find Butler a credible role, but felt that it was one of managing the education service during the exigencies of war rather than promoting reform. There are signs that Butler had been angling for the post, as he sought an advanced copy of a confidential discussion document being prepared by Board officials on the grounds that he provided a link with the central committee of the Conservative Party.[37]

As the ferment for reform developed the officials at the Board who had largely decamped to Bournemouth for the duration continued their pre-emptive planning. The outcome was the Green Book, as it became known, because of the colour of its covers, officially titled *Education after the War*, but which internally was given the ironic title 'the New Testament'.[38] It was given a limited circulation to named representatives, under a code of secrecy.[39] The knowledge that discussions were taking place in the Board had raised protests. The TUC and interested MPs sought and were denied copies.[40] The atmosphere of secrecy engendered by the process of preparing the Green Book led to suspicions that something sinister was occurring. In April 1941 the Association of Directors and Secretaries of Education claimed that Local Education Authorities (LEAs), teachers, education officers all had the right to be consulted, and called for a Consultative Committee.[41]

The circulation of *Education after the War* in July 1941 to twenty-nine undisclosed bodies was described as 'mystifying' by *The Times Educational Supplement*. 'The country does not favour reform by cabal in camera.'[42] *The Journal of Education* was content, however, because the document was merely a basis for discussion with the representatives of local government, teachers, and the other interests concerned.[43] In the middle of this controversy about the extent to which the discussions on reform should be transparent and wide-ranging, Ramsbotham was dismissed, and the radicals demanding greater openness assumed it was because he had mishandled the process of consultation. A more likely explanation is that he was dismissed by Churchill because he had stoked up expectations of educational reform and had upset Tory MPs whose support Churchill needed. Butler had heard whispers that he could be substituted for Ramsbotham because of the concern in certain quarters about Ramsbotham's advanced educational ideas.[44]

After his appointment Butler released the list of bodies to whom the proposals had been distributed.[45] Only at the end of October 1941, four months after his appointment, did he publish the Green Book against the protests of officials. Butler insisted to Holmes that keeping the discussions confined to the twenty-nine accredited partners of the Board meant 'we shall neither produce a scheme of educational reform in which we can be sure that the whole English character is represented, nor shall we be able to hold the confidence of the country, since fears will grow that a "corner" is being effected'.[46]

Education after the War contained a tentative sketch of a further education strategy. It suggested day-continuation schools for school leavers up to the age of eighteen; full-time education in technical and commercial colleges; part-time day and evening technical and commercial education; and adult education.[47]

While the discussions between conservatives and radicals continued after the publication of the Green Book on such issues as tripartite versus multilateral (comprehensive) secondary schools, the future of the Public School system, the role of the voluntary church schools, the survival of Part 3 authorities which simply provided elementary schools, and equal pay for women teachers, Butler operated politically to achieve a measure of educational reform. After intense and skilfully conducted negotiations he proposed a single set of regulations for secondary schools, but resisted promoting multilateral or comprehensive schools; dealt with the Public Schools through setting up the Fleming Committee to ensure 'the first-class carriage had been shunted on to an immense siding'; compromised between secularists and church leaders with partial financial support for church schools; effectively removed Part 3 authorities; and resisted equal pay by invoking Churchill to make it an issue of confidence in the government.[48]

Since these negotiations dominated, it is clear that the importance of further education slipped between 1941 and the publication of the White Paper in July 1943. Butler had proceeded to prepare his legislation without formal government support, and it was here that the role of the pressure groups was important, in providing a momentum which government found difficult to resist. The atmosphere in the parliamentary Conservative Party, however, fuelled by the popular expectations roused by the publication of the Beveridge Report on the future of the welfare state, came to Butler's aid. Government whips were persuaded that with the war beginning to move in the right direction militarily, there was a need for a major piece of legislation to keep backbench members occupied, and if a reformist measure was required then an Education Act was 'preferable to having to enact an equally complex, and far more expensive, measure based on the contents of the Beveridge Report'.[49] Contrary to the writings of many historians of education, the public were less enthusiastic about educational reform than they were about issues of employment, housing, and health. Fortunately for Butler, public opinion mattered less than the opinion of the Chancellor of the Exchequer, Kingsley Wood, who preferred the longer-term financial commitments implied by educational reform to the immediate expenditure implied by the implementation of the Beveridge Report.[50] To secure Wood's support, however, Butler had to convince him that education was the one social reform which should be endorsed. Before he would sanction it, Wood sought a financial estimate from Butler who cited £20 million, but even then the Chancellor demanded a full analysis before he committed the Government.[51] Wood reiterated the competing demands on social expenditure at a meeting of the Lord President's Committee on postwar reconstruction in December 1942, to which Butler and Holmes were summoned. Ernest Bevin supported Butler, particularly on technical and continued education.[52] His cause was assisted, because the folk hero status acquired by Beveridge carried little weight with leading Tories in the government, who naturally preferred a reform fronted by a Conservative Minister. When Wood saw a draft of the White Paper, he urged the removal of a reference to Britain only appearing to make improvements to the education system in times of war as it presented 'too pessimistic a picture of the British achievement' and 'this page will be read overseas and in America'.[53] Wood also stressed the need to convince the Treasury and advised Butler not to include reforms which could not be delivered.

The green light for reform only came formally in March 1943 when Butler visited Churchill at Chequers. Butler told him that he was preparing a Bill, and reluctantly Churchill expressed some interest.[54] Butler had Labour support within the government, and Bevin presciently argued that if the school-leaving age was not lifted to sixteen, 'we should not have another opportunity for another twenty years'.[55]

Butler followed up the White Paper with a bill, published in December 1943, as a self-contained and comprehensive measure superseding all existing Acts. With the fending off of the proposal to introduce equal pay, the parliamentary stage began in January 1944 and the Act received the Royal Assent in August.

THE CAMPAIGNS FOR CONTINUED AND TECHNICAL EDUCATION

It is widely assumed that the 1944 Education Act had little to say about further education.[56] There is also a presumption that it generated little controversy.[57] In reality there was intense controversy and pressure group activity. While the context of war stimulated educational reform, further education might well not have appeared in the Act at all but for the efforts of pressure groups.

There was a vigorous campaign to promote technical education, yet while the war demonstrated its necessity, it was the activities of committed individuals and organizations which ensured that it was not legislatively ignored. The marginalization of technical education is surprising because when Butler first attempted to interest Churchill in reform he stressed the need to link up education and industry and to promote technical training.[58] He urged the renewal of the apprenticeship system and 'the linking up of schools closely with employment'.[59]

War revealed the pitiful inadequacy of British technical education to the point where it threatened to jeopardize the war effort. *The Times* congratulated the technical colleges for their 'heroic efforts in trying to address the desperate shortages of skilled manpower'.[60] Officials also made the connection between the response of the technical education sector to the need for rapid training to produce skilled workers for the munitions factories, and postwar reform. 'Technical colleges have shown, during the war, a remarkable degree of resiliency and capacity for coping with the new demands and . . . we can, I think, do a great deal on that side.'[61] Ernest Bevin, who as Minister of Labour was a doughty supporter of technical training, blamed the desperate shortage not upon working people themselves, but upon past errors in public policy.[62] He met Butler to push the case for continued and technical education.[63] By early 1941 the problem was officially acknowledged and coincided with the growing interest by reformers in the inclusion of technical education in the reform process.[64]

Even when the emergency needs of wartime were being addressed, policy makers began to consider postwar challenges, and there was a consensus that an expansion in the number of skilled workers was essential. The Green Book invited responses to the proposition that there was a need for 'an improved and extended system of technical training' and for 'closer relations between education, industry, and commerce'. This led to many organizations passing resolutions, sending delegations, issuing statements, and publishing pamphlets urging more technical education.[65] But it was informal meetings of industrialists which proved most effective in retaining technical education on the political agenda. Various *ad hoc* groups of educators and enlightened industrialists met to press for more technical education during 1942.[66]

This aspect of reform interested the Conservative Party which set up a sub-committee on industrial affairs, which concluded 'industry stands keenly in need of trained men and women who can display broad intelligence as well as technical competence. . . . In these matters Britain cannot afford not to lead the world'.[67] The perspective was utilitarian as the report was sprinkled with comments such as 'industry needs' and 'the requirements of industry'. There was also a Conservative slant in its support for training as a means of discovering 'natural leaders'. Many Conservative parliamentarians were also industrialists and strongly supported technical education. Sir Harold Webbe asserted that it was not even necessary to make the case for the importance of technical education.[68] Other forceful contributions were made by R. Morgan who was a director of Manbre and Garton Ltd; Sir George Schuster who was chairman of Allied Suppliers, Maypole, The Home and Colonial, Liptons and the Westminster Bank; Sir Patrick Hannon who was president of the National Union of British Industries and the Institute of Export, and vice-president of the Federation of British Industries; and Arthur Colegate, chairman of W.H. Allen and Sons.[69] The Conservatives were enthusiastic about this reform as the party of industry and management, and the newer, reformist Conservatives were concerned about promoting technical efficiency.

The disappointment over the small financial allocation proposed in the White Paper galvanized the lobby into strenuous efforts. *The Times* headed its correspondence column with a letter written by the Principal of Bradford Technical College deploring the low priority given to technical education in the financial appendix. The letter regretted that since a bill was being prepared there was an opportunity for the 'vast leeway' of inadequate expenditure to be made up.[70] It triggered an instant response within the Board. 'We are getting a number of complaints from various quarters, both educational and industrial, that Technical Education is inadequately dealt with in the White Paper.'[71] The concern was over the lack of additional spending for technical education and its omission from the first four-year plan. The press was asking the Board if it had any response to the letter in *The Times*. An official noted that the problem resulted from 'pressure from the Treasury'.[72]

A group of inspectors from within the technical branch of the Board of Education added their protest about the insufficient funds in an internal memorandum.[73] It drew from the work of a committee investigating the engineering industry which was concerned about the deferment of expenditure. Fearing the impact of postwar competition, it urged that 'Sweden and Switzerland clearly indicated what must be done by way of technical education to achieve and maintain pre-eminence in engineering'.[74] Technical Colleges were 'neither equipped nor staffed to deal adequately with modern demands'. The memorandum claimed the position was the same in many other industries. It regretted the emphasis on other parts of education as mere political expedience. It also urged a subsidy from central to local government to cover the costs as the United States was planning extra support for technical education from federal funds.[75]

R.S. Wood noted the criticism that 'the additional expenditure . . . is in no way commensurate with the expansion that ought to be contemplated if the requirements of the country in regard to the needs of industry and commerce are in any degree adequately to be met'.[76] The Board's deputy secretary urged Wood to produce a few paragraphs for Butler to include in a speech to quell the controversy.[77] Meanwhile, officials were drafting a letter for Butler to send to Sir John Anderson, the Lord President, asking for a change in the financial allocation to technical education. The draft conveys the first signs of a retreat on commitments to provide continued education. It stressed the appreciation by industry and commerce that 'the quality of British labour and production are attended to', in order to 'secure a great increase of vocational training for young workers in advance of any scheme of compulsory part-time continued education'. The version of the letter sent by Butler protested that 'the figures do scant justice to our intentions. . . . The war-time technical training of service and industrial personnel has shown what can be done'.[78] Butler asked for Anderson's agreement that he should promise that technical provision 'will be pressed forward to meet the requirements of industry and commerce, to assist them in the tasks of readjustment and recovery'.[79] Anderson assented, demonstrating that pressure group campaigns involving the interests of business can yield substantive outcomes.[80]

The White Paper was firm enough in its rhetorical commitment. It asserted that technical education:

. . . has not hitherto made that advance which the needs of a highly industrialised community demand. The standards of building and equipment in use have often been deplorably low, and comparison with what can be seen in many other countries which have been our competitors in the world markets can leave little cause for satisfaction.[81]

No expenditure was allocated until the second year of the Act's implementation, however, and only a slight increase between 1949 and 1953. In 1948 only £30,000 was to be spent and this paltry sum would slowly rise to £1.2 million in 1953; moreover these figures were to cover both technical and adult education.

The furore over the financial appendix was such that Butler announced that the money allocated was not the sum total of the government's ambitions.[82] The figures proposed in the bill, published in December 1943, were notably more generous. They represented a substantial increase in expenditure. While the precise division between technical and adult education was not apparent, James Chuter Ede, the Parliamentary Secretary to the Board, asserted that there was to be a fourteen-fold increase in technical education within the overall sum, attributing this shift to consultations with industrialists, workers, and local authorities.[83] Chuter Ede's claim is plausible given the extent of the pressure which the Board received.

While the most effective pressure derived from 'insider' groups, others were vociferous in exerting indirect pressure.[84] A plethora of organizations advanced the case for technical education. Given its still limited financial endorsement in the Act, doubts must be raised as to how far it would have appeared at all had there not been intense lobbying.[85]

The British Association for Commercial and Industrial Education (BACIE), for example, urged that education for commerce and industry should claim the attention of parents, educators and industrialists. A leading company spokesman stated that working life is the third and most important stage of education, so industry should not evade its own responsibilities.[86]

Much pressure came from individual industrialists. An official recalls, 'Mr Butler had his contacts with Courtaulds and he had more than one meeting with Sir Raymond Street, who was chairman of the Cotton Board'.[87] Street described his role as that of a 'professional lobbyist' for cotton. He was a natural contact for Butler as he had met him when he was a minister at the India Office to discuss tariffs; and Street recalls many meetings with Butler on technical education. He recalls that Butler, who had married into the Courtauld family, joined him in proselytizing employers in the cotton industry, as technical education was necessary to prevent a decline in the numbers entering that industry.[88] Lord Eustace Percy told BACIE's 1943 conference of its pressure group responsibilities.[89] Speakers were under no illusion that their task was to convert both Butler and his officials to the cause; they also recognized the mammoth task of converting employers to the virtues of investing in employee training.[90] An MP described BACIE as 'an active pressure group'.[91] Some of its members joined with other industrialists in a letter to *The Times* supporting the extension of technical and adult education. 'These reforms may be said to involve financial burdens on industry. We should accept that burden gladly; because we believe that industry will thereby gain in efficiency and the country in well-being'.[92] If not typical of their contemporaries they were clearly 'policy influentials' among British employers.

Butler was enthusiastic about technical education, Sir Robert Wood was the chief author of the Act's further education clauses, and Chuter Ede's favourite theme was the need for technicians to secure a higher social status. H. C. Dent referred to 'extensive consultations' by both Wood and Butler, but points out that those urging the expansion of technical education were 'pressing against an open door'. They realized that in the postwar world 'Britain must produce or perish'.[93]

The technical education network could claim credit for ensuring a tangible commitment to technical education through the raising of the financial allocation. By revealing the inadequacies of the existing system, however, it was the circumstances of war which created the climate in which the lobby could lend Butler support within the core executive. In the medium term, however, the Treasury resisted the clamour. The Board of Education had proved to be more pliable.

Technical education was less severely damaged by the Treasury, however, than was continued education. The failure to implement the day continuation schools after the war was poignant as this was the second time that legislation to provide educational leave for one day a week for 15- to 18-year-old school-leavers withered for financial reasons. It appears that R. S. Wood was a true believer, the Green Book restored the idea to the forefront of the debate, and even by the end of 1942 the Board was still promoting the idea. Butler informed the Lord President's Committee that the failure to implement the earlier proposals 'inflicted serious loss in the training and well-being of our adolescent population'.[94] Bevin too wanted local authorities to be responsible for young workers' welfare up to the age of twenty, and Butler claimed that continued education provided a form of the industrial supervision which Bevin sought.[95] Yet there were signs that some of the supporters of continued education were being branded as extremists. H.C. Dent had a high public profile in the overall reform campaign, but an official advised Butler that Dent 'talks of a rather vague kind of control of young people up to twenty years of age'.[96] The CEA appreciated that vigilance was necessary to prevent the 'vista' of reform from degenerating to a 'mirage'.[97] The NUT urged that 'all young workers who finish their secondary education at the age of sixteen shall have some time every week free from their employment to attend the day continuation school'.[98] Dent described the NUT as 'undoubtedly the most influential body'.[99] If he is correct, then that influence was primarily exercised on behalf of the interests of its members in schools.

The lobby for continued education ultimately proved the weakest in the field as it was unable to secure its gains. The episode reveals the shallowness of governmental wartime benevolence.

THE CAMPAIGN FOR ADULT EDUCATION

The campaign for adult education was mounted on the back of the general campaign for educational reform. The war itself promoted the education of adults. Between Munich and the outbreak of war, many thousands attended classes to learn about war gases, first aid, home nursing, fire-fighting, and civilian duties in the event of an air raid. The demand embraced both academic subjects and recreational activities.[100] Recreational classes were more popular, however, and by 1942 the figures for adults attending local authority evening institutes was 129,642.[101]

The most significant impact of war on the demand for adult education occurred in the Armed Forces. In January 1940 the Central Advisory Council for Education in His Majesty's Forces was set up, to coordinate the adult educational resources of the country and place them at the disposal of the Services.[102] The Army was itself forced to appreciate the need to organize its own provision, and the War Office appointed a committee to investigate.[103] The original purpose was 'to help morale', or 'to keep the troops quiet after the fall of France', but once the civilian educators began their teaching, unintended consequences resulted. It was appreciated at the time that the process had 'a significance for the future'.[104]

By 1943 the Army Bureau of Current Affairs (ABCA) was set up to provide one hour a week of the soldiers' time to discuss current affairs.[105] The Army and the War Office approved the programme so that a soldier should know 'the purpose behind his duty'.[106] It is evident that ABCA's activities revealed the ignorance of soldiers about politics and the reasons for Britain's involvement in the war. This was analogous to the effect on technical education of the discovery that Britain faced a shortage of skilled manpower. The alarm about the political illiteracy of members of the services led to the establishment of the British Way and Purpose Scheme (BWP) to provide citizenship training and make soldiers aware of their place in society.[107] The BWP had a propagandist intent: the representation of British democracy as a cause worthy of fighting for as a defence against the challenges of such ideologies as Nazism and communism. In harnessing adult educators to the task, its stated aim demonstrated a socially reformist message, concerned not simply to defend civil and religious liberties, parliamentary institutions and the legacy of social legislation, but also that 'we must all take the offensive. Democracy is a dynamic idea. It implies that every man . . . should be given an equal opportunity of realising the best that is in him'.[108]

The reformist message went hand in hand with vigorous political instruction. The mood was captured by Lady Rhys Williams who asserted that Britain needed a new *esprit de corps* to counter that of Fascist regimes.[109] While the expansion of technical education reflected concern about the country's productivity, adult education was perceived as relevant to concerns about future social stability. Butler informed the War Cabinet that interest in adult education had been stimulated by Army schemes and expressed his concern that provision was 'sporadic and haphazard'.[110] The 1943 White Paper explicitly mentioned the educational work in the services. It also asserted that through adult education a proper training in democratic citizenship could occur.[111]

The Beveridge Report caught the mood and canvassed the idea of educating adults as a responsibility of the education services and an integral part of the new postwar social order. Beveridge wrote that 'adult education on a greatly extended scale is almost as important as, if not more important than, more education of the young'.[112] Despite the rhetoric of adult education's friends, however, the publication of the financial appendix to the White Paper provoked concerns that adult education would be shelved. The conflation of the expenditures for technical, adult, and continued education fed these concerns. When the expressions of anxiety by the proponents of technical education led to the provision of more money, nothing similar happened about adult education. Butler reassured those anxious about the funding of technical education, but ignored the claims for adult education.[113] When Wood was urging, after the White Paper's publication, that the Treasury should find more funds for technical education with 'all possible energy', he advised leaving adult education to one side, '*pace* the Master of Balliol Sir Richard Livingstone'. Butler was equivocal during the parliamentary debates on the bill, and he recognized that his critics thought he was always in a 'minor key' when it came to adult education.[114]

The inchoate lobby on behalf of adult education was slower in being launched, less forthright, and divided by an unnecessary conflict which weakened its voice. An official suggests that there were only limited consultations.[115] Professor Waller recollects 'pretty close contact' arguing that 'all bodies were concerned to make representations (I was involved myself) and were listened to courteously and sometimes with good effect'. Lady Simon of Wythenshawe affirms that negotiations took place between the Board and the WEA.[116] Ernest Green, the Secretary of the WEA, argued the case and Sir Richard Livingstone protested the inadequacy of the White Paper for Adult Education; but all to no avail.[117]

The conflict within the adult education lobby was signalled by the WEA's complacent response to the financial appendix. It derived pleasure from the Act's language but, as a voluntary body, it was sceptical about the growth of statutory, publicly funded provision. The British Institute of Adult Education (BIAE) was also concerned to defend the role of voluntary organizations, and publicly eschewed any wish to 'send deputations to the Board of Education or to start a crusade in the columns of *The Times*'.[118] Civil servants were present at the committee's meetings, however, and BIAE members also met Butler. Their report described the interview as encouraging, gaining '. . . the impression . . . that he was of our mind . . . and was really going ahead with Adult Education further and faster than might appear from the White Paper'.[119]

The CEA called for 'ample provision for Adult Education'.[120] R.H. Tawney and H.C. Dent argued that the education of adults was more valuable than school education since adults were in charge of society.[121] The NUT proposed that a minister should assume responsibility for developing adult education.[122] While some groups softened their demand for adult education after the White Paper, both the NUS and the TUC maintained their pressure.[123] An aspect of the campaign for adult education was the enthusiasm of women's groups, foreshadowing women's greater use of provision after the war. This demand was successfully predicted by the National Council of Women (NCW).[124] The NCW recognized that adult education was an area where the Government would require considerable 'prodding' and promised to supply it.[125]

Influential individuals spasmodically promoted adult education. A conference in January 1944 comprising William Temple, Archbishop of Canterbury, W.M. Beveridge (later Lord Beveridge), Sir Fred Clarke (London Institute of Education), Sir Richard Livingstone (Master of Balliol, Oxford), Sir George Schuster (the industrialist), and the educationalist Mary Stocks produced a statement defining adult education as 'an indisputable part of national reconstruction'.[126] Some pressure was maintained in the debates on the bill, with MPs protesting at the shabby treatment of adult education, but Butler said he was constrained owing to alternative demands on resources.[127] So adult education proved to be dispensable. Even idealists concentrated their efforts where they were likely to be fruitful. Adult education's fate was to be swamped by a campaign seeking equality of educational opportunity through the reform and extension of the secondary system of education. Its lobby gained publicity, but more effective efforts were made in the field of technical education where the lobbying was largely covert.

The case for adult education was weakened by divisions within the lobby group. Divided campaigns suffer a serious disadvantage. The conflict was reflected in the educational press. While *The Times Educational Supplement* criticized the government for failing to grasp the magnitude and variety of the provision required for adults, *Adult Education*, reflecting the views of the WEA, asserted that 'the scant attention given to Adult Education in the Butler Bill is to be welcomed rather than deplored'.[128] A lack of legislative attention meant that the position of the voluntary agencies would be safeguarded. Adult education was 'a movement unsullied by statutory influences'. The WEA's concern was that the voluntary bodies should expand their role after the war.[129] Tawney defined the voluntary principle as the key to vitality and dynamism.[130] This, despite the injunction on

LEAs in the White Paper to prepare their schemes for the future, taking note of what was already provided. In 1940 Wood had seen the need to 'overhaul the present rather messy and unsatisfactory system of adult education. Any cleaning up here will mean rather hammer blows to people who are reluctant to be upset'.[131] Yet even in 1919 a national committee had recommended that LEAs should become involved in the provision of adult education.[132]

The WEA's position was curious since its own membership and funds were declining.[133] Any expansion of adult education required more public money, yet the WEA feared that public investment would threaten voluntarism. The WEA looked unsuccessfully to the TUC for money.[134] The TUC declined, blaming the WEA for losing 'the idealism of its early days'.[135] The WEA was anxious to preserve the privilege, which it had enjoyed since 1924, of receiving state subsidies while retaining its independence. Even Tawney warned the WEA of the danger of becoming a vested interest preoccupied by a 'proprietary defensiveness against new entrants into a sphere that it considers its own'.[136] It continued to argue the need for social and political education, however, which could best be provided by 'the voluntary bodies experienced in Adult Education'.[137] Close association with the state would make the WEA subject to official direction:

> The WEA has always considered that a high standard of work in Adult Education is of much greater importance than either the volume of its work or even its variety . . . any plan which would put the general direction and guidance of Adult Education into the hands of the Local Education Authority would be fatal.[138]

Ultimately the Act reassured the WEA by maintaining its special status, despite the requirement that LEAs take cognizance of all existing provision before preparing schemes for adult education.[139] The political success of the WEA occurred because 'a number of the department's officials had more practical experience of the WEA's sort of extended education'.[140] It appears that the Board was persuaded that in backing the WEA it was not taking a risk with public money. Negatively, officials could enjoy the advantages of dividing and ruling, as the LEA and voluntary sectors squabbled about the future of adult education.

Parliamentary advocates of adult education were more concerned with the role of the WEA than with overall growth. George Griffiths (Hemsworth) admitted that his defence of the WEA resulted from his having been one of its students.[141] William Temple, the Archbishop of Canterbury, explained his defence as being that he had been its president for sixteen years.[142] James Maxton (Fife) opposed the idea of LEAs supervising schemes of adult education, praising the WEA, the Fabian Society, the Co-operative Society, and the National Council of Labour Colleges (NCLC).[143] Lewis Silkin (Peckham) sought LEA financial assistance for responsible bodies.[144] While it was Labour MPs who were keener to promote adult education, they were also enthusiasts for the WEA. One Labour member pointed to their ideological inconsistency. S.O. Davies (Merthyr Tydfil) argued that voluntary bodies had only assumed a substantial role because of the imperfections in statutory provision, and had long outlived their usefulness. If they continued it would be because postwar adult education continued to be imperfect.[145] Davies adopted a clearer socialist stance than the others, who signified the peculiarities of the British socialist tradition which is ethical rather than statist.

Parliamentary pressure reflected the general pattern of the further education lobby; the greatest clamour was for continued education; the most effective efforts were made in the field of technical education; while adult education remained the preserve of a small but dedicated contingent. While the adult education lobby was vociferous, it gained publicity rather than resources. With both LEAs and the WEA proclaiming their capacities, both were 'satisfied' by a compromise which gave the supervisory role to the LEAs while preventing them from encroaching upon WEA territory. In short, the lobby appears as a curious amalgam of idealism and self-interest. The war alerted policy-makers to the need for adult education, but there were more urgent needs to satisfy within further education: the increase of skills in war industries and postwar economic development.

CONCLUSION

The importance of pressure groups in the policy-making process has been asserted since 1908.[146] Pressure groups are diverse phenomena, and encompass organizations either totally or incidentally involved in exerting pressure. Their methods range from letters to the newspapers to demonstrations. The most effective groups are those which act directly upon parliament, government departments, and ministers. The theories which asserted the role of external pressure groups in shaping policy were superseded by newer conceptualizations: inter-governmentalism in the 1980s and network theories during the 1990s.[147]

Network theory was developed by Rhodes who distinguished between 'issue networks' and 'policy communities'. Issue networks include all participants in a political issue regardless of their status, access or influence; while policy communities describe a relatively closed circle of groups and individuals who share values, exchange resources, enjoy a stable relationship, and are mutually dependent.[148] R.A. Manzer describes an 'educational sub-government' in the making of education policy: a triumvirate of the ministry, the local authorities, and the teacher unions.[149]

Certainly, the concepts of the 'policy community' or 'the educational sub-government' capture the Board of Education's preferred consultation strategy before the publication of the Green Book. Holmes described the process as one where officials lay out their plans before they 'bring our partners into the fullest consultation'.[150] Ramsbotham also pointed out the impracticality of negotiations based on a 'blank piece of paper', and acknowledged that the central state was the main activist in the policy-making process; a phenomenon which both R. Rhodes and Manzer under-estimate. Ramsbotham strongly defended the confining of consultations to the three major 'accredited' partners in public education, despite the protests, which included members of an 'outsider' group claiming that 'to secure a voice in . . . postwar educational plans they must get into the right association'.[151]

If the 1944 Act had emerged solely through a narrow policy community then Rhodes and Manzer would be vindicated. Yet Rhodes exaggerates the all-pervasiveness of networks as it is clear that such arrangements are sometimes challenged.[152] While the discussions based on the Green Book were used 'as the basis upon which ministers and civil servants jointly arrived at decisions about the shape of possible legislation during 1942 and 1943', between 1941 and 1944 the inner circle was challenged by the educational journals speaking on behalf of the excluded groups, and by the emergence of mass organizations such as the CEA.[153] While the partner groups wielded influence, the background of war, placing a premium on agreement, made the government rather more anxious than normal to carry groups drawn from the wider society along with it, and to convince them of its genuine commitment to serious reform. This is not to disregard the 'mountain of idealistic blather which preceded the Education Act of 1944'.[154] Confronted with the bureaucratic authority of the work of the officials by 1941, 'the open-minded Butler, let alone the more radical voices of the time, made little impact'.[155] Together they helped ensure, however, that educational reform actually went ahead. In the more normal times after the war, building on the framework established by the 1944 Act, there emerged a stable settlement in which the key players of the sub-government dominate.[156]

The debate about whether the 1944 Act was radical has been largely answered by the evidence that it was the 'insider' groups, responding to the initiatives of officials, who devised it. The activities of Butler and the officials have been described as 'manipulation and control', at a time when far-reaching changes were widely canvassed.[157] This keeps in perspective the understanding that war produces a reformist and rationalizing outlook. It is significant that the Act was the only significant measure of reform to become law during the war, and contained conservative features. There were advances in the Act, but all had been on the agenda before 1939. It took the war to bring them to fruition.

The demands generated by war were mainly stifled, with the possible exception of technical education. In further education, the hopes generated by the Act were dashed by the circular issued by the Minister two weeks later stating that LEAs were not required to submit schemes for Further Education. The Conservative-dominated wartime coalition followed Hogg's advice to Conservatives: confronted with a tide towards fundamental change, they kept cool and diverted it.[158]

Notes

The author would particularly like to thank research assistants at the University of Huddersfield: Richard Esp, who undertook some reading on behalf of the author, and Steve Miller, for the valuable loan of a chapter in a shortly to be submitted PhD thesis on the relationship between R.A. Butler and Harold Macmillan.

1   S. Andrzjewski, *Military Organisation and Society* (London, Routledge & Kegan Paul, 1954).

2   A.L. Bowley, *Some Economic Consequences of the Great War* (London, Home University Library, 1930), p. 22.

3   R.H. Tawney, 'The Abolition of Economic Controls 1918–1921', *Economic History Review*, 23, 1943, *passim*.

4   A. Marwick, *The Deluge* (London, Penguin, 1965), pp. 297–8.

5   R.H. Titmuss, 'Problems of Social Policy' (London, HMSO, 1950), p. 506.

6   Corelli Barnett, *The Audit of War: The Illusion and Reality of Britain as a Great Nation* (London, Macmillan, 1986), p. 304.

7   A. Toynbee, *War and Civilisation* (Oxford, Oxford University Press, 1951), p. 3.

8   A. Havighurst, *Twentieth Century Britain* (London, Harper, 1962), p. 116.

9   P. Abrams, 'The Failure of Social Reform: 1918–1920', *Past and Present*, April 1963.

10   A.S. Millward, 'The Economic Effects of the World Wars on Britain' in *Economic History Society* (London, Macmillan, 1970), p. 24.

11   Angus Calder, *The People's War, Britain 1939–45* (London, Jonathan Cape, 1969), p. 18.

12   *Hansard*, 12 May 1944, col. 2247.

13   N. Middleton, 'Lord Butler and the Education Act of 1944', *British Journal Of Educational Studies*, xx, 2, 1972. Lord Butler at the opening of Holly Royde College at the University of Manchester, October 1967.

14   Public Record Office, ED136/212. Letter from Permanent Secretary Maurice Holmes to Board officials, 5 November 1940.

15   Ibid.

16   Ibid., Holmes to Sir George Chrystal, KCB, Secretary to the War Cabinet, 24 January 1941.

17   PRO, ED136/212, D.J. Wood, Memorandum.

18   PRO, ED136/212.

19   Brian Simon, *Education and the Social Order 1940–1990* (London, Lawrence & Wishart, 1991), p. 35.

20   Barnett, *The Audit of War*, pp. 20–1.

21   H.M.D. Parker, *A Study of Wartime Policy and Administration* (London, HMSO, 1957).

22   M. Bruce, *The Coming of the Welfare State* (London, Batsford, 1961), p. 263.

23   H.C. Dent, *Education in Transition* (London, Kegan, Paul, Trench, Trubner and Co., 1944), p. 6.

24   Ibid., pp. 8–10.

25   P.H.J.H. Gosden, *Education in the Second World War* (London, Methuen, 1976), p. 13.

26   F.A. Iremonger, *William Temple, Archbishop of Canterbury* (Oxford, Oxford University Press, 1948), p. 569.

27   M. Barber, *The Making of the 1944 Education Act* (London, Cassell, 1994), p. 3.

28   Simon, *Education and the Social Order*, p. 36.

29 *The Times Educational Supplement*, 21 June 1941.

30 *The Times Educational Supplement*, 21 June and 30 May, 1941.

31 Brendan Evans, 'Pressure Groups, Further Education and the 1944 Act' (unpublished M.Ed. thesis of the University of Manchester, 1971), p. 54.

32 José Harris, 'Political Ideas and Social Change', in Harold L. Smith (ed.), *War and Social Change* (Manchester, Manchester University Press, 1986), pp. 240–5.

33 Kevin Jeffreys, 'Chuter Ede Diaries, entries for 7 August and 27 November 1942, pp. 92 and 109–10' quoted in *War and Reform: British Politics during the Second World War* (Manchester, Manchester University Press, 1994), p. 92.

34 *The Times Educational Supplement*, 28 November 1942, p. 578.

35 R.A. Butler, *The Art of the Possible* (London, Hamish Hamilton, 1971), p. 95.

36 Anthony Howard, *RAB* (London, Cape, 1986), p. 107.

37 PRO, ED136/547, Butler to Ramsbotham, 12 July 1941.

38 PRO, ED136/547.

39 Simon, *Education and the Social Order*, p. 58.

40 PRO, ED136/547. For example, a letter to the Board from Walter Citrine, General Secretary of the TUC, 3 July 1941.

41 *The Journal of Education*, Vol. 73, April 1941, p. 118.

42 *The Times Education Supplement*, 12 July 1941.

43 *The Journal of Education*, Vol. 73, August 1941, p. 326.

44 Barber, *The Making of the 1944 Education Act*, p. 31.

45 The bodies were the Association of Education Committees, the County Councils' Association, the Association of Municipal Corporations, the Federation of Welsh Local Education Authorities, the London County Council, the Association of Directors and Secretaries of Education, the Federation of part 3 Education Authorities, the National Union of Teachers, the Association of Headmasters and Headmistresses, the Association of Principals of Technical Institutes, the Association of Teachers in Technical Institutions, the National Society of Art Manufacturers, the Tutorial Classes Joint Advisory Committee, the Joint Standing Committee of Training Colleges, the Association of Principals of Training Colleges, the University Consultative Committee of Vice-Chancellors and Principals, the Association of Principals of Recognised Training Colleges of Domestic Subjects, the National Froebel Foundation, the National Society, the Catholic Education Council, the National Free Churches Council, the Workers' Educational Association, the Trades Union Congress, the British and Foreign Schools Society.

46 PRO, ED136/212. Letter from Butler to Holmes, 2 September 1941.

47 Board of Education, 'Education after the War', *Board of Education Green Book* (London, HMSO, 1941), para. 5.

48 Butler's own account of this, and his admission that he managed to stall on the reform of the Public Schools at a time when there was a clamour for their removal, in *The Art of the Possible*, chapter 6, p. 120.

49 Howard, *RAB*, p. 132.

50 P. Addison, *The Road to 1945* (London, Cape, 1975), p. 238.

51 PRO, ED136/212. Note by Butler, 9 September 1941.

52   PRO, ED136/378. Note by Butler of meeting held on 18 December 1942. It was also attended by Sir John Anderson the Lord President, Attlee, Bevin, Morrison, and Cranborne. Butler was accompanied by Holmes for this agenda item.

53   PRO, ED136/378. Note by Butler, 8 June 1943.

54   Butler, *The Art of the Possible*, p. 115.

55   PRO, ED136/312.

56   Lord Butler in conversation with the author in 1967.

57   Lord Eccles in correspondence with the author in 1970.

58   M. Barber, *The Making of the 1944 Education Act*, p. 37.

59   PRO, ED136/312. Letter from Butler to Churchill, 12 September 1941.

60   *The Times*, 16 April 1943.

61   PRO, ED136/547. Internal notes.

62   *The Times Educational Supplement*, 8 November 1940, p. 534.

63   PRO, ED136/547. Note of meeting on 13 January 1943.

64   H.M.D. Parker, *Manpower*, p. 210.

65   These organizations included the Association of Head Teachers in Technical Institutions, the National Union of Teachers, the National Association of Head Teachers, the Association of Education Committees, London County Council, the Workers Educational Association, the City and Guilds Institute, the National Union of Students, the Trades Union Congress, the National Council of Commercial Education, the British Association for Commercial and Industrial Education, the Association of Scientific Workers, and ad hoc groups of industrialists.

66   Certain individuals always attended: for example, Basil Blackball the industrialist, Fred Clarke the educationalist, the National Labour politician Kenneth Lindsay, the college director E.W. Woodhead, and the editor of the Journal of Education, Salter Davies.

67   *Looking Ahead, The Conservative Party* (London, 1943), p. 27.

68   *Hansard*, Vol. 398, Col. 1115.

69   *Dod's Parliamentary Companion* (1944).

70   *The Times*, 30 September 1943.

71   PRO, ED136/427. Note to deputy Secretary of the Board from H.B. Wallis.

72   Idem.

73   Gosden, *Education in the Second World War*, p. 417.

74   PRO, ED136/427. Memorandum dated 1 September 1943.

75   Ibid.

76   Ibid. Note from R.S. Wood to Butler, 5 October 1943.

77   Ibid. Note dated 19 October 1943.

78   Ibid. Letter from Butler to Anderson, 19 October 1943.

79   Ibid.

80   Ibid., 23 October 1943.

81   White Paper (CND 6458), 'Educational Reconstruction in England and Wales' (London, HMSO, 1943), p. 21.

82   *The Times Educational Supplement*, 11 September 1943, p. 483.

83   Ibid., 8 January 1944.

84 Ibid., No. 1413, 30 May 1942, p. 259.

85 Among the organizations publicly demanding better provision of technical education were the Association of Teachers in Technical Institutions, the National Union of Teachers, the National Association of Head Teachers, the Association of Principals in Technical Institutions, the Association of Directors and Secretaries of Education, the Association of Education Committees, the Workers' Educational Association, the National Council of Labour Colleges, the National Union of Students, the Trades Union Congress, and the British Association for Commercial and Industrial Education.

86 *The Times Educational Supplement*, No. 1405, 14 April 1942.

87 R.N. Heaton, in correspondence with the author, 8 December 1969.

88 *Education Weekly*, Vol. 81, No. 2009, 2 April 1943. Also in discussions with the author, summer 1971.

89 'Young Workers and Their Education', report of the BACIE conference held in Manchester, April 1943, introduction. Percy was President of the Board of Education 1924–29, and in 1943 was Rector of King's College, Newcastle-on-Tyne.

90 'Young Workers and Their Education', p. 22.

91 In correspondence with the author, 1969.

92 *The Times*, 22 January 1944.

93 In correspondence with the author, c. 1970.

94 PRO, ED136/378.

95 PRO, ED136/312. Letter from Butler to Bevin, 6 November 1941.

96 PRO, ED136/312, 8 May 1942.

97 Ibid., 6 February 1943.

98 Ibid., 19 July 1941.

99 In correspondence with the author, c. 1970.

100 Dent, *Education in Transition*, p. 147.

101 H.C. Dent, *Part-Time Education in Britain* (London, Turnstile Press, 1949) p. 52.

102 A. Hawkins and Y. Brimble, *The Record of the British Army* (London, Macmillan, 1947) pp. 97–9. The three members of the Council were Sir Walter Mobberly (Chairman), Dr A.D. Lindsay (Master of Balliol), and Dr Basil Yeaxlee (Reader in Educational Psychology, Oxford).

103 Dent, *Education in Transition*, p. 152.

104 C.D. Legge, an active participant in wartime education (later Head of Department of Adult Education in the University of Manchester) in conversation with the author. Also see the *Times Educational Supplement*, 22 November 1941, p. 533.

105 Dent, *Education in Transition*, p. 153.

106 Ibid., p. 154.

107 C. Lloyd, *British Services Education* (London, Routledge, 1950), pp. 19–21.

108 The British Way and Purposes Committee, *The British Way and Purpose, Consolidated Edition* (London, 1941), p. 1.

109 Lady Rhys Williams, *Something to Look Forward To* (London, Macdonald, 1943), p. 52.

110 PRO, ED136/378. Note to Lord President's Committee of the War Cabinet, not dated.

111 'Educational Reconstruction in England and Wales', CMD 6458 (London, HMSO, 1943) p. 85.

112 Sir William Beveridge, *Pillars of Society* (London, 1942), p. 85.

113 *The Times Educational Supplement*, 18 December 1943, p. 602.

114 *Hansard*, Vol. 396, Col. 221.

115 R.N. Heaton in conversation with the author, 1969.

116 Professor Waller and Lady Simon of Wythenshawe in correspondence with the author, *c*. 1970.

117 *The Times Educational Supplement*, 31 July 1943, p. 367. Other influentials were Sir Fred Clarke (the educationalist), R.F. Brettle (Director of Education for Hornsey), H.C. Dent (the writer), Peter Venables (a College Principal).

118 *Adult Education*, December 1942 (25), 41 p. 66.

119 'Adult Education after the War', report of the British Institute of Adult Education Committee on Postwar Adult Education, pp. 9–61.

120 *The Times Educational Supplement*, 28 November 1942, p. 578.

121 Ibid., 27 March 1943, p. 138.

122 *Education after the War*, the National Union of Teachers *Education After the War* (London, 1942), pp. 16–18.

123 *The Times Educational Supplement*, 15 January 1944, p. 29; and 22 January, 1944, p. 40.

124 *Newsletter of the National Council of Women*, 1943.

125 *The Times Educational Supplement*, 24 October 1942, p. 516.

126 *The Times*, 15 January 1944, p. 40.

127 *Hansard*, Vol. 396, Cols. 247–9.

128 *Adult Education*, 17: 1 March 1944, p. 104.

129 Ibid., June 1941, *passim*.

130 R.H. Tawney, 'Education, the Task Before Us', WEA, p. 7.

131 PRO, ED136/427, R.S. Wood to Maurice Holmes, undated.

132 Final Report of the Adult Education Committee of the Ministry of Reconstruction, 1010, p. 170.

133 'Educational Problems in Wartime', a report on three regional conferences of the WEA, April–May 1941, p. 8.

134 Ibid., p. 15.

135 Ibid., p. 11.

136 R.H. Tawney, 'Education', p. 6.

137 WEA Annual Report, 1944, p. 10.

138 'Adult Education after the War', report (London, 1943), pp. 35–44.

139 Public General Acts and Measures of 1944, Chapter 31, 287, Clause 41, subsection 4.

140 A Board official in correspondence with the author, 1971.

141 *Hansard*, Vol. 398, Col. 1092.

142 Ibid., Lords, Vol. 132, Col. 36.

143 Ibid., Vol. 398, Cols 806–8. His concern may have been to protect the Marxist NCLC which refused any association with the capitalist state.

144 Ibid., Col. 1075.

145 Ibid., Vol. 398, Col. 1091.

146 A.F. Bentley, discussed in A. Potter, *Organised Groups in British Politics* (London, Faber, 1958), p. 39.

147 R. Rhodes, 'The Changing Face of Public Administration', *Politics*, 15: 2. See also A. Gamble, 'The New Political Economy', *Political Studies*, 43: 3.

148 This literature is discussed in the context of education and training policy in B.J. Evans,

The Politics of the Training Market (London, Routledge, 1992), Chapter 8.

149 R.A. Manzer, *Teachers and Politics: the Role of the National Union of Teachers in the Making of Educational Policy* (Manchester, Manchester University Press, 1970) pp. 64–5.

150 PRO, ED136/21.

151 *The Times Educational Supplement*, 29 September 1941, p. 477 and Saturday 26 July 1941, p. 351.

152 R. Rhodes, 'From Marketisation to Diplomacy: it's the Mix that Matters', in *Australian Journal of Public Administration*, 56: 2, p. 51.

153 Jeffreys, 'Chuter Ede Diaries', p. 419.

154 Calder, *The People's War, Britain 1939–45*, p. 543.

155 R.G. Wallace, 'The Origins and Authorship of the 1944 Education Act', *History of Education*, 10: 4, 1981, p. 290.

156 T. Ling, *The British State Since 1945* (Cambridge, Polity Press, 1998) p. 107.

157 Simon, *Education and the Social Order*.

158 Calder, *The People's War*, p. 545.

INDEX